THE HOME BOOK
OF IRISH HUMOR

THE HOME BOOK OF
Irish Humor

SELECTED AND EDITED WITH COMMENTARIES

by John McCarthy

DODD, MEAD & COMPANY

NEW YORK

TO EVELYN

First published as a Dodd, Mead Quality Paperback in 1984
Fifteen printings in hardcover

Copyright © 1968 by John McCarthy

Published by Dodd, Mead & Company, Inc.
79 Madison Avenue, New York, N.Y. 10016
Distributed in Canada by
McClelland and Stewart Limited, Toronto
Manufactured in the United States of America

Library of Congress Cataloging in Publication Data

Main entry under title:
The Home book of Irish humor.
  Includes index.
  1. Irish wit and humor. I. McCarthy, John,
1898- . II. Title.
PN6178.I6H57 1984   827'.008   84-8048
ISBN 0-396-08426-5
ISBN 0-396-08426-5 (pbk.)

Thanks are due the following for permission to reprint the material indicated: Harper & Row, Publishers, Inc.: for "A Bachelor's Life" and "A Book Review" from *Mr. Dooley's Philosophy* by Finley Peter Dunne. Charles Scribner's Sons: for excerpt from "St. Patrick's Day" from *Mr. Dooley on Making a Will and Other Necessary Evils* by Finley Peter Dunne. Copyright 1919 by Charles Scribner's Sons; renewal copyright 1947 by David Leonard Dunne and Finley Peter Dunne. The Sterling Lord Agency: for "In a Dublin Pub: Poetry and People" by Jimmy Breslin. Copyright © 1966 by Jimmy Breslin. C.J. Fallon Ltd.: for "Pub Types" by T.P. O'Rourke. The Associated Press: for "A Bar for Every Eight Drinkers" by Eddy Gilmore. *The New Yorker:* for "Atheist Hit By Truck" by John McNulty. Copyright 1941 by John McNulty. (Appeared originally in *The New Yorker.*) The Devin-Adair Company: for "All the Sweet Buttermilk . . ." by Donagh MacDonagh and "The Burial" by St. John Ervine from *44 Irish Short Stories,* edited by Devin Garrity. Copyright © 1955 by Devin-Adair Company. McIntosh and Otis, Inc.: for "Lincoln's Irish Soldiers" from *The Coming of the Green* by Leonard Wibberley. Published by Holt, Rinehart & Winston, Inc. Copyright © 1958 by Leonard Wibberley. John Farquharson Ltd.: for "Trinket's Colt" from *Some Experiences of an Irish R M* by E. O. Sommerville and Martin Ross. Eamon Kelly: for "A Matter of Opinion," "The Looking Glass" and "The Umbrella." Dublin Opinion: for "Way of Women" by Paul Jones. Hubert Butler: for "Naming a Street." The Hutchinson Publishing Group Ltd.: for "Ireland's Different to England—See?" from *Brewing Up in the Basement* by Patrick Campbell. Copyright © Patrick Campbell 1963. The Viking Press, Inc.: for "Ivy Day in the Committee Room"

Acknowledgments

In assembling *The Home Book of Irish Humor,* I am indebted for help on the research to Kathleen Cohalen, librarian of the American Irish Historical Society, New York; Louis A. Rachow of The Walter Hampden Memorial Library at The Players, New York; Newman Mallon of the Public Library, Toronto; and Margaret Gale of the library of the Australian Consulate, New York. For the typing and assembling of the manuscript, I am grateful to Lee Anderson, Barbara Burns, Kathleen Doyle and Dorothy Jenkins. I appreciate no end the time and trouble taken by my wife, Evelyn Boyle McCarthy, in double checking my manuscript and the proofs and for her hours of work on the Index. I want to thank too my editor, Raymond T. Bond of Dodd, Mead & Company, for his creative contributions and for having the idea for the book in the first place.

JOHN MCCARTHY

---

from *The Dubliners* by James Joyce. Originally published by B. W. Huebsch, Inc., in 1916. All rights reserved. Lady Dunsany: for "Little Tim Brannehan" by Lord Dunsany. Cyril Daly and *The Sign:* for "Homeward" by Cyril Daly. Reprinted from *The Sign*, National Catholic Magazine, Union City, New Jersey. January, 1967 issue. Alfred A. Knopf, Inc.: for "Peasants" from *The Stories of Frank O'Connor.* Copyright 1936 by Frank O'Connor. Atlantic-Little, Brown and Company: for "Two of a Kind" from *I Remember, I Remember* by Sean O'Faolain. Copyright © 1959, 1961 by Sean O'Faolain. "World's Worst Juggler Goes Down Under" from *Much Ado About Me* by Fred Allen. Copyright © 1956 by Portland Hoffa Allen. "The Governor Was There" from *The Last Hurrah* by Edwin O'Connor. Copyright © 1956 by Edwin O'Connor. A. P. Watt & Son, Collins-Knowlton-Wing, Inc. and the Estate of Leslie A. Montgomery: for "A Persian Tale" from *Lobster Salad* by Lynn Doyle. Copyright 1922 by Leslie A. Montgomery and Alan A. Montgomery. Detroit Athletic Club: for "Erin Go Bragh!" by Frank Sullivan. Copyright March 1955 by *D.A.C. News,* Detroit, Michigan. Doubleday & Company, Inc.: for "Bird Milligan" from *A Weekend in the Middle of the Week* by Oliver St. John Gogarty. Copyright © 1958 by Oliver D. Gogarty, Executor of the Estate of Oliver St. John Gogarty. The Ryerson Press: for "A Secret Union" from *The Best of Gregory Clark* by Gregory Clark. McClelland and Stewart Ltd.: for "Bumps and a Brogue" from *Imperfectly Proper* by Peter Donovan. Copyright 1920. Harold Matson Company, Inc.: for "A Very Merry Christmas" by Morley Callaghan. Copyright 1937, 1965 by Morley Callaghan. Fred Hana Ltd. (Dublin, Ireland): for some of the Irish Bulls.

Preface

This miscellany of Irish wit and humor makes no attempt to serve as an authoritative anthology. It is solely a very personal selection of stories I have read and tales I have heard over the years—from Israel to Ireland to Idaho, for real humor crosses all state and national lines.

Many of the stories I have heard told firsthand by such famed Dublin wits as Dr. Oliver St. John Gogarty, Brinsley McNamara, and Rabbi Herzog. And I have had the privilege of listening to many other renowned raconteurs (who are hereby thanked for their contributions!) in such congenial clubs as the Players in New York, the Tavern in Chicago, the Bohemian in San Francisco, and the Savage and the Garrick in London.

The stories here have all one thing in common—I thought them worth repeating. Sometimes the humor sublimates into poignancy and pathos, but what are these but the other side of the same golden coin? I leave to the Gaelic scholars the historical background and the interpretation.

And if, as I hope, this book will induce the American reader to explore the vast treasure of Irish literature, humorous or otherwise, then it will help repay my debt for the many hours of pleasure given me by that land and its people the world over.

JOHN MCCARTHY

Rye, New York

Introduction

"Why do you Irish," asked Franklin D. Roosevelt of New York's genial mayor, Jimmy Walker, "always answer a question with a question?"

"Do we now?" promptly answered Jimmy.

FDR was not the first president of the United States to be intrigued by the Irish. The legendary charisma of the unique, witty Irish personality has commanded the interest of American presidents and citizens alike as far back as the Colonial times of George Washington, who, incidentally, was a member of the Friendly Sons of St. Patrick and regularly attended their celebrations.

In fact, it is a matter of record that St. Patrick's Day celebrations were held as early as 1737 in Boston and in 1762 in New York. Claims are made that St. Patrick's Day was first publicly celebrated in New York in 1683 because the Royal British Governor of York Colony then was Thomas Dongan, the Catholic Earl of Limerick, who likely encouraged the honoring of Ireland's patron saint in the colony.

The St. Patrick's Day parade has been held on the 17th of March in New York since 1763, and on Fifth Avenue after the new cathedral was built at 50th Street in 1875. When there was some consideration by the advisors to Mayor John Lindsay that the St. Patrick's Day parade be on the Sunday prior to the Saint's actual feast day on Friday, March 17, 1967, and that the route of march be shunted from Fifth Avenue to Central Park, a huge hue and cry went up all over the metropolis. A big delegation of prominent citizens representing all the City's Irish associations and societies tramped to City Hall and into the Mayor's office, demanding an official explanation.

And the Irish delegation got it pronto. Tersely and officially, said His Honor, Mayor John Lindsay himself: "There will be a St. Patrick's Day parade on the 17th of March, 1967, on Fifth Avenue." The new, young Mayor of New York already had troubles aplenty without taking on a fight with the Irish.

When Abram S. Hewitt, a New York reform mayor elected in 1886, declined to follow the practice of many of his predecessors in that office and fly the Irish flag from City Hall on St. Patrick's Day his political goose was cooked. His successor circumspectly reinstituted the old custom.

After all, it is authoritatively estimated that there are over 30 million Americans with Irish blood in their veins. Proud, too, of every drop of it. In New York City alone, there are at least several million who trace their ancestry back to Ireland. Other major United States cities, such as Boston, Philadelphia, Chicago and San Francisco, also have proportionately large American Irish populations. For the Irish who came here by the millions after the dreadful 1845 potato famine in Ireland settled mainly in the cities rather than in the rural areas.

As a matter of fact, on St. Patrick's Day, most Americans, particularly in the major cities, turn Irish for a day and wear the green. For instance, in New York some restaurants on that day even feature green bagels.

Few descendants of other nationalities who have come to America have maintained consistently through the years the same great pride in their heritage as have those of Irish forebears. They particularly take pleasure in keeping alive and popularizing the witty sayings and writings of those of their blood, expecially of those intensely Irish Irishmen such as Swift, Sheridan, Shaw, Goldsmith, Curran, O'Connell, Joyce, Gogarty, O'Casey, Wilde, O'Neill, Behan, Yeats, Dunsany, Dunne, and Mahaffy. The same is true of the memory of such entertainers as Ned Harrigan and Tony Hart, George M. Cohan, Frank Tinney, Pat O'Brien, Frank McHugh, Walter Kelly, Fred Allen (né John Florence Sullivan), Eddie Dowling, Frank Fay, Jackie Gleason, Art Carney, Barry Fitzgerald and a host of others.

These members of the Irish creative contingent have caught the ready wit, the quick retort, the hundred ingratiating faults, the thousand redeeming weaknesses, the sometimes bitter and usually ironic observations of the Irish which have given this nationality, wherever they have settled, a reputation for good humor and good fellowship.

For instance, take Oliver Gogarty's explanation of why the Irish prefer drink to food—"It interferes less with conversation." Or Finley Peter Dunne's publican Dooley's reply when his bartender asked whether or not patron Hennessy was good for a drink? "Has he had it yet?" sagely inquired owner Dooley. Regard Olympian poet Yeats' observation of a certain character—"He is a terrible bore when he is drunk and even a worse bore when he is sober."

Then there are the many penetrating epigrams of Oscar Wilde's which condense a world of shrewd observations in a few classic sentences. Consider: "Women only call each other sister after they have called each other a lot of other things first." "Long engagements give people the opportunity of finding out each other's character before marriage, which is never advisable." "A cynic is a man who knows the price of everything and the value of nothing." "The only thing to do with good advice is to pass it on. It is never of any use to oneself."

Wilde's instructor at Trinity University, Dublin, was Sir John P. Mahaffy. Once when Sir John was crossing the campus, he was stopped by a girl student and asked what, in his opinion, was the great difference between men and women. "I can't conceive," was his apt retort. Sir John Mahaffy is credited with: "Ireland is a country in which the probable never happens and the impossible always does."

Even in personal tragedy, the Irishman can manage a laugh. When his London Drury Lane Theatre, in which he had put his life's savings, was burning to the ground, playwright Richard Brinsley Sheridan viewed the scene and then entered the Piazza Coffee House. There he calmly watched the conflagration through a window, helped by a bottle or two of his favorite sustenance. A friend expressed astonishment at the tranquillity of his demeanor. "A man may surely be allowed to take a glass of wine at his own fireside," he replied.

When Babe Ruth, the great home-run hitter, was the star of baseball in the early 1920's a booking agent cabled Bernard Shaw and asked his permission to use the title of one of his plays, "Man and Superman," for Babe's billing in vaudeville. Shaw cabled back: "Whose baby is Ruth?" The beautiful Isadora Duncan in her prime as one of the world's greatest ballet dancers proposed to Shaw that they marry and produce the perfect child, which would have his great brains and her great beauty. Typically Irish, Shaw answered with a question: "But what if the child inherited my beauty and your brains?"

Other Shavian comments include: "It takes an Irishman many years in residence in England to learn to respect and like a block-head. An Englishman will not respect or like anyone else." Another: "England cannot do without its Irish and its Scots because it cannot do without at least a little sanity."

At the turn of the century in Manhattan when the term for policemen as "New York's Finest" originated, the force numbered many recent Irish immigrants. A then current story dealt with an Irisher who, just landed, was twitted on the dock by some long-shoremen. Rebutted the new arrival: "If you fellows are around here tomorrow, bedad, I'll run ye all in." Another yarn had a horse dropping dead on Morningside Drive. The Irish immigrant cop could not spell "Morningside Drive" for his report of the accident, so he dragged the horse a block to 72nd Street, which he could write. Such stories were called Irish Bulls in their time. We have included in this book a liberal sampling of them, along with those tales regarded by some eminent critics as classics.

Contents

THE RENAISSANCE

FOR THE BEND IN THE ROAD

NORTH OF THE BORDER AND DOWN UNDER

IRISH SONGS AND BALLADS

OLD IRISH PROVERBS

WAKES AND WAGS

Pubs, Publicans, and Patrons

Pubs, Publicans, and Patrons

Around the world, a great part of Irishmen's lives has been spent in pubs. In fact, as Jimmy Breslin has pointed out, the pub or saloon, as it is commonly called in America, is the Irishman's second living room. Hibernians prefer to give their pub patronage to one of their own. Since their patronage is large, Irish pubs or saloons may be found in goodly numbers in practically every city of Ireland, England, Scotland, U.S.A., Australia, and Canada where the Irish congregate.

The Irish pubs offer what a Hibernian likes most—the company of fellow male Irishmen. True, women go to Irish saloons, but they are not encouraged too much to do so. Once there in the pub, the opportunity to talk, which the average Celt loves to do, is ample. Furthermore, there is a tolerance of word and action which is not common elsewhere. As long as a man does not cause a disturbance, he is welcome. Even if he does occasionally, it's forgotten the next day.

The Irish attitude is that anyone who holds a man responsible for what he did in drink or talks about it later in a reproving tone is no gentleman.

Though the Irish like to talk or even sing in their pubs, withal, there is an air of formality and quiet, particularly if the saloon occasionally remains open after official closing hours. The term "speakeasy," used universally in Prohibition days, comes from the traditional Irish publican's warning to patrons after hours "to spake aisy" so the police would not hear.

Of course, oft such warning was and is not necessary. Not infrequently, "after hours" on bitter cold or blazing hot nights is when the saloonkeeper invites the officer on the beat to come in and get warm or cool off, as the season reckons. Such invitations were or are not always declined by the officer, especially if he is a fellow

Celt. "Aye, after all, Dooley, Dugan or Dolan runs a good house and never gives a mite of trouble at all!"

It is true that the Irish publican, often a bit of a puritan, prides himself on running a good house. Mr. Dooley, the great creation of Finley Peter Dunne, was and is typical of the Irish publican—a knowing, God-fearing man who respects his patrons as long as they remain self-respecting patrons. Usually, a smart businessman, a diplomat extraordinary, the Irish publican considers his public house as a private club and likes to introduce one regular customer to another so they, too, can be friends.

The late Dublin-born Tim Costello, whose bar was and still is at 44th and Third Avenue, New York, was the true publican who liked all his steady patrons to be acquainted and be friends. In league with his late brother Joe, he would make introductions of regular patrons to one another. When Tim or Joe introduced you to James Thurber, John O'Hara, Tom Maloney, John McNulty, Burl Ives, John Steinbeck, Dr. Oliver St. John Gogarty, Brendan Behan, Bob Considine, and other celebrities who went to Costello's regularly, you knew you were in. Such recognition by the Costello brothers was prized by some as greater recognition than being elected to the exclusive Racquet and Tennis Club.

Once accepted by the Costellos, you enjoyed certain privileges. For instance, you could occasionally needle the Costellos or play a practical joke on them. James Thurber, whose drawings decorate the walls of the pub, had a glass eye. He had a gag of removing this glass eye and replacing it with one which had in it a waving American flag. With this eye, Thurber once stood at the bar and stared long and hard at Joe Costello. Joe, who had been brandy-nipping a bit during a long evening of bartending, took one look at Thurber's American flag optic, tore off his apron, and decided to go home.

When brother Tim wanted to know why, Joe said he saw an American flag in Thurber's eye. "I've told ye, Joe," reprimanded Tim, "you shouldn't be drinking on the job. You better go home. I'll take over."

Of course, Tim, who was a friendly lad, too, had had quite a few drinks himself with patrons in the course of the night.

Putting on Joe's apron, Tim went forward to take Thurber's order, stared hard, went back to mix the drink ordered, came back with it, and looked deep into Thurber's eye again. Then Tim took off his apron, told the other bartender to take over, and left, muttering, "I must be nipping as much as Joe when I, too, see an American flag waving in a customer's eye."

Selections from Mr. Dooley

BY FINLEY PETER DUNNE

A FAMILY REUNION

"Why aren't you out attending the reunion of the Dooley family?" Mr. McKenna asked the philosopher.

"Thim's no rel-ations to me," Mr. Dooley answered. "Thim's farmer Dooleys. No wan iv our fam'ly iver lived in th' counthry. We live in th' city, where they burn gas an' have a polis foorce to get on to. We're no farmers, divvle th' bit. We belong to th' industhreel classes. Thim must be th' Fermanagh Dooleys, a poor lot, Jawn, an' always on good terms with th' landlord, bad ciss to thim, says I. We're from Roscommon. They'se a Dooley family in Wexford an' wan near Ballybone that belonged to th' constabulary. I met him but wanst. 'Twas at an iviction; an', though he didn't know me, I inthrajooced mesilf be landin' him back iv th' ear with a bouldher th' size iv ye'er two fists together. He didn't know me afterwards, ayether.

"We niver had but wan reunion iv th' Dooley fam'ly, an' that was tin years ago. Me Cousin Felix's boy Aloysius—him that aftherwards wint to New York an' got a good job dhrivin' a carredge f'r th' captain iv a polis station—he was full iv pothry an' things; an' he come around wan night, an' says he, 'D'ye know,' he says, ' 'twud be th' hite iv a good thing f'r th' Dooleys to have a reunion,' he says. 'we ought to come together,' he says, 'an' show the people iv this ward,' he says, 'how sthrong we are,' he says. 'Ye might do it betther, me buck,' says I, 'shovellin' slag at th' mills,' I says, 'an' I'll attind to havin' the' polis there,' I says, 'f'r I have a dhrag at th' station.'

"Well, he sint out letters to all th' Roscommon Dooleys; an' on a Saturdah night we come together in a rinted hall an' held th' reunion. 'Twas great sport f'r awhile. Some iv us hadn't spoke frindly to each other f'r twinty years, an' we set around an' tol' stories iv Roscommon an' its green fields, an' th' stirabout pot that was niver filled, an' th' blue sky overhead an' th' boggy ground undherfoot. 'Which Dooley was it that hamsthrung th' cows?' 'Mike Dooley's Pat' 'Naw such thing: 'twas Pat Dooley's Mike. I mane Pat Dooley's Mike's Pat.' F'r 'tis with us as with th' rest iv our people. Ye take th' Dutchman: he has as manny names to give to his childher as they'se nails in his boots, but an Irishman has th' pick iv on'y a few. I knowed a man be th' name iv Clancy —a man fr'm Kildare. He had fifteen childher; an', whin th' las' come, he says, 'Dooley, d'ye happen to know anny saints?' 'None iv them thrades here,' says I. 'Why?' says I. 'They'se a new kid at th' house,' he says; 'an', if somewan don't come to me assistance, I'll have to turn th' child out on th' wurruld without th' rag iv a name to his back,' he says.

"But I was tellin' ye about th' reunion. They was lashins iv dhrink an' story-tellin', an' Felix's boy Aloysius histed a banner he had made with 'Dooley Aboo' painted on it. But, afther th' night got along, some iv us begun to raymimber that most iv us hadn't been frinds f'r long. Mrs. Morgan Dooley, she that was Molly Dooley befure she married Morgan, she turns to me, an' says she, ' 'Tis sthrange they let in that Hogan woman,' she says—that Hogan woman, Jawn, bein' th' wife iv her husband's brother. She heerd her say it, an' she says, 'I'd have ye to understand that no wan iver come out iv Roscommon that cud hold up their heads with th' Hogans,' she says. ' 'Tis not f'r th' likes iv ye to slandher a fam'ly that's iv th' landed gintry iv Ireland, an' f'r two pins I'd hit ye a poke in th' eye,' she says. If it hadn't been f'r me bein' between thim, they'd have been trouble; f'r they was good frinds wanst. What is it th' good book says about a woman scorned? Faith, I've forgotten.

"Thin me uncle Mike come in, as rough a man as iver laid hands on a polisman. Felix Dooley was makin' a speech on th' vartues iv th' fam'ly. Th' Dooleys, says he, 'can stand befure all th' wurruld, an' no man can say ought agin ayether their honor or their integrity,' says he. 'Th' man that's throwin' that at ye,' says me uncle Mike, 'stole a saw fr'm me in th' year sivinty-five.' Felix paid no attintion to me uncle Mike, but wint on, 'We point proudly to th' motto, "Dooley aboo—Dooley f'river." ' 'Th' saw aboo,' says me uncle Mike. 'Th' Dooleys,' says Felix, 'stood beside Red Hugh O'Neill; an', whin he cut aff his hand—' 'He didn't cut if off with anny wan else's saw,' says me uncle Mike. 'They'se an old sayin',' wint on Felix. 'An' ol' saw,' says me uncle Mike. 'But 'twas new whin ye stole it.'

" 'Now look here,' says Aloysius, 'this thing has gone far enough. 'Tis an outrage that this here man shud come here f'r to insult th' head iv th' fam'ly.' 'Th' head iv what fam'ly?' says Morgan Dooley, jumpin' up as hot as fire. 'I'm th' head iv th' fam'ly,' says he, 'be right iv histhry.' 'Ye're an ol' cow,' says me uncle Mike. 'Th' back iv me hand an' th' sowl iv me fut to all iv ye,' he says. 'I quit ye,' he says. 'Ye're all livin' here undher assumed names'; an' he wint out, followed be Morgan Dooley with a chair in each hand.

"Well, they wasn't two Dooleys in th' hall'd speak whin th' meetin' broke up; an' th' Lord knows, but I don't know to this day, who's th' head iv th' Dooley fam'ly. All I know is that I had wan th' nex' mornin'."

A WINTER NIGHT

Any of the Archey Road cars that got out of the barns at all were pulled by teams of four horses, and the snow hung over the shoulders of the drivers' big bearskin coats like the eaves of an old-fashioned house on the blizzard night. There was hardly a soul in the road from the red bridge, west, when Mr. McKenna got laboriously off the platform of his car and made for the sign of somebody's celebrated Milwaukee beer over Mr. Dooley's tavern. Mr. Dooley, being a man of sentiment, arranges his drinks to conform with the weather. Now anybody who knows anything at all knows that a drop of "J.J." and a whisper (subdued) of hot water and a lump of sugar and lemon peel (if you care for lemon peel) and nutmeg (if you are a "jood") is a drink calculated to tune a man's heart to the song of the wind slapping a beer-sign upside down and the snow drifting in under the door. Mr. Dooley was drinking this mixture behind his big stove when Mr. McKenna came in.

"Bad night, Jawn," said Mr. Dooley. There hasn' been a can in tonight but wan, an' that was a pop bottle. Is the snow-ploughs out, I dinnaw?"

"They are," said Mr. McKenna.

"I suppose Doherty is dhrivin'," said Mr. Dooley. "He's a good dhriver. They do say he do be wan iv th' best dhrivers on th' road. I've heerd that th' prisdent is dead gawn on him. He's me cousin. Ye can't tell much about what a man'll be fr'm what th' kid is. That there Doherty was th' worst omadhon iv a boy that iver I knowed. He niver cud larn his a-ah-bee, abs. But see what he made iv himself! Th' best dhriver on th' road; an', by dad, 'tis not twinty to wan he won't be stharter befure he dies. 'Tis in th' fam'ly to make their names. There niver was anny fam'ly in th' ol' counthry that turned out more priests than th' Dooleys. By gar, I believe we hol' th' champeenship iv th' wurruld. At M'nooth th' profissor that called th' roll got so fr'm namin' th' Dooley la-ads that he came near bein' tur-rned down on th' cha-arge that he was whistlin' at vespers. His mouth, d'ye mind, took that there shape fr'm sayin' Dooley,' 'Dooley,' that he'd looked as if he was whistlin'. D'ye mind? Dear, oh, dear, 'tis th' divvle's own fam'ly f'r religion."

Mr. McKenna was about to make a jeering remark to the effect that the alleged piety of the Dooley family had not penetrated to the Archey Road representative, when a person, evidently of wayfaring habits, entered and asked for alms. Mr. Dooley arose, and, picking a half-dollar from the till, handed it to the visitor with great unconcern. The departure of the wayfarer with profuse thanks was followed by a space of silence.

"Well, Jawn," said Mr. Dooley.

"What did you give the hobo?" asked Mr. McKenna.

"Half a dollar," said Mr. Dooley.

"And what for?"

"Binivolence," said Mr. Dooley, with a seraphic smile.

"Well," said Mr. McKenna, "I should say that was benevolence."

"Well," said Mr. Dooley, " 'this a bad night out, an' th' poor divvle looked that mis'rable it brought th' tears to me eyes, an'—"

"But," said Mr. McKenna, "that ain't any reason why you should give a half dollar to every tramp who comes in."

"Jawn," said Mr. Dooley, "I know th' ma-an. He spinds all his money at Schneider's, down th' block."

"What of that?" asked Mr. McKenna.

"Oh, nawthin'," said Mr. Dooley, "on'y I hope Herman won't thry to bite that there coin. If he does—"

ST. PATRICK'S DAY

"If there's wan thing that St. Patrick did f'r Ireland that I like betther thin annything else," said Mr. Dooley, " 'tis th' day he fixed f'r his birthday. . . . Bein' an injanius man as well as holy an' well read in th' calendar, he named a day that was sure to fall somewheres in th' middle iv Lent. . . . About the end iv th' first month I begin to feel that I'm too healthy an' far betther thin anny man ought to be in this sinful wurruld. . . . I begin readin' up relijous books to see whether th' rewards is akel to me heeroyic sacrifices. An' I'm almost ready to offer to thrade in a couple iv millyon years f'r wan pipe full iv kinnikinnick whin th' corner iv me eye catches th' date on th' top iv a pa-aper. It's on'y two days to Pathrick's Day an' a dauntless man can stick it out. But, dear me th' sixteenth iv March is a long day. It's th' longest day in th' year. Haythen asthronomers say it ain't, but I know betther. An' be th' same token th' siventeenth is th' shortest. It's like a dhream. It don't last more thin a minyit but a millyon things can happen in it. Annyhow it comes ar-round at last. Many iv me frinds goes out to meet it. Not me, mind ye. But ye can bet I'm standin' on th' dure step waitin' f'r it with me pipe in me hand."

A BACHELOR'S LIFE

"A man with a face that looks as if some wan had thrown it at him in anger nearly always marries befure he is old enough to vote. He feels he has to an' he cultivates what Hogan calls th' graces. How often do ye hear about a fellow that he is very plain but has a beautiful nature. Ye bet he has. If he hadn't an' didn't always keep it in th' show-case where all th' wurruld cud see he'd be lynched be th' Society f'r Municipal Improvement. But it's diff'rent with us comely bachelors. Bein' very beautiful, we can afford to be haughty an' peevish. . . . Th' best lookin' iv us niver get marrid at all."

MARRIAGE

"A marrid man gets th' money, Hinnissy, but a bachelor man gets th' sleep. Whin all me marrid frinds is off to wurruk poundin' th' ongrateful sand an' wheelin' th' rebellyous slag, in th' heat iv th' afthernoon, ye can see ye'er onfortchinit bachelor frind perambulatin' up an' down th' shady side iv th' sthreet, with an umbrelly over his head an' a wurrud iv cheer fr'm young an' old to enliven his lonliness."

"But th' childher?" asked Mr. Hennessy slyly.

"Childher!" said Mr. Dooley. "Sure I have th' finest fam'ly in th' city. Without scandal I'm th' father iv ivry child in Ar-rchey Road fr-m end to end."

"An' none iv ye'er own," said Mr. Hennessy.

"I wish to hell, Hinnissy," said Mr. Dooley savagely, "ye'd not lean again that mirror, I don't want to have to tell ye agin."

"Ye know a lot about marredge," said Mr. Hennessy.

"I do," said Mr. Dooley.

"Ye was niver marrid?"

"No," said Mr. Dooley. "No, I say, givin' three cheers. I know about marredge th' way an asthronmer knows about th' stars. I'm studyin' it through me glass all th' time."

"Ye're an asthronomer," said Mr. Hennessy, "but," he added, tapping himself lightly on the chest, "I'm a star."

"Go home," said Mr. Dooley crossly, "befure the mornin' comes to put ye out."

In a Dublin Pub–Poetry and People

By Jimmy Breslin

His tie was loose and the long end thrown over his shoulder. He had on two pairs of eyeglasses. Both of them sat cockeyed and were steamed up in the hot pub. He sat hunched over in his rumpled overcoat with his arms folded and the pint of stout in front of him. His shoes were open and the laces were caught under the soles. His name is Patrick Kavanagh, and he can write like hell. In Ireland, where the poet is important, Paddy Kavanagh is considered the best today. To find him, you go to this pub called McDaid's, right off Grafton Street, near Trinity College, Dublin. Any hour of the day that the pub is open will do. Paddy Kavanagh drinks.

He sits with his stout and listens to old women talking about a remedy for lumbago a doctor had given them. Paddy Kavanagh thunders at the old ladies. "There's millions of Muslims, from Khartoum to Calcutta, and they cure their ailments by . . ." The old ladies hide their heads while he finishes his speech.

He goes back and sits down. His doctor's son comes into the pub. "Your father!" Paddy Kavanagh says. "Your father has me lung in his laboratory. It's the finest in the whole . . . laboratory."

A college student talks about a track and field meet and Paddy Kavanagh says, "Fiberglass poles, they use. 'Tisn't a pole vault anymore, it's a . . . catapult."

Paddy Kavanagh is rude and rough and delightful and profane, and his book *Tarry Flynn* has some important ways of using words. He is in McDaid's pub, traveling the route of the Irish poet. In Dublin, the drink goes with the words. So many of them drink their masterpieces and die unnoticed. But so many of them have produced, too. Many experts have come here and spent this Easter week pulling the Irish apart to see what they are. One thing is certain. They are a people who pick words out of the night wind.

Dublin is a city of 500,000. It was much smaller in the past. But even a quick list of those who have written here becomes an index for a literature textbook. In the 1700's, the names are Swift, Goldsmith, Congreve, Sheridan. Coming forward, there are Shaw and Wilde and Synge and Yeats and Joyce and O'Casey. Today, Brendan Behan and Frank O'Connor have just died, but Padraic Colum is alive and so is Sean O'Faolain. Then there is Liam O'Flaherty, who wrote the best movie I ever saw, "The Informer."

Brian Friel, from Donegal, has his Braodway play, "Philadelphia, Here I Come." And in the pubs they tell you that John Keane, a pub owner in Kerry, has genius. "He is the playwright they'll remember as great," Ulick O'Connor, another writer, said over dinner last night.

Everybody uses words here. In the midst last night, a working-man in a cap came out into Gardiner Street and found his bicycle gone. His voice shrieked at the tenements about him:

"They shteal the Cross from behind Jesus' back and leave him hangin' in midair."

The ones who take their words into a vocation get help and harm from what they are. Theirs is the drink. The dreaming can be terrible, too. They dream their lives away casually here. But at the same time the dreaming is what makes them. Dreaming of sex comes out as far better than sex. Anyway, the Irish are too lazy to chase girls. They also have their official attitude toward sex. The other morning, at a little church out in the suburbs, twelve great-grandmothers and three men too old to see sat in the pews while the parish priest warned them about sins of the flesh. But the dreaming and illusions counteract any holding down. And beyond the religion, there are the little men, the leprechauns. You'll find sophisticated Irishmen who will not totally believe that they don't exist.

The people here are great for writers to be around. The people love words. And the Irish have so much natural spite for anybody's success that it is exhilarating to succeed around them.

Many of the writers never make it through this. Flann O'Brien, a fine comic writer, just died of the drink without getting much done. Behan had so much further to go. Now the poet Paddy Kavanagh sits in McDaid's, and it is up to him and the stout and the life in front of him.

Now at this time a new enemy arises. The worship of the car and the machine has started in Dublin. The narrow streets are becoming clogged with cars and the fumes rise in the air with the noise, and more is to come. If there is anything that can kill the romance and the lilt of a place it is a good auto salesman with a full showroom. In America, Detroit announces proudly that it is turning out nine million cars this year. The place is becoming a metal India. And with all these machines, the country's idea of a poet is Robert Lowell. It should be a felony for anybody to give him a sheet of paper. He is absolutely awful. And while men genuflect in front of computers, they listen, mouths open, to the mechanical age romance of a Marshall McLuhan.

In Dublin, where the machines have not yet ruined the air, the dreamer and poet still matters, and it is he the people want to listen to. Last night, in a place called Baker's, an old pub on Thomas Street, a working section, the people were crowded into the family room, grandmothers, mothers and daughters, all with their men, sitting at tables along the walls and drinking pints of stout and singing songs together loudly while a gas burner hung from the ceiling to warm them.

They all recognized Ulick O'Connor when he came in. One of the old women screamed in the middle of the song, "Tell us somethin' " and they all stopped singing and turned to Ulick.

"I'll give a recitation."

"Good!" they yelled.

He got up and walked into the middle of the room.

"This is a poem about a murder," he said.

"Oh, wonderful!"

"About a murder in Belfast!"

"Hurrah!"

They hung on his words while he recited his poem about a man in Belfast who slit his wife's throat and was glad he had done what he had and he tied his wife's nightgown around his neck and hung himself. He died promptly, but the wife lived.

". . . For the razor blade was Dublin-made, but the gown was Belfast linen." O'Connor finished.

They all shrieked and jumped up and crowded around him to thank him for his words. At half-eleven, closing time, they went out the side door into the street, singing into the night wind that carries words.

Pub Types

By T. P. O'Rourke

LISTEN TO THE GLOOMY MAN

Every Irish pub has its Gloomy Man in varying degrees of gloom. It may be the result of leaden skies and lonesome rain. The

Gloomy Man puts his elbow slowly and sadly on the counter and, having opened his paper, goes straight for the Death column. Not that he is hopefully looking for the demise of a creditor, or that he is at all interested in any particular death; it is merely the quiet melancholy reading ". . . At his residence, Thady . . . beloved husband of . . . Deeply regretted by his sorrowing wife . . . Remains will be removed . . . R.I.P."

There is a nice soothing solace in this mournful monotony of beloved, deeply regretted and mourned; and there is not an editor in Ireland who will accept anything as factual as, say, "At last, at her residence, Julia, aged 105 . . . to the inexpressible delight of her son-in-law and everybody else. Deo gratias. Remains will be galloped to . . ."

Having finished this solacing feature, the Gloomy Man will take a slow, philosophic sip from his pint as if wondering whether it is worthwhile finishing the drink at all, and proceed to search for earthquakes, plane crashes, shipwrecks, strikes, bankruptcies and other indications that life is not worth living.

Now, the Gloomy Man is by no means a silent, reserved type. He may always be addressed and will take and give a drink. It is just that he sees the futility of earthly life and is solidly opposed to any form of optimistic or hopeful notions.

"What'll win the tote double?" asks the Young Customer.

"I'll tell you, son," says the Gloomy Man. "I'll tell you—Mirrelson and Kilmartin, the bookies." He then goes on to give a sermon on bookies, jockeys, trainers, owners and the ruination caused by racing. By now the Sedate Man butts in to agree with the Gloomy Man and advises the Young Customer to put his money in the post office. The Gloomy Man does not agree.

"No use at all, son. No use. D'ye know that the value of the pound is fallin' day by day. Anyhow, when the Chinese take over this country in two years' time, they'll seize every penny that's in the banks, every penny." Turning to the Sedate Man. "D'ye remember ould Mulligitawny that had the pub over the way? Thirty-five thousand solid he had salted away. Never took a drink in his life. What d'ye think happened? The Income Tax crowd sailed in on him and took the lot—the whole bloody lot. Drank himself to death. Divil a wan at the funeral only a rate collector and two summons servers."

There is a lull as his hearers ponder the tragedy, suddenly broken by the roar of a 'plane overhead. The Gloomy Man shakes his head sadly.

"Them 'planes. I'll tell ye what: wan o' these days, wan o' them'll crash down on us. Did ye see the case in England? Woman havin' her dinner in her own house. In her own house, mind ye. Down on top of her it falls. Can ye believe it? Knife and fork in her hands."

The Sedate Man hastens to assure him that although this sounds incredible, he nevertheless believes it. Also agrees possibility of it happening to the pub. Goes further and says 'planes should be forbidden to fly over public houses or within ten miles of a pub. Opens a packet of fags and offers one to the Gloomy Man. The Gloomy Man declines. Asks him does he have a cough in the morning. The Sedate Man says he does.

"I thought so," says the Gloomy Man. "I'll tell you what about them cigarettes and the cough. Remember Hennessy? About your age he was. Just felt tired and began to lose weight. All over in three months. Wouldn't take no heed . . . and, d'ye know, the doctor—a divil for the fags—went off himself in six months after."

The Sedate Man surreptitiously tops his fag and feels less sedate.

"Let's talk about drink," he says.

"Drink is right," says the Gloomy Man. "Drink is right. D'ye see them bloody beer cans? D'ye see all them yokes for pumping gas into the beer? Mother of God, sure it can't be right. Did ye see Moriarity lately? A divil for the pints. Full up of the gas—and the size of the belly on him—goin' round like a maternity case. I tells him to take out an insurance policy. Too late—no company'd take him."

"A fact," says the Young Customer.

"Ye see," continues the Gloomy Man, "the ould porter swells the liver—swells it up till it's like a sponge."

"Something to be said for the whiskey after all," comments the Sedate Man.

The Gloomy Man surveys him with a look of half pity, half contempt.

"Have ye any idea how the whiskey works? D'ye know anything at all? Well, the whiskey shrivels up the liver into a little ball until it gets smaller an' smaller. What they call the cirrhosis. Five weeks it took Mularkey to die and the bawling out of him was somethin' ferocious to hear."

By now a deep gloom has descended on the bar. The sad, silent rain is running down the pub windowpanes and the Gloomy Man is beginning to explain how the crops will be ruined and the country bankrupt, when the Sedate Man and the Young Customer decide to leave.

"Good luck now," they say to the Gloomy Man. "See you tomorrow."

"If we live," replies the Gloomy Man. "If we live."

PORTRAIT OF THE FORGETFUL MAN

Every barman has at some time come across the Forgetful Man; and so has every customer.

The Forgetful Man is to be found at all levels of society, more especially in the upper circles. When alone, he is usually reading a book or a newspaper. He calls for a drink from out of the middle of Chapter Twenty-two or from the racing page. He never notices that the drink has been served—how could he when the wicked duke has just thrown his arms around the peasant girl, hoarsely muttering a false promise to marry her the very next morning?

If and when he is asked to pay for the drink, he looks up with a start. It takes several moments and much effort to recall that he is, in fact, in a public house; and that, in fact, he did call for a drink; and that, in fact, he didn't pay for it.

If, on the other hand, he is not asked for payment he will absentmindedly consume the drink in a mood of utter detachment. After all, the human brain was never intended to be able to take in the form of ten horses and pay for a drink at the same time. Perhaps a bookie could, but a gentleman—no, sir!

In a praiseworthy endeavour to avoid the embarrassment of being asked to pay for a drink at the wrong moment and in the wrong circumstances, the Forgetful Man will often take the precaution of putting out the money in advance on the counter. But he doesn't put it out vulgarly or ostentatiously. On the contrary, he delicately places it in the shadow of an ashtray or donation box.

where it will not unduly distract the attention of a barman who is already too busy with other items of currency.

If the barman, having in due course served the drink, takes the money, the Forgetful Man doesn't notice it. He is too immersed. If he doesn't take it, the Forgetful Man, still deeply engrossed, but somehow prompted by his subconscious mind, picks up the money and puts back in his pocket what he believes to be his change. It is these little failings and lack of mental activity which endear the Forgetful Man to the barman, to the publican, and to society in general.

Sometimes the Forgetful Man arrives at the pub having utterly forgotten to bring any money with him. In which case he may offer to "see" the barman again. When he does, it will be to point out that the barman is looking remarkably well and to hope that the weather will continue to hold up. Or he may borrow a pound from somebody, or have a pound tendered to him by an acquaintance who is touched by his plight.

But the sadness of this disease of forgetfulness is that it is progressive—what the doctors call galloping amnesia. The Forgetful Man can never remember the pound. To remind him of it makes his memory worse. It further injures the brain cells; and, if repeated from time to time, has the effect that not only can the unfortunate man not remember the pound but he also fails to remember even the person who lent him the pound. And he may be absent for several months because he cannot remember the premises in which he got the pound.

Instead of borrowing a pound or expressing his determination to see the barman again, the Forgetful Man may use a check book. This generally doesn't help matters, as he is inclined to forget what year it is and may use the date 1916 or 1976. Even when the error in timing is brought to his notice and rectified, the check will usually bounce—not that there is anything more wrong with his account than that he forgot to lodge money into it—which, after all, is something that can happen to anybody, except a bishop.

Frequently and tragically the Forgetful Man suffers from kidney disease. Whenever it comes to his turn to stand a round, he has to go to the toilet, where he may spend up to five minutes contemplating and demonstrating the ultimate fate of all drinks consumed on or off the premises. Or he may suddenly remember that he has to make an urgent telephone call involving the most terrible and immediate consequences. "Quick, quick," he cries to the barman, "gimme four coppers." He may, or may not return, depending on whether the round has been completed.

Mental experts had for years been puzzled by the extraordinary behaviour of the Forgetful Man until recently Professor Goodhead of the Guinness Laboratory discovered that man has two sets of memory cells—one of which enables him to remember anything which is due to him, and the other anything which he owes.

In the sad case of the Forgetful Man the latter cells have, as a result of some shock in childhood, become paralysed. It is said that a society is being formed to help to soften this tragedy by having donation boxes placed in all pubs to aid the Forgetful Man.

Actually this subject of memory is an involved one, having various shades of meaning, such as remembering, recalling, recollecting, and so on. Some time ago a Forgetful Man, who had several university degrees, was challenged by an illiterate man in the bar.

"What," he demanded, "is the precise difference between 'remember' and 'recollect'?"

We were all a bit puzzled, but finally the dopey man replied:

"Well, it's like this. Six months ago I remember I lent you ten bob, but I don't recollect havin' got it back!"

NOBODY LIKES THE HEARTY MAN

The Hearty Man is not always welcome in the pubs: as a rule he is too hearty. He breezes in noisily and upsets the Sick Man, the Gloomy Man and the Quiet Man. He is full of loud good mornings, nice-day-to-days and how's-every-bit-of yous. His head is erect, his feet firm and he is disgustingly healthy.

He arouses jealousy and envy, and can draw even dangerous hatred from the man who has two up out of a treble at ten to one each and finds that the third money on nag has been beaten a short head. He calls for his drink loudly, rattles the money on the counter and has something pleasantly derogatory to say about the barman and the premises.

His special techniques are the slap on the back, the dig in the ribs and the poke in the chest. The slap on the back is usually accompanied by a shout of "The bould Pat," which nearly knocks the bould Pat off his stool. Shocked to his foundations, he twists around and his lips move noiselessly to respond suitably and tersely in language which is not tolerated in this house.

The dig in the ribs is always part of the "D'ye see now!" while the poke in the chest backs up "D'ye get me!" All this is accompanied by loud laughter; but it is not laughter at all, for genuine laughter makes others laugh, and nobody laughs when the Hearty Man laughs. He laughs alone and the world weeps.

The Hearty Man often has a very strong cough which deafens the bar and makes the timid man's little "ahem" seem like a whisper. This type of cough has the medical profession baffled. It doesn't come from the lungs at all but from somewhere unknown in the back of the head or the neck.

The Hearty Man requires an immense amount of space because he has the habit of stretching out his arms and flinging them all over the place. Even when he sits at the counter and places his elbows on it, the distance between the elbows is about seven feet. Another unusual feature is that he nearly always wears an overcoat of great thickness. This must be psychological, because the bigger he feels, the heartier he is.

The Hearty Man is fatal for conversation. He breaks it up by taking it over and switching the subject to no subject or ten subjects. Suppose you are talking about hens . . . history and habits thereof. The Hearty Man will break in loudly and clearly: "Hens! Is it hens? I'll tell you about a horse . . . And talking of horses reminds me of a man who had a mother-in-law . . . D'ye know Mullinger, which talking of horses reminds me of a dog . . . not of horses . . . of the fellow who sez that's a horse of a different cow (dig in the ribs), d'ye get me?" Loud laughter from the Hearty Man while the man with the fractured rib tries to remember on what date he joined the Voluntary Health Scheme.

The Hearty Man generally takes his stance opposite the cash register, a focal point where he has the best chance of interrupting the barman. But he has no difficulty in moving from group to group and from bar to lounge. Even the man in the toilet is not safe from his attentions. "Is that you in there. Mick? How's tricks?

How's the mother? Did I tell you about the two monkeys . . ."

From group to group goes the Hearty Man, encouraging, interrupting, admonishing, fortifying the faithful and loudly advising. When the Quiet Man in the back lounge has been at last persuaded by his friends to sing "I Hear You Calling Me" and the eyes of the listeners are moistening at "hearing your voice through all the years to be," etc., the Hearty Man bursts in with "Give us 'Boolavogue,' ould stock."

Maybe it is because the world is so full of troubles and cares that we all put up with the Hearty Man. It seems unlucky to try to silence him or ignore him. There is something of the west wind about him—he can't be kept out or kept quiet. He belongs to a race apart. He seems to have no troubles and incapable of having them, and accordingly doesn't know how the rest of us feel.

Essentially, the Hearty Man has no heart.

MEET THE CONTRADICTOR

It is not certain that there are any solid grounds for believing that the Contradictor started to argue with his mother five seconds after he was born. However, it is clear why his mother is a widow. His affected father drowned himself.

The Contradictor looks at the world with utter suspicion. He is convinced that the more something looks to be right, the more it must be wrong. This outlook is mostly due to his having found out in later life that everything he was taught at school proved to be wrong and even idiotic. For example, that honesty is the best policy. The patent lunacy behind this extraordinary notion galls him whenever he sees an opulent building contractor dangling the keys of his Rolls-Royce and throwing back a glass of brandy with the ease and abandon of a gull swallowing a mackerel.

Nor, to give a further example, can he tolerate the long-unlearnt yarn that the policeman is your friend. As he seeks to get into a pub five minutes before opening time, he throws a baleful eye at the Garda standing nearby, at a point where there is no trace of a bank, and where obviously he is on pint duty.

"What," he curses, "is the so-an'-so guarding? Is it me, or the pub, or himself, or the whole bloody universe? Wouldn't you think that with every man having two Guardian Angels, that'd be enough?"

Having shuffled around the block for the necessary eternity of 300 seconds and millions of sub-seconds, and having cast a cold and challenging eye on such assorted cheering objects as open dustbins, stray cats and dog droppings, he enters the pub, prepared for the strife of the day.

The barman, having served him with his pint, adds, free of charge, the information that it's a nice day now. The Contradictor begs to be informed why. What's nice about it? Whether the barman sees anything particularly nice about a biting east wind running up your legs and taking the skin off the backs of your ears. Whether . . .

The barman is luckily spared by the entry of the Sedate Man and the Scrounger, whose conversation is remarkably affable, for the reason that the Scrounger thoroughly agrees with everything the Sedate Man says. The Contradictor allows South Vietnam, the Gold Standard and the high price of periwinkles to pass as trivial; but when the Sedate Man asks if today is Tuesday and the Scrounger confirms it, the Contradictor denies it loudly, pointing out that in China it is Wednesday.

This leads to a vigorous discussion of the movement—or non-movement—of the sun, whether there is a sun at all or an earth at all or a pub at all. So strong are the denials of the Contradictor that the Scrounger, beginning to doubt the reality of his pint, takes the precaution of instantly swallowing it.

The Contradictor is generally a fairly poor man, since there are little prospects of promotion for a man who always contradicts his boss; or for the barrister who does not defer to the judge. But, by way of compensation, he has escaped the ravages of matrimony simply for the reason that were he asked was he taking the wench to be his lawful wedded wife, he would contradict the clergyman and say "No."

He is at heart a lonely man, gazing at an imcomprehensible universe woven of wealth and poverty, light and darkness, love and hate, good and bad, birth and death, beauty and ugliness, pints and no pints. Nor can he pal up with a fellow contradictor, since it would be a case of plus one added to minus one. Often he is barred from the pub for causing rows, but has to be re-admitted to bring a bit of life into the place.

It is at nighttime, when the customers are a little more than relaxed, that the Contradictor is at his best—or rather his worst. He then soars to the eight of opposition. For example, the talk all around may be about the chances of the local football team and the strategy it must employ to win. The Hearty Man is loudly proclaiming that the essential thing is to keep the ball in the air and avoid ground play. "Keep the ball in the air," he keeps on repeating. "The important thing is to keep the ball in the air."

The Contradictor gives a loud challenging bellow: "No! No! The important thing is to keep the air in the ball."

When the time comes for the Contradictor to die, he will be somewhat at a disadvantage in so far as a corpse finds it difficult to maintain any kind of intelligent discussion with the undertaker. His hope of Heaven is nil, for the reasons that he has contradicted the clergy all his life and that St. Peter likes a quiet undisturbed kind of a life.

What, of course, will happen is that when the Contradictor goes down below, he will draw a chair a little nearer to the fire, warm and rub his cold hands and, turning his face directly to the Devil, will say: "God, this is Heaven."

A Bar for Every Eight Drinkers

BY EDDY GILMORE

High, but far from dry, on the westernmost tip of Ireland, Dingle is one of the world's great oases for the drinking man.

With a population of less than 1,000 men, women and children, Dingle has 48 licensed bars.

It even has bars in butcher shops and groceries.

"And why not?" asked dark-eyed Margaret O'Grady. "Suppose you're in the butcher's. You're waiting for your order. Now, what's more natural than stepping over to the other side of the shop and buying a drink?"

Down by the waterfront there is one little stretch of downtown

Dingle where there are nine full-fledged bars, huddling together like old friends supporting one another, with nothing to separate them but walls.

Jimmy Flahive's bar is down at the far end, out where the wild Atlantic winds pound in to Dingle Bay.

Why does one small town have so many bars?

"Ah," Jimmy Flahive said, "you're looking at Dingle with prejudice, with a one-sided point of view. Be objective, sir. Look at it logically and say to yourself, 'It's London, and New York and Paris what's wrong. They don't have enough bars. Dingle's got the proportion right.' "

A short, broad-shouldered man, with a face as brown as a whisky bottle, joined the discussion, reasoning:

"Look at it this way, sir. With a population just under 1,000, and a number of bars just under 50, we have a drinking place for every 20 souls—men, women and children. But as many of the women don't, and as none of the children do, we figure we've got one bar for every eight full-grown drinking men.

Up the road from James Flahive's bar, another foreigner was drinking in Nora Kennedy's bar. He was from Cahirciveen, 18 miles across Dingle Bay, and for that reason a foreigner in Dingle.

Dingle lays claim to being the most westerly town in Europe, to being closer to the United States than any other town in Europe.

"That's not so," said the man from across Dingle Bay. "Cahirciveen's closer to America than Dingle."

A tall man with a rain-soaked overcoat and a blue-red nose looked up from his stout at the far end of the bar and said: "You talk like a fool. All but an idiot would know that Dingle is more west than Cahirciveen. Look at the bloody map."

As tempers flared, I intervened, offering to go to a shop that advertised "Tourist Information" to settle the question.

The shop also sold dry goods and, as the door opened, a bell clanged somewhere well back in the unlighted interior. Finally a woman appeared.

"Is this the tourist office?"

"It is."

"You have some information on Dingle?"

"We closed on October 15."

"But you're open."

"The shop's closed," she said.

"Have you any pamphlets about Dingle?"

"They collected them and took them away," she replied, "but if you want to know anything, just write me a letter."

She disappeared into the gloom of the shop.

Outside an Atlantic storm raged—as no doubt the argument still did—down in one of Dingle's 48 licensed bars.

Concerning Whiskey and Whisky

"The Irish claim to have invented whiskey is true, and the Scots themselves acknowledge it," Mr. Michael O'Reilly, secretary of the Irish Whiskey Distillers in Dublin, told us.

"I have a copy of a paper read to the Licensed Vintners' Association in London in 1948 by a Scots manager from Elgin in the Highlands. He admits that whisky did not come to Scotland until long after we invented it in Ireland. Uisge Beatha (the Irish word for whiskey or water of life) is mentioned in the Annals of the Four Masters. In Dr. Samuel Johnson's original dictionary, published in 1755, he mentions Uisge Beatha, but significantly there is no mention of whiskey. This is not mentioned until a later edition."

We asked that famous Scotsman, author of Whisky Galore and connoisseur of tobacco and good whisky, Sir Compton Mackenzie. He said:

"Real whisky, my boy, comes from the Scottish Highlands. Only the Scottish streams and genius can produce such a sublime drink. Although the Scots drank a great deal of brandy in former generations, it was they who invented whisky. They had to invent it because of the climate and the chills of the Highlands. I have heard of the other beverages claiming to be whisky, but there's only one whisky—Scotch."

The secretary of the Scotch Whisky Distillers' Association, Mr. James Woodhouse, said dryly:

"We wouldn't want to fall out with our good friends in Ireland. Let's just say we in Scotland were the first to produce Scotch whisky."

Cead Míle Fáilte
(A Hundred Thousand Welcomes)

Housed in a few of the old mansions are some of the old Irish land-lords whose incomes are gone, but who persist in living in their decaying homes. As a result, some of them are quite eccentric. Take the old gentleman in County Cork whose once beautiful mansion was filled with mice. Occasionally, he would whistle, and his favorite mouse would come out and he'd give it a drop of whiskey.

Once when he had an English visitor, the mouse got drunk, shook his paw and said, "Call in the dog and I'll fight him." "How extraordinary," said the English visitor.

"Yes, it is, rather," replied the old man. "It's usually the cat he wants to fight."

An Irishman, working on a building, fell four stories to the pavement below. He awoke to find a doctor holding forth a glass of water. "Begorrah," he exclaimed, "how far must a man fall here before he gets whiskey?"

McGuire walked into a saloon and asked the bartender for a drink. The bartender seeing that Mac already had too much to drink said, "Sorry, sir, I cannot serve you." McGuire left by a side exit and returned again through a back door, again sat at the bar and asked the same bartender for a drink—and received the same answer—"Sorry, but I can't serve you." Leaving through another exit and returning again through the front door, he again asked the same bartender for a drink. The bartender became very angry—"Sir, I've told you once, I've told you twice, and now I'm telling you for the third time—you're too drunk, and I can't serve you—now get out of here!" McGuire looked up and replied, "Hey, fellow, what do you do—work in every joint in town?"

A true gentleman is one who offers you a drink of Irish whiskey and doesn't watch while you pour it from the bottle, according to comedian Davy Crockett.

A man obviously under the influence of drink was about to enter his car in Grafton Street, Dublin, when he was stopped by a guard, who asked him: "Surely you are not going to drive that car?"

"Certainly, I'm going to drive it," was the reply. "I'm in no condition to walk."

There is another famous Donegal-born Connolly at the Players. He is the head steward, Charles Connolly, whose half century of sterling service there evoked a unanimous vote from the members to make him an honorary Player. He is credited with originating the celebrated Gibson drink. Some years ago, Player Charles Dana Gibson, the artist, asked Charley to concoct a different kind of gin potion than a Martini, and today's so popular Gibson was the result.

When Dublin's favorite actor, Cyril Cusack, was a guest at the Players, he enjoyed a Gibson so well he asked Charley Connolly for the recipe. Charley complied. Later back home, Cyril went into his favorite Dublin pub and orally gave Murphy, the proprietor, the Gibson recipe and asked him to make him one. When it came, the drink was practically all gin and instead of the traditional onion, there was a radish. After a sip, Cusack said, "That's no Gibson; that's a Murphy." However, today, according to Cusack, the Murphy has become a popular drink in Dublin or at least in Murphy's pub.

John Donahue, editor emeritus of *Columbia,* the magazine of the Knights of Columbus, tells about Slattery who worked as a bartender in some twelve saloons in a town in Southern Ireland. After tending bar for years in these twelve pubs, Slattery had scraped enough together to open his own saloon, making it the thirteenth bar in a town which had about 1300 people.

On the night that Slattery opened up, the other twelve bars closed down and their owners as well as their customers all flocked to Slattery's. It was a great night, with everyone spending freely, particularly Slattery's old bosses.

After closing up around daybreak, Slattery retired to his room upstairs, and as he was taking off his coat he noticed that the upper left-hand pocket of his vest was bulging with half crowns. Slattery glanced down solemnly at the bulging vest pocket and said, "Ah, you can't teach an old dog new tricks."

For all evening Slattery had been following his custom of many years when he worked for his employers. One for the house and one for meself. He didn't know it but all night long Slattery had been robbing himself.

Away back there was a thriving Irish saloon on the New York waterfront operated by one Matt Kinsella. According to Frank B. Clancy, who has been connected with the New York shipping interests for years, the secret of Kinsella's success as a publican was that he usually had a drink with every customer. He not only bought customers drinks freely but joined them himself and always accepted a courtesy drink from a patron.

When it came to order his own drink, Matt would signal the bartender and say, 'Give me some of that special Holland gin which the doctor ordered." The Holland gin was in a solid crock and the bartender would always pour Matt a fairly generous amount of straight gin. "The amazing thing," says Frank Clancy, "was that Kinsella through the years never seemed to show the effects of the drinks although he must have had several dozen a day with the longshoremen who appreciated his hospitality."

However, after Matt's death, his bartender, who didn't share in his will, leaked out the fact that it actually wasn't Holland gin which he served Kinsella; rather it was plain water.

Publisher representative Jack Curley relates of his visit on a summery day to a quaint pub in a remote section of Ireland. He asked for a Scotch on the rocks. The publican shook his head and asked Jack to explain. When he finished explaining that the rocks were simply ice, the publican replied: "Sorry, sir, but this isn't the season for ice."

Once in a Dublin pub where Dr. Oliver St. John Gogarty, famed poet and raconteur, was standing, a friend entered with a patch over his eye. Promptly, the good Doctor said: "Drink to me with thine only eye."

Another time, Davy Byrne, the publican mentioned in Joyce's *Ulysses*, spotted Gogarty in a bar and said: "Dr. Gogarty, I often served you from the other side of the counter, so it is now my turn to stand you a drink." "Yes," replied Gogarty, "they also stand who only serve and wait."

Once interrupted in the middle of an anecdote by a prominent financier who commented: "You can't believe eighty per cent of what Gogarty says." "The trouble about you," came back Gogarty, "is that you can never forget your percentage!"

The sage of Bray, the lovely little seaside town just outside of Dublin, is Patrick Lyne. For some years before World War II, Lyne was the New York representative of British-Irish Railways. He recalls that once when attending Mass in St. Patrick's Cathedral in Manhattan, Oliver Gogarty joined him in the same pew. Pat was very much impressed as Gogarty took out a Missal from his pocket and began following the Mass attentively with his lips moving as if in deep prayer.

Out of Celtic curiosity, Pat Lyne stole a glance at Gogarty's Missal and discovered he was reading Horace's *Odes*.

That congenial conductor, John Whyte, who is responsible for the daily 5:23 P.M. New Haven train which takes commuters from New York to Larchmont and Rye, was offered a half-fare ticket by an Irish mother for her long-haired son, a large glob of a lad, togged out in tight-fitting dirty denims. Conductor Whyte asked the boy's age and was told he was 9 years old.

"He looks 18 to me," remarked Conductor Whyte, an Irisher himself and father of a large family.

"Indade," tartly answered the mother. "Can I help if if he worries?"

Boat Train

Back in the early 1930's, when we made our first trip to Ireland, the boat train from Cobh to Dublin was quite an event. That was in the times when Prohibition still reigned in the United States. Besides, there were no transatlantic airplanes, and all traffic from America to Ireland came by boat.

When we took the train, it was thronged with returning Irish who had been working in the States and were using their vacations for visits to their families and friends at home in Ireland. The holiday atmosphere prevailed. Many of the returning natives were met at the boat in Cobh by families and friends who accompanied them on the boat train to Dublin. Private and public drinking parties broke out everywhere on the train the moment we got under way.

Much to our surprise, when the first stop came at Limerick Junction, the train emptied suddenly. Everyone seemed to be dashing pell-mell toward the station, leaving their baggage behind in their seats. Naturally, out of curiosity, we joined the stampede to the station. As surmised, we thought with the drinking already being done, the lavatories were the passengers' destination. Instead, it was the station bar.

Incidentally, in these local Irish railway stations, the bar premises occupied almost three-quarters of the space. The ticket and baggage offices seemed like small annexes.

At the bar, not only were the passengers ordering single drinks but pints and quarts which they wanted to carry back on the train. Evidently, many of the Irishers who had been in America wanted to quench that long, long thirst with good old John Jameson's or Power's Irish whiskey which Prohibition had forbidden them to partake of for so long.

At the first stop in Limerick Junction, we noticed a tumblerful of Jameson which the barmaid poured and laid to one side. While the crowd were drinking at the bar, in came the conductor holding his watch in his hand and shouted: "Come on now, drink up, you have only a minute more before we take off."

With that, the barmaid reached for the glassful of whiskey set aside, and handed it to the conductor with a wonderful smile and said: "Here, Mr. O'Leary, the compliments of the house!"

With that, Conductor O'Leary glanced at his watch again, "Aye, I figured wrong, ye all got five minutes more. That's because of the good service we give ye. We are way ahead of time."

Cheers and laughter greeted Conductor O'Leary's remarks. As he leisurely drained his own glass, re-orders went to the bar from the throng. Finally, in due course, all got back on the boat train.

The same procedure was followed at the next and every other

stop we made en route to Dublin, and there must have been at least six more in the several hours' ride. It was quite evident to all that the Dublin Boat Train was no longer "way ahead of time." One crabby passenger, an Englishman likely, who had a timetable, angrily berated Conductor O'Leary with: "What good are the figures printed on these timetables?" O'Leary wearily explained: "My dear sir, if we didn't have these figures, how would we ever know how late the Dublin Boat Trains were?"

Atheist Hit by Truck

BY JOHN McNULTY

This drunk came down the "L" stairs, and at the bottom he made a wrong turn. This led him into the gutter instead of onto the sidewalk, and a truck hit him and knocked him down.

It is a busy corner there at Forty-second Street and Second Avenue, in front of the Shanty, and there's a hack line there. Naturally, a little crowd and a cop gathered around the drunk and some hackies were in the crowd.

The cop was fairly young. After he hauled the guy up and sat him on the bottom step of the "L" stairs, he saw there wasn't much wrong with him. His pants were torn and maybe his knee was twisted slightly—maybe cut.

The cop got out his notebook and began asking questions and writing the answers down. Between questions he had to prop the man up. Fellow gave his name—Wilson, Martin, some noncommittal name—and his address. Everybody around was interested in these facts.

The blind man in the newspaper hut under the stairs felt a little put out because nobody was telling him what was going on, and he could hear beguiling fragments of it. "What happen? What happen?" the blind man kept asking, but the event wasn't deemed sensational enough for anybody to run and tell him, at least until afterward.

"What religion are yuh?" the policeman asked the man, who

propped himself up this time and blurted out, "Atheist! I'm an atheist!"

For some reason, a lot of people laughed.

"Jeez, he's an atheist!" one of the hackies said. He shouted to a comrade who was still sitting behind the wheel of a parked cab at the corner, "Feller says he's an atheist!"

"Wuddaya laughing at?" the cop asked, addressing himself to the crowd generally. "Says he's an atheist, so he's an atheist. Wuddaya laughing at?" He wrote something in the book.

Another policeman, from over by Whelan's drugstore, where there was a picket line, strolled up. He was an older cop, more lines in his face, bigger belly, less humps around his hips, because the equipment—twisters, mace, and all that stuff—fitted on him better after all these years. "Wuzzamadder with 'im?" he asked his colleague.

"This here truck hit him. He isn't hurt bad. Says he's an atheist."

"I am an atheist!" the man yelled.

The crowd laughed again.

"Did you put that down—atheist?" the older cop asked.

"Yuh, I put it in where it says 'religion.' "

"Rubbid out. Rubbid out. Put in Cat'lic. He looks like a Cat'lic to me. He's got an Irish name? Anyway rubbid out. When he sobers up, he'll be sorry he said that atheist business. Put in Cat'lic. We gotta send him to Bellevue just for safety's sake." The young cop started for the drugstore to put in a call.

"Never mind safety's sake. I'm an atheist, I'm telling you," the drunk said, loud as he could.

"Cuddid out, cuddid out," the older cop said. Then he leaned over like a lecturer or somebody. "An' another thing—if you wouldn't go round sayin' you're an atheist, maybe you wouldn't be gettin' hit by trucks."

The crowd sensed a great moral lesson and didn't laugh.

"Jeez! The guy says he's an atheist," the hackie said again.

A little later the Bellevue ambulance came.

"I yam a natheist," the man kept muttering as they put him into the ambulance.

"All the Sweet Buttermilk . . ."

By Donagh MacDonagh

The most lonesome place I was ever posted to was a little town twenty miles from the nearest railway, in the County Mayo, where there was neither cinema, theater nor anything else; the only entertainment was a chat and a smoke, a drink and an occasional dance. I was always a great one to fish and take life easy, so it suited me fine, but the Sergeant didn't fancy it at all.

Sergeant Finnegan was a dour-looking man and very close. I never rightly discovered what it was had him shifted to that place, but it can't have been want of zeal. He was the most energetic man and the most enthusiastic man in his search for crime that ever I met. Of course he was wasting his time looking for crime in Coolnamara, but what he couldn't find he invented.

Hanlon and Flaherty and myself used to have a grand easy life of it in old Sergeant Moloney's time; there wasn't a bicycle lamp in the district, the pubs closed when the last customer went home, and that was earlier than you'd think, and if there was any poteen made, nobody came worrying us about it. But Sergeant Finnegan soon changed all that. He wasn't a month in the place till every lad in the county had a lamp on his bike, I even bought one myself; and there was such a row kicked up about the pubs staying open that nobody went home till midnight. They suddenly realized that there must be a great charm in after-hours drinking.

The Sergeant used to have me cross-eyed chasing round the country in search of illicit stills, and as soon as ever I'd get settled down for the evening with my pipe going nicely and the wireless behind my head, he'd be in with some new list of outrages, cattle straying on the road, a camp of tinkers that whipped a couple of chickens, or some nonsense like that.

"Take your feet down off that mantelpiece," he'd say, "and get out on patrol. Who knows what malicious damage or burglary or larceny is going on under the cover of night!" And up I'd have to get, put on my coat and go in next door to listen to the news.

He was a great man for objecting to dance-hall licenses, and if he'd had his way there wouldn't have been a foot put on a floor within the four walls of Ireland. On the night of a dance he'd be snooping around to see was there any infringement of the regulations, and his finger itching on the pencil to make notes for a prosecution.

One night there was an all-night dance over in Ballyduv and he sent me over to keep an eye on it.

"I think I better go in mufti, Sergeant," says I. "There's no use in drawing their attention to the Civic Guards being present."

"True. True. Quite true!" says he. So up I went and changed, chuckling to myself. I could have worn a beard and a major-general's outfit and every hog, dog and devil in the place would have known me. But I always enjoyed a dance and I didn't want to be encumbered with a uniform for the stretch of the evening.

When I got to the dance-hall, it was about half-ten but hardly anyone had arrived yet. At an all-night dance they're never in much of a hurry to get started, and besides, the lads have to get washed and changed after the day's work. I stood chatting to Callaghan, that owned the hall, for a bit, and then we went over to Hennessy's for a couple of pints. Of course it was well after hours by this time, but with the Sergeant safe in Coolnamara nobody was worrying too much about that. Around about half-eleven we heard the band getting into its stride, so we came back to see how the fun was going.

As soon as I stepped in through the door I saw the grandest-looking girl you'd want to see, bronze-colored hair, green eyes, and an American dress that was made for her figure.

"Who's that?" says I to Callaghan. "She must be down from Dublin."

"Dublin nothing!" says he. "She's from the mountain beyond. There's a whole family of them, and they're as wild as a lot of mountain goats. Lynch's they are."

"Give us a knock-down," says I. "I'll surely die if I don't meet that one!"

"I will," says he, "but I better say nothing about you being in the Guards."

"And why not?"

"Now never mind. It's what I'm telling you." So he brought me over and introduced me to her.

Well, we got on grand. There was a waltz just starting and I asked her out, and we danced from that out without a break, and when we were tired dancing we went out for a bit of a walk, and I can tell you I wasn't wasting my time.

She told me all about the sister in America, and how anxious she was to get to Dublin, and I could see she was dying down dead to find out what I was, but after Jack Callaghan's warning, I made her no wiser.

On about one o'clock we were whirling around when what should I see sloping in through the door but the Sergeant, and he in mufti, too. He gave me a very cold nod and I didn't pretend to take the least bit of notice of him.

"Who's your friend?" says she. "I never saw him before."

"Any more than you saw me!" says I, giving her a squeeze and avoiding the question.

"Who is he, though?" she said again, so I saw there was no way out of it.

"That's Sergeant Finnegan from Coolnamara," says I, "and a greater trouble maker there isn't in the country."

"And what else would he be only a trouble maker, if he's a Guard. If there's one thing I hate in this world it's a Guard, and if there's a thing I hate more it's a Sergeant." I could see I was on very delicate ground and took all the trouble I could not to be any way awkward with my big feet.

"And why is that?" says I, but she only tossed her head and shot the Sergeant dead with both her green eyes.

After a bit some great gawk of a countryman managed to prise her away from me, and off she went, though I felt she'd rather stay.

No sooner had she gone than I could feel the Sergeant breathing down the back of my neck.

"Come outside here till I talk to you," says he, and I could see she had her eyes buried in us as we went out the door.

"Do you know what that is?" says he.

"That's a girl called Maeve Lynch," says I. "Isn't she a grand-looking thing."

"Her father's the greatest poteen maker in the County of Mayo, and I thought you were long enough in the county to know that."

"Well, that's news to me. He was never prosecuted in my time.

How do you know?"

"From information received. Now you keep away from that girl, or it might be worse for you. And keep your mind on your business. Don't you know you have no right to be dancing?"

"I was just seeing could I pick up any information. But things are very quiet."

"Things are never as quiet as they appear. I hope you investigated Hennessy's after closing time."

"You can be bound I did!" says I without a smile.

We went back into the hall, and as soon as I got the Sergeant's back turned I gave Maeve the beck to come on out. As she passed the Sergeant, she gave him a glare that must have rocked him back on his heels.

"Are you not going to dance?" says she to me, but instead of an-swering I drew her out into the dark and slipped an arm around her. We walked along for a while without saying a word. Then she gave my hand a squeeze.

"What did the Sergeant want with you?"

"Ah, he was just chatting."

"You seem to be terrible great with him."

"I wouldn't say that. I just know him."

"Did he say anything about me?"

"What would he say? He doesn't know you, does he?"

"Oh, the dear knows. They're a very nosy crowd, the Guards. Come on back and dance."

"No," I said, "I'm tired. Let's sit down." So we sat down.

When we got back to the dance, it was near breaking up and the Sergeant was gone. I was all for taking her home, but there were some cousins of hers there who said they'd take her in a trap, so I arranged to meet her the next Sunday at a dance a few miles aways, and away I went singing "The Red-Haired Girl" and whis-tling back at the birds.

I had an early breakfast and was off to the lake with my rod and line long before the Sergeant or Hanlon or Flaherty were stirring. I spent half the day fishing and half the day dreaming, and when I got back in the afternoon the Sergeant was fit to be tied.

"Where were you all day?" says he. "I'll report you to the Super-intendent for being absent without leave."

"Oh, indeed I wasn't, Sergeant," says I, "I was on duty all day. I was down at the lake keeping an eye open for poachers." It was fortunate that I had left the half-dozen trout down the town on my way home.

"Poachers!" says he. "And who ever heard of poachers on Cool Lake?"

"You never know when they might start. I took the precaution of bringing along a rod as a camouflage!" I could see he was only half convinced, but he let it go.

"Get up on your bike there," says he. "We have work to do." But I told him I'd have to get something to eat first. I had such an appetite that minute that I'd have nearly eaten the sour face off himself. I downed a good meal in record time and the two of us started off.

For a couple of miles the Sergeant never said a word, and I said no more. After a bit I realized we were heading up towards the mountains, a part of the world I wasn't very well acquainted with.

"Where are we off to, Sergeant?" says I.

"We're off on a job that may get you your Sergeant's stripes if you play your cards right. It's that old Maurice Lynch. I have information that he's after running enough poteen to set the whole countryside drunk. He thinks he's as safe as Gibraltar, stuck up here on his mountainside, but it isn't old Sergeant Moloney he has to deal with now. Callaghan told me last night the daughter didn't know about you being in the Guards."

"That's true enough."

"Well, maybe it's just as well you were so busy chasing after her. You'll be able to keep them in chat while I have a look around. You can pretend you came on a social call."

I cursed my day's fishing when I realized that it was too late now to get any word to Maeve. If I'd been in the station when the Sergeant first decided on this expedition, I could have sent a message through Callaghan, but here I was now on an empty bog road with the Sergeant glued to my side and ever stroke on the pedals bringing us nearer. There was a big push being made against poteen all through the country, and I knew it would go hard with old Lynch if he was caught.

At last we got into the mountains, and after a while we had to get down and walk, and heavy climbing it was.

"There it is now," says the Sergeant. "We'll have to dump the bikes and take to the fields. But you go ahead and I'll follow after at a safe distance."

Here's my chance, said I to myself, and I started hot-foot for the farmhouse. Just as I got to the gate, a fine handsome girl with red hair came out the door and leaned against the jamb, showing off her figure. I was just going to wave to her when I realized that it wasn't Maeve.

"What can we do for you?" says she, looking very bold at me.

"Listen!" says I. "This is urgent. If you have any poteen about the place, for God's sake tell me where it is till I get rid of it. There's a Sergeant of the Guards on his way across the fields now."

"Poteen?" says she. "Poteen? I seem to have heard of the stuff."

"Look!" I said. "This is no time for fooling. Show me where it is quick till I destroy it. God knows I'm taking enough risk." She stretched her arms over her head and yawned.

"Is your father here?" I said.

"He is not."

"Is Maeve?"

"She is not."

"Well then, show me where it is quick. The Sergeant will be in on top of us in a minute."

"He'll find nothing here."

"Very well then, I give up. But you'll be a sorry girl if your father gets six months or a year in jail."

"Be off with you now, you have the look of a spy about you. By the big boots I'd take you for a peeler. Go on now before I let out Shep."

I gave a sigh and turned out the gate again. The Sergeant was just coming up the field, his uniform standing out against the country like a scarecrow in the corn.

"Why aren't you inside keeping them out of the way?" says he.

"There's no one there."

"Better and better. Come on and help me now." And he was off like a retriever for the barn. I pretended to help him in his search, but he found no more than I did.

"I'll tell you a little trick I know," says he, and he caught up a dung-fork that was lying against the wall. "Come out here now and I'll show you." So I followed him out again. He went across to the heap of manure that was lying in the back yard and started to probe around in it with the fork. I was just standing, admiring the fine sight of a Sergeant at work when there was the noise of the fork striking something, and the next moment the Sergeant was standing up holding a two-gallon jar. He pulled out the cork and gave the first real smile I ever saw on his face.

"Poteen!" says he, and the way he said it you'd think it was a poem. Then he whipped it behind his back and I looked round and saw Maeve's sister just coming round the corner of the house. When she saw the Sergeant's uniform, she shook her fist at the two of us.

"I knew what you were," she said. "I knew! Let you get out of this now before my father gets back or it'll be the worse for the pair of you."

"Be careful, young woman!" says the Sergeant. "It is a very dangerous thing to obstruct a Guard officer in the discharge of his duty. We are here in search of illicit spirits, and if there is any on the premises it is wiser to tell us now."

I was leaning against the door of the barn, looking out over the Mayo mountains, and wondering how long would poor old Lynch get at the District Court when what should I see peeping up over the hedge but another red head. And this time it Maeve sure enough. She had been there all the time watching every move. She gave me a wicked glare. I winked back. The Sergeant was standing with his back turned to her, rocking from his heels to his toes playing cat-and-mouse with the sister, and waggling the jar gently behind his back. There wasn't a prouder Sergeant on the soil of Ireland that minute.

I could see that Maeve wasn't quite sure whether I was just a pal of the Sergeant's that came out to keep him company, or a Guard on duty, and she kept glancing from me to the jar that the Sergeant was so busy hiding. She seemed to be asking me a question with her eyes. As there wasn't anything I could do to help her, I gave her another wink and a big grin. She looked hard at me, then ducked out of sight behind the hedge. I was just beginning to wonder what had happened to her when she stood up straight, and my heart nearly stopped when I saw the big lump of a rock she had

in her fist. I'm not a very narrow-minded man, and I had no particular regard for the Sergeant, but I wasn't going to have him
murdered in cold blood before my eyes. If a thing like that came
out at the inquest it would look very bad on my record. I was in
two minds whether to shout out or not, weighing the trouble
Maeve and her family would get into if I did against the trouble
I'd get into if I didn't, when she drew back her arm, took wicked
and deliberate aim, and let fly. I closed my eyes tight and turned
away. When I heard a scream of agony from the Sergeant, I closed
them even tighter, but I opened them again when I heard what
he was shouting.

"Blast it! Blast it! Blast it to hell!" he was roaring, and then I
saw the heap of broken crockery at his feet. The sister was in kinks
of laughter and there wasn't a sign of a Maeve. There was a most
delightful smell of the very best poteen on the air, and when the
Sergeant threw the handle of the jar on the ground in a rage, I
realized that it was the jar and not the Sergeant's head that had
received the blow. I burst out laughing.

"Who did that?" he shouted at me. "Who did that, you grinning
imbecile?" But I shook my head.

"I was just day-dreaming," I said. "I didn't see a thing."

"You'll pay for this!" he said. "You'll pay dearly for this, you
inefficient lout! Dereliction of duty! Gross imbecility! Crass stupidity! I'll have the coat off your back for this day's work!" Of
course the poor man didn't know what he was saying, but in a way
I was nearly sorry for him. He was so sure that he had the case all
sewn up. But now, without the contents of the jar, any chance of a
prosecution was ballooned from the beginning. The Law requires
very strict proof in these matters.

The Sergeant and myself searched all through the farm that day.
And every day for a week afterwards Flaherty and Hanlon and myself searched it again. But it was labor in vain. It was great
weather, though, and I used to spend most of the day lying out in
the hay, and after the first day I managed to get Maeve to join me.
I had a terrible job persuading her that all Guards aren't as bad as
she thought, and that the Sergeant was quite exceptional. Fortunately, Flaherty and Hanlon were in no great hurry to get the
searching finished, so I had plenty of time to devote to persuading
her. For some reason old Lynch didn't seem to care if we searched

till doomsday, and himself and myself struck up a great friendship when I told him about my conversation with Maeve's sister Mary. So that when Maeve agreed to marry me he put up no objection.

The Sergeant did his level best to have me drummed out of the Guards for marrying a poteen-maker's daughter, but, as I pointed out to the Superintendent, there was no proof that Maurice Lynch ever ran a drop of poteen, and even if he did, wouldn't a Guard in the family be the greatest deterrent against illicit distilling? The Superintendent saw my point, but I'm not so sure that I was right. I've often said that my father-in-law makes the smoothest run of mountain dew it has ever been my good luck to taste.

It was just as well the Sergeant was moved soon after. He was very bitter about the broken jar and would have stopped at nothing to get a conviction. Things have been very quiet and peaceful since he left, and crime has practically disappeared from the district.

Irish Bulls and
Pure Poteen

Irish Bulls

The great famine occurred in Ireland in 1845. Following that, began the great waves of Irish immigration to America. Starting with the late 1840's, up until the turn of the century in 1900, the Irish arrived in the United States in the millions, practically cutting their nation's population in half. In 1840, Ireland's population was over 8,000,000. Today, it is scarcely half of that.

Though the Irish had the advantage over other immigrants from other European countries in that they spoke English, they were, in the main, poor, uneducated, and untrained. The best they could hope for were jobs as low-paid laborers or domestics. Many went to work in the coal mines of Pennsylvania or joined the gold rushes to Colorado, California and Alaska. Others quickly enlisted in both the Union and Confederate Armies. There were many brigades composed entirely of Irish immigrants in both the Union and Confederate Armies.

Withal, up to 1900, the Irish were regarded almost everywhere in the U.S.A. as newly arrived immigrants, unfamiliar with the country or the customs. Certain segments of American citizenry for whose jobs they competed were openly resentful of the Irish, made them the butt of many jokes, and to a degree persecuted them.

However, this was nothing unusual to these new American Irish. They had known the effects of penal laws, lack of privileges and persecution in their own dear old Erin. So in America, they met the challenge by playing it safe, as they had done at home, but in a way which would not give offense to anybody. In short, the Irish were not as dumb as their critics would make them out to be. Basically, they possessed an earthy shrewdness and showed it repeatedly. Being uneducated, untrained and new to America, naturally, they made mistakes—plenty. However, the Irish were able with innate charm and cheerfulness to laugh along with those who found them inexperienced and amusing.

It was these Hibernian mistakes in language, customs, and manners which were called "Irish Bulls." For almost a half century in America, "Irish Bulls" formed a major part of American entertainment on the stage, in cartoons, in magazine and newspaper articles, and in the daily conversation of most Americans. The "Irish Bulls" or the Pat and Mike jokes were daily favorites with all.

Sir Boyle Roche is claimed by Irishmen as father of the bulls, though one Aladich Bull, an Irish lawyer in London, is said to have made his name famous by his blundering. Sir Boyle was the son of a Limerick gentleman, served with the British army against the French in Canada, was later in the Irish Revenue department and represented various boroughs in parliament. He died in Dublin in 1807. Perhaps his most celebrated bull is: "Why should we beggar ourselves to benefit posterity? What has posterity done for us?" Inviting a friend to visit him, he wrote: "If you ever come within a mile of our house, will you stop there all night?" One of his most cherished bulls was: "Along the untrodden paths of the future, I can see the footprints of an unknown hand." In a message to a friend he declared: "While I write this letter, I have a pistol in one hand and a sword in the other."

The following gems are connected by long usage with Sir Boyle's name:

"I smell a rat. I see him floating in the air but mark me, I shall nip him in the bud."

"Many thousands of them were destitute of even the goods they possessed."

To guard the Shannon he proposed: "Sir, I would anchor a frigate off each bank of this river, with strict orders not to stir, and so, by cruising up and down, put a stop to smuggling." But not all the bulls are Sir Boyle's.

Sir John Parnell, in a debate in the Irish House of Commons in 1795, advised that "in the prosecution of the present war every man ought to be ready to give his last guinea to protect the remainder."

R. J. Mecredy in *Irish Cyclist* advised that "the best way to pass a cow on the road when cycling is to keep behind it," and an anonymous do-gooder has suggested that "there is nothing keeps the feet warm like an empty petrol tin full of hot water."

An Irish farmer returning from the market where he sold his pig reported: "Well, I didn't get as much as I expected, but then I didn't expect I would."

Pure Poteen

The other day a little red-faced Irishman approached a post office which had three letter boxes outside. One was labeled "City," another "Domestic," and the third "Foreign." He looked at the three in turn and then as a puzzled expression crossed his face, scratched his head.

"Faith," he was heard to mutter, "I don't know in which wan to put th' letter. Sure, Katie's a domestic, an' she lives in the city alright, an' she's a furriner, too; but, begobs, how can th' thing go in both of the three holes at wance?"

"Pat, if Mr. Jones come back before I return, tell him that I will meet him at two o'clock."

"Aye, aye, sir; but what shall I tell him if he doesn't come?"

An Irishman, describing the trading powers of the genuine Yankee, said, "Bedad, if he was cast away on a desolate island, he'd get up the next morning and go round selling maps to the inhabitants."

In a meeting years ago, Lord Erne in Ireland was attempting to shut off a speaker who was away off base in his remarks.

"Mr. O'Leary," said he, "I regret very much to say that you are out of order."

"I thank you for your anxiety, my lord," answered O'Leary, "but I assure I never felt in better health."

Among the conditions of sale by an Irish auctioneer was the following: "The highest bidder to be the purchaser, unless some gentheman bids more."

Mr. Hogan (after hammering on the door for five minutes) : "Is it dead or alive ye are?"

Mr. Grogan (within) : "Nayther; I'm shlapin'."

At a legal investigation of a liquor seizure the judge asked an unwilling witness: "What was in the barrel that you had?" The reply was: "Well, your honor, it was marked 'whisky' on one end of the barrel and 'Pat Duffy' on the other end, so that I can't say whether it was whisky or Pat Duffy was in the barrel, being as I am on my oath."

The Prosecuting Attorney: "Was the prisoner in the habit of singing when he was alone?"

Pat McGuire (witness) : "Shure, an' I can't say, for Oi was niver with him when he was alone."

Pat Kelly came home one night a little to the bad from whisky and went to bed with a somewhat hazy idea of things. In the night he was aroused by the cry of "Fire!" and in his anxiety to make a hasty toilet, and not wholly recovered from the effects of his indiscretion earlier in the evening, he donned his trousers hind side before. As he started down the stairs he slipped and fell, rolling to the bottom of the flight. A friend rushed to his assistance and exclaimed, "Are you hurted, Pat?" Kelly got on his feet slowly, and after an intent and analytical examination of his trousers said, "No, but I got a hell of a twist."

"Dennis," said a gentleman to his janitor, "you are late this morning. What's your trouble?"

"I wor obliged to go to court this mornin' where they wor investigating a little occurrence that happened last night."

"Well, did they find anything?"

"Yes, they fined me."

Casey and Riley agreed to settle their dispute by a fight, and it was understood that whoever wanted to quit should say "Enough." Casey got Riley down and was hammering him unmercifully when Riley called out several times, "Enough!" As Casey paid no attention, but kept on administering punishment, a bystander said,

"Why don't you let him up? Don't you hear him say that he's got enough?" "I do," says Casey, "but he's such a liar, you can't believe him."

An Irish provincial paper inserted the following notice: "Whereas, Patrick O'Connor lately left his lodgings, this is to give notice that if he does not return immediately and pay for the same, he will be advertised."

"Doctor: "Begorra and I've knocked the fever out of him. That is one good thing."
Wife of Patient: "Oh, doctor, do you think there is any hope?"
Doctor: "Small chance of that, marm; but ye'll have the satisfaction of knownin' that he died cured."

An Irish editor congratulates himself that "half the lies told about him are not true."

In hearing an Irish case of assault and battery, counsel, in cross-examining one of the witnesses, asked him what they had the first place they stopped at.
"Four glasses of ale," was the reply.
"Next?"
"Two glasses of whisky."
"Next?"
"One glass of brandy."
"Next?"
"A fight."

The following is a resolution of an Irish corporation: "That a new jail should be built, that this be done out of the materials of the old one, and the old jail to be used until the new one be completed."

An Irishman, apologizing for running away from a fight, said, "Bedad, I'd rather be a coward fifteen minutes than a corpse the rest of my life."

This passage is from the report of an Irish Benevolent Society:

'Notwithstanding the large amount paid for medicine and medical attendance, very few deaths occurred during the year."

Mike: "I saw a man fall from a roof on a wagonload of soda water yesterday."
Pat: "Killed, I suppose?"
Mike: "No; he landed on soft stuff."

An Irishman, upon being asked "What is an Irish bull, anyway?" replied:
"Well, it's like this: Supposing there were thirteen cows lying down in a field, and one of them was standing up; that would be a bull."

"Faith, Mrs. O'Hara, how d'ye till thim twins apart?"
"Aw, 'tis aisy. I sticks me finger in Dinnis' mouth, an' if ee bites I know it's Moike."

Minister (writing a certificate at a christening, and trying to recall the date) : "Let me see, this is the thirtieth?"
Indignant Mother: "Indade, an' it's only the elivinth."

Mike: "The trouble with Casey is he has no backbone."
Pat: "Faith, he has backbone enough if he'd only bring it to the front."

An Irishman was brought to task by his employer for being absent from his work one day, and his excuse was that he "wint to a funeral." His employer asked him who was dead, and he replied, "Divil a know I know—who it was. I jist wint for the ride."

"Pat," said one Catholic friend to another, "how would you like to be buried in a Protestant graveyard?" "Faith, an' I'd die first!"

"Dennis, I'm told ye was the best man at Mike's marriage." "The same is a lie," answered Dennis, "but I was as good as any man was there."

"Did you have any trouble with black ants in Ireland, Bridget?"

"No, ma'am, but I had some trouble onc't with a white uncle."

Pat: "Do yez belave in ghosts, Moike?"

Mike: "Oi do. Oi don't think thur's a ghost of a chance av me iver becomin' prisidint av Amerikey."

"I presume, Mrs. Murphy, you carry a memento of some sort in that locket of yours?"

"Indeed I do, sir; it's a lock of my Dan's hair."

"But your husband is still alive."

"Yes, sir, but his hair is all gone."

"Who lives in that big house on the corner, Dennis?"

"The widdy O'Malley, sor, who is dead."

"Indeed! When did she die?"

"If she had lived till next Sunday she would have been dead a year."

"Your money or your life!" growled the footpad.

"Take me life," responded the Irishman. "I'm savin' me money for me old age."

"Good morning, Mr. Cassidy," said the undertaker's humorous friend. "I suppose business is dead with you?"

"Faith, it is so," replied Cassidy, with great seriousness. "I haven't buried a livin' soul for nearly a month."

An Irishman got out of his carriage at a railway station for refreshments, but the bell rang and the train left before he had finished his repast.

"Hould on!" cried Pat, as he ran like a madman after the car. "Hould on, ye murthen ould stame injin—ye've got a passenger on board what's left behind."

Two Irishmen who had just landed in this country had taken rooms in one of the downtown hotels in New York. In the middle of the night they were awakened by a great noise in the street. One of the Irishmen got up and looked out of the window. Two fire engines tore along, belching smoke and fire and leaving a trail of sparks.

"Phwat is ut?" asked the chap who remained in bed.

"They're movin' hell," said the man at the window, "and two loads have just gone by."

An Irish sergeant in a volunteer corps, being doubtful whether he had distributed rifles to all the men, called out: "All of ye that are without arms hold up your hands!"

Cassidy: "Brace up, man! Troth, ye luk as if ye didn't hov a frind in the whole wur'rld."

Hogan: "Oi hovn't."

Cassidy: "G'wan. If it ain't money ye want t' borry Oi'm as good a frind as iver ye had."

His Honor: "What made you steal this gentleman's doormat?"

Pat: "Shure, yer honor, isn't 'Welcome' on it in letters as long as yer a-r-rm?"

"And how's yer wife, Pat?"

"Sure, she do be awful sick."

"Is ut dangerous she is?"

"No, she's too weak t' be dangerous anymore!"

A young lady went into a well-known establishment a few days ago and said to the floorwalker,

"Do you keep stationery?"

"No, ma'am," replied the floorwalker; "if I did I should lose me job."

"I hear O'Reilly is going to prove an alibi at his trial."

"What's an alibi, Pat?"

"Shure and it's being in two places at wanst!"

When Dr. John Cairns went from Scotland to Ireland for rest and travel in 1864, he was at once delighted by discovering from the guides who showed him about that most of the landed gentry were "Sunday folks."

"That's a fine castle," he would say, pointing to a big house set like a crown on some rocky hill.

"Yes, sorr," said his guide. " 'Tis Sir John O'Connor's" or " 'Tis Sir Rory O'Moore's." He always added, "He's a Sunday mon."

At last Dr. Cairns grew curious.

"What is a Sunday man?" he asked.

"Well, sorr, it do be a mon thot has so many writs out agin him for debt that he stays shut up tight in his house all the week, and only comes out on Sunday, when the law protects him."

Two Irish servants were quarreling. "Shure," said the one, "an' didn't Oi hear yer masther comin' in after half-pasht four av the noight." "An' shure," retorted the other, "an' didn't Oi hear yer masther not comin' home at all lasht noight."

An Irish lover remarks that it is a great comfort to be alone, "especially when yer swateheart is wid ye."

Mike: "Say, Mrs. Nolan, I hear you are keeping company with a man, an' your husband is only dead six months."

Widow Nolan: "True for you, Mike, I am, an' glad of it."

Mike: "Sure, I am ashamed to hear you say so, and indeed you ought to have more respect for his memory."

Widow Nolan: "Whist, now, Mike; you can't take a memory in your arms of a cowld night."

The judge asked an Irish policeman named O'Connell, "When did you last see your sister?" The policeman replied: "The last time I saw her, judge, was about eight months ago, when she called at my home, and I was out." "Then you did not see her on that occasion?" "No, judge, I wasn't there."

Mike: "Shure, Pat, health is a good thing to have."

Pat: "Yis, Moike, especially when yez is sick!"

Inquisitive Party: "And do you go up that ladder all day long?"

Pat: "No, sur; half of the toime Oi come down."

Employer: "Don't you see what's on the door?"

Pat: "A bit ov paper, sir."

Employer: "It says, 'Please shut the door.' "
Pat: "Faith, I didn't hear it, sir!"

An American was boasting of Niagara Falls. "There!" cried Jonathan to a newly arrived Paddy, as he waved his hand in the direction of the Horseshoe Falls. "There! Now, isn't that wonderful?"

"Wontherful?" replied Pat. "What's wontherful?"

"Why, to see all that water coming over them rocks."

"Faith, then, to tell ye the honest truth," was the response, "I can't see anything very wontheerful in that. Why, what the divil is there to hinther it?"

An Irishman, hearing of a friend who had a stone coffin made for himself, exclaimed:

"Faith, that's good; shure, an' a shtone coffin w'ud lasht a man a loife-toime!"

Foreman: "Look here, Pat, you heard the governor say that job must be finished tonight?"

Pat: "All roight, sur, I'll have it done tonight if it takes me till tomarrow marnin'."

An Irish lady was up before a judge for assault on one Patrick Gihooly.

Judge: "The testimony proves that you threw a brick at this man."

The Lady: "The testimony proves more nor that, judge. It proves I hit him!"

O'Brien: "An' poor Flanagan got sixteen years in Sing Sing."

Murphy: "For phwat?"

O'Brien: "For hommycide, I belave."

Murphy: "Oh, shure that's nothing. I thought it might be for killin' somebody."

Grady (after Riley has fallen five stories) : "Are yez dead, Pat?"

Riley: "Oi am."

Grady: "Shure, yer such a liar Oi don't know whither to believe yez or not."

Riley: "Shure, thot proves Oi'm dead. Ye wudn't dare call me a liar if Oi wur aloive!"

Pat O'Brien gave a dinner, to which he invited three or four of his neighbors. Pat had allowed his wife to cook only one chicken. When dinner was served, Pat took possession of the carving knife and, in a hospitable tone, said to Mrs. Dugan: "What part of the fowl will you have?"

"A leg, if you please," was the answer.

"An' what part will yez have? Would yez loike some of the white?" Pat inquired of Mrs. O'Hooligan.

"An' a leg will do me," she answered. As each answered, the part of the fowl she desired was given her.

"What part will yez have, Moike Walsh?" Pat blandly inquired of his neighbor.

"Oi belave Oi will take a leg, too," said Mike, in his most modest way, wishing to follow in the footsteps of the rest of the company.

"Begorra," said Pat to Mickey, "what does yez think Oi'm carving—a spider?"

An Irishman was planting shade trees when a passing lady said:
"You're digging out the holes, are you, Mr. Haggerty?"
"No, mum, Oi'm diggin' out the dirt an' lavin' the holes."

Pat: "Did you attend Casey's funeral?"
Mike: "Oi did."
Pat: "Was you wan av th' mourners?"
Mike: "Oi was—somebody stole my hat."

Casey: "How do you tell the age of a turkey?"
Pat: "By the teeth."
Casey: "A turkey hasn't got teeth!"
Pat: "No; but I have."

Casey: "Oi see there's bin another railroad wreck due to an open switch."
Cassidy: "Aye, 'tis a pity somewan don't invint a switch thot'll stay shut when it's open."

An Irish couple, whose married bliss was not without a few "squalls," received a homely lecture from their spiritual adviser regarding their disgraceful quarrels.

"Why, that dog and cat you have agree better than you."

"If yer riverence'll toie them tigither, ye'll soon change yer moind."

Lincoln's Irish Soldiers

By Leonard Patrick O'Connor Wibberley

The Irish 9th New York was one of the toughest regiments in the Union army. It had been raised in the Bowery and the Five Points sections, and many of the men had been members of the Dead Rabbits and other clubs that terrorized the polling places in favor of Tammany candidates. That was undoubtedly a bad mark against them, but they redeemed themselves on the battlefield and won the respect of more law-abiding soldiers. Accustomed to the paving-stone and shillelagh fighting of the New York slums, the Irishmen were great at clubbing their muskets and going into the Rebel lines roaring and swinging with delight.

Their colonel, when they came to the Mason-Dixon line, is reported to have taken out a large and beautiful gold watch and showed it to his men.

"Boys," he said, "every fine gentleman south of the line on which you are now standing has a watch such as this. Every man jack of you ought to be able to bring one back when we go marching home again."

Two hours later the colonel missed his watch and he never did recover it.

Quite often Irish regiments of the Federal army faced Irish units of the Confederate army. This had happened at the slaughter on Marye's Heights at Fredericksburg, where the Irish Brigade had charged the stone wall behind which were Irish companies from North Carolina and Georgia. They gave each other no quarter.

Like their fellow Americans, their fight was to the finish, and however difficult it may have been for the Rebel Irish units to fire on the green flag of Ireland, fire they did. But sometimes, as at the deadlock in the Petersburg campaign, the soldiers of both armies would call an unofficial truce. There the Irish Brigade of the North found itself opposite Mahone's Confederate division, also Irish.

"Are there any Limerick men among ye?" someone sang out.

"Enough to take care of the whole of County Cork."

"Ah, the divil with war. We're short of tobacco. Have ye a pipe to spare?"

In no time the men were meeting in no man's land, trading tobacco, newspapers, or whatever comforts they had. Rifles left behind, they had an Irish get-together in which the war was dropped and no mention made of the possibilities of the morrow. They sang songs like "Colleen Bawn" and "Where the River Shannon Flows," and did a jig or two, for there was always a fiddle to be found among the Irish, though there might be but two strings to it. Then at dusk, the men returned to their own trenches. When the fighting resumed, both sides, according to the historian of the Irish Brigade, fought "like bulldogs."

The Southern Irish soldiers, like their Northern fellows, carried the green flat of Erin. An Irishman was questioned on whether he didn't think it shameful to fire on the Irish flag.

"Sure it isn't a greater shame for an Irishman to fire on Irish colors than for an American to fire on American colors," he replied, and torpedoed his questioner.

The Irish had no use for firing on enemy pickets. They could not be brought to indulge in this shooting of single Rebel soldiers, regarding the act as murder. The Rebels soon discovered this Irish peculiarity and when the Irish regiments had picket duty, there was no firing done on either side. If they had to fire, under the orders of an ambitious officer, they would call out "Down, Johnnie!" and lose a round high in the air. Finally, even the most strict of officers resigned themselves to the situation.

In action, however, the Irish (like the rest of the Union army) would kill their own brothers. Dr. Thomas Ellis commented on the Irish attitude in his *Leaves from the Diary of an Army Surgeon*. "Other men," he wrote, "go into fights finely, sternly, or indifferently, but the only man that loves it, after all, is the green, immortal Irishman. [They] fought and joked as if it was the finest fun in the world."

Toward the end of the war an Irish color bearer, Mike Scannel of the 19th Massachusetts (not an Irish regiment), got ahead of his line and was captured in a thrust on the Jerusalem Plank Road before Petersburg.

"Hand over those colors, Yankee," a Confederate ordered, pointing a pistol at Mike and reaching for the flag.

"Yankee is it, now," said Mike in slow wonder. "Faith I've been twenty years in this country and nobody ever paid me the compliment before." And he handed over the flag.

That was it. The Irish had gone into the Civil War the helots of the nation—alien, Catholic, clannish, unlettered, and poor. And now they were Americans: Yankees. A hundred and forty thousand of them had picked up arms and fought for their new country and their country had now adopted them. They had fought to preserve the Union and they now had become part of that Union.

Born Politicos

Born Politicos

Ambrose Higgins left his cabin in County Meath, Ireland, and emigrated to South America. There, he became Don Ambrosia O'Higgins, patriot and founder of a political dynasty which ruled in Chile and Peru. Charles Gavan Duffy departed from his home in County Monaghan after a disagreement with Liberator Daniel O'Connell and went to Australia, where he rose to be Sir Charles and Premier of Victoria. Hugh Roe O'Donnell fled to Spain rather than be taken prisoner by the British. In Spain, he became prominent in the government and his descendants are still famous. In the exile of those who were in the Irish uprising of 1798 were several Hennessys and MacMahons who later won distinction in Napoleon's armies and in public life in France.

Wherever the Irish went, they seemed eventually to enter politics in their adopted lands and many became very successful politicians. Certainly, plenty did in the United States. Here the Irish in politics really flourished from their landing down to the present. The Mansfields, Kennedys, McCarthys, the Dempseys, the Hugheses, the McCormicks, Farleys, Reagans and others of Irish descent are still today very much in the American political limelight.

It has often been said that the Irish are born politicos. The Irish are in the main extroverts, gregarious, pragmatic, possess a sense of humor, like people, mix well generally in any gathering, and employ blarney in their talks, some of which are eloquent and many amusing. Besides, the Irish are clannish. All of these qualities are real assets in seeking and building a political career.

In America, the Irish got the jump politically because they settled en masse in the major cities, such as New York, Boston, Philadelphia, Chicago and San Francisco. Frequently in settling in the cities, the Irish located where others from the same county in Ireland had gone. Typical, for instance, those from Donegal went mainly to Philadelphia. Those from Clare to Chicago. Emigrants from Galway preferred New York because " 'Twas the closest place to home." Old home folks back in Galway did not want their loved ones too far away—"just across there," they said, pointing to the Atlantic.

The Irish were not entirely among strangers. They knew each other from back home or they knew their neighbors and where they came from originally. This knowledge was helpful in organizing the Irish in the political sense. Another factor in organizing them was the handicaps and opposition they had from the native-born Americans' anti-attitude on immigrants.

The Democratic Party was the first to welcome the Irish and lend them assistance. This loyalty to the Democrats has continued. In fact, some Irishers do not admit that there is any other party, so intense is their Democratic loyalty.

The Catholic Church, too, was a big factor in keeping the Irish organized and maintaining their heritage. For example, unlike other immigrants, few Irish changed their names or Americanized them. The few who did were highly criticized. Cardinal O'Connell of Boston used to describe those who did assume Anglo-Saxon names to get on in the American world as "contemptible toadies." Life to the early Irish arrivals here revolved around the Catholic parish church. This life was not all spiritual. The parish organized dramatic, debating and elocution contests. Amateur plays were staged regularly. Al Smith and many another successful politician got his early training on how to handle himself on the platform in these parish plays.

By holding together in their respective districts and wards in the big city, the Irish, who became citizens almost on arrival, were able to elect their own political leaders who, of course, were usually "one of their own" and thereby controlled the ward and district. From this, the Irish branched out to the cities and states, making their voices heard. Since they were in the major cities and states with large electoral votes, the Irish finally emerged into the national picture!

In their climb up the political ladder the Irish immigrants produced many colorful characters and left many amusing anecdotes to mark their progress upward.

A Book Review

By Finley Peter Dunne

In the land attack upon Santiago, the Rough Riders, under the command of Theodore Roosevelt, had played a significant part. Not long after the war was over, Roosevelt wrote a history of the regiment which he and Leonard Wood had raised and commanded. Mr. Dooley's review brought the consolation from Senator Lodge that such a notice indicated that Roosevelt had "advanced far on the high road to fame." Roosevelt replied ruefully, "How he does get at any joint in the harness." To F. P. Dunne he wrote, "I regret to state that my family and intimate friends are delighted with your review of my book."

"Well, sir," said Mr. Dooley, "I jus' got hold iv a book, Hinnissy. It suits me up to th' handle, a gran' book, th' grandest iver seen. Ye know I'm not much throubled by lighrachoor, havin' manny worries iv me own, but I'm not prejudiced agin books. I am not. Whin a rale good book comes along I'm as quick as anny wan to say it isn't so bad, an' this here book is fine. I' tell ye 'tis fine."

"What is it?" Mr. Hennessy asked languidly.

" 'Tis 'Th' Biography iv a Hero be Wan Who Knows.' 'Tis 'Th' Darin' Exploits iv a Brave Man be an Actual Eye Witness.' 'Tis 'Th' Account iv th' Desthruction iv Spanish Power in th' Ant Hills,' as it fell fr'm th' lips iv Tiddy Rosenfelt an' was took down be his own hands. Ye see 'twas this way, Hinnissy, as I r-read th' book. Whin Tiddy was blowed up in th' harbor iv Havana he instantly con-cluded they must be war. He debated th' question long an' earnestly an' fin'lly passed a jint resolution declarin' war. So far so good. But there was no wan to carry it on. What shud he do? I will lave th' janial author tell th' story in his own wurruds.

" 'Th' sicrety iv war had offered me,' he says, 'th' command of a rig'mint,' he says, 'but I cud not consint to remain in Tampa while perhaps less audacious heroes was at th' front,' he says.

'Besides,' he says, 'I felt I was incompetent f'r to command a rig'mint raised be another,' he says. 'I detarmined to raise wan iv me own,' he says. 'I selected fr'm me acquaintances in th' West,' he says, 'men that had thravelled with me acrost th' desert an' th' storm-wreathed mountain,' he says, 'sharin' me burdens an' at times confrontin' perils almost as gr-raet as anny that beset me path,' he says. 'Together we had faced th' turrors iv th' large but vilent West,' he says, 'an' these brave men had seen me with me trusty rifle shootin' down th' buffalo, th' elk, th' moose, th' grizzly bear, th' mountain goat,' he says, 'th' silver man, an' other fero-cious beasts iv thim parts,' he says. 'An they niver flinched,' he says. 'In a few days I had thim perfectly tamed,' he says, 'an' ready to go annywhere I led,' he says. 'On th' thransport goin' to Cubia,' he says, 'I wud stand beside wan iv these r-rough men threatin' him as an akel, which he was in ivrything but birth, education, rank, an' courage, an' together we wud look up at th' admirable stars iv that tolerable southern sky an' quote th' Bible fr'm Walt Whitman,' he says. 'Honest, loyal, thrue-hearted la-ads, how kind I was to thim,' he says.

" 'We had no sooner landed in Cubia than it become nicissry f'r me to take command iv th' ar-rmy which I did at wanst. A number of days was spint be me in reconnoitring, attinded on'y be me brave an' fluent bodyguard, Richard Harding Davis. I discovered that th' inimy was heavily inthrenched on th' top iv San Joon hill immejiately in front iv me. At this time it became apparent that I was handicapped by th' prisence iv th' ar-rmy,' he says. 'Wan day whin I was about to charge a block house sturdily definded by an ar-rmy corps undher Gin'ral Tamale, th' brave Castile that I aftherwards killed with a small ink-eraser that I always carry, I r-ran into th' entire military force iv th' United States lying on its stomach. 'If ye won't fight,' says I, 'let me go through,' I says. 'Who ar're ye?" says they. 'Colonel Rosenfelt,' says I 'Oh, excuse me,' says the gin'ral in command (if me mimry serves me thrue it was Miles) , r-risin' to his knees an' salutin'. This showed me 'twud be impossible f'r to carry th' war to a successful con-clusion unless I was free, so I sint th' ar-rmy home an' attackted San Joon hill. Armed on'y with a small thirty-two which I used in th' West to shoot th' fleet prairie dog, I climbed that precpitous ascent in th' face iv th' most gallin' fire I iver knew or heered iv. But I had a few r-rounds iv gall mesilf an' what cared I? I dashed madly on, cheerin' as I wint. Th' Spanish throops was dhrawn up in a long line in th' formation known among military men as a long line. I fired at th' man nearest to me an' I knew be th' expression iv his face that th' trusty bullet wint home. It passed through his frame, he fell, an' wan little home in far-off Catalonia was made happy be th' thought that their riprisintative had been kilt be th' future governor iv New York. Th' bullet sped on its mad flight an' passed through th' intire line fin'lly imbeddin' itself in th' abdomen iv th' Ar-rch-bishop iv Santago eight miles away. This ended th' war."

" 'They has been some discussion as to who was th' first man to r-reach th' summit iv San Joon hill. I will not attempt to dispute th' merits iv th' manny gallant sojers, statesmen, corryspondints, an' kinetoscope men who claim th' distinction. They ar-re all brave men an' if they wish to wear me laurels they may. I have so manny annyhow that it keeps me broke havin' thim blocked an' irned. But I will say f'r th' binifit iv posterity that I was th' on'y man I see. An' I had a tillyscope.'

"I have thried, Hinnissy," Mr. Dooley continued, "to give you a fair idee iv th' contints iv this remarkable book, but what I've tol' ye is on'y what Hogan calls an outline iv th' principal pints. Ye'll have to r-read th' book ye'ersilf to get a thrue conciption. I haven't time f'r to tell ye th' wurruk Tiddy did in ar-rmin' an' equippin' himsilf, how he fed himsilf, how he steadied himsilf in battle an' encouraged himsilf with a few well chosen wurruds whin th' sky was darkest. Ye'll have to take a squint into th' book ye'ersilf to larn thim things."

"I won't do it," said Mr. Hennessy. "I think Tiddy Rosenfelt is all r-right an' if he wants to blow his hor-rn lave him do it."

"Thrue f'r ye," said Mr. Dooley, "an' if his valliant deeds didn't get into this book 'twud be a long time befure they appeared in Shafter's histhry iv th' war. No man that bears a gredge agin himsilf will iver be governor iv a state. An' if Tiddy done it all he ought to say so an' relieve th' suspinse. But if I was him I'd call th' book 'Alone in Cubia.' "

Happy Hooleys

Previous to World War I, there were two notable Tammany sachems, namely Big Tim and little Tim Sullivan. Both had their New York East Side districts in their pockets. One election Big Tim carried his district with a majority of 8,571 Democrats to two Republicans.

Naturally, the day after election, his Tammany followers thought he would be very happy with the results. Instead, Big Tim was quite glum and nasty. When asked why, Tim explained, "Last week, Joe Doyle came to me and said that the fellow running on the Republican ticket was a relative of his wife's, and the women in his family were at him to vote for him. So I told Joe to go ahead and vote for him. What I want to know is, who was the s.o.b. who voted Republican without my permission."

Little Tim Sullivan knew a couple of pretty good political tricks in arguing for his success. For instance, before each election, he would go over the individual amounts received from people. After adding the entire amount, he would deduct 10 per cent and put it in a separate savings account. Then after the elections were over, and just prior to collecting new donations, Little Tim would write a letter to the donors telling them that all debts had been paid and because everything had been handled in such a businesslike way, a dividend of 10 per cent was being given to all donors. For instance, one who gave $1,000 received a $100 dividend.

This made quite an impression on the recipients, who never expected to get anything from their political gifts. The word went around that Little Tim was not only an honest man, but a very good businessman. Therefore, the contributors were glad to make a political donation again.

The Sullivans operated in the days before machine voting. Whenever Big Tim Sullivan was suspicious of someone being Republican when he was going to pay two dollars for him to vote Democratic, he would ask him to prove that he voted his way by tearing off the "chicken" as he called it. This was the eagle on the Republican ballot.

The bribed voter was not to be paid until he tore off the "chicken" and brought it to Big Tim for payment. Naturally, when he tore off the "chicken" and turned it in, his ballot was declared mutilated and therefore nullified the Republican vote and made the Sullivan Democratic majority still larger.

Several decades ago, Tammany Hall New York was dominated by the Irish. This group selected the late Jimmy Walker, the charming, witty but irresponsible Mayor of New York. Shortly after Jimmy was nominated for Mayor, a local politician, who hadn't heard of Walker, arrived late at a meeting. He found the whole room wildly cheering Walker. Since he knew nothing about Jimmy Walker, he said to a Tammany leader—"This Jimmy Walker, will he make a good mayor?" "He'll be a terrible mayor," replied the Tammanyite, "but what a candidate! What a candidate!"

In Wilkes Barre, Pa., there flourished before World War I, one John Jay McDevitt, known as the "Millionaire for a Day." Actually, McDevitt was a self-educated miner who got a nest egg of a few thousand dollars. In those days, a few thousand dollars went a long way. Instead of saving the money for his old age, McDevitt decided to spend it in a dramatic way. He did.

Hiring a special Lehigh Valley train, McDevitt went to New York, took a room at the Waldorf Astoria, had a champagne bath, bought a box at the theater, went to Delmonico's, and then went home broke the next day in a caboose.

Of course, McDevitt had invited newspapermen on his special. From then on, until he died some twenty-five years later, John Jay McDevitt was known as the "Millionaire for a Day."

How this Irisher, McDevitt, got the nest egg to become a "Millionaire for a Day" is an amusing political story.

In Pennsylvania in those days, anybody could file for office. However, the Democratic Party which controlled Wilkes Barre and the county usually picked a slate which was equally divided between the Irish and the Germans. That year, one George Schmidt, a German contractor, was scheduled to be the county treasurer. The Democratic bosses asked McDevitt to withdraw. McDevitt just said that he only went in the race for fun. Instead of withdrawing, he volunteered to do what he could to help Schmidt be elected.

He asked Schmidt for a number of his cards so he could pass them out in the Irish saloons during the campaign.

McDevitt would go into these Irish saloons in the city and out-skirts and hand out Schmidt's cards to everyone and introduce himself as Schmidt to all the miners. It was customary for the can-didate in those Irish sections to buy drinks all around. Instead of buying drinks, McDevitt would go up to the bar and order himself a seltzer water. While the Irish miners looked on with disgust, McDevitt would lecture them on the evils of drink and say that when he, Schmidt, was elected he would see that the saloons would all be closed down. He, Schmidt, was against parochial schools and believed that the Catholic Irish should be put in their place. After a while, McDevitt, who had plenty of courage as well as gall, would then hand out besides Schmidt's cards, prison-made cigars. All the Irish miners were union men and hated these "scab see-gars."

Of course, McDevitt would have a shill in the audience, who, as McDevitt was about to leave, would ask, "Mr. Schmidt, who is running against you?" Then McDevitt would turn and address the Irish ensemblage with: "I am sorry to report that my opponent is one John Jay McDevitt, an Irish Catholic union miner, a man who does not believe in Prohibition and likes to drink himself. Imag-ine, he believes that drink is good for a man. He also has the strange idea that parochial schools are worthwhile and he likes to help the Catholic shanty Irish. I want you people to remember his name so that you can vote against him. His name is John Jay McDevitt—again, John Jay McDevitt."

With that, McDevitt would make a quick exit to the next sa-loon, where he would put on the same act.

Schmidt was badly beaten in the primary. The Democrats had to pay off McDevitt to resign from the ticket. It was this payoff which enabled him to assume his "Millionaire for a Day" role.

Family expenditures was the topic at the family dinner of the mil-lionaire clan of Joseph P. Kennedy one evening back in 1959. "No one," said the patriarch Joe, then worth at least $250 million, "ap-pears to have the slightest concern for what they spend." The chastened familial silence that greeted this was at length broken by one of his sons. Said the then Senator John F. Kennedy, "We've come to the conclusion that the only solution is to have Dad work harder."

During his journey to Ireland, President John Fitzgerald Kennedy was given an honorary degree by the nation's two leading universities, namely, Trinity and the National University. Both are traditionally bitter rivals. Trinity, established by Queen Elizabeth in 1591, has long been regarded as the Protestant establishment, while the National University, founded much later, is the seat of Catholic culture.

In commenting upon the awarding of the degrees, President Kennedy told the Trinity group that having a degree from each of such bitter rivals might pose a dilemma for himself later when he returned to Dublin as a private citizen, particularly if he should be back on the day on which the two universities had their annual rugby game.

"However, I have solved that dilemma," asserted JFK. "I will cheer for the National University and pray for Trinity."

Prior to his election in 1960 as President, John F. Kennedy, in addressing the National Press Club, Washington, D.C., at the Gridiron Dinner, read an alleged telegram from his multi-millionaire father, Joseph P. Kennedy, which stated: "Buy all the votes you can, but remember I am not paying for any landslides."

The late President John F. Kennedy was not the only one in that famed Boston family to inherit the gift of Irish wit. His two Senatorial brothers, Robert and Ted, have it also.

Senator Robert Kennedy, noting that two Rockefellers were running for governor, jibed, "If there is anything I hate in politics, it's someone who runs on a famous name."

The New York Times reported before Christmas that Kennedy's secretaries were driven so hard that they had little time for lunch and were expected to subsist on "loyalty pills." So for Christmas, Kennedy gave them gold charms in the shape of pills. On one side was engraved: "One a day—R.F.K." On the reverse side was the word "Loyal."

When Bobby was told that author Lasky, whose critical book about President Kennedy—*JFK;The Man and the Myth,* a 1963 best seller, was doing a book on him, R.F.K. said with a laugh: "Somebody suggested the title should be 'R.F.K.: The Boy and the Myth,' but I don't think that the publishers will approve. You can say, however, that it's not going to be a friendly book."

During the campaign, a questioner in a crowd asked Kennedy, "How do you feel about these high prices?"

"I'm against them," Kennedy shot back. He paused, then added derisively, "Another brave stand taken by Senator Kennedy."

When a youthful admirer asked Kennedy how he felt about lowering the voting age, R.F.K., who has a houseful of children, deadpanned, "I really favor lowering it to twelve."

Senator Ted Kennedy, referring to his own rich birth, happily quotes a factory worker who confronted him while campaigning. "Senator," the man said, "I hear you have never worked a day in your life, and this is what a lot of people have against you. I want to tell you, you haven't missed a thing."

James Reston in *The New York Times* News Service, Oct. 26— "'He [Robert Kennedy] starts each political talk with the kind of self-mocking wit, quiet, brief and conversational . . . Observing that the President, the Vice President and the Congress are all out of Washington, he says he has just had a wire from his brother Teddy:

" 'Everybody's gone: Have just seized control.' "

Irv Kupcinet in the *Chicago Sun-Times*, Oct. 30—"Sen. Ted Kennedy, who addressed a Democratic rally at O'Hare Inn the other morning, told of the kidding that goes on between him and his brother, Sen. Robert Kennedy, and then read a gag telegram he had received from Bobby: "With President Johnson out of the country and Congress adjourning, I have seized power."

In 1938, John Danaher became the first Irish Catholic ever elected as a Republican to the U.S. Senate. Of Danaher's father, who switched the family allegiance to the G.O.P., the story was told of an old Irish lady who said to her friend: "Have you heard the news? John Danaher has become a Republican." The other replied: "It can't be true. I saw him at Mass last Sunday."

Quiet Arthur Griffith, the first provisional president of the Irish

Free State, was once described by Churchill as that "rare phenomenon, a silent Irishman."

Several years ago this writer was called to go on jury duty in the Federal building in New York.

It so happened at that time, the Jewish Holidays were starting that same week. As a result many of the citizens of Jewish faith were asking to be excused from serving. The Irisher clerk was very highly annoyed, so when he came to me he said, "I suppose you want to be excused, too."

"No, sir, I don't. I can understand what you're up against this week with so many people asking to be excused. I will be very happy to serve."

So he said to me, in a loud voice, so that everyone in the room could hear, "I like that spirit. I wish a few more people would be as considerate."

About an hour later, this same clerk came up quietly and said, "Quite a few of the judges won't be sitting this week and if you would like to be excused, I can arrange it."

Some fifteen minutes later the clerk in a very loud voice said, "Because of the Jewish Holiday, the following people are excused: Abner Rubin, Harry Shapiro, George Weissman, Harry Isaacs, John J. McCarthy, Milton Enzer, Murray Sachs, etc."

Having an Irish name does come in rather handy sometimes, and I learned this very early in New York.

In 1922 I had just come to New York and was living at the University of Pennsylvania's club, then at 35–37 East 50th Street. My roommate was Dr. Thomas B. R. Webster, now a prominent Manhattan dentist.

At that time Park Avenue was beginning to fill up with apartments and with the coming of wealthier people, the district was filling up with Republicans.

However, Tammany was doing its best to stave off the Republican invasion. One way was to keep them from registering. When Webster and I went over to register, we found the Tammany clerk was giving many people a hard time. For instance, if a lady said she was Mrs. Mildred Joyce Smith, the clerk would say, "How could your husband have the name of Mildred?" and when she would lean over and quietly say that she was divorced, the clerk would say in a loud voice, "Divorced, are you!"

Webster started to register ahead of me and the clerk really went at him and made a point of wanting to know exactly where he lived, what room, what floor and what was the club like and how long he had lived in New York. The clerk had guessed, and rightly so, that the Doctor was a Republican.

When my turn came, he snarled and said, "What's your name?" "John Sylvester Joseph McSweeney McCarthy." says I. With that, the hardboiled Irish clerk looked up with a broad grin and said, "Where do you live, Mac?"

Although Theodore Roosevelt was a fast man with the retort proper, an Irisher, who was feeling no pain at the time, got the better of him in a Boston campaign speech exchange.

Republican candidate TR was constantly interrupted by the inebriated Irisher, who kept shouting, "I'm a Democrat." Finally, Roosevelt asked the Irisher why he was a Democrat. "My grandfather was a Democrat," replied the Irisher, "my father was a Democrat, and I am a Democrat." Sarcastically, TR then asked, "My friend, suppose your grandfather had been a jackass, and your father had been a jackass. What would you be?"

Instantly, the Irisher replied, "A Republican."

Coming from New York's tough lower East Side, Governor Al Smith knew how to handle hecklers. Once, when Smith paused because a heckler kept interrupting him, the man shouted, "Go ahead, Al, don't let me bother you. Tell 'em all you know. It won't take you long."

Immediately Smith responded, "If I tell 'em all we both know, it won't take me any longer."

In discussing hecklers, Al Smith would cite the story of the lady temperance orator who concluded her vibrant pleading speech with: "I would rather commit adultery than take a glass of beer."

"Who wouldn't?" came a clear voice from her audience.

In the rough-and-tumble political times before World War I, it was almost customary to heave some vegetables when a candidate

was making a speech. While talking in the Bronx, Al Smith narrowly missed being hit by a head of cabbage. As the cabbage rolled
on the platform, Al looked at it and commented: "Whoever threw
that lost his head."

Once while attending a convention in Atlantic City, Al Smith
and Jimmy Walker had to rise very early to attend Mass on a Sunday before the opening meeting at 8:30 A.M.

When they went down to the lobby, it was still dark and nobody
was around, for they were still sound asleep in their rooms. Referring to the sleeping guests, Smith remarked sadly: "Suppose,
Jimmy, they're right and we're wrong?"

Governor Alfred E. Smith was once the guest of a friend at the
round table at The Players Club in New York. The Governor was
not one to put on airs. In fact, he was rather proud of his humble
background. This day, there was a Columbia professor of literature at the table. Much to the annoyance of the other Players at
the table, the pedagogue attempted to bring out the Governor's
lack of formal education.

"What is your favorite book, Governor?" asked the Columbia
professor.

"*The Life and Times of John L. Sullivan,*" promptly and
proudly replied the Governor, much to the merriment and satisfaction of all save the Columbia professor.

In our reportorial days in Philadelphia, there was a colorful ward
boss named William P. Carey, a self-educated Hibernian. A great
talker, Carey's political observations contained some classic mala-
props. Here are a few: "I know every cranny and crook in Philly."
"I've been keeping my ear to the grindstone." "That kind of
business gets my dandruff up." "We've got to do something to get
a toehold in the public eye." "It's just a matter of whose ox is
being goosed."

The *Daily News* columnist, Ed Sullivan, maintains that De Gaulle
always reminds him of Ireland's De Valera.

Comments Ed:

"Dealing with the Irish is like trying to catch quicksilver on a fork," once said a British statesman. Snapped De Valera: "Try a spoon." Eamon De Valera was born in New York City, son of a Spanish planter from Cuba and Limerick's Catharine Coll. He was rescued from a British jail by fabled Michael Collins.

Later, in the London home of Irish painter Sir John Lavery and his American wife, Collins met Lord French, who escorted him to Churchill. Collins studied a Boer placard in Churchill's office. "Five pounds, dead or alive, for Winston Churchill."

Said Churchill: "My apologies, Mr. Collins. The Boers only offered five pounds for me. We offered five hundred pounds for you."

Collins laughed: "Prices have gone up since your day, Mr. Churchill."

Few Irish politicians could match Boston's James Michael Curley when it came to pulling off political tricks, uncorking eloquence or giving with the blarney. Those who have read the novel *The Last Hurrah*, or who saw the movie in which Spencer Tracy portrayed Skeffington, the hero, will get some idea of what Curley's career was like. Naturally, James Michael in his lifetime denied that he was Skeffington, except when he was running for office and there were some write-in votes marked for Skeffington. Immediaetly, James Michael claimed them for his own.

Curley rose from a grocery clerk to Governor of Massachusetts, from a tenement in the Roxbury slums in Boston to a handsome mansion in Jamaica Plains. As a young man he went to jail for taking an examination for postman for another man also named Curley. The examiners found that James Michael's paper was so perfect that they got suspicious, because so few applicants ever did so well.

With many politicians this jail sentence would have ended their careers, but it helped to make Curley's. He capitalized on it no end. For instance, James Michael would always tell the Irish that he did this for a friend who was a man with a large family and needed the job. The Irish in South Boston liked that.

Back in the early 1920's when we were a reporter on a Philadelphia paper, we were assigned to Boston to cover a Curley campaign. Making the rounds with him one evening, our first stop was in South Boston. There Curley was dressed in an ordinary, rumpled, crumpled business suit.

Right in the middle of the Curley talk, a big bulky Irishman stood up and shouted, "Jail bird." The audience almost wanted to lynch him; however, Curley raised his hands as if in Christian charity and asked them to desist. He said the man was right, that he did serve a term in jail, but he did it for a friend. Then James Michael went on tearfully to tell how he did this to get his friend a needed job. The Celtic crowd ate it up and cheered him to the rafters.

Later he spoke in the Back Bay district, which was then the aristocratic section of Boston. The crowd was quite different. So was Curley, now dressed in a cutaway and striped trousers. Sure enough, right in the middle of his speech, I was rather surprised to see the same big bulky Irishman who had stood up at the South Boston meeting make his appearance here in Back Bay and go into his same routine by shouting "Jail bird" again.

Here again the crowd wanted to usher him out. Again Curley came to his rescue. However, Curley's talk in Back Bay was far different from the one he gave in South Boston. In Back Bay, Curley said that the man was right that he had committed a wrong, but that he had paid his debt to society. James Curley asked the people for their consideration since he was most contrite and had served his sentence. Now Curley was asking for fair play.

In this campaign, his opponent was an eminent Catholic who had been picked by Cardinal O'Connell. Curley knew how to defeat him. For instance, Curley would ask the crowd, "Where was my worthy opponent last Friday night? Well, I will tell you. He was at the Copley Plaza eating a big steak. Where was I? I won't tell you." However, Curley would have a stooge in the audience who would shout: "I know where you were, Boss. You were over at the cathedral attending the Stations of the Cross." Then, Boston Catholic Irish would have none of one of their own who would eat meat on Friday.

Once while returning from Europe on the *Bremen,* one of the passengers, a well-known attorney, said to Curley, "So you are from Boston where the Cabots speak only to the Lowells, and the Lowells speak only to God." Added James Michael: "And where the Caseys speak only to the Curleys, and the Curleys speak only to whom they damn well please."

Like many Celts in politics, Harold Hughes, the only Iowa Democrat ever elected Governor of his state three times, has that certain
toughness and humor so necessary for success in public life. Visiting a prison, Governor Hughes asked an inmate what he did. "I'm
a burglar, Governor," he said. "But I mean, what's your job?
What do you do for a living?" "I told you, Governor, I'm a burglar." "How many terms have you served?" the Governor asked.
He said, "This is my third." "Well, then," Hughes said, "you must
not be a very damn good burglar."

A few years ago Jack McCarthy had run several times for City
Councilman in Rye, New York, on the Democratic ticket. Just before one election, he met several of the Irish lads.

"Now, Jack," said one of them, "I see you are running again on
next Tuesday. I want you to know that all the boys from the Donegal Society are with you. We voted for you last time and we're
going to vote for you again. However, we want to ask you a return
favor."

"I don't know whether I can do any favors," said McCarthy,
"because I don't know whether I will be elected or not. Maybe
we'd better discuss it next Wednesday. What is it you want?"

"First of all, I want for you to help us to make out our first citizenship papers. We would like to apply for citizenship."

That same Jack McCarthy, after two defeats for Councilman, had
the effrontery to run a third time. This was for Supervisor, the top
spot on the local Democratic slate. However, McCarthy did not
think it was such a great honor because the Rye Democrats could
not actually persuade any really prominent citizen to stick out his
neck and run for Supervisor against the popular Republican Supervisor Lester Cook, who was seeking a third term. Faithful
Democrat McCarthy was really helping to fill out the ticket. He
did not believe his nomination worthwhile enough to tell his wife
and family.

After all, at the time McCarthy was candidate, the Rye Democrats had not yet won a single election since John Jay went to the
Continental Congress of 1774.

When the weekly *Rye Chronicle* broke with a front-page headline, "McCarthy Leads Democrats Again," Jack's family, especially his wife, showed surprise.

"Jack McCarthy," exclaimed his wife, "why are you running again?" His four children, standing by, agreed unanimously with their mother.

"Well," Jack tried to explain, "it's an old political axiom. The more you run, the greater publicity you get. With your name repeatedly on the ballot, more people get to know you and eventually, knowing you, they vote for you."

"But, Jack," replied his wife wearily, "that's not your problem at all. We have lived in Rye for over twenty-five years. We have raised four children here and all have gone through the local schools. We have participated in all the parish and community affairs. Everybody in Rye already knows you. That's why they don't vote for you."

In my boyhood, many years ago, I chided my grandfather for championing an old crony of his who was prominent in Philadelphia politics. This particular politician had come from the same village in Ireland as did Grandfather. Since his arrival to the City of Brotherly Love, the politician had become a millionaire many times over as a contractor doing entirely work for the city. His local reputation bordered on the notorious.

"I cannot understand," I remember telling my grandfather, "why you think this politician so wonderful. It is common knowledge that he takes graft."

"Now, lad," replied my grandfather kindly, "he only takes honest graft."

In the many intervening years since, I have heard other Irishmen than my grandfather repeatedly defending fellow Celts in politics who have been accused of misappropriation of funds, taking bribes while in office, or overcharging a government for work with the expression that, after all, " 'Twas honest graft." It seems to be a common Celtic quirk with some Irishmen that when a man goes into politics, he is entitled to get all he can. For instance, when a dedicated reformer asked old-time Irisher Tammany boss Richard Croker if he were working for his own pocket, Croker growled, "All the time, the same as you."

It was during Croker's regime as Tammany's Supreme Sachem

in the 1880's that the term "honest graft" originated. Croker succeeded Honest John Kelly who in turn had taken over Tammany when Boss William Marcy Tweed went to jail for stealing millions from the treasury of New York City. Ironically, Tweed had been named after Senator William Marcy, a big-time dealer when Martin Van Buren held forth in Albany. Senator Marcy defended patronage at a price with his classic "To the victor belong the spoils." Throughout his political life, Boss Tweed certainly emulated his namesake when he got into public life.

When Honest John Kelly followed after Tweed in Tammany Hall, he set the stage for honest graft instead of outright robbery such as practiced by Tweed. Honest John accepted an unsalaried post of Sheriff of New York County. The no-salary angle for this job was offset by the fees garnered. During his six years as Sheriff, Honest John personally was said to have cleared about $800,000 "honestly and fairly." Also Honest John Kelly thought he was being strictly within his rights when he billed the City of New York at 133 per cent over the legal rate for transporting prisoners to Blackwell's Island. *The Times* uncovered this excessive charge.

However, the *Star* and the *Evening Express* editorially thought Honest John had shown admirable restraint in this regard when compared to his predecessor, Boss Tweed. Of course, the praise from the *Star* and *Evening Express* was understandable. Honest John Kelly was one of their largest stockholders.

Like Honest John and unlike Tweed, Boss Richard Croker used his Tammany connections to edge into outside interests such as railroads, banks, ice companies, and other firms serving New York City. Before he retired to a castle in his native Ireland, Croker made enough to support several mansions and to raise thoroughbreds able to win the English Derby. Hence, by not stealing from the public treasury, as Tweed had done, Croker's personal code was regarded as "honest graft."

Actually, Croker's tactics regarding income inspired his contemporary, State Senator George Washington Plunkitt, an amusing Irisher then known as "Tammany's Philosopher," to coin the term "honest graft." Said Plunkitt: "The politician who steals is worse than a thief. He is a fool. With the grand opportunities all around for the man with a political pull, there's no excuse for stealing a cent."

That shrewd Philadelphia political observer, Edward F. Britt, offers the explanation given by an old-time Irish district leader in an investigation on city officials accepting bribes for favors rendered. When this Irisher, who was on the city's payroll at $7,000 per year, was asked how on his salary he was able to bank $40,000 annually, he testified: "Thrift."

Whenever that peppery Hibernian, Chicago's perennial Mayor Richard Daley, competent boss of the Democratic Party in Illinois, wins an election, and that's pretty often, Raymond J. Ryan, popular publisher's representative in the Windy City, waxes nostalgic and eloquent about the long-time Irish ascendancy in politics in his home town. He loves to tell of the Dunnes, the Glynns and other Irishers who, like Daley, reached the political pinnacle.

One of Ryan's favorite reminiscences concerns two colorful Celtic characters known as Bath House John and Hinky Dink, who long represented in the Chicago City Council two predominantly Irish wards in the early years of the present century. Both made no bones about the fact that their personal politics always were serving their own best personal interests. This frankness evoked the bitterest denunciations from the Chicago Bar Association, Better Government League and all reform associations, but brought only admiration from their Irish constituents

As a matter of fact, Ray Ryan gleefully points out that if the Chicago Bar Association or the Better Government League neglected at election time to issue a public rebuke, Bath House John and Hinky Dink would seek same and pull all kinds of strings to secure it.

The reason they did was because the nastier and more official condemnations which Bath House John and Hinky Dink received publicly from the Chicago Bar Association and the Better Government League, the greater was the vote of confidence from their Irish constituents.

The Great Georgians

The Great Georgians

During the period from 1714 to 1830 which encompassed the reigns of the four King Georges of Great Britain and Ireland, a group of remarkable Irishmen appeared—men whose works and words have come down through posterity. Among these native Irishmen were Dean Jonathan Swift, John Philpot Curran, Daniel O'Connell, Richard Brinsley Sheridan, and Oliver Goldsmith. All achieved greatness in their chosen fields. All were wits supreme.

The Dour Dean

A keener satire upon the cant and sham of courts, parties and statesmen has yet to be written than *Gulliver's Travels,* published in 1726 by Jonathan Swift, then Dean of St. Patrick's, Dublin.

Personally, a disappointed, bitter clergyman who felt that he should have gotten more recognition and reward from His Majesty's Government, Dean Swift was a constant crusader to right the wrongs inflicted by the English in those times upon the Irish people. In one of his many ironical tracts, "A Modest Proposal," he suggested to the English Government "to utilize children by fattening and eating them."

Generous, gregarious Swift traveled all over Ireland. He gave one-third of his income to charities—something rarely done in those Georgian times. His great interest in Ireland's welfare made Dean Swift a hero with the Irish.

The wit of Jonathan Swift is sometimes caustic and scalding; here his irony is by contrast gentle and playful.

Directions to the Cook

By Jonathan Swift

Altho' I am not ignorant that it hath been a long Time, since the Custom began among People of Quality to keep Men Cooks, and generally of the *French* Nation; yet because my Treatise is chiefly calculated for the general Run of Knights, 'Squires, and Gentlemen both in Town and Country, I shall therefore apply myself to you, Mrs. Cook, as a Woman: However, a great Part of what I intend may serve for either Sex; and your Part, naturally follows the former, because the Butler and you are join'd in Interest; your Vails are generally equal, and paid when others are disappointed: You can junket together at Nights upon your own Progue, when the rest of the House are abed; and have it in your Power to make every Fellow-servant your Friend; you can give a good Bit or a good Sup to the little Masters and Misses, and gain their Affections: A Quarrel between you is very dangerous to you both, and will probably end in one of you being turned off; in which fatal Case, perhaps, it will not be so easy in some Time to cotton with another. And now Mrs. Cook, I proceed to give you my Instructions, which I desire you will get some Fellow-servant in the Family to read to you constantly one Night in every Week when you are going to Bed, whether you serve in Town or Country, for my Lessons shall be fitted for both.

Never send up a Leg of a Fowl at Supper, while there is a Cat or a Dog in the House that can be accused of running away with it: But, if there happen to be neither, you must lay it upon the Rats, or a strange Greyhound.

It is ill Housewifry to foul your Kitchen Rubbers with wiping the Bottom of the Dishes you send up, since the Table-cloth will do as well, and is changed every Meal.

If you are employed in Marketing, buy your Meat as cheap as you can; but when you bring in your Accounts, be tender of your Master's Honour, and set down the highest Rate; which besides is but Justice, for no body can afford to sell at the same Rate that he buys, and I am confident that you may charge safely; swear that you gave no more than what the Butcher and Poulterer asked. If your Lady orders you to set up a Piece of Meat for Supper, you are not to understand that you must set it up all, therefore you may give half to yourself and the Butler.

Good Cooks cannot abide what they justly call fidling Work, where Abundance of Time is spent and little done: Such, for Instance, is the dressing small Birds, requiring a World of Cookery and Clutter, and a second or third Spit, which by the way is absolutely needless; for it will be a very ridiculous Thing indeed, if a Spit which is strong enough to turn a Surloyn of Beef, should not be able to turn a Lark; however, if your Lady be nice, and is afraid that a large Spit will tear them, place them handsomely in the Drippingpan, where the Fat of roasted Mutton or Beef falling on the Birds, will serve to baste them, and so save both Time and Butter: for what Cook of any Spirit would lose her Time in picking Larks, Wheatears, and other small Birds; therefore if you cannot get the Maids, or the young Misses to assist you, e'en make short Work, and either singe or flay them; there is no great Loss in the Skins, and the Flesh is just the same.

The Kitchen Bellows being usually out of Order with stirring the Fire with the Muzzle to save the Tongs and Poker, borrow the Bellows out of your Lady's Bed-chamber, which being least used, are commonly the best in the House; and if you happen to damage or grease them, you have a Chance to have them left entirely for your own Use.

Always keep a large Fire in the Kitchen when there is a small Dinner, or the Family dines abroad, that the Neighbours seeing the Smoak, may commend your Master's Houskeeeping: But, when much Company is invited, then be as sparing as possible of your Coals, because a great deal of the Meat being half raw will be saved, and serve next Day.

When you have Plenty of Fowl in the Larder, leave the Door open, in Pity to the poor Cat, if she be a good Mouser.

If you find it necessary to market in a wet Day, take out your

Mistress's Riding-hood and Cloak to save your Cloaths.

To keep troublesome Servants out of the Kitchen, always leave the Winder sticking on the Jack to fall on their Heads.

If a Lump of Soot falls into the Soup, and you cannot conveniently get it out, stir it well in, and it will give the Soup a *French* Taste.

Scrape the Bottoms of your Pots and Kettles with a Silver Spoon, for fear of giving them a Taste of Copper.

When you send up Butter for Sauce, be so thrifty as to let it be half Water; which is also much wholesomer.

Never make use of a Spoon in any thing that you can do with your Hands, for fear of wearing out your Master's Plate.

When you find that you cannot get Dinner ready at the Time appointed, put the Clock back, and then it may be ready to a Minute.

You are to look upon your Kitchen as your Dressing-room; but, you are not to wash your Hands till you have gone to the Necessary-house, and spitted your Meat, trussed your Fowl, picked your Sallad; not indeed till after you have sent up your second Course; for your Hands will be ten times fouler with the many things you are forced to handle; but when your Work is over, one Washing will serve for all.

There is but one Part of your Dressing that I would admit while the Victuals are boiling, toasting, or stewing, I mean the combing your Head, which loseth no Time, because you can stand over your Cookery, and watch it with one Hand, while you are using your Comb in the other.

As soon as you have sent up the second Course, you have nothing to do in a great Family until Supper: Therefore scoure your Hands and Face, put on your Hood and Scarf, and take your Pleasure among your Cronies, till Nine or Ten at Night—But dine first.

Let there be always a strict Friendship between you and the

Butler, for it is both your Interests to be united: The Butler often wants a comfortable Tit-bit, and you much oftener a cool Cup of good Liquor. However, be cautious of him, for he is sometimes an inconstant Lover, because he hath great Advantage to allure the Maids with a Glass of Sack or White Wine and Sugar.

When you roast a Breast of Veal, remember your Sweetheart the Butler loves a Sweetbread; therefore set it aside till Evening: You can say, the Cat or the Dog has run away with it, or you found it tainted, or fly-blown; and besides, it looks as well at the Table without it as with it.

If your Dinner miscarries in almost every Dish, how could you help it? You were teized by the Footmen coming into the Kitchen; and, to prove it true, take Occasion to be angry, and throw a Ladlefull of Broth on one or two of their Liveries; besides, *Friday* and *Childermass-day* are two cross Days in the Week, and it is impossible to have good Luck on either of them; therefore on those two Days you have a lawful Excuse.

To save Time and Trouble, cut your Apples and Onions with the same Knife; and well-bred Gentry love the Taste of an Onion in everything they eat.

Lump three or four Pounds of Butter together with your Hands, then dash it against the Wall just over the Dresser, so as to have it ready to pull by Pieces as you have occasion for it.

When you send up a Mess of Broth, Water-gruel, or the like, to your Master in a Morning, do not forget with your Thumb and two Fingers to put Salt on the side of the Plate; for if you make use of a Spoon, or the End of a Knife, there may be Danger that the Salt would fall, and that would be a Sign of ill Luck. Only remember to lick your Thumb and Fingers clean, before you offer to touch the Salt.

Short Comments on Swift

Dean Swift, in his journeys on foot, was accustomed to stop for refreshment or rest at the neat little alehouse on the road's side.

One of these, between Dunchurch and Doventry, was distinguished by the sign of three crosses, in reference to the three intersecting ways which fixed the site of the house. At this house the Dean called for breakfast, but the landlady being engaged with accommodating her more constant customers, some wagoners, and staying to settle an altercation which unexpectedly arose, kept the dean waiting and ignored his repeated requests for some service.

Before he left the inn, Swift took a diamond from his pocket and scratched on every pane of glass in the best room in the inn:

TO THE LANDLORD
There hang three crosses at thy door
Hang up thy wife, and she'll make four.

Happening to be in company with a petulant young man, who prided himself on saying pert things and who informed Dean Swift that "I'm set up around here as a wit," "Are you now," replied the dour Dean. "Take my advice and sit down again!"

One day, the dour Dean Swift waited at the Dublin Castle, for an audience with the Lord Lieutenant, Lord Carteret. After an hour's wait, his patience was exhausted. Thereupon, the Dean wrote the following couplet on a window and went away:

My very good Lord, 'tis very hard task
For a man to wait here who has nothing to ask.

Lord Carteret, after reading same, immediately wrote underneath:

My very good Dean, there are few who came here
But have something to ask, or something to fear.

The last thing Dean Swift wrote was an epigram on the building of an arsenal. During one of his exercises while a mental case, this arsenal (or magazine) was pointed out to him. The not so crazy Dean whipped out a pencil and on the side of the building wrote:

Behold a proof of Irish sense;
Here Irish wit is seen;

When nothing's left that's worth defence;
They build a magazine!

Lady Carteret, wife of Ireland's Lord Lieutenant, was once prais-
ing with great unction the atmosphere and climate of Ireland.
"Oh, for goodness' sake, madam," Dean Swift exclaimed, "do not
mention it in the presence of any member of the Government. If
you do, they certainly will tax it."

Once Dean Swift preached a lengthy sermon on charity at St. Patrick's Dublin. Wide criticism was made of it. The next time the
Dean spoke of charity, he began with "Dearly beloved Brethern, I
am instructed by my text that he who giveth to the church lendeth
to the Lord." This he repeated in an emphatic tone and proceeded: "Now beloved brethern, if you like the terms and approve
the security, down with your money," He then descended from the
pulpit and had the satisfaction to find that his pithy oration was
followed by a very liberal collection.

A Witty, Wise Counselor

Toward the close of the eighteenth and early nineteenth centuries,
John Philpot Curran was the idol of the Irish masses. A Protestant
patriot, he defended in court persecuted Catholic priests, rebels
and vagrants. A member of the Irish Parliament, he was a brilliant
orator, an ardent advocate, an extraordinary humorist and a
charming conversationalist.

His daughter Sarah was the betrothed of Robert Emmet, the
Irish hero who was hanged by the British in 1803. Sarah died
shortly afterward at twenty-four. Thomas Moore has enshrined
her memory in his beautiful ballad "She is far from the land."

As a crossexaminer, Curran was unrivaled in the Irish courts of
his day. He took particular pleasure in baiting British judges,
many of whom in Curran's time were remittance men from England and were not too knowledgeable about the law. Once while
raking a witness with speedy perplexing questions, the victim cried

out, "My lord, I cannot answer Mr. Curran; he is putting me in such a doldrum." "A doldrum," exclaimed the judge. "What is a doldrum, Mr. Curran?"

"Oh, my lord," replied Curran, "it is a common complaint with persons like the witness. It is the confusion of the head arising from a corruption of the heart."

"No man," said a wealthy Irish landlord, "should be admitted to the bar who has not an independent landed property." "May I ask, sir," said John Philpot Curran, "how many acres make a wise-acre?"

A barrister entered one of the Four Courts, Dublin, with his wig so much awry as to cause a titter. Seeing J. P. Curran smile, he said, "Do you see anything ridiculous in my wig?" "No," replied Curran, "nothing but the head!"

Another Curran story dealt with an Irishman refusing to prosecute a man who had beaten him almost to death on St. Patrick's night, saying that he be let off "in honor of that night."

Bills of indictment had been sent up to a grand jury in the finding of which Curran was interested. After delay and much hesitation, one of the grand jurors came into court to explain the reason why it was ignored. Vexed by the stupidity of this juror, Curran commented: "You, sir, can have no objection to write upon the back of the bill 'ignoramus; for self and fellow jurors;' it will then be a true bill!"

Lund Foot, a prominent Dublin tobacconist, bought himself a fancy carriage and applied to Curran to give him a motto to be painted on the side. Since Foot was not of the landed gentry, he feared that people might laugh at any motto which was too commercial and not scholarly, but at the same time, he wanted the carriage to symbolize his success in the tobacco trade. In fact, he preferred a motto in Latin.

"I have it," quickly said Curran. "The motto is only two words, but will explain your elevation in the world and has the advantage of being in two languages, Latin or English, as the reader chooses. Put *Quid Rides* (Why do you laugh?) upon your carriage."

A farmer attending a fair with a hundred pounds in his pocket took the precaution of depositing it with a pub owner. Next day, he applied for his money, but Mine Host claimed to know nothing about it.

Consulting Counsel Curran, he was told to "continue to be civil to the pub owner and convince him you must have left the money with someone else. Then take a friend with you and lodge with the pub owner another hundred pounds in the presence of your friend. Then, later, go alone and ask the pub owner for your hundred." He did so and got it. "Now," advised Counsel Curran, "take your friend with you and ask the pub owner for the hundred pounds your friend saw you leave with him."

The farmer did. The swindling pub owner, completely taken by surprise, quickly came up with the second hundred pounds.

As an admirer of Curran's celebrated art, Justice Frank S. McCullough of the Supreme Court of Westchester County, New York, relays Curran's response to Lord Norbury, known as Ireland's "hanging judge." At a Dublin dinner, Norbury turned to the famous Irish barrister and asked: "Is this meat well hung, Curran?"

"It will be after your lordship has tried it," was the reply

Superlative Sheridan

The wittiest and most fascinating of all the Georgians was Richard Brinsley Sheridan. Even today, his plays "School for Scandal" and "The Rivals" are staged all over the world. Modern audiences find these Sheridan plays just as charming and delightful as those who saw them over two hundred years ago.

What is remarkable about Sheridan is that he wrote these wonderful comedies when he was in his early twenties. Besides being a great playwright, he was a first-rate director and became owner of the Drury Lane Theatre, the best in London in his time.

Apart from his theatrical activities, Richard Brinsley Sheridan had an outstanding career of thirty years in the British Parliament as a leading member of the Whig party.

While in Parliament, Sheridan delivered some memorable speeches. One against Warren Hastings lasted for five and a half hours and bowled everyone over. The three most famous orators of the times—Edmund Burke, Charles James Fox and William Pitt—witnessed its effect and were lavish in their praise of the speech. For instance, Burke called it "the most astonishing effort in eloquence, argument and wit united, of which there is any record or tradition."

Aside from making great speeches, Sheridan frequently contributed to the merriment of Parliament with barbs at stuffy opponents and quick retorts to jeers or heckles from back benches. Socially and in personal contact, Sherry, as he was popularly known, was a superb spinner of funny tales, fast on quips and great fun.

Sheridan had a reputation for brilliant impromptus. His off-hand and casual manner of delivery seemed to fulfill Sydney Smith's definition of wit, "in a midwife's phrase, a quick conception and an easy delivery."

Unfortunately, his extravagances in dress, entertainment, gambling, and drinking kept Sheridan constantly in debt. In fact, he died a pauper at sixty-five, but was buried with great pomp and ceremony in Westminster Abbey.

His funeral was attended by dukes, earls, lords, bishops and all the literary and stage stars.

Sheridan's father had been a well-known actor and a friend of Dr. Samuel Johnson. His mother, Frances Sheridan, was a successful novelist and playwright. His grandfather was a friend of Swift, and it was in his home in Ireland that the Dean wrote his *Gulliver's Travels*.

Some of Sherry's comments included: "A fluent tongue is the only thing a mother doesn't like her daughter to resemble her in." "If it is abuse, why, one is always sure to hear of it from one damned good-natured friend or another." "He was not only a chip off the old block but the old block itself." And "He is indebted to his memory for his jests and to his imagination for his facts."

Once asked by a pompous parliamentarian, "How is it that your name has not an 'O' prefixed to it as have all illustrious Irish family names?" "No family," replied Sherry, "has a better right to an 'O' than our family, for, in truth, we owe everybody."

After Sheridan uncorked a merry tale at his club, one Lord Belvedere remarked: "Sherry, that's a good one. I think I'll repeat it." "Pray, my lord," said Sheridan, "please do not, for a joke in your mouth is no laughing matter."

One of the great actresses at the Drury Lane Theatre was Mrs. Sarah Siddons. There was something awesome in her beauty which audiences found fascinating and at the same time disturbing. Since Sheridan cast her in a number of plays in his theater and was profuse in his praise of her acting, some suspected he was having an affair with her. Sherry denied this with: "One would as soon make love to the Archbishop of Canterbury as to Mrs. Siddons."

Of a prominent judge who slept through much of Sheridan's play "Pizarro," the author said, "Poor fellow, I suppose he fancied he was on the bench."

Pretending to defend the lawyer Clifford, who constantly abused and attacked him, Sheridan said, "I hardly expect you to believe me, but I pledge you my word that once, if not twice, but most assuredly once, I did meet him in the company of gentlemen."

Once when walking in St. James's Street, Sheridan met two royal dukes and was asked by one, "I say, Sherry, we have just been discussing whether you are a greater fool or rogue. What is your opinion?" Taking each by the arm, Sheridan replied, "Why, in faith, I believe I am between both."

One day in Parliament, which had long been plagued by a member who constantly interrupted every speaker with cries of "Hear, hear!" Sheridan rose and, in a speech, asked rhetorically, "Where, oh where shall we find a more foolish knave or a more knavish fool than this?" When from the usual bench Sheridan heard the shout of "Hear, hear," he turned and, amidst the general laughter of the House, thanked the honorable gentleman for the answer to his question.

Sheridan's son Tom inherited both his feeling for independence and his wit. When the boy decided to seek a seat in the Commons, he said to his father: "I think that many men who are called great patriots in the House of Commons are great humbugs. For my own part, if I get into Parliament, I will pledge myself to no party, but write upon my forehead in legible characters, 'To let.' "

"And under that, Tom," his father suggested, "write 'unfurnished.' "

After Tom's marriage, and at a time when Sheridan was angry with his son, he met him and said he had made a will and cut him off with a shilling. Tom said he was sorry, but he asked, "You don't happen to have the shilling about you now, sir, do you?"

Three Poems

By Oliver Goldsmith

In a piece called "Retaliation," Oliver Goldsmith wrote this suggested epitaph for David Garrick, regarded as one of the greatest actors in the history of the English stage. Some contemporaries of Goldsmith felt that the same epitaph could be used for Edmund Burke, the eminent statesman as well as Sir Joshua Reynolds, the famed portrait painter. Goldsmith, Garrick, Burke, and Reynolds were founding fellow members of the London Literary Club and knew each other intimately.

Here lies David Garrick, describe me who can
An abridgement of all That was pleasant in man
As an actor, confessed without rival to shine;
As a wit, if not first, in the very first line;
Yet with talents like these, and an excellent heart,
The man had his failings, a dupe to his art.
Like an ill-judging beauty, his colors he spread
And beplastered with rouge his own natural red.
On the stage, he was natural, simple, affecting;
'Twas only that when he was offstage, he was acting.

AN ELEGY

On that glory of her Sex, Mrs. Mary Blaize

Good people all, with one accord,
Lament for Madam Blaize,
Who never wanted a good word—
From those who spoke her praise.

The needy seldom passed her door,
And always found her kind;
She freely lent to all the poor—
Who left a pledge behind.

She strove the neighborhood to please
With manners wondrous winning;
And never followed wicked ways—
Unless when she was sinning.

At church, in silks and satins new,
With hoop of monstrous size,
She never slumbered in her pew—
But when she shut her eyes.

Her love was sought, I do aver,
By twenty beaux and more;
The King himself has followed her—
When she has walked before.

But now, her wealth and finery fled,
Her hangers-on cut short all;
The doctors found, when she was dead—
Her last disorder mortal.

Let us lament, in sorrow sore,
For Kent Street well may say,
That had she lived a twelvemonth more—
She had not died today.

AN ELEGY ON THE DEATH
OF MAD DOG

Good people all, of every sort,
Give ear unto my song;
And if you find it wondrous short,
It cannot hold you long.

In Islington there was a man
Of whom the world might say,
That still a godly race he ran,
Whene'er he went to pray.

A kind and gentle heart he had,
To comfort friends and foes:
The naked every day he clad,
When he put on his clothes.

And in that town a dog was found,
As many dogs there be,
Both mongrel, puppy, whelp, and hound,
And curs of low degree.

This dog and man at first were friends;
But when a pique began,
The dog, to gain some private ends,
Went mad, and bit the man.

Around from all the neighboring streets
The wondering neighbors ran,
And swore the dog had lost his wits,
To bite so good a man.

The wound it seemed both sore and sad
To every Christian eye:
And while they swore the dog was mad,
They swore the man would die.

But soon a wonder came to light,
That showed the rogues they lied:
The man recovered of the bite,
The dog it was that died.

The Liberator

Daniel O'Connell was responsible for getting the Catholic Emancipation Act through the British Parliament in 1829. This gave Irish Catholics the right to hold property and vote. It also earned him the title of "The Liberator."

Prior to getting into politics, O'Connell had been a lawyer on the circuit courts throughout Ireland. He knew the Irish and was fully familiar with all of the cute tricks they might try to pull in court.

A very blunt man, O'Connell had a picturesque style of talking. Once he called the great Wellington "a stunted corporal." Another time he said that Prime Minister Peel's smile "was like a silver plate on a coffin." O'Connell referred to a judge who was ninety-eight as "preserving his intellect unimpaired, such as it is."

In Cork, O'Connell was prevented by the bench from entering certain evidence. In the morning, the court relented. Impatiently, O'Connell burst out with, "Had your Lordship known as much law yesterday as you do today, you would have spared me a vast amount of time and trouble and my client a considerable amount of injury."

O'Connell called Lord Alvanley a bloated buffoon and the younger Peel the "Orange Peel."

Once a perjuring witness in a will case kept on saying that the testator was alive when his hand signed the will. O'Connell noticed that the witness used the same phrase over and over, namely, "There was life in him when he signed the will."

After battering with the man for over an hour, O'Connell suddenly challenged the witness to deny by his God that there was a live fly in the deceased's mouth when his hand was put to the will. In terror, the witness admitted the conspiracy.

"The Lord spare you to me, Mr. O'Connell," said a highwayman. "What would happen to me if anything happened to you?"

This was the man O'Connell had defended for burglary in Dublin and had then gone down to Cork and gotten him off a second time. He came back to Dublin, only to find that he had stolen a boat, was selling the cargo, and buying arms and pirating along the coast. Again O'Connell freed him by arguing that the case should have gone before the Admiralty because the crime was committed on the high seas.

In his bar career, O'Connell always seemed to take on cases for the underdog. As he once said, "As for myself, to my last hours at the bar, I ultimately kept the clerks in constant laughter."

Patriot John Mitchel hailed O'Connell with: "He took all Ireland as his clients."

"Twist" was the commonest form of Irish tobacco in former times. It was usually sold by length rather than by weight. When Daniel O'Connell won a case for a client, a sailor against a shopkeeper, he prompted the client to ask, as damages, "as much twist as would reach from the sole of his foot to the tip of his ear."

When the shopkeeper agreed to what seemed to be a token of payment, it was revealed to him that the tip of the sailor's ear had been cut off in a knife brawl in a South American seaport years before, and he was glad to pay over a hundred pounds to escape the impossible task of providing so much tobacco.

One of the drollest scenes that O'Connell ever figured in took place in the early part of his life.

His talent for vituperative language was early developed, and by some he was considered, even in those days, a matchless scold.

There was, however, in Dublin at that time a certain woman, Biddy O'Houlihan by name, who had a huckster's stall on one end of the quay, nearly opposite the Four Courts. She was a virago of the first order. From one end of Dublin to the other she was notorious for her powers of abuse. And even in the provinces Mrs. O'Houlihan's language had passed into currency.

Some of O'Connell's friends, however, thought he could beat her at the use of her own weapons.

Of this, however, O'Connell himself had some doubt. But when one of the company rather too freely ridiculed the idea of the young Kerry barrister's ability to cope with the famous Mrs. O'Houlihan, O'Connell, who never liked the idea of being put down, professed himself ready to encounter his famous rival. It was decided that the contest should come off at once.

The party adjourned to the huckster's stall, and there they

found the owner herself superintending the sale of her small wares. A few ragged loungers and idlers were hanging round her stall, for Biddy was a "character," and, in her way, one of the sights of Dublin.

O'Connell was very confident of success. He had laid a very ingenious plan for overcoming her, and with all the anxiety of an ardent experimentalist, waited to put it in practice. He resolved to open the attack.

"What's the price of this walking-stick, Mrs. What's-your-name?"

"O'Houlihan, sir, is my name; and a good one it is, and what have you to say ag'in' it? And one and sixpence is the price of the stick, and it's cheap as dirt, so it is."

"One and sixpence for a walkingstick, whew! whew! Why, you are no better than an impostor to ask one and sixpence for what only cost you fourpence."

"Fourpence your grandmother! Do you mane to say it's chatin' people I am? Impostor, indeed!"

"Aye, impostor! And it's that I call ye to your teeth."

"Come, cut your shtick, you cantankerous ould jackanapes."

"Keep a civil tongue in your head, you old diagonal."

"Stop your jaw! you pug-nosed badger, or by this an' by that, I'll make you go quicker than you came."

"Don't be in a passion, my old radius; anger will only wrinkle your beauty."

"By the hooky! if you say another wurrud of your impidence, I'll tan your hide for you—an' sorry I'll be for to soil my hands wid such a common good-for-nothin' scrub."

"Oho, boys! what a passion old Biddy is in. I protest as I'm a gentleman—"

"A gintleman! a gintleman! the likes of you a gintleman! Wisha, that bangs Banagher. Why, you potato-faced pippen-sneezer! When did a Madagascar monkey like you pick up enough common decency to hide his Kerry brogue?"

"Aisy now, don't choke yourself with fine language, you antiquated whisky-drinking parallelogram."

"What's that you call me, you murtherin' ould villain?"

"I call you a parallelogram; and a Dublin judge and jury would support me in saying it's no libel to call you so."

"Tare-an-ouns! That a dacent, honest 'ooman like me should be

called a parybellygrums, you rascally gallows-bird, you cowardly,
sneaking, plate-licking blaggard."

"Oh, not you, indeed! I suppose you'll deny that you keep a
hypothenuse in your house?"

"It's a lie for you, you rascally robber, I never had such a thing
in my house, you swindling thief."

"Why, sure all your neighbors know very well that you keep a
hypothenuse in your house but also that you have two diameters
locked up in your garret, and that you go to walk with them every
Sunday—you heartless old heptagon, you unmitigated individual!"

"Oh, hear that—ye saints in glory! There's bad language from a
fellow that wants to pass himself for a gintleman! May the divil fly
away wid you, you mitcher from Munster!—you flannel-mouth
bog trotter!"

"But you cannot deny the charge, you miserable old sub-
multiple of a duplicate ratio."

"Go rinse your mouth in the river! After all the bad words you
shpake it ought to be dirtier than your face, you cantankerous
ould chicken of Beelzebub!"

"Rinse your own mouth, you wicked-minded old polygon! To
the dickens I pitch you, you blustering intersection of an antique
superficies!"

"You saucy tinker's apprentice! If you don't cease your jaw,
I'll—" But here she lost her breath, and likewise lost her temper;
for the last volley from O'Connell had nearly settled her. O'Connell continued nevertheless to berate her without mercy:

"While I have a tongue, I'll abuse you, you most inimitable
peripher. Look at her, boys! There she stands, a convicted perpen-
dicular in petticoats. There's contamination in her circumference,
and she trembles with guilt down to the extremities of her corol-
laries. Ah, ha; you're found out, you rectilinear antecedent and
equiangular old hag! 'Tis with you the divil will fly away, you
porter-swipin' similitude of the bisection of a vertix."

At this juncture Mrs. O'Houlihan was so overcome with her
emotions that she could no longer contain herself. Catching up a
saucepan, she aimed it at O'Connell's head; and he was forced to
beat a hasty retreat. It was decided, however, O'Connell had won
the victory!

The Landed Gentry

The Landed Gentry

Following the Georgian period which ended in 1830 and after the 1845 famine, life in Ireland revolved around the so-called "Big House" which was owned by the British landlord. The landlords were dubbed "The Landed Gentry." Aside from a short-lived rebellion in 1848, Irish life moved leisurely. The Victorian Age had come in, and with it, a certain placidness for the Irish people.

Acceptance of the landlord and his privileges seemed to be in order with the Irish people. Bitterness between the Irish and the Landed Gentry seemed to be buried until the emergence of Parnell with his calculated policy of obstruction and the starting of the Land League in 1879. However, a number of the Landed Gentry were very popular locally.

In this period, Charles Lever, Samuel Lover, Canon Patrick A. Sheehan and Joseph Sheridan Le Fanu, in his special field of the supernatural, were the leading novelists, and their tales dealt with the status quo of the Big House and the Irish villages.

However, in the late 1880's Edith Somerville began collaborating with her cousin, Violet Florence Martin, whose pen name was Martin Ross. Between them, they produced vivid, amusing tales of Irish life. Since both of these writers were of the Landed Gentry themselves, their stories were written from their status viewpoint. However, in fairness, Somerville and Ross knew their Irish neighbors of that period. Their sketches can still be read today with pleasure.

Sir Dominick's Bargain

By J. Sheridan Le Fanu

In the early autumn of the year 1838, business called me to the south of Ireland. The weather was delightful, the scenery and people were new to me, and sending my luggage on by the mail-coach route in charge of a servant, I hired a serviceable nag at a posting-house, and, full of the curiosity of an explorer, I commenced a leisurely journey of five-and-twenty miles on horseback, by sequestered cross-roads, to my place of destination. By bog and hill, by plain and ruined castle, and many a winding stream, my picturesque road led me.

I had started late, and having made a little more than half my journey, I was thinking of making a short halt at the next convenient place, and letting my horse have a rest and a feed, and making some provision also for the comforts of his rider.

It was about four o'clock when the road, ascending a gradual steep, found a passage through a rocky gorge between the abrupt termination of a range of mountain to my left and a rocky hill, that rose dark and sudden at my right. Below me lay a little thatched village, under a long line of gigantic beech-trees, through the boughs of which the lowly chimneys sent up their thin turf-smoke. To my left, stretched away for miles, ascending the mountain range I have mentioned, a wild park, through whose sward and ferns the rock broke, time-worn and lichen-stained. This park was studded with straggling wood, which thickened to something like a forest, behind and beyond the little village I was approaching, clothing the irregular ascent of the hillsides with beautiful, and in some places discoloured, foliage.

As you descend, the road winds slightly, with the grey park-wall built of loose stone, and mantled here and there with ivy, at its left, and crosses a shallow ford; and as I approached the village, through breaks in the woodlands, I caught glimpses of the long front of an old ruined house, placed among the trees, about half-way up the picturesque mountainside.

The solitude and melancholy of this ruin piqued my curiosity, and when I had reached the rude thatched public-house, with the sign of St. Columbkill, with robes, mitre, and crozier displayed over its lintel, having seen to my horse and made a good meal myself on a rasher and eggs, I began to think again of the wooded park and the ruinous house, and resolved on a ramble of half an hour among its sylvan solitudes.

The name of the place, I found, was Dunoran; and beside the gate a stile admitted to the grounds, through which, with a pensive enjoyment, I began to saunter towards the dilapidated mansion.

A long grass-grown road, with many turns and windings, led up to the old house, under the shadow of the wood.

The road, as it approached the house, skirted the edge of a precipitous glen, clothed with hazel, dwarf-oak, and thorn, and the silent house stood with its wide open hall-door facing this dark ravine, the further edge of which was crowned with towering forest; and great trees stood about the house and its deserted court-yard and stable.

I walked in and looked about me, through passages overgrown with nettles and weeds; from room to room with ceilings rotted, and here and there a great beam dark and worn, with tendrils of ivy trailing over it. The tall walls with rotten plaster were stained and mouldy, and in some rooms the remains of decayed wainscoting crazily swung to and fro. The almost sashless windows were darkened also with ivy, and about the tall chimneys the jackdaws were wheeling, while from the huge trees that overhung the glen in sombre masses at the other side, the rooks kept up a ceaseless cawing.

As I walked through these melancholy passages—peeping only into some of the rooms, for the flooring was quite gone in the middle, and bowed down toward the centre, and the house was very nearly un-roofed, a state of things which made the exploration a little critical—I began to wonder why so grand a house, in the midst of scenery so picturesque, had been permitted to go to decay; I dreamed of the hospitalities of which it had long ago been the rallying place, and I thought what a scene of Redgauntlet revelries it might disclose at midnight.

The great staircase was of oak, which had stood the weather wonderfully, and I sat down upon its steps, musing vaguely on the transitoriness of all things under the sun.

Except for the hoarse and distant clamour of the rooks, hardly audible where I sat, no sound broke the profound stillness of the spot. Such a sense of solitude I have seldom experienced before. The air was stirless, there was not even the rustle of a withered leaf along the passage. It was oppressive. The tall trees that stood close about the building darkened it, and added something of awe to the melancholy of the scene.

In this mood I heard, with an unpleasant surprise, close to me, a voice that was drawling, and, I fancied, sneering, repeat the words: "Food for worms, dead and rotten; God over all."

There was a small window in the wall, here very thick, which had been built up, and in the dark recess of this, deep in the shadow, I now saw a sharp-featured man, sitting with his feet dangling. His keen eyes were fixed on me, and he was smiling cynically, and before I had well recovered my surprise, he repeated the distich:

"If death was a thing that money could buy,
    The rich they would live, and the poor they would die."

"It was a grand house in its day, sir," he continued, "Dunoran House, and the Sarsfields. Sir Dominick Sarsfield was the last of the old stock. He lost his life not six foot away from where you are sitting."

As he thus spoke he let himself down, with a little jump, on to the ground.

He was a dark-faced, sharp-featured, little hunchback, and had a walkingstick in his hand, with the end of which he pointed to a rusty stain in the plaster of the wall.

"Do you mind that mark, sir?" he asked.

"Yes," I said, standing up, and looking at it, with a curious anticipation of something worth hearing.

"That's about seven or eight feet from the ground, sir, and you'll not guess what it is."

"I dare say not," said I, "unless it is a stain from the weather."

" 'Tis nothing so lucky, sir," he answered, with the same cynical smile and a wag of his head, still pointing at the mark with his stick. "That's a splash of brains and blood. It's there this hundred years; and it will never leave it while the wall stands."

"He was murdered, then?"

"Worse than that, sir," he answered.

"He killed himself, perhaps?"

"Worse than that, itself, this cross between us and harm! I'm oulder than I look, sir; you wouldn't guess my years."

He became silent, and looked at me, evidently inviting a guess.

"Well, I should guess you to be about five-and-fifty."

He laughed and took a pinch of snuff, and said:

"I'm that, your honour, and something to the back of it. I was seventy last Candlemas. You would not'a' thought that, to look at me."

"Upon my word I should not; I can hardly believe it even now. Still, you don't remember Sir Dominick Sarsfield's death?" I said, glancing up at the ominous stain on the wall.

"No, sir, that was a long while before I was born. But my grandfather was butler here long ago, and many a time I heard tell how Sir Dominick came by his death. There was no masther in the great house ever sinst that happened. But there was two sarvants in care of it, and my aunt was one o' them; and she kep' me here wid her till I was nine year old, and she was lavin' the place to go to Dublin; and from that time it was let to go down. The wind sthript the roof, and the rain rotted the timber, and little by little, in sixty years' time, it kem to what you see. But I have a likin' for it still, for the sake of ould times; and I never come this way but I take a look in. I don't think it's many more times I'll be turnin' to see the ould place, for I'll be undher the sod myself before long."

"You'll outlive younger people," I said.

And, quitting that trite subject, I ran on:

"I don't wonder that you like this old place; it is a beautiful spot, such noble trees."

"I wish ye seen the glin when the nuts is ripe; they're the sweetest nuts in all Ireland, I think," he rejoined, and with a practical sense of the picturesque. "You'd fill your pockets while you'd be lookin' about you."

"These are very fine old woods," I remarked. "I have not seen any in Ireland I thought so beautiful."

"Eiah! your honour, the woods about here is nothing to what they wor. All the mountains along here was wood when my father was a gossoon, and Murroa Wood was the grandest of them all. All oak mostly, and all cut down as bare as the road. Not one left here that's fit to compare with them. Which way did your honour come hither—from Limerick?"

"No. Killaloe."

"Well, then, you passed the ground where Murroa Wood was in former times. You kem undher Lisnavourra, the steep knob of a hill about a mile above the village here. 'Twas near there that Murroa Wood was, and 'twas there Sir Dominick Sarsfield first met the devil, the Lord between us and harm, and a bad meeting it was for him and his."

I had become interested in the adventure which had occurred in the very scenery which had so greatly attracted me, and my new acquaintance, the little hunchback, was easily entreated to tell me the story, and spoke thus, so soon as we had each returned to his seat:

It was a fine estate when Sir Dominick came into it; and grand doings there was entirely, feasting and fiddling, free quarters for all the pipers in the counthry round, and a welcome for every one that liked to come. There was wine, by the hogshead, for the quality; and poteen enough to set a town a-fire, and beer and cidher enough to float a navy, for the boys and girls, and the likes of me. It was kep' up the best part of a month, till the weather broke, and the rain spoilt the sod for the moneen jigs, and the fair of Allybally Killudeen comin' on they wor obliged to give over their divarsion, and attind to the pigs.

But Sir Dominick was only beginnin' when they wor lavin' off. There was no way of gettin' rid of his money and estates he did not try—what with drinkin', dicin', racin', cards, and all soarts, it was not many years before the estates wor in debt, and Sir Dominick a distressed man. He showed a bold front to the world as long as he could; and then he sould off his dogs, and the most of his horses, and gev out he was going to thravel in France, and the like; and so off with him for a while and no one in these parts heard tale or tidings of him for two or three years. Till at last quite unexpected, one night there comes a rapping at the big kitchen window. It was past ten o'clock, and old Connor Hanlon, the butler, my grandfather, was sittin' by the fire alone, warming his shins over it. There was a keen east wind blowing along the mountains that night, and whistling cowld enough through the tops of the trees, and soundin' lonesome through the long chimneys.

(And the story-teller glanced up at the nearest stack visible from his seat.)

So he wasn't quite sure of the knockin' at the window, and up he gets, and sees his master's face.

My grandfather was glad to see him safe, for it was a long time since there was any news of him; but he was sorry, too, for it was a changed place and only himself and old Juggy Broadrick in charge of the house, and a man in the stables, and it was a poor thing to see him comin' back to his own like that.

He shook Con by the hand, and says he:

"I came here to say a word to you. I left my horse with Dick in the stable; I may want him again before morning, or I may never want him."

And with that he turns into the big kitchen, and draws a stool, and sits down to take an air of the fire.

"Sit down, Connor, opposite me, and listen to what I tell you, and don't be afeard to say what you think."

He spoke all the time lookin' into the fire, with his hands stretched over it, and a tired man he looked.

"An' why should I be afeard, Masther Dominick?" says my grandfather. "Yourself was a good masther to me, and so was your father, rest his sould, before you, and I'll say the truth, and dar' the devil, and more than that, for any Sarsfield of Dunoran, much less yourself, and a good right I'd have."

"It's all over with me, Con," says Sir Dominick.

"Heaven forbid!" says my grandfather.

" 'Tis past praying for," says Sir Dominick. "The last guinea's gone; the ould place will follow it. It must be sold, and I'm come here, I don't know why, like a ghost to have a last look round me, and go off in the dark again."

And with that he tould him to be sure, in case he should hear of his death, to give the oak box, in the closet off his room to his cousin, Pat Sarsfield, in Dublin, and the sword and pistols his grandfather carried in Aughrim, and two or three thrifling things of the kind.

And says he, "Con, they say if the divil gives you money over-night, you'll find nothing but a bagful of pebbles, and chips, and nutshells, in the morning. If I thought he played fair, I'm in the humour to make a bargain with him tonight."

"Lord forbid!" says my grandfather, standing up with a start, and crossing himself.

"They say the country's full of men, listin' sogers for the king o' France. If I light on one o' them, I'll not refuse his offer. How contrary things goes! How long is it since me and Captain Waller fought the jewel at New Castle?"

"Six years, Masther Dominick, and ye broke his thigh with the bullet the first shot."

"I did, Con," says he, "and I wish, instead, he had shot me through the heart. Have you any whisky?"

My grandfather took it out of the buffet, and the masther pours out some into a bowl, and drank it off.

"I'll go out and have a look at my horse," says he, standing up. There was a sort of a stare in his eyes, as he pulled his riding-cloak about him, as if there was something bad in his thoughts.

"Sure, I won't be a minute running out myself to the stable, and looking after the horse for you myself," says my grandfather.

"I'm not goin' to the stable," says Sir Dominick; "I may as well tell you, for I see you found it out already—I'm goin' across the deer-park; if I come back you'll see me in an hour's time. But, anyhow, you'd better not follow me, for if you do I'll shoot you, and that'd be a bad ending to our friendship."

And with that he walks down this passage here, and turns the key in the side door at that end of it, and out wid him on the sod into the moonlight and the cowld wind; and my grandfather seen him walkin' hard towards the park wall, and then he comes in and closes the door with a heavy heart.

Sir Dominick stopped to think when he got to the middle of the deerpark, for he had not made up his mind, when he left the house and the whisky did not clear his head, only it gev him courage.

He did not feel the cowld wind now, nor fear death, nor think much of anything, but the shame and fall of the old family.

And he made up his mind, if no better thought came to him between that and there, so soon as he came to Murroa Wood, he'd hang himself from one of the oak branches with his cravat.

It was a bright moonlight night, there was just a bit of a cloud driving across the moon now and then, but, only for that, as light a'most as day.

Down he goes, right for the wood of Murroa. It seemed to him every step he took was long as three, and it was no time till he was among the big oak-trees with their roots spreading from one to another, and their branches stretching overhead like the timbers of a naked roof, and the moon shining down through them, and casting their shadows thick on the ground as black as my shoe.

He was sobering a bit by this time, and he slacked his pace, and he thought 'twould be better to list in the French king's army, and thry what that might do for him, for he knew a man might take his own life any time, but it would puzzle him to take it back again when he liked.

Just as he made up his mind not to make away with himself, what should he hear but a step clinkin' along the dry ground under the trees, and soon he sees a grand gentleman right before him comin' up to meet him.

He was a handsome young man like himself, and he wore a cocked-hat with gold-lace round it, such as officers wear on their coats, and he had on a dress the same as French officers wore in them times.

He stopped opposite Sir Dominick, and he cum to a stand-still also.

The two gentlemen took off their hats to one another, and says the stranger:

"I am recruiting, sir," says he, "for my sovereign, and you'll find my money won't turn into pebbles, chips, and nutshells, by tomorrow."

At the same time he pulls out a big purse full of gold.

The minute he sets eyes on that gentleman, Sir Dominick had his own opinion of him; and at those words he felt the very hair standing up on his head.

"Don't be afraid," says he, "the money won't burn you. If it proves honest gold, and if it prospers with you, I'm willing to make a bargain. This is the last day of February," says he; "I'll serve you seven years, and at the end of that time you shall serve me, and I'll come for you when the seven years is over, when the clock turns the minute between February and March; and the first of March ye'll come away with me, or never. You'll not find me a bad master, any more than a bad servant. I love my own; and I command all the pleasures and the glory of the world. The bargain dates from this day, and the lease is out at midnight on the last day I told you; and in the year"—he told him the year, it was easy reckoned, but I forget it—"and if you'd rather wait," he says, "for eight months and twenty-eight days, before you sign the writin', you may, if you meet me here. But I can't do a great deal for you in the meantime; and if you don't sign then, all you get from me up to that time, will vanish away, and you'll be just as you are tonight, and ready to hang yourself on the first tree you meet."

Well, the end of it was, Sir Dominick chose to wait, and he came back to the house with a big bag full of money, as round as your hat a'most.

My grandfather was glad enough, you may be sure, to see the master safe and sound again so soon. Into the kitchen he bangs again, and swings the bag o' money on the table; and he stands up straight, and heaves up his shoulders like a man that has just got shut of a load; and he looks at the bag, and my grandfather looks at him, and from him to it, and back again. Sir Dominick looked as white as a sheet, and says he:

"I don't know, Con, what's in it; it's the heaviest load I ever carried."

He seemed shy of openin' the bag; and he made my grandfather heap up a roaring fire of turf and wood, and then, at last, he opens it, and, sure enough, 'twas stuffed full of golden guineas, bright and new, as if they were only that minute out o' the Mint.

Sir Dominick made my grandfather sit at his elbow while he counted every guinea in the bag.

When he was done countin', and it wasn't far from daylight when that time came, Sir Dominick made my grandfather swear not to tell a word about it. And a close secret it was for many a day after.

When the eight months and twenty-eight days were pretty near spent and ended, Sir Dominick returned to the house here with a troubled mind, in doubt what was best to be done, and no one alive but my grandfather knew anything about the matter, and he not half what had happened.

As the day drew near, towards the end of October, Sir Dominick grew only more and more troubled in mind.

One time he made up his mind to have no more to say to such

things, nor to speak again with the like of them he met with in the wood of Murroa. Then, again, his heart failed him when he thought of his debts, and he not knowing where to turn. Then, only a week before the day, everything began to go wrong with him. One man wrote from London to say that Sir Dominick paid three thousand pounds to the wrong man, and must pay it over again; another, in Dublin, denied the payment of a thundherin' big bill, and Sir Dominick could nowhere find the receipt, and so on, wid fifty other things as bad.

Well, by the time the night of the 28th of October came round, he was a'most ready to lose his senses with all the demands that was risin' up agains' him on all sides, and nothing to meet them but the help of the one dhreadful friend he had to depind on at night in the oak-wood down there below.

So there was nothing for it but to go through with the business that was begun already, and about the same hour as he went last, he takes off the little crucifix he wore round his neck, for he was a Catholic, and his gospel, and his bit o' the thrue cross that he had in a locket, for since he took the money from the Evil One he was growin' frightful in himself, and got all he could to guard him from the power of the devil. But tonight, for his life, he daren't take them with him. So he gives them into my grandfather's hands without a word, only he looked as white as a sheet o' paper; and he takes his hat and sword, and telling my grandfather to watch for him, away he goes, to try what would come of it.

It was a fine still night, and the moon—not so bright, though, now as the first time—was shinin' over heath and rock, and down on the lonesome oak-wood below him.

His heart beat thick as he drew near it. There was not a sound, not even the distant bark of a dog from the village behind him. There was not a lonesomer spot in the country round, and if it wasn't for his debts and losses that was drivin' him on half mad, in spite of his fears for his soul and his hopes of paradise, and all his good angel was whisperin' in his ear, he would 'a' turned back, and sent for his clargy, and made his confession and his penance, and changed his ways, and led a good life, for he was frightened enough to have done a great dale.

Softer and slower he stept as he got once more, in undher the big branches of the oakthrees; and when he got in a bit, near where he met with the bad spirit before, he stopped and looked round him, and felt himself, every bit, turning cowld as a dead man, and you may be sure he did not feel much betther when he seen the same man steppin' from behind the big tree that was touchin' his elbow a'most.

"You found the money good," says he, "but it was not enough. No matter, you shall have enough and to spare. I'll see after your luck, and I'll give you a hint whenever it can serve you; and any time you want to see me you have only to come down here, and call my face to mind, and wish me present. You shan't owe a shilling by the end of the year, and you shall never miss the right card, the best throw, and the winning horse. Are you willing?"

The young gentleman's voice almost stuck in his throat, and his hair was rising on his head, but he did get out a word or two to signify that he consented; and with that the Evil One handed him a needle, and bid him give him three drops of blood from his arm; and he took them in the cup of an acorn, and gave him a pen, and bid him write some words that he repeated, and that Sir Dominick did not understand, on two thin slips of parchment. He took one himself and the other he sunk in Sir Dominick's arm at the place where he drew the blood, and he closed the flesh over it. And that's as true as you're sittin' there!

Well, Sir Dominick went home. He was a frightened man, and well he might be. But in a little time he began to grow aisier in his mind. Anyhow, he got out of debt very quick, and money came tumbling in to make him richer, and everything he took in hand prospered, and he never made a wager, or played a game, but he won; and for all that, there was not a poor man on the estate that was not happier than Sir Dominick.

So he took again to his old ways; for, when the money came back, all came back, and there were hounds and horses, and wine galore, and no end of company, and grand doin's, and divarsion, up here at the great house. And some said Sir Dominick was thinkin' of gettin' married; and more said he wasn't. But, anyhow, there was somethin' troublin' him more than common, and so one night, unknownst to all, away he goes to the lonesome oak-wood. It was something, maybe, my grandfather thought was troublin' him about a beautiful young lady he was jealous of, and mad in love with her. But that was only guess.

Well, when Sir Dominick got into the wood this time, he grew more in dread than ever; and he was on the point of turnin' and lavin' the place, when who should he see, close beside him, but my gentleman, seated on a big stone undher one of the trees. In place of looking the fine young gentleman in goold lace and grand clothes he appeared before, he was now in rags, he looked twice the size he had been, and his face smutted with soot, and he had a murtherin' big steel hammer, as heavy as a half-hundhred, with a handle a yard long, across his knees. It was so dark under the tree, he did not see him quite clear for some time.

He stood up, and he looked awful tall entirely. And what passed between them in that discourse my grandfather never heered. But Sir Dominick was as black as night afterwards, and hadn't a laugh for anything nor a word a'most for any one, and he only grew worse and worse, and darker and darker. And now this thing, whatever it was, used to come to him of its own accord, whether he wanted it or no; sometimes in one shape, and sometimes in another, in lonesome places, and sometimes at his side by night when he'd be ridin' home alone, until at last he lost heart altogether and sent for the priest.

The priest was with him a long time, and when he heered the whole story, he rode off all the way for the bishop, and the bishop came here to the great house next day, and he gev Sir Dominick a good advice. He toult him he must give over dicin', and swearin' and drinkin' and all bad company, and live a vartuous steady life until the seven years' bargain was out, and if the divil didn't come for him the minute afther the stroke of twelve the first morning of the month of March, he was safe out of the bargain. There was not more than eight or ten months to run now before the seven years wor out, and he lived all the time according to the bishop's advice, as strict as if he was "in retreat."

Well, you may guess he felt quare enough when the mornin' of the 28th of February came.

The priest came up by appointment, and Sir Dominick and his raverence wor together in the room you see there, and kep' up their prayers together till the clock struck twelve, and a good hour after, and not a sign of a disturbance, nor nothing came near them, and the priest slep' that night in the house in the room next Sir Dominick's, and all went over as comfortable as could be, and they shook hands and kissed like two comrades after winning a battle.

So now, Sir Dominick thought he might as well have a pleasant evening, after all his fastin' and prayin'; and he sent round to half a dozen of the neighbouring gentlemen to come and dine with him, and his raverence stayed and dined also, and a roarin' bowl o' punch they had, and no end o' wine, and the swearin' and dice, and cards and guineas changin' hands, and songs and stories, that wouldn't do any one good to hear, and the priest slipped away, when he seen the turn things was takin', and it was not far from the stroke of twelve when Sir Dominick, sitting at the head of his table, swears, "This is the best first of March I ever sat down with my friends."

"It ain't the first o' March," says Mr. Hiffernan of Ballyvoureen. He was a scholard, and always kep' an almanack.

"What is it then?" said Sir Dominick, startin' up, and dhroppin' the ladle into the bowl, and starin' at him as if he had two heads.

" 'Tis the twenty-ninth of February, leap year," says he. And just as they were talkin', the clock strikes twelve; and my grandfather, who was half asleep in a chair by the fire in the hall, openin' his eyes, sees a short square fellow with a cloak on, and long black hair bushin' out from under his hat, standin' just there where you see the bit o' light shinin' again' the wall.

(My hunchback friend pointed with his stick to a little patch of red sunset light that relieved the deepening shadow of the passage.)

"Tell your master," says he, in an awful voice, like the growl of a baist, "that I'm here by appointment, and expect him downstairs this minute."

Up goes my grandfather, by these very steps you are sittin' on.

"Tell him I can't come down yet," says Sir Dominick, and he turns to the company in the room, and says he with a cold sweat shinin' on his face, "For God's sake, gentlemen, will any of you jump from the window and bring the priest here?" One looked at another and no one knew what to make of it, and in the meantime, up comes my grandfather again, and says he, tremblin', "He says, sir, unless you go down to him, he'll come up to you."

"I don't understand this, gentlemen, I'll see what it means," says

Sir Dominick, trying to put a face on it, and walkin' out o' the room like a man through the press-room, with the hangman waitin' for him outside. Down the stairs he comes, and two or three of the gentlemen peeping over the banisters, to see. My grandfather was walking six or eight steps behind him, and he seen the stranger take a stride out to meet Sir Dominick, and catch him up in his arms, and whirl his head against the wall, and wi' that the hall-doore flies open, and out goes the candles, and the turf and wood-ashes flyin' with the wind out o' the hall-fire, ran in a drift o' sparks along the floore by his feet.

Down runs the gentlemen. Bang goes the hall-doore. Some comes runnin' up, and more runnin' down, with lights. It was all over with Sir Dominick. They lifted up the corpse, and put its shoulders again' the wall; but there was not a gasp left in him. He was cowld and stiffenin' already.

Pat Donovan was comin' up to the great house late that night and after he passed the little brook, that the carriage track up to the house crosses, and about fifty steps to this side of it, his dog, that was by his side, makes a sudden wheel, and springs over the wall, and sets up a yowlin' inside you'd hear a mile away; and that minute two men passed him by in silence, goin' down from the house, one of them short and square, and the other like Sir Dominick in shape, but there was little light under the trees where he was, and they looked only like shadows; and as they passed him by he could not hear the sound of their feet and he drew back to the wall frightened; and when he got up to the great house, he found all in confusion, and the master's body, with the head smashed to pieces, lying just on *that spot.*

The narrator stood up and indicated with the point of his stick the exact site of the body, and, as I looked, the shadow deepened, the red stain of sunlight vanished from the wall, and the sun had gone down behind the distant hill of New Castle, leaving the haunted scene in the deep grey of darkening twilight.

So I and the story-teller parted, not without good wishes on both sides, and a little "tip" which seemed not unwelcome, from me.

It was dusk and the moon up by the time I reached the village, remounted my nag, and looked my last on the scene of the terrible legend of Dunoran.

Trinket's Colt

By SOMERVILLE AND ROSS

It was Petty Sessions day in Skebawn, a cold grey day of February, A case of trespass had dragged its burden of cross summonses and cross swearing far into the afternoon, and when I left the bench my head was singing from the bellowing of the attorneys, and the smell of their clients was heavy upon my palate.

The street still testified to the fact that it was market day, and I evaded with difficulty the sinuous course of carts full of soddenly screwed people, and steered an equally devious one for myself among the groups anchored round the doors of the public-houses. Skewbawn possesses, among its legion of public-houses, one establishment which timorously, and almost imperceptibly, proffers tea to the thirsty. I turned in there, as was my custom on court days, and found the little dingy den, known as the Ladies' Coffee-room, in the occupancy of my friend Mr. Florence McCarthy Knox, who was drinking strong tea and eating buns with serious simplicity. It was a first and quite unexpected glimpse of that domesticity that has now become a marked feature in his character.

"You're the very man I wanted to see," I said as I sat down beside him at the oilcloth-covered table; "a man I know in England who is not much of a judge of character has asked me to buy him a four-year-old down here, and as I should rather be stuck by a friend than a dealer, I wish you'd take over the job."

Flurry poured himself out another cup of tea, and dropped three lumps of sugar into it in silence.

Finally he said, "There isn't a four-year-old in this country that I'd be seen dead with at a pig fair."

This was discouraging, from the premier authority on horseflesh in the district.

"But it isn't six weeks since you told me you had the finest filly in your stables that was ever foaled in the County Cork," I protested; "what's wrong with her?"

"Oh, is it that filly?" said Mr. Knox with a lenient smile; "she's gone these three weeks from me. I swapped her and six pounds for a three-year-old Ironmonger colt, and after that I swapped the colt and nineteen pounds for that Bandon horse I rode last week at your place, and after that again I sold the Bandon horse for seventy-five pounds to old Welply, and I had to give him back a couple of sovereigns luck-money. You see I did pretty well with the filly after all."

"Yes, yes—oh, rather," I assented, as one dizzily accepts the propositions of a bimetallist; "and you don't know of anything else—?"

The room in which we were seated was closely screened from the shop by a door with a muslin-curtained window in it; several of the panes were broken, and at this juncture two voices that had for some time carried on a discussion forced themselves upon our attention.

"Begging your pardon for contradicting you, ma'am," said the voice of Mrs. McDonald, proprietress of the tea-shop, and a leading light in Skebawn Dissenting circles, shrilly tremulous with indignation, "if the servants I recommend you won't stop with you, it's no fault of mine. If respectable young girls are set picking grass out of your gravel, in place of their proper work, certainly they will give warning!"

The voice that replied struck me as being a notable one, well-bred and imperious.

"When I take a barefooted slut out of a cabin, I don't expect her to dictate to me what her duties are!"

Flurry jerked up his chin in a noiseless laugh. "It's my grand-mother!" he whispered. "I bet you Mrs. McDonald don't get much change out of her!"

"If I set her to clean the pigsty I expect her to obey me," continued the voice in accents that would have made me clean forty pigsties had she desired me to do so.

"Very well, ma'am," retorted Mrs. McDonald, "if that's the way you treat your servants, you needn't come here again looking for them. I consider your conduct is neither that of a lady nor a Christian!"

"Don't you, indeed?" replied Flurry's grandmother. "Well, your opinion doesn't greatly distress me, for, to tell you the truth, I don't think you're much of a judge."

"Didn't I tell you she'd score?" murmured Flurry, who was by this time applying his eye to a hole in the muslin curtain. "She's off," he went on, returning to his tea. "She's a great character! She's eighty-three if she's a day, and she's as sound on her legs as a three-year-old! Did you see the old shandryhan of hers in the street a while ago, and a fellow on the box with a red beard on him like Robinson Crusoe? That old mare that was on the near side— Trinket her name is—is mighty near clean bred. I can tell you her foals are worth a bit of money."

I had heard of old Mrs. Knox of Aussolas; indeed, I had seldom dined out in the neighbourhood without hearing some new story of her and her remarkable menage, but it had not yet been my privilege to meet her.

"Well, now," went on Flurry in his slow voice, "I'll tell you a thing that's just come into my head. My grandmother promised me a foal of Trinket's the day I was one-and-twenty, and that's five years ago, and deuce a one I've got from her yet. You never were at Aussolas? No, you were not. Well, I tell you the place there is like a circus with horses. She had a couple of score of them running wild in the woods, like deer."

"Oh, come," I said, "I'm a bit of a liar myself—"

"Well, she has a dozen of them anyhow, rattling good colts too, some of them, but they might as well be donkeys, for all the good they are to me or to anyone. It's not once in three years she sells one, and there she has them walking after her for bits of sugar, like a lot of dirty lapdogs," ended Flurry with disgust.

"Well, what's your plan? Do you want me to make her a bid for one of the lapdogs?"

"I was thinking," replied Flurry, with great deliberation, "that my birthday's this week, and maybe I could work a four-year-old colt of Trinket's she has out of her in honour of the occasion."

"And sell your grandmother's birthday present to me?"

"Just that, I suppose," answered Flurry with a slow wink.

A few days afterwards a letter from Mr. Knox informed me that he had "squared the old lady, and it would be all right about the colt." He further told me that Mrs. Knox had been good enough to offer me, with him, a day's snipe shooting on the celebrated Aussolas bogs, and he proposed to drive me there the following Monday, if convenient. Most people found it convenient to shoot the Aussolas snipe bog when they got the chance. Eight o'clock on the following Monday morning saw Flurry, myself, and a groom packed into a dogcart, with portmanteaus, gun-cases, and two rampant red setters.

It was a long drive, twelve miles at least, and a very cold one. We passed through long tracts of pasture country, fraught, for Flurry, with memories of runs, which were recorded for me, fence by fence, in every one of which the biggest dog-fox in the country had gone to ground, with not two feet—measured accurately on the handle of the whip—between him and the leading hound; through bogs that imperceptibly melted into lakes, and finally down and down into a valley, where the fir-trees of Aussolas clustered darkly round a glittering lake, and all but hid the grey roofs and pointed gables of Aussolas Castle.

"There's a nice stretch of a demesne for you," remarked Flurry, pointing downwards with the whip, "and one little old woman holding it all in the heel of her fist. Well able to hold it she is, too, and always was, and she'll live twenty years yet, if it's only to spite the whole lot of us, and when all's said and done goodness knows how she'll leave it!"

"It strikes me you were lucky to keep her up to her promise about the colt," I said.

Flurry administered a composing kick to the ceaseless strivings of the red setters under the seat.

"I used to be rather a pet with her," he said, after a pause; "but mind you, I haven't got him yet, and if she gets any notion I want to sell him I'll never get him, so say nothing about the business to her."

The tall gates of Aussolas shrieked on their hinges as they admitted us, and shut with a clang behind us, in the faces of an old mare and a couple of young horses, who, foiled in their break for the excitement of the outer world, turned and galloped defiantly on either side of us. Flurry's admirable cob hammered on, regardless of all things save his duty.

"He's the only one I have that I'd trust myself here with," said his master, flicking him approvingly with the whip; "there are plenty of people afraid to come here at all, and when my grandmother goes out driving, she has a boy on the box with a basket full of stones to peg at them. Talk of the dickens, here she is herself!"

A short, upright old woman was approaching, preceded by a white woolly dog with sore eyes and a bark like a tin trumpet; we both got out of the trap and advanced to meet the lady of the manor.

I may summarize her attire by saying that she looked as if she had robbed a scarecrow; her face was small and incongruously refined, the skinny hand that she extended to me had the grubby tan that bespoke the professional gardener, and was decorated with a magnificent diamond ring. On her head was a massive purple velvet bonnet.

"I am very glad to meet you, Major Yeates," she said with an old-fashioned precision of utterance; "your grandfather was a dancing partner of mine in old days at the Castle, when he was a handsome young aide-de-camp there, and I was— You may judge for yourself what I was."

She ended with a startling little hoot of laughter, and I was aware that she quite realized the world's opinion of her, and was indifferent to it.

Our way to the bogs took us across Mrs. Knox's home farm, and through a large field in which several young horses were grazing.

"There now, that's my fellow," said Flurry, pointing to a fine-looking colt, "the chestnut with the white diamond on his forehead. He'll run into three figures before he's done, but we'll not tell that to the old lady!"

The famous Aussolas bogs were as full of snipe as usual, and a good deal fuller of water than any bogs I had ever shot before. I was on my day, and Flurry was not, and as he is ordinarily an infinitely better snipe shot than I, I felt at peace with the world and all men as we walked back, wet through, at five o'clock.

The sunset had waned, and a big white moon was making the eastern tower of Aussolas look like a thing in a fairy tale or a play when we arrived at the hall door. An individual, whom I recognized as the Robinson Crusoe coachman, admitted us to a hall, the like of which one does not often see. The walls were panelled with dark oak up to the gallery that ran around three sides of it, the balusters of the wide staircase were heavily carved, and blackened portraits of Flurry's ancestors on the spindle side stared sourly down on their descendants as he tramped upstairs with the bog mould on his hobnailed boots.

We had just changed into dry clothes when Robinson Crusoe shoved his red beard round the corner of the door, with the information that the mistress said we were to stay for dinner. My heart sank. It was then barely half-past five. I said something about having no evening clothes and having to get home early.

"Sure the dinner'll be in another half hour," said Robinson Crusoe, joining hospitably in the conversation; and as for evening clothes—God bless ye!"

The door closed behind him.

"Never mind," said Flurry, "I dare say you'll be glad enough to eat another dinner by the time you get home." He laughed. "Poor Slipper!" he added inconsequently, and only laughed again when I asked for an explanation.

Old Mrs. Knox received us in the library, where she was seated by a roaring turf fire, which lit the room a good deal more effectively than the pair of candles that stood beside her in tall silver candlesticks. Ceaseless and implacable growls from under her chair indicated the presence of the woolly dog. She talked with confounding culture of the books that rose all round her to the ceiling; her evening dress was accomplished by means of an additional white shawl, rather dirtier than its congeners; as I took her in to dinner she quoted Virgil to me, and in the same breath screeched an objurgation at a being whose matted head rose suddenly into view from behind an ancient Chinese screen, as I have seen the head of a Zulu woman peer over a bush.

Dinner was as incongruous as everything else. Detestable soup in a splendid old silver tureen that was nearly as dark in hue as Robinson Crusoe's thumb; a perfect salmon, perfectly cooked, on a chipped kitchen dish; such cut glass as is not easy to find nowadays; sherry that, as Flurry subsequently remarked, would burn the shell off an egg; and a bottle of port, draped in immemorial cobwebs, wan with age, and probably priceless. Throughout the vicissitudes of the meal Mrs. Knox's conversation flowed on undismayed, directed sometimes at me—she had installed me in the position of friend of her youth—and talked to me as if I were my own grandfather—sometimes at Crusoe, with whom she had several heated arguments, and sometimes she would make a statement of remarkable frankness on the subject of her horse-farming affairs to Flurry, who, very much on his best behaviour, agreed with all she said, and risked no original remark. As I listened to them both, I remembered with infinite amusement how he had told me once that a pet name she had for him was "Tony Lumpkin," and no one but herself knew what she meant by it. It seemed strange that she made no allusion to Trinket's colt or to Flurry's birthday, but mindful of my instructions, I held my peace.

As, at about half-past eight, we drove away in the moonlight, Flurry congratulated me solemnly on my success with his grandmother. He was good enough to tell me that she would marry me tomorrow if I asked her, and he wished I would, even if it was only to see what a nice grandson he'd be for me. A sympathetic giggle behind me told me that Michael, on the back seat, had heard and relished the jest.

We had left the gates of Aussolas about half a mile behind when, at the corner of a by-road, Flurry pulled up. A short squat figure rose from the black shadow of a furze bush and came out in the moonlight, swinging its arms like a cabman and cursing audibly.

"Oh, murdher, oh, murdher, Misther Flurry! What kept ye at all? 'Twould perish the crows to be waiting here the way I am these two hours—"

"Ah, shut your mouth, Slipper!" said Flurry, who, to my surprise, had turned back the rug and was taking off his driving coat. "I couldn't help it. Come on, Yeates, we've got to get out here."

"What for?" I asked, in not unnatural bewilderment.

"It's all right. I'll tell you as we go along," replied my companion, who was already turning to follow Slipper up the by-road. "Take the trap on, Michael, and wait at the River's Cross." He waited for me to come up with him, and then put his hand on my arm. "You see, Major, this is the way it is. My grandmother's given me that colt right enough, but if I waited for her to send him over to me I'd never see a hair of his tail. So I just thought that as we were over here we might as well take him back with us, and maybe you'll give us a help with him; he'll not be altogether too handy for a first go off."

I was staggered. An infant in arms could scarcely have failed to discern the fishiness of the transaction, and I begged Mr. Knox not to put himself to this trouble on my account, as I had no doubt I could find a horse for my friend elsewhere. Mr. Knox assured me that it was no trouble at all, quite the contrary, and that, since his grandmother had given him the colt, he saw no reason why he should not take him when he wanted him; also, that if I didn't want him he'd be glad enough to keep him himself; and finally, that I wasn't the chap to go back on a friend, but I was welcome to drive back to Shreelane with Michael this minute if I liked.

Of course I yielded in the end. I told Flurry I should lose my job over the business, and he said I could then marry his grandmother, and the discussion was abruptly closed by the necessity of following Slipper over a locked five-barred gate.

Our pioneer took us over about half a mile of country, knocking down stone gaps where practicable and scrambling over tall banks in the deceptive moonlight. We found ourselves at length in a field with a shed in one corner of it; in a dim group of farm buildings a little way off a light was shining.

"Wait here," said Flurry to me in a whisper; "the less noise, the better. It's an open shed, and we'll just slip in and coax him out."

Slipper unwound from his waist a halter, and my colleagues glided like spectres into the shadow of the shed, leaving me to meditate on my duties as Resident Magistrate, and on the questions that would be asked in the House by our local member when Slipper had given away the adventure in his cups.

In less than a minute three shadows emerged from the shed, where two had gone in. They had got the colt.

"He came out as quiet as a calf when he winded the sugar," said Flurry; "it was well for me I filled my pockets from grandmamma's sugar basin."

He and Slipper had a rope from each side of the colt's head; they took him quickly across a field towards a gate. The colt stepped daintily between them over the moonlit grass; he snorted occasionally, but appeared on the whole amenable.

The trouble began later, and was due, as trouble often is, to the beguilements of a short cut. Against the maturer judgment of Slipper, Flurry insisted on following a route that he assured us he knew as well as his own pocket, and the consequence was that in about five minutes I found myself standing on top of a bank hanging on to a rope, on the other end of which the colt dangled and danced, while Flurry, with the other rope, lay prone in the ditch, and Slipper administered to the bewildered colt's hind quarters such chastisement as could be ventured on.

I have no space to narrate in detail the atrocious difficulties and disasters of the short cut. How the colt set to work to buck, and went away across a field, dragging the faithful Slipper, literally ventre à terre, after him, while I picked myself in ignominy out of a briar patch, and Flurry cursed himself black in the face. How we were attacked by ferocious cur dogs, and I lost my eye-glass; and how, as we neared the River's Cross, Flurry espied the police patrol on the road, and we all hid behind a rick of turf while I realized in fullness what an exceptional ass I was, to have been beguiled into an enterprise that involved hiding with Slipper from the Royal Irish Constabulary.

Let it suffice to say that Trinket's infernal offspring was finally handed over on the high road to Michael and Slipper, and Flurry drove me home in a state of mental and physical overthrow.

I saw nothing of my friend Mr. Knox for the next couple of days, by the end of which time I had worked up a high polish on my misgivings, and had determined to tell him that under no circumstances would I have anything to say to his grandmother's birthday present. It was like my usual luck that, instead of writing a note to this effect, I thought it would be good for my liver to walk across the hills to Tory Cottage and tell Flurry so in person.

It was a bright, blustery morning, after a muggy day. The feeling of spring was in the air, the daffodils were already in bud, and crocuses showed purple in the grass on either side of the avenue. It was only a couple of miles to Tory Cottage by the way across the hills; I walked fast, and it was barely twelve o'clock when I saw its pink walls and clumps of evergreens below me. As I looked down at it the chiming of Flurry's hounds in the kennels came to me on the wind; I stood still to listen, and could almost have sworn that I was hearing again the clash of Magdalen bells, hard at work on May morning.

The path that I was following led downwards through a larch plantation to Flurry's back gate. Hot wafts from some hideous cauldron at the other side of a wall apprised me of the vicinity of the kennels and their cuisine, and the fir-trees round were hung with gruesome and unknown joints. I thanked heaven that I was not a master of hounds, and passed on as quickly as might be to the hall door.

I rang two or three times without response; then the door opened a couple of inches and was instantly slammed in my face. I heard the hurried paddling of bare feet on oil-cloth, and a voice, "Hurry, Bridgie, hurry! There's quality at the door!"

Bridgie, holding a dirty cap on with one hand, presently arrived and informed me that she believed Mr. Knox was out about the place. She seemed perturbed, and she cast scared glances down the drive while speaking to me.

I knew enough of Flurry's habits to shape a tolerably direct course for his whereabouts. He was, as I had expected, in the training paddock, a field behind the stable yard, in which he had put up practice jumps for his horses. It was a good-sized field with clumps of furze in it, and Flurry was standing near one of these with his hands in his pockets, singularly unoccupied. I supposed that he was prospecting for a place to put up another jump. He did not see me coming, and turned with a start as I spoke to him. There was a queer expression of mingled guilt and what I can only describe as divilment in his grey eyes as he greeted me. In my dealings with Flurry Knox, I have since formed the habit of sitting tight, in a general way, when I see that expression.

"Well, who's coming next, I wonder!" he said, as he shook hands with me. "It's not ten minutes since I had two of your d——dpeelers here searching the whole place for my grandmother's colt!"

"What!" I exclaimed, feeling cold all down my back. "Do you mean the police have got hold of it?"

"They haven't got hold of the colt anyway," said Flurry, looking sideways at me from under the peak of his cap, with the glint of the sun in his eye. "I got word in time before they came."

"What do you mean?" I demanded. "Where is he? For heaven's sake don't tell me you've sent the brute over to my place!"

"It's a good job for you I didn't," replied Flurry, "as the police are on their way to Shreelane this minute to consult you about it. You!" He gave utterance to one of his short diabolical fits of laughter. "He's where they'll not find him, anyhow. Ho ho! It's the funniest hand I ever played!"

"Oh yes, it's devilish funny, I've no doubt," I retorted, beginning to lose my temper, as is the manner of many people when they are frightened; "but I give you fair warning that if Mrs.

Knox asked me any questions about it, I shall tell her the whole story."

"All right," responded Flurry; "and when you do, don't forget to tell her how you flogged the colt out on to the road over her own bounds ditch."

"Very well," I said hotly, "I may as well go home and send in my papers. They'll break me over this—"

"Ah, hold on, major," said Flurry soothingly, "it'll be all right. No one knows anything. It's only on spec the old lady sent the bobbies here. If you'll keep quiet it'll all blow over."

"I don't care," I said, struggling hopelessly in the toils; "if I meet your grandmother, and she asks me about it, I shall tell her all I know."

"Please God you'll not meet her! After all, it's not once in a blue moon that she—" began Flurry. Even as he said the words his face changed. "Holy fly!" he ejaculated. "Isn't that her dog coming into the field? Look at her bonnet over the wall! Hide, hide for your life!" He caught me by the shoulder and shoved me down among the furze bushes before I realized what had happened.

"Get in there! I'll talk to her."

I may as well confess that at the mere sight of Mrs. Knox's purple bonnet my heart had turned to water. In that moment I knew what it would be like to tell her how I, having eaten her salmon, and capped her quotations, and drunk her best port, had gone forth and helped to steal her horse. I abandoned my dignity, my sense of honour; I took the furze prickles to my breast and wallowed in them.

Mrs. Knox had advanced with vengeful speed; already she was in high altercation with Flurry at no great distance from where I lay; varying sounds of battle reached me, and I gathered that Flurry was not—to put it mildly—shrinking from that economy of truth that the situation required.

"Is it that curby, long-backed brute? You promised him to me long ago, but I wouldn't be bothered with him!"

The old lady uttered a laugh of shrill derision. "Is it likely I'd promise you my best colt? And still more, is it likely that you'd refuse him if I did?"

"Very well, ma'am." Flurry's voice was admirably indignant. "Then I suppose I'm a liar and a thief."

"I'd be more obliged to you for the information if I hadn't known it before," responded his grandmother with lightning speed; "if you swore to me on a stack of Bibles you knew nothing about my colt, I wouldn't believe you! I shall go straight to Major Yeates and ask his advice. I believe him to be a gentleman, in spite of the company he keeps!"

I writhed deeper into the furze bushes, and thereby discovered a sandy rabbit run, along which I crawled, with my cap well over my eyes, and the furze needles stabbing me through my stockings. The ground shelves a little, promising profounder concealment, but the bushes were very thick, and I laid hold of the bare stem of one to help my progress. It lifted out of the ground in my hand, revealing a freshly cut stump. Something snorted, not a yard away; I glared through the opening, and was confronted by the long, horrified face of Mrs. Knox's colt, mysteriously on a level with my own.

Even without the white diamond on his forehead I should have divined the truth; but how in the name of wonder had Flurry persuaded him to couch like a woodcock in the heart of a furze brake? For a full minute I lay as still as death for fear of frightening him, while the voices of Flurry and his grandmother raged on alarmingly close to me. The colt snorted, and blew long breaths through his wide nostrils, but he did not move. I crawled an inch or two nearer, and after a few seconds of cautious peering I grasped the position. They had buried him.

A small sandpit among the furze had been utilized as a grave; they had filled him up to his withers with sand, and a few furze bushes, artistically disposed around the pit, had done the rest. As the depth of Flurry's guile was revealed, laughter came upon me like a flood; I gurgled and shook apoplectically, and the colt gazed at me with serious surprise, until a sudden outburst of barking close to my elbow administered a fresh shock to my tottering nerves.

Mrs. Knox's woolly dog had tracked me into the furze, and was now baying at the colt and me with mingled terror and indignation. I addressed him in a whisper, with perfidious endearments, advancing a crafty hand towards him the while, made a snatch for the back of his neck, missed it badly, and got him by the ragged fleece of his hindquarters as he tried to flee. If I had flayed him alive, he could hardly have uttered a more deafening series of yells, but, like a fool, instead of letting him go, I dragged him towards me, and tried to stifle the noise by holding his muzzle. The tussle lasted engrossingly for a few seconds, and then the climax of the nightmare arrived.

Mrs. Knox's voice, close behind me, said, "Let go my dog this instant, sir! Who are you—"

Her voice faded away, and I knew that she also had seen the colt's head.

I positively felt sorry for her. At her age there was no knowing what effect the shock might have on her. I scrambled to my feet and confronted her.

"Major Yeates!" she said. There was a deathly pause. "Will you kindly tell me," said Mrs. Knox slowly, "am I in Bedlam, or are you? And what is that?"

She pointed to the colt, and that unfortunate animal, recognizing the voice of his mistress, uttered a hoarse and lamentable whinny. Mrs. Knox felt around her for support, found only furze prickles, gazed speechlessly at me, and then, to her eternal honour, fell into wild cackles of laughter.

So, I may say, did Flurry and I. I embarked on my explanation and broke down; Flurry followed suit and broke down too. Overwhelming laughter held us all three, disintegrating into our very souls. Mrs. Knox pulled herself together first.

"I acquit you, Major Yeates, I acquit you, though appearances are against you. It's clear enough to me you've fallen among thieves." She stopped and glowered at Flurry. Her purple bonnet was over one eye. "I'll thank you, sir," she said, "to dig out that horse before I leave this place. And when you've dug him out, you may keep him. I'll be no receiver of stolen goods!"

She broke off and shook her fist at him. "Upon my conscience, Tony, I'd give a guinea to have thought of it myself!"

The Bians

In the 1830's, Charles Bianconi, who came to Ireland from Italy as a peddler, revolutionized the transport system with a line of coaches. His establishment consisted of more than 1300 horses and 100 vehicles, each capable of carrying from four to twenty passengers, according to type, at an average speed of between eight and nine miles per hour, including stops, and at an average of one penny farthing per mile. These Bianconi coaches or "Bians," as they were popularly called, covered at one period no less than 3800 miles per day, reaching even remote Donegal in the North and all main points such as Limerick and Cork in the South, carrying passengers and mail.

Trollope, Thackeray, Dickens and a host of other celebrities rode the Bians and praised them highly.

Notable among the Bian drivers was one colorful McCluskie. Once Trollope traveled with him and spent most of the trip extolling the virtues and usefulness of the donkey only to get the devastating comment from McCluskie, "Ah, well, sir, a fellow feeling makes us wondrous kind."

Another time, McCluskie suspected an English passenger of stealing his sandwiches while he had alighted to hand over his mails. So he promptly pretended to have lost some poisoned bait which he was taking to a gamekeeper. When the culprit began to turn green with apprehension, McCluskie, with great solicitude, insisted on his stopping at the next stage to take a strong emetic.

One evening, owner Bianconi and his deputy, Dan Hearn, returning from a horse fair, stopped at a so-called hotel run by one Biddy Minehan. Tired as they were, neither of the two men could get to sleep, largely on account of a cold draft in their room.

At length, Hearn exclaimed, "Shure, there must be an iceberg below," and put his hand under the bed as if to prove his point. Immediately, he leaped out of bed and, speechless with terror, fled downstairs in his nightshirt to the bar below. There, he hollered up to Bianconi to come out of the room, "because the Devil was in it." Promptly, taking his advice, Bianconi, also in his nightshirt, joined Hearn.

"The Devil?" asked Bianconi. "Where did you see him?"

"Under the bed," hoarsely replied Dan.

Then Boniface Biddy Minehan herself, not at all embarrassed by her guests in their nightshirts in the bar, came forward full of apologies, explaining, "Indeed, I had no place to put it, your Honor."

"Put what?" asked Bianconi.

"The corpse, your Honor."

"Do you mean there is a corpse under our bed?"

"Oh, your Honor," came back Biddy, with her best ingratiating smile, "we were going to have a wake when you asked for a night's lodging. The House of Minehan would niver disappoint yourself, so we put the corpse under the bed temporarily because we had no place else to put it. Besides, your Honor, you wouldn't begrudge a poor widowed woman like meself the chance of making a few shillings, now, would ye, the grand man you are!"

Billy Traynor as Orator

BY CHARLES LEVER

Three weeks rolled over: an interval not without its share of interest for the inhabitants of the little village of Leenane, since on one morning Mr. Craggs had made his appearance on his way to Clifden, and after the absence of two days returned to the Castle. The subject for popular discussion and surmise had not yet declined, when a boat was seen to leave Glencore heavily laden with trunks and travelling gear, and, as she neared the land, the "lord" was detected amongst the passengers; looking very ill—almost dying; he passed up the little streets of the village, scarcely noticing the uncovered heads which saluted him respectfully. Indeed, he scarcely lifted up his eyes, and, as the acute observers remarked, never once turned a glance towards the opposite shore where the Castle stood.

He had not reached the end of the village, when a chaise with four horses arrived at the spot. No time was lost in arranging the trunks and portmanteaus, and Lord Glencore sat moodily on a bank, listlessly regarding what went forward. At length Craggs came up, and touching his cap in military fashion, announced all was ready.

Lord Glencore arose slowly, and looked languidly around him; his features wore a mingled expression of weariness and anxiety, like one not fully awakened from an oppressive dream. He turned his eyes on the people, who at a respectful distance stood around, and in a voice of peculiar melancholy said, "Good-bye."

"A good journey to you, my lord, and safe back again to us," cried a number together.

"Eh—what—what was that?" cried he, suddenly, and the tones were shrill and discordant in which he spoke.

A warning gesture from Craggs imposed silence on the crowd, and not a word was uttered.

"I thought they said something about coming back again," muttered Glencore, gloomily.

"They were wishing you a good journey, my lord," replied Craggs.

"Oh, that was it, was it?" And so saying, with bent-down head he walked feebly forward and entered the carriage. Craggs was speedily on the box, and the next moment they were away.

It is no part of our task to dwell on the sage speculations and wise surmises of the village on this event. They had not, it is true, much "evidence" before them, but they were hardy guessers, and there was very little within the limits of possibility which they did not summon to the aid of their imaginations. All, however, were tolerably agreed upon one point—that to leave the place, while the young lord was still unable to quit his bed, and too weak to sit up, was unnatural and unfeeling; traits which, "after all," they thought "not very surprising, since the likes of them lords never cared for anybody."

Colonel Harcourt still remained at Glencore, and under his rigid sway the strictest blockade of the coast was maintained, nor was any intercourse whatever permitted with the village. A boat from the Castle, meeting another from Leenane, half way in the lough, received the letters and whatever other resources the village supplied. All was done with a rigid exactness of a quarantine regulation, and if the mainland had been scourged with plague, stricter measures of exclusion could scarcely have been enforced.

In comparison with the present occupant of the Castle, the late one was a model of amiability; and the village, as is the wont in the case, now discovered a vast number of good qualities in the "lord," when they had lost him. After a while, however, the guesses, the speculations, and the comparisons all died away, and the Castle of Glencore was as much dreamland to their imaginations as, seen across the lough in the dim twilight of an evening autumn, its towers might have appeared to their eyes.

It was about a month after Lord Glencore's departure, of a fine, soft evening in the summer, Billy Traynor suddenly appeared in the village. Billy was one of a class who, whatever their rank in life, are always what Coleridge would have called "noticeable men." He was soon, therefore, surrounded with a knot of eager and inquiring friends, all solicitous to know something of the life he was leading; what they were doing "beyant at the Castle."

"It's a mighty quiet studious kind of life," said Billy, "but agrees with me wonderfully; for I may say that until now I never was able to give my 'janius' fair play. Professional life is the ruin of the student; and being always obleeged to be thinkin' of the bags destroyed my taste for letters." A grin of self-approval at his own witticism closed this speech.

"But is it true, Billy, the lord is going to break up house entirely, and not come back here?" asked Peter Slevin, the sacristan, whose rank and station warranted his assuming the task of cross-questioner.

"There's various ways of breakin' up a house," said Billy; "ye may do so in a moral sinse, or in a physical sinse; you may obliterate, or extinguish, or, without going so far, you may simply obfuscate—do you perceave?"

"Yes!" said the sacristan, on whom every eye was now bent, to see if he was able to follow subtleties that had outwitted the rest.

"And whin I say obfuscate," resumed Billy, "I open a question of disputed etymology, bekase tho' Lucretius thinks the word obfuscator original, there's many supposed it comes from ob, and fucus, the dye the ancients used in their wool, as we find in Horace, lana fuco medicata; while Cicero employs it in another sense, and says, facere fucum, which is as much as to say, humbuggin' somebody—do ye mind?"

"Begorra, he might guess that anyhow!" muttered a shrewd little tailor, with a significance that provoked hearty laughter.

"And now," continued Billy, with an air of triumph, "we'll proceed to the next point."

"Ye needn't trouble yerself then," said Terry Lynch, "for Peter has gone home."

And so, to the amusement of the meeting, it turned out to be the case; the sacristan had retired from the controversy. "Come in here to Mrs. Moore's, Billy, and take a glass with us," said Terry; "it isn't often we see you in these parts."

"If the honourable company will graciously vouchsafe and condescind to let me trate them to a half-gallon," said Billy, "it will be the proudest event of my terrestrial existence."

The proposition was received with a cordial enthusiasm, flattering to all concerned; and in a few minutes after, Billy Traynor sat at the head of a long table in the neat parlour of "The Griddle," with a company of some fifteen or sixteen very convivially-disposed friends around him.

"If I was Caesar, or Lucretius, or Nebuchadnezzar, I couldn't be prouder," said Billy, as he looked down the board. "And let moralists talk as they will, there's a beauutiful expansion of sentiment— there's a fine genial overflowin' of the heart in gatherin's like this, where we mingle our feelin's and our philosophy; and our love and our learning walk hand in hand like brothers—pass the spirits, Mr. Shea. If we look to the ancient writers, what do we see? Lemons! Bring in some lemons, Mickey. What do we see, I say, but that the very highest enjoyment of the haythen gods was—hot wather! why won't they send in more hot wather?"

"Begorra, if I was a haythen god, I'd like a little whisky in it," muttered Terry, dryly.

"Where was I?" asked Billy, a little disconcerted by this sally, and the laugh it excited. "I was expatiatin' upon celestial convivialities. The noctes coenaeque deum—them elegant hospitalities, where wisdom was moistened with nectar, and wit washed down with ambrosia. It is not, of coorse, to be expected," continued he, modestly, "that we mere mortals can compete with them elegant reflections. But, as Ovid says, we can at least diem jucundam decipere."

The unknown tongue had now restored to Billy all the reverence and respect of his auditory, and he continued to expatiate very eloquently on the wholesome advantages to be derived from convivial intercourse, both amongst gods and men; rather slyly intimating that either on the score of the fluids, or the conversation, his own leanings lay towards "the humanities."

"For after all," said he, " 'tis our own wakenesses is often the source of our most refined enjoyments. No, Mrs. Cassidy, ye

needn't be blushin'. I'm considerin' my subject in a high ethno-
logical and metaphysical sinse." Mrs. Cassidy's confusions, and the
mirth it excited, here interrupted the orator.

"The meeting is never tired of hearin' you, Billy," said Terry
Lynch; "but if it was plazin' to ye to give us a song, we'd enjoy it
greatly."

"Ah!" said Billy, with a sigh. "I have taken my partin' kiss with
the Muses—non mihi licet increpare digitis lyram:

> "No more to feel poetic fire,
> No more to touch the soundin' lyre;
> But wiser coorses to begin,
> I now forsake my violin."

An honest outburst of regret and sorrow broke from the assembly, who eagerly pressed for an explanation of this calamitous
change.

"The thing is this," said Billy, "if a man is a creature of mere
leisure and amusement, the fine arts—and by the fine arts I mean
music, paintin', and the ladies—is an elegant and very refined subject of cultivation; but when you raise your cerebrial faculties to
grander and loftier considerations, to explore the difficult ragions
of polemic or political truth, to investigate the subtleties of the
schools, and penetrate the mysteries of science, then, take my word
for it, the fine arts is just snares—devil a more than snares! And
whether it is soft sounds seduces you, or elegant tints, or the union
of both—women I mane—you'll never arrive at anything great or
tri-um-phant till you wane yourself away from the likes of them
vanities. Look at the haythen mythology; consider for a moment
who is the chap that represents Music—a lame blackguard, with
an ugly face, they call Pan. Ay, indeed, Pan! If you wanted to see
what respect they had for the art, it's easy enough to guess, when
this crayture represints it; and as to Paintin', on my conscience,
they haven't a god at all that ever took to the brush. Pass up the
spirits, Mickey," said he, somewhat blown and out of breath by
this effort; "maybe," said he, "I'm wearin' you."

"No, no, no," loudly responded the meeting.

"Maybe I'm imposin' too much of personal details on the
house," added he, pompously.

"Not at all; never a bit," cried the company.

"Because," resumed he, slowly, "if I did so, I'd have at least the excuse of sayin', like the great Pitt, 'These may be my last words from this place.'"

An unfeigned murmur of sorrow ran through the meeting, and he resumed:

"Ay, ladies and gintlemin, Billy Traynor is takin' his 'farewell benefit'; he's not humbuggin'; I'm not like them chaps that's always positively goin', but stays on at the unanimous request of the whole world. No; I'm really goin' to leave you."

"What for? Where to, Billy?" broke from a number of voices together.

"I'll tell ye," said he; "at least so far as I can tell; because it wouldn't be right nor decent to 'print the whole of the papers for the house,' as they say in parliamint. I'm going abroad with the young lord; we are going to improve our minds, and cultivate our janiuses, by study and foreign travel. We are first to settle in Germany, where we're to enter a University, and commince a coorse of modern tongues, French, Sweadish, and Spanish; imbibin' at the same time a smatterin' of science, such as chemistry, conchology, and the use of the globes."

"Oh, dear! oh, dear!" murmured the meeting in wonder and admiration.

"I'm not goin' to say that we'll neglect mechanics, metaphysics, and astrology; for we mane to be cosmonopolists in knowledge. As for myself, ladies and gintlemin, it's a proud day that sees me standin' here to say these words. I, that was ragged, without a shoe to my foot—without breeches—never mind, I was, as the poet says, nudus nummis ac vestimentis—

"I haven't sixpence in my pack,
    I haven't small clothes to my back,

carryin' the bag many a weary mile, through sleet and snow, for six pounds tin per annum, and no pinsion for wounds or superannuation; and now I'm to be—it isn't easy to say what—to the young lord, a spacies of humble companion, not manial, do you mind, nothing manial. What the Latins called a famulus, which was quite a different thing from a servus. The former bein' a kind of domestic adviser, a deputy-assistant, monitor-general, as a body might say. There now, if I discoorsed for a month, I couldn't tell you more about myself and my future prospects. I own to you that I'm proud of my good luck; and I wouldn't exchange it to be Emperor of Jamaica, or King of the Bahamia Islands."

If we have been prolix in our office of reporter to Billy Traynor, our excuse is, that his discourse will have contributed so far to the reader's enlightenment as to save us the task of recapitulation. At the same time, it is but justice to the accomplished orator that we should say, we have given but the most meagre outline of an address, which, to use the newspaper phrase, "occupied three hours in the delivery." The truth was, Billy was in vein; the listeners were patient, the punch strong; nor is it every speaker who has had the good fortune of such happy accessories.

Handy Andy

By Samuel Lover

Andy Rooney was a fellow who had the most singularly ingenious knack of doing everything the wrong way; disappointment waited on all affairs in which he bore a part, and destruction was at his fingers' ends: so the nickname the neighbours stuck upon him was Handy Andy, and the jeering jingle pleased them.

Andy's entrance into this world was quite in character with his after achievements, for he was nearly the death of his mother. She survived, however, to have herself clawed almost to death while her darling babby was in arms, for he would not take his nourishment from the parent fount unless he had one of his little red fists twisted into his mother's hair, which he dragged till he made her roar; while he diverted the pain by scratching her till the blood came, with the other. Nevertheless she swore he was "the loveliest and sweetest craythur the sun ever shined upon"; and when he was able to run about and wield a little stick, and smash everything breakable belonging to her, she only praised his precocious powers, and used to ask, "Did ever any one see a darlin' of his age handle a stick so bowld as he did?"

Andy grew up in mischief and the admiration of his mammy; but, to do him justice, he never meant harm in the course of his life, and was most anxious to offer his services on all occasions to those who would accept them; but they were only the persons who had not already proved Andy's peculiar powers.

There was a farmer hard by in this happy state of ignorance, named Owen Doyle, or as he was familiarly called, Owny na Coppal, or, "Owen of the Horses," because he bred many of these animals, and sold them at the neighbouring fairs; and Andy one day offered his services to Owny when he was in want of some one to drive up a horse to his house from a distant "bottom," as low grounds by a river side are always called in Ireland.

"Oh, he's wild, Andy, and you'd never be able to ketch him," said Owny.

"Troth, an' I'll engage I'll ketch him if you'll let me go. I never seen the horse I couldn't ketch, sir," said Andy.

"Why, you little spridhogue, if he took to runnin' over the long bottom, it 'ud be more than a day's work for you to folly him."

"Oh, but he won't run."

"Why won't he run?"

"Bekaze I won't make him run."

"How can you help it?"

"I'll soother him."

"Well, you're a willin' brat, anyhow; and so go, and God speed you!" said Owny.

"Just gi' me a whisp o' hay an' a han'ful iv oats," said Andy, "if I should have to coax him."

"Sartinly," said Owny, who entered the stable and came forth with the articles required by Andy, and a halter for the horse also.

"Now, take care," said Owny, "that you're able to ride that horse if you get on him."

"Oh, never fear, sir. I can ride owld Lanty Gubbins's mule betther nor any o' the other boys on the common, and he couldn't throw me th' other day, though he kicked the shoes av him."

"After that you may ride anything," said Owny: and indeed it was true; for Lanty's mule, which fed on the common, being ridden by all the young vagabonds in the neighbourhood, had become such an adept in the art of getting rid of his troublesome customers, that it might be well considered a feat to stick on him.

"Now, take grate care of him, Andy, my boy," said the farmer.

"Don't be afeard, sir," said Andy, who started on his errand in that peculiar pace which is elegantly called a "sweep's trot"; and as the river lay between Owny Doyle's and the bottom, and was too deep for Andy to ford at that season, he went round by Dinny Dowling's mill, where a small wooden bridge crossed the stream.

Here he thought he might as well secure the assistance of Paudeen, the miller's son, to help him in catching the horse; so he looked about the place until he found him, and, telling him the errand on which he was going, said, "If you like to come wid me, we can both have a ride." This was temptation sufficient for Paudeen, and the boys proceeded together to the bottom, and they were not long in securing the horse. When they had got the halter over his head, "Now," said Andy, "give me a lift on him;" and accordingly, by Paudeen's catching Andy's left foot in both his hands clasped together in the fashion of a stirrup, he hoisted his friend on the horse's back; and, as soon as he was secure there, Master Paudeen, by the aid of Handy's hand, contrived to scramble up after him; upon which Andy applied his heels to the horse's side with many vigorous kicks, and crying "hurrup!" at the same time, endeavoured to stimulate Owny's steed into something of a pace as he turned his head towards the mill.

"Sure aren't you going to crass the river?" said Paudeen.

"No, I'm going to lave you at home."

"Oh, I'd rather go up to Owny's, and it's the shortest way across the river."

"Yes, but I don't like."

"Is it afeard you are?" said Paudeen.

"Not I, indeed," said Andy; though it was really the fact, for the width of the stream startled him; "but Owny towld me to take grate care o' the baste, and I'm loth to wet his feet."

"Go 'long wid you, you fool! what harm would it do him? Sure he's neither sugar nor salt, that he'd melt."

Well, I won't anyhow," said Andy, who by this time had got the horse into a good high trot, that shook every word of argument out of Paudeen's body; besides, it was as much as the boys could do to keep their seats on Owny's Bucephalus, who was not long in reaching the miller's bridge. Here voice and halter were employed to pull him in, that he might cross the narrow wooden structure at a quiet pace. But whether his double load had given him the idea of double exertion, or that the pair of legs on each side sticking into his flanks (and perhaps the horse was ticklish) made him go the faster, we know not; but the horse charged the bridge as if an Enniskilliner were on his back, and an enemy before him; and in two minutes his hoofs clattered like thunder on the bridge, that did not bend beneath him. No, it did not bend, but it broke; proving the falsehood of the boast, "I may break, but I won't bend"; for, after all, the really strong may bend, and be as strong as ever; it is the unsound, that has only the seeming of strength, which breaks at last when it resists too long.

Surprising was the spin the young equestrians took over the ears of the horse, enough to make all the artists of Astley's envious; and plump they went into the river, where each formed his own ring, and executed some comical "scenes in the circle," which were suddenly change to evolutions on the "flying cord" that Dinny Dowling threw the performers, which became suddenly converted into a "tight rope" as he dragged the voltigeurs out of the water; and for fear their blood might be chilled by the accident, he gave them both an enormous thrashing with the dry end of the rope, just to restore circulation; and his exertions, had they been witnessed, would have charmed the Humane Society.

As for the horse, his legs stuck through the bridge, as though he had been put in a chiroplast, and he went playing away on the water with considerable execution, as if he were accompanying— himself in the song which he was squealing at the top of his voice. Half the saws, hatchets, ropes, and poles in the parish were put in requisition immediately; and the horse's first lesson in chiroplastic exercise was performed with no other loss than some skin and a good deal of hair. Of course Andy did not venture on taking Owny's horse home; so the miller sent him to his owner with an account of the accident. Andy for years kept out of Owny na Coppal's way; and at any time that his presence was troublesome, the inconvenienced party had only to say, "Isn't that Owny na Coppal coming this way?" and Andy fled for his life.

A Retrospect

By Canon Patrick A. Sheehan

Long ago, when I used to read an occasional novel, if the author dared to say: "But I am anticipating; we must go back here twenty years to understand the thread of this history," I invariably flung down the book in disgust. The idea of taking you back to ancient history when you were dying to know what was to become of the yellow-haired Blumine, or the grand chivalrous Roland. Well, I am just going to commit the very same sin; and, dear reader, be patient just a little while.

It is many years since I was appointed to the parish of Kilronan. It happened in this wise. The Bishop, the old man, sent for me, and said, with what I would call a tone of pity or contempt, but he was incapable of either, for he was the essence of charity and sincerity:

"Father Dan, you are a bit of a litterateur, I understand. Kilronan is vacant. You'll have plenty of time for poetizing and dreaming there. What do you say to it?"

I put on a little dignity, and though my heart was beating with delight, I quietly thanked his Lordship. But, when I had passed beyond the reach of episcopal vision, which is far-stretching enough, I spun my hat in the air, and shouted like a schoolboy: "Hurrah!"

You wonder at my ecstasies! Listen. I was a dreamer, and the dream of my life, when shut up in musty towns, where the atmosphere was redolent of drink, and you heard nothing but scandal, and saw nothing but sin—the dream of my life was a home by the sea, with its purity and freedom, and its infinite expanse, telling me of God. For, from the time when as a child the roar of the surges set my pulse beating, and the scents of the weed and the brine would make me turn pale with pleasure, I used to pray that some day, when my life's work would be nearly done, and I had put in my years of honest labour in the dusty streets, I might spend my declining years in the peace of a seaside village, and go down to my grave, washed free from the contaminations of life in the daily watching and loving of those

"Moving waters at their priestlike task
Of pure ablution round earth's human shores."

My wish was realized, and I was jubilant.

Returning home by train, when my emotion had calmed down, my mind could not help recurring to the expression used by the Bishop; and it suggested the following reflections: How has it come to pass in Ireland that "poet" and "saint" are terms which denote some weakness or irregularity in their possessors? At one time in our history we know that the bard was second only to the King in power and influence; and are we not vaguely proud of that title the world gives us—Island of Saints? Yet, nowadays, through some fatal degeneracy, a poet is looked upon as an idealist, an impractical builder of airy castles, to whom no one would go for advice in an important matter, or intrust with the investment of a five-pound note. And to speak of a man or woman as a "saint" is to hint at some secret imbecility, which it would be charitable to pass over in silence. I was quite well aware, therefore, on that day, when I had the secret pleasure and the sublime misfortune of seeing my name in print over some wretched verses, that I was ruining my prospects in life. The fact of being a litterateur, although in the most modest and hidden manner, stamped me as a volatile, flighty creature, who was no more to be depended upon than a feather in the wind; or, as the Italians say, qu' al piume al vento. It is a curious prejudice, and a purely insular one. And sometimes I think, or rather I used to think, that there was something infinitely grotesque in these narrow ideas, that shut us out from sympathy with the quick-moving subtle world as completely as if we were fakirs by the banks of the sacred Ganges. For what does modern literature deal with? Exactly those questions of philosophy, ethics, and morality which form the staple material of theological studies and discussion in our own colleges and academies. Novels, poetry, essays, lectures, treatises on the natural sciences— all deal with the great central questions of man's being, his origin, and his conduct. And surely it is folly to ignore these discussions in the market places of the world, because they are literature, and not couched in scholastic syllogisms. Dear me! I am philosophizing—I, old Daddy Dan, with the children plucking at my coat-tails and the brown snuff staining my waist-coat, and ah, yes! the place already marked in my little chapel, where I shall sleep at last. I must have been angry, or gloomy, that day, thirty years ago, when I stepped on the platform at M—— after my interview with the Bishop, and met my friends, who had already become aware that I was elevated out of the junior ranks, and had become an independent officer of the Church Militant.

"You don't mean to say that you have accepted that awful place?" said one.

"You'll have nothing but fish to eat," said another. "The butcher's van goes there but once a week."

"And no society but fishermen," said a third. "And they speak nothing but Irish, and you know you cannot bless yourself in Irish."

"Well," I replied, "my Job's comforters, I have accepted Kilronan, and am going there. If all things go well, and you are good boys, I may ask for some of you as curate—"

"You'll be glad to get a curacy yourself in six months," they shouted in chorus.

And so I came to Kilronan, and here have I been since. The years have rolled by swiftly. Life is a coach, whose wheels move slowly and painfully at the start; but once set moving, particularly when going down the deep decline of life, the years move so swiftly you cannot see the spokes in the wheels, which are the days we number so sadly. What glorious resolutions I made the first months of my residence here! How I would read and write and burn the midnight oil, and astonish the world, and grow from dignity to dignity into an honoured old age! Alas! circumstances are too much for us all, and here I am, in my seventieth year, poor old Daddy Dan, with no great earthly trouble, indeed, and some few consolations—my breviary and the grand psalms of hope—my daily Mass and its hidden and unutterable sweetness—the love of little children and their daily smiles—the prayers of my old women, and, I think, the reverence of the men. But there comes a little sting sometimes, when I see young priests, who served my Masses long ago, standing in cathedral stalls in all the glory of purple and ermine, and when I see great parishes passing into the hands of mere boys, and poor old Daddy Dan passed over in silence. I know, if I were really good and resigned, I would bless God for it all, and I do. But human nature will revolt sometimes, and people will say,

"What a shame, Father Dan; why haven't you the red buttons as well as so and so?" or, "What ails the Bishop, passing over one of the most learned men in the diocese for a parcel of gossoons!" I suppose it was my own fault. I remember what magnificent ideas I had. I would build factories, I would pave the streets, I would establish a fishing station and make Kilronan the favourite bathing resort on the western coast; I would write books and be, all round, a model of push, energy, and enterprise. And I did try. I might as well have tried to remove yonder mountain with a pitchfork, or stop the roll of the Atlantic with a rope of sand. Nothing on earth can cure the inertia of Ireland. It weighs down like the weeping clouds on the damp heavy earth, and there's no lifting it, nor disburthening of the souls of men of this intolerable weight. I was met on every side with a stare of curiosity, as if I were propounding something immoral or heretical. People looked at me, put their hands in their pockets, whistled dubiously, and went slowly away. Oh, it was weary, weary work! The blood was stagnant in the veins of the people and their feet were shod with lead. They walked slowly, spoke with difficulty, stared all day at leaden clouds or pale sunlight, stood at the corners of the village for hours looking into vacuity, and the dear little children became old the moment they left school, and lost the smiles and the sunlight of childhood. It was a land of the lotus. The people were narcotized. Was it the sea air? I think I read somewhere in an old philosopher, called Berkeley, that the damp salt air of the sea has a curious phelgmatic effect on the blood, and will coagulate it and produce gout and sundry disorders. However that be, there was a weary weight on everything around Kilronan. The cattle slept in the fields, the fishermen slept in their coracles. It was a land of sleep and dreams.

I approached the agent about a foreshore for the pier, for you cannot, in Ireland, take the most preliminary and initial step in anything without going, cap in hand, to the agent. I explained my intentions. He smiled, but was polite.

"Lord L——, you know, is either in Monte Carlo or yachting in the Levant. He must be consulted. I can do nothing."

"And when will his Lordship return?"

"Probably in two years."

"You have no power to grant a lease to the foreshore, or even give temporary permission to erect a pier?"

"None whatever,"

I went to the Presentment Sessions about a grant for paving or flagging the wretched street. I woke a nest of hornets.

"What! More taxation! Aren't the people crushed enough already? Where can we get money to meet rates and taxes? Flagging Kilronan! Oh, of course! Wouldn't your reverence go in for gas or the electric light? Begor, ye'll be wanting a water supply next," etc., etc.

I applied to a factory a few miles distant to establish a local industry by cottage labour, which is cheap and remunerative.

"They would be delighted, but—" And so all my castles came tumbling down from the clouds, and left them black and lowering and leaden as before. Once or twice, later on, I made a few spasmodic efforts to galvanize the place into life; they, too, failed, and I accepted the inevitable. When Father Laverty came as my curate, he helped me to bear the situation with philosophical calmness. He had seen the world, and had been rubbed badly in contact with it. He had adopted as his motto and watchword the fatal Cui bono. And he had printed in large Gothic letters over his mantelpiece the legend:

'TWILL BE ALL THE SAME IN A HUNDRED YEARS.

Tales from the Irish Countryside

Tales from the Irish Countryside

The traditional Irish storyteller was known as the Shanachie. In the far gone days, he would visit cottages in the evenings and spin his sagas by the light of a candle and a peat fire. Eamon Kelly, the well-known Dublin actor who appeared as the father in the long Broadway run of the Irish play "Philadelphia, Here I Come" and on tour too, has resurrected some of these Shanachie tales which he first heard as a lad in his grandfather's home. Besides re-creating them in writing, Eamon Kelly also has ably recited them much to the enjoyment of his audiences, Irish or not. Here are a few of his own Shanachie stories which now make their first appearance in print.

A Matter of Opinion

By Eamon Kelly

A scholar and a poet were debating. The scholar was a big lump of a man of a very serious turn of mind. The poet was the direct opposite and thin, the Lord save us, if he turned sideways he'd be marked absent. They were debating how long it was since the first Irishman set foot in America. Weren't they short taken for a topic of conversation! The scholar said, "I suppose that honour will have to go to St. Brendan the Sailor. Wasn't it he discovered America, though this fact is not too widely known? St. Brendan kept his mouth shut about it."

"Maybe," says the poet, "the world might be a happier place today if the other man did the same thing."

The scholar never smiled, so the poet said, "How long ago is it now since St. Brendan set foot in America?"

"Well," says the scholar, "I think I can work that out." He settled himself in his chair and then he said with great weight. "St. Brendan was born near Fenit in the County Kerry in the year 532 —that's A.D. of course—and after a lifetime spent sailing the high seas spreading the good word, he died in Anach Chuain on the shores of Lough Corrib, where he built that big monastery, in the year 580. Now if we take it that the bulk of St. Brendan's exploring was done in his prime, I would say that it is every day of fourteen hundred years since the first Irishman set foot in America."

"Is that all you know!" says the poet. "Irishmen were going to America before that."

"Can you prove it?" says the scholar.

"To be sure I can," says the poet. "When my great-granduncle was going to America before the famine—in a sailing vessel he was, and a couple of hundred miles out from the coast of Clare what happened this evening but the ship was becalmed. The captain threw out the anchor and they all went to bed for the night. What did they want up for?

"Came the morning and there was a nice breeze blowing. The captain drew in the anchor and do you know what was tied on to it? The wheel of a horse car."

"And what does that prove?" says the scholar.

"It proves," says the poet, "that Irish people were going to America by road before the flood!"

The Looking Glass

By Eamon Kelly

'Tis always a mystery to me how the women got on before the looking glass was invented, or indeed the men if it went to that; they are often enough in front of it. Well, the looking glass was invented and there was this man ignorant of the fact. He was living in an out-of-the-way place.

There was an excursion and he availed himself of the cheap fare to travel out, and when he landed in the city he went down the main street and into this shop where he saw a heap of shiny things on the counter. Little oblongs they were, no bigger than a small fag box. He took up one and held it up that way in front of his face.

"Will you look at that," says he, "a picture of my father where-ever they got it."

Turning to the girl inside the counter, he said, "What are these selling for?"

She told him. Ah, 'twas only a trifle, so he bought the looking glass and put it in his inside pocket and brought it home. Every opportunity he got he'd take it out to admire what he thought was a picture of his father—a man he had great respect for and who was dead this long time. But he was always very careful not to let the wife see him, for indeed she didn't have the same respect for the father-in-law. Which of 'em have!

As we all know very little goes unknown to the women. And she saw him and she wondered greatly what it was was taking him to the pocket and what it was he was admiring. Curiosity was killing her. Finally her chance came. What happened this day but a neighbour's chimney to go on fire. Her husband, when he heard all the *hilaboherk,* dashed out and in the excitement he forgot his coat. Well, his back was hardly turned when his wife went to his pocket and took out the looking glass and held it in front of her face.

"Well," says she, "could you be up to him! or who is this old hairpin? And, indeed, wherever he met her, she's no great shakes. I tell you," says she, "if that is the attraction that's drawing him away to the city, I'll soon put a halt to his gallop!"

So she put the looking glass back in his pocket and geared her-self for battle. And we all know what women in a like situation can be. Her husband came in after doing the good turn for the neighbour. She said what was on her mind. Was he getting tired of her? He denied it.

"And what are you doing so," she said, "with this other Dolly Varden inside in your pocket?"

Now that the cat was out of the bag, he thought it would be just as well to admit what was in his pocket. So he said, "That's only a picture of my father."

And do you think did she believe him? She did not. "You'll

hear more about this," she said, putting on her coat and bonnet and going to the priest's house. That was the court of appeal at the time.

Well, the parish priest when he heard her story you could knock him down with a feather. Her husband was well known to him. A nice, quiet, sober, natural, pious, devout man, exactly what Father John said.

"God help your head, father," says she; "he has me fooled up to the ball of my eye, and what's more he has a picture of this strange woman in his pocket pretending 'tis his father."

"Oh, in that case," says Father John, "I'll have to go to the house and reprimand him." And of course Father John was right. Wouldn't this be a nice headline to be giving his congregation!

Away to the house went the two, Father John and the woman and, lifting the latch, the parish priest said:

"Here now, my good man, this is gone far enough. Hand me out the picture of that strange woman you have in your pocket."

Well, the poor man, he was praying for the ground to open and swallow him, he was so ashamed and upset at the turn things were taking. He went to his coat pocket and took out the looking glass and gave it to the parish priest. Father John put it up in front of his face, and when he saw who was staring out at him, he had to smile and, turning to the man's wife, he said, "No doubt in life but you'd want to have your eyes examined. Isn't that the parish priest that was here before me!"

The Umbrella

By Eamon Kelly

Once every five years the people of this townland collect into Larry's house and the priest comes and hears confessions and says Mass there.

This function is called the station. It is an old custom going back to the penal times when people of our way of thinking had to worship in holes and corners. Twice a year the station would take place in the Spring and in the harvest. It was a movable feast going to a different house each time, and as there are ten houses in our townland, once ever five years it came to Larry's turn to take the station. "Often enough," Larry used to say, "if you look at it from the point of view of expense!" Like many another good Christian, he was a man of limited resources, and the house had to be painted inside and out, provisions had to be laid in, as well as a little light refreshment for the people. All of which, Larry used to say, did not take place unknown to his pocket.

Well, to get on with the story, it so happened one year that the station was published for Larry. I don't remember this too well myself. My father I heard talking about it, and what kept it so fresh in his memory was something comical that took place the morning of the station. It seems the priest we had here at the time was a trifle hasty, a little impatient and stern of demeanor. Signs on it, innocent people were peppering afraid of him. Although to go to his house, I was told, you couldn't meet a nicer man. Jermiah Horgan that was telling me. Jermiah was at the house for a letter of freedom. He was marrying some bird from an outside community. He got the letter—as things turned out, he'd be better off if he didn't.

Come the morning of the station and all the neighbors were waiting in Larry's yard for Father John. The morning turned out very wet, but of course country people don't mind the rain, they say it never melted anyone. With that a son of Johnny Dan Tadhgeen's put his head around the corner of the house and said, "He's coming!" the yard emptied itself into the kitchen, leaving only Larry to welcome Father John, and Larry'd rather any other job—he'd rather be draining the Dead Sea with a silver spoon—for he was a very shy, distant sort of an individual. He hadn't long to wait. Father John came riding into the yard on a saddle horse, holding over his head a black round roof on top of a walking cane.

This strange object left poor Larry speechless, for it was the first umbrella that was seen in this townland. He didn't say "Good morning" or "Good day" or "It was good of you to come," only took the priest's horse and put him in the stable. Father John made off into the kitchen, and when those inside saw the doorway darkening, every man turned his back, making himself small behind his neighbor in case any awkward question should be put to him.

When they turned around again, Father John had opened the umbrella at the bottom of the kitchen so as that the rain'd be running off it and that it'd be nice and dry when he'd be going home bye 'n' bye, that is when confessions'd be heard, Mass'd be said, breakfast'd be ate and dues'd be collected.

The morning wore on and all these things came to pass and the grace of God, glory be to Him, was in the house and Father John was in the room having his breakfast. The women were up and down on him, taking the legs off one another with excitement, and Larry's wife said and her face as red as a coal of fire, "If you saw the look he gave me when he took the top off the egg!"

"Were they too done?" says Cait.

"Bullets, girl! And I wouldn't mind, but I told that daughter of mine not to take her eyes off the eggs. But there you are the morning you'd want a thing to go right for you, that's the morning everything'd break the melt in you."

The men were in the kitchen around the umbrella the same as if it was a German bomber. And they were saying that for such a simple thing, wasn't it a great wonder someone didn't think of it long 'go. And how handy it would be, they said, to prop it over the mouth of the barrel in the yard a wet day where you'd have a goose hatching. On the heel of that remark Father John came up from the room. They all backed toward the fire.

"Morning, men," he said. "What's the day doing?"

" 'Tis brightening, Father," says John Cronin, a forward class of a man anyway.

"I'll be going," he said. "There's many the thing I could be doing."

"Good morning, Father," they all said, and said it very loud and with great relief, for they knew that the bottle wouldn't be opened till he was gone.

Larry took the priest's horse from the stable and conveyed Father John down the passageway to the main road. They were nearly halfway down when Father John thought of his umbrella. "Run up to the house," he said to Larry, "and bring me out my parasol."

He didn't have to say this secondly. Larry ran up to the house and into the kitchen breathless. He took the umbrella by the leg, 'twas open, and brought it after him to the door, but it wouldn't go out. He came inside it and tried to shove it out before him, but the devil a out it'd go. He looked at those in the kitchen and they looked at him and they had pity for him. He took the door off the hinges—that'd give him an extra inch—but the umbrella wouldn't go out. Little beads of perspiration began to stand out on his forehead at the thought of Father John waiting in the passageway. He began muttering to himself, saying, "If it came in, it must go out."

Well, there was a small man there and, wanting to be of help, he said, "I wonder would it be any value if we kicked out the two sides of the door frame." The two sides of the frame were driven out in the yard, but the umbrella remained inside. "Well," says Larry, "there's nothing for it now only knock down the wall." A sledge hammer was procured and when Father John heard all the pounding, he doubled back to the house. And when he saw what was happening, 'twas as good as a tonic to him. He roared out laughing. "What are you at?" says he. "Well, do you know now, Father," says Larry, "I think myself that if I got the cornerstone there down, the mushroom'd sail out—no trouble."

"Move into the kitchen from me," says he. They did. Father John took the umbrella by the leg—'twas open, as I said—and brought it to the door in front of him. He was a fierce big man, God bless him, overcoat and all on a wet day, and they couldn't see what was happening. When he came to the door, like lightning he shut the umbrella and opened it again outside and walked out the yard holding it over his head, leaving them there spellbound.

When he was gone, Larry turned to his neighbors and said, "Say what ye like, *they* have the power!"

Way of Women

By Paul Jones

"I hear your daughter's all packed up to go on her holidays, " said Hennessey.

"She is," said Hogan.

"That's more than you and I were ever able to do when we were her age," said Hennessey.

"It is," said Hogan.

"Extraordinary how the years roll by!" said Hennessey. "It seems only yesterday when she was climbing over the wall in a little pink frock down on top of my rhubarb to get her ball back, and now I suppose she's a young lady with a half-pitying smile when old fogeys like you and I express an opinion about anything."

"She is," said Hogan, "and maybe she's right."

"Maybe she is," said Hennessy. "I'll say this for her. She's a nice girl and a great credit to her mother. Where's she going?"

"To Ballybunion," said Hogan. "I hope it's a nice place. She deserves a holiday after twelve months in a solicitor's office. What kind of a place is it?"

"Listen, Hogan," said Hennessey. "It doesn't matter what sort of a place it is. Would you like me to tell you eternal truth about girls and holidays?"

"I would," said Hogan.

"When a girl," said Hennessey, "says that such and such a place is a lovely place for a holiday, all she means is that she met a nice young fellow there, or two or three nice young fellows, and preferably, nice young fellows with a car. It doesn't matter if the place itself is devoid of scenic or historic or any other attraction and is as flat as the back of me hand. I don't know what sort of a place Ballybunion is, but I'll tell you this. If, two days after she arrives there, you get a post card of a hunk of the local landscape with 'Having a lovely time here, Love, Peggy' scrawled on it, and fivepence to pay because she's forgotten the stamp, you'll know she's met one already. And if she comes home and says, 'Ballybunion's a lovely place for a holiday!' all that'll mean will be that she'll be staying in at night waiting for the telephone to ring and getting up early in the morning to see if there's a letter."

Always the Card

On the wharf in Burtonport in Donegal, a man walked into the restaurant and asked, "Do you serve crabs?" The kindhearted col-

leen waitress said quickly, "Now you sit right down here and nobody will recognize you."

"I never can understand," said a Mayo lady to her friend, "why a
fine strapping lad like Patrick whould marry a plain-looking
woman twenty years his senior."

"When you want bank notes," tartly replied her companion,
"you don't look at their dates."

Michael came home with his first report card from the new trade
school in Wicklow, where he had taken up carpentry. His report
read, "Give Michael the job and he will finish the tools."

"I shall hold this case in camera," said the Irish judge.

"What does that mean?" asked the witness.

"Well," said the judge, "I know what it means, and the jury
knows what it means—you just tell us what happened on the night
of June 1st."

"I went to a dance," related the witness, "and Mary asked me to
see her home. It was a fine evening and after we'd crossed a field
we sat on a stile in the moonlight and I put my arm around her.
After that, there was a little mushy, sweety-pie palaver."

"And what, pray, does that mean?" asked the judge.

The reply came quickly: "I know what it means, the jury knows
what it means, and if you'd been there with your camera, judge,
you'd know what it means!"

Advice to farmers given in an Irish country newspaper: "One of
the best investments a farmer can make is money spent on paint.
He can put the paint on himself and in so doing brighten up the
home."

There is an old Kerry saying: "Show me an Irishman without a
cause and I'll show you an incomplete man."

On a visit to the village in Tipperary where his grandparents were
born, Major General Patrick J. Ryan, former Chief of Chaplains,
U.S. Army, stopped in to see the local Canon.

As the General was ushered into the rectory, he found the

Canon busily engaged in discussion with an elderly parishioner.
As the Canon got up to greet the General, he ordered the parishioner to wait in the next room. When the parishioner left, the
General explained that he was simply on holiday and in no hurry
and that he would gladly wait until the Canon had finished talking
to the parishioner.

"Aye, General," said the Canon, "there is no need to. You see
this parishioner has a problem and he is a bit finicky about it.
After all, he is getting married tomorrow."

"Getting married!" commented General Ryan. "Why, he looks
to me to be in his eighties."

"He is!"

"Well," said the General, "What's his trouble?"

"Aye," replied the Canon, "his trouble is he, a man of eighty-
six, is marrying a widow of seventy-eight and he is faced with his
dilemma. He wants her to come as a bride to his house alone. She,
having three wee sons, wants him to come and live in her house.
Now if he refuses to go to live in her house and insists that she
come to live in his house alone, she will have to turn out to the
cruel, hard world three wee boys to shift for themselves. Why, the
youngest is only forty-nine!"

Naming a Street

By Hubert Butler

On the principle of "ex pede Hercules" a small Irish town of
10,000 inhabitants is quite a good place to study the tangled loyal-
ties of our country. For Ireland is run by countrymen, who reveal
themselves with fewest inhibitions in rural surroundings. The
revelation is of more than Irish importance, for our emigrants
never quite forget the domestic pattern. Senator Joe McCarthy did
not really surprise us, and Jimmy Walker, the famous Tammany
mayor of New York, was one of our own, returning once or twice
to Kilkenny, the town of his childhood. Men very much like these
world figures, reduced in size, still walk our streets. Perhaps Providence tries them out as small-scale models in tiny towns. Will they

work? Yes, they do! And then they are recast in a gigantic, transatlantic mold.

Our town, which has been admirably described by the novelist
Francis Hackett, was built by the Normans. It is dominated by the
now empty castle of the Dukes of Ormonde, by the thirteenth-
century Protestant cathedral, by two other large Protestant
churches, St. Mary's and St. John's, and a number of modern
Roman Catholic churches, convents and monasteries. It is, as one
would assume, a stronghold of institutional Christianity and it is
not surprising that ecclesiastical considerations often intrude into
the deliberations of our public bodies.

For example, not long ago the residents of Asylum Road informed the corporation that they would like the name of their
street changed. The corporation discussed it at great length and two
names were suggested, Nuncio Street and Berkeley Street. For the
Papal Nuncio had recently visited the town and his name had
been inscribed on the Roll of Freemen; Bishop Berkeley, the
philosopher, had been born near the town and, like Swift and
Congreve, educated at Kilkenny College.

The principal champion of Berkeley was a councillor who goes
as near Communist views as it is wise for an Irish official, and that
is not far at all. A great deal of middle-aged unorthodoxy in Kilkenny is aristocratic in origin, for the old Countess of Desart, who
was wealthy and philanthropic, started, some forty years ago, political economy classes. Before the classes were taken over by the
local seminary and safely harnessed to the Papal Encyclicals, some
disturbing, though ancient, books were handled, and the views of
Robert Owen are not unknown to our citizens.

Anyway the councillor's suggestion, because of his "Red" association, was regarded with suspicion; it was privately whispered that
Berkeley himself was a "Kind of Communist" (and, in fact, "The
Querist" is full of subversive and even equalitarian suggestions) ;
there were outraged letters in the local press and a hasty retreat by
the Berkeleyites; a prominent citizen who had seconded the proposal hurriedly explained that he had only done so "to start a discussion." The liveliest of the letter-writers argued:

"Philosophy is all very well for the gentry, but for the working class people of Upper Patrick Street the Faith of Our Fa-

thers and a reasonable rent for the new council houses are more to the purpose. And why should a Protestant bishop be commemorated in Kilkenny when the Blessed Oliver Plunkett would certainly not get a street named after him in Belfast?"

The street was without more ado called "Nuncio Street."

It is sadly characteristic that our local Protestants held aloof from the controversy, though a couple of years ago they had canvassed the academies of Europe and America in the name of Berkeley for funds to build a new hall at Kilkenny College. Though they are influential, they are cautious and do not believe in "getting mixed up in things," and they chose to forget that Berkeley had expressly stated that "the Protestant gentry" could not flourish "exclusive of the bulk of the natives" and that he would not have relished a purely sectarian homage.

Only one eccentric Protestant, suspected like the councillor and the great Bishop of Cloyne of being a Communist, took up the cudgels for Berkeley and said that it was a disgrace that in the States a town of a quarter of a million had been called after him, though he had never lived there, while the town where he had been born and bred grudged him a single street. "Also the Blessed Oliver had no connection with Belfast, while Berkeley had the closest with Kilkenny."

The councillor who had first proposed Berkeley saw he was getting into bad company, but a lucky chance soon gave him an opportunity of restoring his reputation. Something was said at a Dublin meeting by the eccentric Protestant at which the Papal Nuncio took offence, a special meeting of the corporation was held to denounce him, and the "Red" Berkeleyite joined cordially in the denunciations.

But the Berkeleyites had underestimated their strength. A few weeks later Mr. De Valera was addressing an election meeting at Cloyne, at which he bestowed the highest of praise upon Bishop Berkeley. "He was," he said, "the first economic Sinn Feiner . . . a wonderfully cultured, enlightened and kindly gentleman, who rose high above the prejudices of his class, and loved his country and his people." He quoted a series of observations from "The Querist," which do, in fact, justify Mr. De Valera's claim to be a practical exponent of Berkeleyism. Berkeley was, like De Valera, a strong believer in economic self-sufficiency and had asked for "a wall of brass a thousand cubits high round Ireland." He would have supported De Valera in his demands for native wheat and sugar, bacon and boots, which have for many years drawn upon De Valera the hostility of the majority of the bishop's co-religionists.

Ireland's Different to England–See?

By Patrick Campbell

The summer was in progress one morning last year in the village of Rooskey, on the River Shannon, in Co. Longford. The rain was descending vertically on the deck of a cabin-cruiser in which, at the early hour of 9:45, I was taking breakfast in bed.

All at once, unexpected as the roaring of a lion, an English accent established itself on the jetty. "I say!" it cried. "I say, is anyone there?"

We love strangers in Ireland. You never know what they're going to be like. With high expectation I drew back the six inches of chintz concealing the porthole, and there he was—a splendid specimen of English holiday male, fully grown with all his distinguishing marks ablaze.

He wore, in the downpour, his wife's transparent plastic mackintosh, and a transparent pixie hood. Under the mackintosh I could see a striped Shaftesbury-Avenue-Italian jersey and a pair of white shorts. On his feet he wore yellow socks and new, brown leather sandals. "I say," he called. "I say, is anyone there?"

I let him know, through the porthole, that a fellow human was present, while warning him that it was practically the middle of the night. "Or perhaps," I said, "you're still on the way to bed." There had been, the previous evening, a Grand Gala Ball in aid of the church in a fancy palais called Dreamland on the other side of the river, which had terminated round about 4 A.M., a normal social occasion in Irish rural life.

He knelt down on the jetty, presenting me with a close-up through the frame of the porthole of the pixie hood, and a pale, anxious face. "Hello, there," he said. "Actually, I was looking for some milk." He held up a small, plastic jug, making his mission clear. The rain poured into it as though from a tap.

We love strangers in Ireland. It's the last place left in the British Isles where you'll find a deeply appreciative audience if you want to talk about yourself. I invited him to fill in the details of how he came to be standing on Tony Fallon's jetty at the stark hour of 9:45, wearing a pixie hood and carrying a plastic jug.

He provided some facts. He was cruising with his wife and family, and had made an early start, to cover twenty miles before breakfast, as they had only a week and wished to see as much of the Shannon as possible in this short space of time. His wife and children were very hungry, but they couldn't start breakfast until they had some milk. He gestured with the jug toward Tony Fallon's. "The shop," he said, "doesn't seem to be open."

It's always a pleasure to us in Ireland to give information to a stranger, because he can scarcely ever believe his ears.

"Owing to the licensing laws," I said, "the shop doesn't open until the legal hour of 10:30, but when it does, you'll be able to buy not only a bottle of milk but also a packet of aspirin, a bar of cut-plug, a tin of peaches, a rat-trap, a screwdriver, half a pound of streaky bacon, a length of clothes-line, a jar of honey, a fishing rod, a morning paper, and a bottle of stout with which to wash it down. What's more, Tony's got a piano in the back lounge, so that while waiting you'll be able to play and sing. In addition, you'll be able to deal in all these commodities and pleasures for thirteen hours without a break, because the place doesn't shut until 11:30 tonight."

"I see," he said, though the concept was obviously new to him. "I suppose," he suggested after a moment, "there isn't a sort of dairy where I could just buy a bottle of milk?"

"There's one on the other side of the river," I told him, "but you'd have to walk nearly half a mile in the rain, and then it mightn't be open. The butcher, for instance, only comes to Rooskey once a week, and then he chops up carcasses in a rented sitting-room, with floral paper on the walls. Ireland's different to England, you see. The individual runs the country here, not the country the individual, and no individuals are up and about yet, so if I were you, I'd go back to bed until they get the place aired."

Ireland is beautiful to look at, the beauty of desolation. Long, white roads, the only traveller for miles an old woman in a black shawl on a donkey cart. The light is ever changing on the distant mountains, as the tall clouds sail in from the Atlantic. There is complete silence. A curlew pipes suddenly, but there is nothing else. A shaft of sunlight turns the bog to gold. Then the clouds darken again over the purple hills and the soft rain comes down and everything turns to pearly grey and luminous green. Machines and houses, brick walls and concrete and barbed wire died out before they got here. It's the uttermost, empty edge of Europe, the silent prehistoric land of Hy Brazil. It makes a haunting, quite unforgettable impression even on jolly, orange-sucking coach-parties from Manchester, Scunthorpe and Hull, so that, once bitten by it, they always come back, to recapture the strange feeling of being one's own man in a lost and dreamlike world, where there's no need to do anything in a hurry because you can be perfectly certain that no one else will be there to do it for you or with you . . . until we've got the place aired, and then there's a fair chance there'll be no need to do it at all.

It's a slowing down of the tempo that the English find difficult to get in step with at first, and even when they find the beat, they're never quite happy, being a people overconcerned with immediate practicalities, but on the other hand it provides them with an experience they never forget.

Take, for instance, the case of this milk-seeking Englishman. I went over to Tony Fallon's pub at about eleven o'clock, having a number of urgent commissions on my mind, to find him, still in his pixie hood and transparent mac, stamping up and down the light hardware and tinned comestibles department of the shop, and still calling, though on a more strained note than before, "I say, there—I say!" He had his plastic jug with him, but it was empty.

He was glad to see me. "I say," he said, "there seems to be no one here. A girl opened the shop at half-past ten, but she's disappeared."

I was able to clarify the position. "Our genial host," I said, "Mr. Tony Fallon, is heir-apparent to the resident undertaker, so he's gone to a funeral to polish up his technique with the ropes that go round the coffin. The beautiful girl who opened the door is his sister Patty, and she is now putting ten gallons of petrol into a lorry across the road, because Tony Fallon owns the filling station as well. She may be there for some time because the lorry driver has just arrived from Belturbet and she has a natural desire to know what's going on in a metropolis of that size. I don't know where Mrs. Fallon is, but she's got two small children, and is probably attending to them. Have a bottle of stout."

"But I haven't had breakfast yet," he said. "We've no milk."

I went into the bar at the back and pulled two bottles of stout, leaving the money in an ashtray. "But what about breakfast?" he said. "We want to get provisioned up, and make a start—"

"If you're going downstream," I said, "there's no point in leaving now because I'm meeting the lock-keeper here at midday, and giving him a lift. He's seventy-eight, but he's never been in a cabin-cruiser and wants to broaden his mind. He might be here earlier, but that won't help because we've lost a child and can't start without her."

He became overconcerned with practicalities. "You've lost a child? Where? How? Have you told the police?"

"The police," I said, "are in the back bar. He's having a bottle of stout and reading the paper. The child went into Longford on the nine o'clock bus to buy some comics—she hates boats. She should have been back here by ten, but she didn't arrive, so she's obviously lost."

He forgot about his milk troubles. "What are you doing about it?"

"Nothing," I said. "She's got plaits and she's wearing leopard-skin trousers. Someone in Longford is bound to fall into conversation with such an interesting-looking visitor, and then they'll ring up about her. What I'm really worried about is getting some flexible cable to repair the steering gear, but the police thinks he knows a man in Mohill who might have some, so we're going there as soon as Tony comes back from the funeral with the car. There's one little difficulty about the car. Tony's just sold it, in his function as garagist, to a man who's coming to collect it, but if he turns up before we leave for Mohill, he can take us there himself."

He sifted through it, and came up with a matter which he considered affected himself. "This lock-keeper," he said. "Do you mean I can't get through without him? We wanted to start in about ten minutes."

"You'd better have another bottle of stout," I said. "The lock-keeper is coming up from the lock in the new water-bus, because it can't get past here until the lock-keeper opens the swing bridge. He doesn't want to come up on his bicycle because he's going back to the lock with me. But in any case," I said, "there's no great hurry because a man's dropping in here on his way to Sligo to show me some new charts of the river, and there's a strong rumour that he broke down last night in Mullingar."

"I see," said the Englishman. "I think," he said tightly, "I'd better go and tell my wife."

It turned out to be a wonderful day, the kind of day you get only in Ireland where past, present and future, and day and night, blend into an endless, whirling dream, into which new characters constantly intrude and stay a while and vanish, unexplained—a dream of comings and goings and long talks with total strangers, of songs and loud laughter, of sudden friendships with people entirely unknown, and everything wrapped in this feeling of time-lessness and buoyant, floating ease.

The Englishman, the lock-keeper, the policeman, the postman and I spent a good deal of it in the distant town of Mohill, nego-tiating for flexible steel cable in perhaps twelve different pubs. When we got back to Rooskey, the lockkeeper opened the swing-bridge for the water-bus. We stood on it, while he wound the han-dle, wondering at the power of machinery. In Tony Fallon's we found that the Englishman's wife and my wife had set off in a speedboat at thirty-five knots for Carrickway to Sligo. He had, it seemed, been compelled to make a detour, for business or social reasons, to Longford, where general rumour quickly led him to a child in leopardskin trousers, contentedly browsing in a bookshop, having spent her return fare.

"That," as I explained to the Englishman, "is the wonderful thing about Ireland, our passionate interest in life, and in human beings. For twenty miles all up and down the river, people have heard there are two cabin-cruisers in Rooskey, and there's a young one missing, in leopardskin trousers. A man we met in Mohill passed it on to a fella in Dumlish, who met another fella at the crossroads in Ballinalee, so it's a wonder they didn't hear in Long-ford that a tiger was loose from Dublin Zoo. I bet you," I said, "there's fellas as far away as Sligo town itself who have heard there might be a bit of a do tonight in Tony Fallon's, and they're coming here now by way of Galway."

A car pulled up at the filling station. A head came out of the window. It was a man I hadn't seen for ten years. "I heard," said he, "below in Athlone you were up this way. Are you buying?" We brought him inside.

Timelessness and buoyancy and ease. The wives and the man with the speedboat came back, and he played the piano, so they started another gala ball in the back room. A middle-aged and studious American couple came in, Pennsylvania Quakers by persuasion, touring Ireland in search of Celtic crosses. Within a few moments they were absorbed in conversation with a very old farmer whose brother, during the Jimmy Walker administration, had been a policeman in New York. There was a Swedish couple as well, who suddenly materialised from the wind and the rain of the Irish night. You'd have thought the whole world was gathered together. By 11:30, and closing time, the back room and the bar and the shop were packed so tightly we could only stand, shoulder to shoulder, and sing. And it had really all begun twelve hours before with an Englishman in a pixie hood looking for a small jug of milk.

That's what happens in Ireland, where the machines and mass entertainment haven't reached, where every man is his own man and makes the day go by as he wishes.

It's what people come to Ireland for.

The Renaissance

The Renaissance

In the 1880's a new spirit of national pride came into being in Ireland. No longer did Irishmen pay homage to the Anglo-Irish Ascendancy. The Big House of the English gentry faded in prestige and power as the Irish began to emerge as a united force to have Ireland take once more its rightful place among the nations of the world.

This new spirit for independence, as enkindled by the political success of Charles Stewart Parnell in getting through the British Parliament a commitment for Home Rule for Ireland, was not without its effect upon the Irish artists and writers of the period.

Through his herculean feat of uniting all Irish political factions, Parnell gained strong parliamentary power—in fact, enough to bring about the defeat of the Gladstone government in 1885. Upon Gladstone's return to power in 1886, Parnell was able to exact the coveted commitment from his government for Home Rule.

This was no easy achievement. Parnell was tough, unyielding with the British and made good his threats, even when imprisoned. When the English outlawed the Irish Land League, Parnell from prison told the Irish tenants to pay no rent. They didn't. When an Irish landlord evicted a tenant, Parnell called upon the Irish countryside to ignore him as if he were dead. One Captain Charles Boycott in County Mayo did evict tenants for failure to pay rent. The neighboring Irish cut the Captain dead. Servants left his house. Farmers in his fields stopped work. Tradesmen refused to sell him any food or supplies. Nobody spoke to him. Captain Boycott finally fled Ireland under armed guard. Anyway, the Captain had the consolation of giving a new word to the language, namely: "boycott."

Heartened by the emergence of Ireland politically, the literary

Renaissance began. A movement to revive Gaelic, the native language, was started and met with response. A modern Irish theater, The Abbey, got under way headed by Lady Gregory, William Butler Yeats, and Edward Martyn. The new theater produced some highly original plays, and attracted international interest.

Among the successful Abbey playwrights are Synge, O'Casey, Behan, McNamara, Friel, Beckett, St. John Ervine, and Lord Dunsany. Many fine actors, including the Faheys, Digges, Corrigan, McKenna, Fitzgerald, Cusack, and others owe their start to stardom to the Abbey.

With the Renaissance also came Oscar Wilde and George Bernard Shaw. Both were born and educated in Ireland.

To shatter any illusions that he was not Irish, G.B.S. has written: "I have no trace in me of the commercially imported North Spanish strain which passes for aboriginal Irish: I am a genuine typical Irishman of the Danish, Norman, Cromwellian and, of course, Scotch invasions. I am violently and arrogantly Protestant by family tradition; but let no English Government therefore count on my allegiance; I am English enough to be an inveterate Republican and Home Ruler. It is true that my grandfather was an Orangeman, but then, his sister was an abbess, and his uncle, I am proud to say, was hanged as a rebel."

When George Bernard Shaw died, he left one third of his sizable estate to the National Gallery of Ireland.

Besides being great writers, both Shaw and Wilde, like most Celts, were great talkers. Though in some of his remarks Shaw could be as savage as Swift, he had a sentimentally witty Irish streak in him, along with a trained musical voice. His overall Celtic charm was such that people did not take offense at his remarks but instead hugely enjoyed them. Though Shaw took himself very seriously, he had that Hibernian knack of making his audience believe he was not serious or stuffy.

For example, once at a Players' Festival in London, a certain Osman Edwards read a paper on "The Superiority of Shaw to Shakespeare." At a point, Shaw rose and begged to say a few words "in favor of his famous rival."

Regarding Wilde, the eminent critic, Desmond McCarthy, who knew him well, states: "Oscar Wilde was probably the greatest self-consciously deliberate master of the Art of Conversation who has talked the English language. The qualification is important as distinguishing him from such talkers as Dr. Johnson or Sydney Smith, in whom there was nothing of the play actor."

William Tachau, the well-known New York architect, who is now still spry, though in his nineties, met Wilde when he was a student in Paris. I have spent many evenings with Bill Tachou at the Players and he has told me what an impressive talker Oscar Wilde really was. According to Tachau, Wilde had a delightful voice, which he could alter to mimic anyone. At the same time, his hands were capable of making effective gentle gestures which would emphasize the points he was making. Wilde was always the superb actor speaking superb lines of his own.

Contemporary in this Irish Renaissance with Lady Gregory, George Moore, and William Butler Yeats came Oliver St. John Gogarty, James Joyce, Padraic Colum, Lynn Doyle, Lord Dunsany, St. John Ervine and then later Frank O'Connor, Sir Shane Leslie, James Stephens, Donagh MacDonagh, Brinsley MacNamara, Paul Vincent Carroll, Sean O'Faolain, Lian O'Flaherty, Brien Friel, Mary Lavin, Daniel Corkey, Brian O'Nolan, and others.

Now with the Republic of Ireland taking its rightful place among the nations of the world, the Renaissance spirit continues more than ever. New wits, poets, authors, and playwrights are appearing constantly on the Irish scene and maintaining that great tradition of Irish wit, humor, and wisdom.

Ivy Day in the Committee Room

BY JAMES JOYCE

Old Jack raked the cinders together with a piece of cardboard and spread them judiciously over the whitening dome of coals. When the dome was thinly covered, his face lapsed into darkness but, as he set himself to fan the fire again, his crouching shadow ascended the opposite wall and his face slowly reemerged into light. It was an old man's face, very bony and hairy. The moist blue eyes blinked at the fire and the moist mouth fell open at times, munching once or twice mechanically when it closed. When the cinders had caught, he laid the piece of cardboard against the wall, sighed and said:

"That's bettter now, Mr. O'Connor."

Mr. O'Connor, a grey-haired young man, whose face was disfigured by many blotches and pimples, had just brought the tobacco for a cigarette into a shapely cylinder, but when spoken to he undid his handiwork meditatively and after a moment's thought decided to lick the paper.

"Did Mr. Tierney say when he'd be back?" he asked in a husky falsetto.

"He didn't say."

Mr. O'Connor put his cigarette into his mouth and began to search his pockets. He took out a pack of thin pasteboard cards.

"I'll get you a match," said the old man.

"Never mind, this'll do," said Mr. O'Connor.

He selected one of the cards and read what was printed on it:

MUNICIPAL ELECTIONS
Royal Exchange Ward
Mr. Richard J. Tierney, P.L.G., respectfully
solicits the favour of your vote and influence
at the coming election in the Royal Exchange Ward.

Mr. O'Connor had been engaged by Tierney's agent to canvass one part of the ward but, as the weather was inclement and his boots let in the wet, he spent a great part of the day sitting by the fire in the Committee Room in Wicklow Street with Jack, the old caretaker. They had been sitting thus since the short day had grown dark. It was the sixth of October, dismal and cold out of doors.

Mr. O'Connor tore a strip off the card and, lighting it, lit his cigarette. As he did so the flame lit up a leaf of dark glossy ivy in the lapel of his coat. The old man watched him attentively and then, taking up the piece of cardboard again, began to fan the fire slowly while his companion smoked.

"Ah, yes," he said, continuing, "it's hard to know what way to bring up children. Now who'd think he'd turn out like that! I sent him to the Christian Brothers and I done what I could for him, and there he goes boosing about. I tried to make him someway decent."

He replaced the cardboard wearily.

"Only I'm an old man now I'd change his tune for him. I'd take the stick to his back and beat him while I could stand over him—as I done many a time before. The mother, you know, she cocks him up with this and that . . ."

"That's what ruins children," said Mr. O'Connor.

"To be sure it is," said the old man. "And little thanks you get for it, only impudence. He takes th' upper hand of me whenever he sees I've a sup taken. What's the world coming to when sons speaks that way to their fathers?"

"What age is he?" said Mr. O'Connor.

"Nineteen," said the old man.

"Why don't you put him to something?"

"Sure, amn't I never done at the drunken bowsy ever since he left school? 'I won't keep you,' I says. 'You must get a job for yourself.' But, sure, it's worse whenever he gets a job; he drinks it all."

Mr. O'Connor shook his head in sympathy, and the old man fell silent, gazing into the fire. Someone opened the door of the room and called out:

"Hello! Is this a Freemason's meeting?"

"Who's that?" said the old man.

"What are you doing in the dark?" asked a voice.

"Is that you, Hynes?" asked Mr. O'Connor.

"Yes. What are you doing in the dark?" said Mr. Hynes, advancing into the light of the fire.

He was a tall, slender young man with a light brown moustache. Imminent little drops of rain hung at the brim of his hat and the collar of his jacket-coat was turned up.

"Well, Mat," he said to Mr. O'Connor, "how goes it?"

Mr. O'Connor shook his head. The old man left the hearth, and after stumbling about the room returned with two candlesticks which he thrust one after the other into the fire and carried to the table. A denuded room came into view and the fire lost all its cheerful colour. The walls of the room were bare except for a copy of an election address. In the middle of the room was a small table on which papers were heaped.

Mr. Hynes leaned against the mantelpiece and asked:

"Has he paid you yet?"

"Not yet," said Mr. O'Connor. "I hope to God he'll not leave us in the lurch tonight."

Mr. Hynes laughed.

"Oh, he'll pay you. Never fear," he said.

"I hope he'll look smart about it if he means business," said Mr. O'Connor.

"What do you think, Jack?" said Mr. Hynes satirically to the old man.

The old man returned to his seat by the fire, saying:

"It isn't but he has it, anyway. Not like the other tinker."

"What other tinker?" said Mr. Hynes.

"Colgan," said the old man scornfully.

"It is because Colgan's a working-man you say that? What's the difference between a good honest bricklayer and a publican—eh? Hasn't the working-man as good a right to be in the Corporation as anyone else—ay, and a better right than those shoneens that are always hat in hand before any fellow with a handle to his name? Isn't that so, Mat?" said Mr. Hynes, addressing Mr. O'Connor.

"I think you're right," said Mr. O'Connor.

"One man is a plain honest man with no hunker-sliding about him. He goes in to represent the labour classes. This fellow you're working for only wants to get some job or other."

"Of course, the working-classes should be represented," said the old man.

"The working-man," said Mr. Hynes, "gets all kicks and no halfpence. But it's labour produces everything. The working-man is not going to drag the honour of Dublin in the mud to please a German monarch."

"How's that?" said the old man.

"Don't you know they want to present an address of welcome to Edward Rex if he comes here next year? What do we want kow-towing to a foreign king?"

"Our man won't vote for the address," said Mr. O'Connor. "Anyway, I wish he'd turn up with the spondulics."

The three men fell silent. The old man began to rake more cinders together. Mr. Hynes took off his hat, shook it and then turned down the collar of his coat, displaying, as he did so, an ivy leaf in the lapel.

"If this man was alive," he said, pointing to the leaf, "we'd have no talk of an address of welcome."

"That's true," said Mr. O'Connor.

"Musha, God be with them times!" said the old man. "There was some life in it then."

The room was silent again. Then a bustling little man with a snuffling nose and very cold ears pushed in the door. He walked over quickly to the fire, rubbing his hands as if he intended to produce a spark from them.

"No money, boys," he said.

"Sit down here, Mr. Henchy," said the old man, offering him his chair.

"Oh, don't stir, Jack; don't stir," said Mr. Henchy.

He nodded curtly to Mr. Hynes and sat down on the chair which the old man vacated.

"Did you serve Aungier Street?" he asked Mr. O'Connor.

"Yes," said Mr. O'Connor, beginning to search his pockets for memoranda.

"Did you call on Grimes?"

"I did."

"Well? How does he stand?"

"He wouldn't promise. He said : 'I won't tell anyone what way I'm going to vote.' But I think he'll be all right."

"Why so?"

"He asked me who the nominators were, and I told him. I mentioned Father Burke's name. I think it'll be all right."

Mr. Henchy began to snuffle and to rub his hands over the fire at a terrific speed. Then he said:

"For the love of God, Jack, bring us a bit of coal. There must be some left."

The old man went out of the room.

"It's no go," said Mr. Henchy, shaking his head. "I asked the little shoeboy, but he said: 'Oh, now, Mr. Henchy, when I see the work going on properly I won't forget you, you may be sure.' Mean little tinker! 'Usha, how could he be anything else?"

"What did I tell you, Matt?" said Mr. Hynes. "Tricky Dicky Tierney."

"Oh, he's as tricky as they make 'em," said Mr. Henchy. "He hasn't got those little pigs' eyes for nothing. Blast his soul! Couldn't he pay up like a man instead of: 'Oh, now, Mr. Henchy, I must speak to Mr. Fanning. . . . I've spent a lot of money.' Mean little schoolboy of hell! I suppose he forgets the time his little old father kept the hand-me-down shop in Mary's Lane."

"But is that a fact?" asked Mr. O'Connor.

"God, yes," said Mr. Henchy. "Did you never hear that? And the men used to go in on Sunday morning before the houses were open to buy a waistcoat or a trousers—moya! But Tricky Dicky's little old father always had a tricky little black bottle up in a corner. Do you mind now? That's that. That's where he first saw the light."

The old man returned with a few lumps of coal which he placed here and there on the fire.

"That's a nice how-do-you-do," said Mr. O'Connor. "How does he expect us to work for him if he won't stump up?"

"I can't help it," said Mr. Henchy. "I expect to find the bailiffs in the hall when I go home."

Mr. Hynes laughed and, shoving himself away from the mantelpiece with the aid of his shoulders, made ready to leave.

"It'll be all right when King Eddie comes," he said. "Well, boys, I'm off for the present. See you later. 'Bye, 'bye."

He went out of the room slowly. Neither Mr. Henchy nor the old man said anything, but, just as the door was closing, Mr. O'Connor, who had been staring moodily into the fire, called out suddenly:

" 'Bye, Joe."

Mr. Henchy waited a few moments and then nodded in the direction of the door.

"Tell me," he said across the fire, "what brings our friend in here? What does he want?"

" 'Usha, poor Joe!" said Mr. O'Connor, throwing the end of his cigarette into the fire. "He's hard up, like the rest of us."

Mr. Henchy snuffled vigorously and spat so copiously that he nearly put out the fire, which uttered a hissing protest.

"To tell you my private and candid opinion," he said, "I think he's a man from the other camp. He's a spy of Colgan's, if you ask me. Just go round and try and find out how they're getting on. They won't suspect you. Do you twig?"

"Ah, poor Joe is a decent skin," said Mr. O'Connor.

"His father was a decent, respectable man," Mr. Henchy admitted. "Poor old Larry Hynes! Many a good turn he did in his day! But I'm greatly afraid our friend is not nineteen carat. Damn it, I can understand a fellow being hard up, but what I can't understand is a fellow sponging. Couldn't he have some spark of manhood about him?"

"He doesn't get a warm welcome from me when he comes," said the old man. "Let him work for his own side and not come spying around here."

"I don't know," said Mr. O'Connor dubiously, as he took out cigarette-papers and tobacco. "I think Joe Hynes is a straight man. He's a clever chap, too, with the pen. Do you remember that thing he wrote . . . ?"

"Some of these hillsiders and fenians are a bit too clever, if you ask me," said Mr. Henchy. "Do you know what my private and candid opinion is about some of those little jokers? I believe half of them are in the pay of the Castle."

"There's no knowing," said the old man.

"Oh, but I know it for a fact," said Mr. Henchy. "They're Castle hacks. . . . I don't say Hynes . . . No, damn it, I think he's a stoke above that. . . . But there's a certain little nobleman with a cock-eye—you know the patriot I'm alluding to?"

Mr. Connor nodded.

"There's a lineal descendant of Major Sirr for you if you like! Oh, the heart's blood of a patriot! That's a fellow now that'd sell his country for fourpence—ay—and go down on his bended knees and thank the Almighty Christ he had a country to sell."

There was a knock at the door.

"Come in!" said Mr. Henchy.

A person resembling a poor clergyman or a poor actor appeared in the doorway. His black clothes were tightly buttoned on his short body and it was impossible to say whether he wore a clergyman's collar or a layman's, because the collar of his shabby frock-coat, the uncovered buttons of which reflected the candlelight, was turned up about his neck. He wore a round hat of hard black felt. His face, shining with raindrops, had the appearance of damp yellow cheese save where two rosy spots indicated the cheekbones. He opened his very long mouth suddenly to express disappointment and at the same time opened wide his very bright blue eyes to express pleasure and surprise.

"Oh, Father Keon!" said Mr. Henchy, jumping up from his chair. "Is that you? Come in!"

"Oh, no, no, no!" said Father Keon quickly, pursing his lips as if he were addressing a child.

"Won't you come in and sit down?"

"No, no, no!" said Father Keon, speaking in a discreet, indulgent, velvety voice. "Don't let me disturb you now! I'm just looking for Mr. Fanning . . ."

"He's round at the Black Eagle," said Mr. Henchy. "But won't you come in and sit down a minute?"

"No, no, thank you. It was just a little business matter," said Father Keon. "Thank you, indeed."

He retreated from the doorway and Mr. Henchy, seizing one of the candlesticks, went to the door to light him downstairs.

"Oh, don't trouble, I beg!"

"No, but the stairs is so dark."

"No, no, I can see. . . . Thank you, indeed."

"Are you right now?"

"All right, thanks. . . . Thanks."

Mr. Henchy returned with the candlestick and put it on the table. He sat down again at the fire. There was silence for a few moments.

"Tell me, John," said Mr. O'Connor, lighting his cigarette with another pasteboard card.

"Hm?"

"What he is exactly?"

"Ask me an easier one," said Mr. Henchy.

"Fanning and himself seem to me very thick. They're often in Kavanagh's together. Is he a priest at all?"

"Mmmyes, I believe so. . . . I think he's what you call a black sheep. We haven't many of them, thank God! but we have a few. . . . He's an unfortunate man of some kind. . . ."

"And how does he knock it out?" asked Mr. O'Connor.

"That's another mystery."

"Is he attached to any chapel or church or institution or—"

"No," said Mr. Henchy, "I think he's travelling on his own account. . . . God forgive me," he added, "I thought he was the dozen of stout."

"Is there any chance of a drink itself?" asked Mr. O'Connor.

"I'm dry, too," said the old man.

"I asked that little shoeboy three times," said Mr. Henchy,

"would he send up a dozen of stout. I asked him again now, but he was leaning on the counter in his shirt-sleeves having a deep goster with Alderman Cowley."

"Why didn't you remind him?" said Mr. O'Connor.

"Well, I couldn't go over while he was talking to Alderman Cowley. I just waited till I caught his eye, and said: 'About that little matter I was speaking to you about. . . .' 'That'll be all right, Mr. H.,' he said. Yerra, sure the little hop-o'-my-thumb has forgotten all about it."

"There's some deal on in that quarter," said Mr. O'Connor thoughtfully. "I saw the three of them hard at it yesterday at Suffolk Street corner."

"I think I know the little game they're at," said Mr. Henchy. "You must owe the City Fathers money nowadays if you want to be made Lord Mayor. Then they'll make you a Lord Mayor. By God! I'm thinking seriously of becoming a City Father myself. What do you think? Would I do for the job?"

Mr. O'Connor laughed.

"So far as owing money goes. . . ."

"Driving out of the Mansion House," said Mr. Henchy, "in all my vermin, with Jack here standing up behind me in a powdered wig—eh?"

"And make me your private secretary, John."

"Yes. And I'll make Father Keon my private chaplain. We'll have a family party."

"Faith, Mr. Henchy," said the old man, "you'd keep up better style than some of them. I was talking one day to old Keegan, the porter. 'And how do you like your new master, Pat?' says I to him. 'You haven't much entertaining now,' says I. 'Entertaining!' says he. 'He'd live on the smell of an oil-rag.' And do you know what he told me? Now, I declare to God, I didn't believe him."

"What?" said Mr. Henchy and Mr. O'Connor.

"He told me: 'What do you think of a Lord Mayor of Dublin sending out for a pound of chops for his dinner? How's that for high living?' says he. 'Wisha! Wisha,' says I. 'A pound of chops,' says he, 'coming into the Mansion House.' 'Wisha!' says I. 'What kind of people is going at all now?' "

At this point there was a knock at the door, and a boy put in his head.

"What is it?" said the old man.

"From the Black Eagle," said the boy, walking in sideways and depositing a basket on the floor with a noise of shaken bottles.

The old man helped the boy to transfer the bottles from the basket to the table and counted the full tally. After the transfer the boy put his basket on his arm and asked:

"Any bottles?"

"What bottles?" said the old man.

"Won't you let us drink them first?" said Mr. Henchy.

"I was told to ask for the bottles."

"Come back tomorrow," said the old man.

"Here, boy!" said Mr. Henchy. "Will you run over to O'Farrells's and ask him to lend us a corkscrew—for Mr. Henchy, say. Tell him we won't keep it a minute. Leave the basket there."

The boy went out and Mr. Henchy began to rub his hands cheerfully, saying: "Ah, well, he's not so bad after all. He's as good as his word, anyhow."

"There's no tumblers," said the old man.

"Oh, don't let that trouble you, Jack," said Mr. Henchy. "Many's the good man before now drank out of the bottle."

"Anyway, it's better than nothing," said Mr. O'Connor.

"He's not a bad sort," said Mr. Henchy, "only Fanning has such a loan of him. He means well, you know, in his own tinpot way."

The boy came back with the corkscrew. The old man opened three bottles and was handing back the corkscrew when Mr. Henchy said to the boy:

"Would you like a drink, boy?"

"If you please, sir," said the boy.

The old man opened another bottle grudgingly, and handed it to the boy.

"What age are you?" he asked.

"Seventeen," said the boy.

As the old man said nothing further, the boy took the bottle, said: "Here's my best respects, sir, to Mr. Henchy," drank the contents, put the bottle back on the table and wiped his mouth with his sleeve. Then he took up the corkscrew and went out of the door sideways, muttering some form of salutation.

"That's the way it begins," said the old man.

"The thin edge of the wedge," said Mr. Henchy.

The old man distributed the three bottles which he had opened and the men drank from them simultaneously. After having drank, each placed his bottle on the mantelpiece within hand's reach and drew in a long breath of satisfaction.

"Well, I did a good day's work today," said Mr. Henchy, after a pause.

"That so, John?"

"Yes. I got him one or two sure things in Dawson Street, Crofton and myself. Between ourselves, you know, Crofton (he's a decent chap, of course), but he's not worth a damn as a canvasser. He hasn't a word to throw to a dog. He stands and looks at the people while I do the talking."

Here two men entered the room. One of them was a very fat man, whose blue serge clothes seemed to be in danger of falling from his sloping figure. He had a big face which resembled a young ox's face in expression, staring blue eyes and a grizzled moustache. The other man, who was much younger and frailer, had a thin, clean-shaven face. He wore a very high double collar and a wide-brimmed bowler hat.

"Hello, Crofton!" said Mr. Henchy to the fat man. "Talk of the devil . . ."

"Where did the boose come from?" asked the young man. "Did the cow calve?"

"Oh, of course, Lyons spots the drink first thing!" said Mr. O'Connor, laughing.

"Is that the way you chaps canvass," said Mr. Lyons, "and Crofton and I out in the cold and rain looking for votes?"

"Why, blast your soul," said Mr. Henchy, "I'd get more votes in five minutes than you two'd get in a week."

"Open two bottles of stout, Jack," said Mr. O'Connor.

"How can I," said the old man, "when there's no corkscrew?"

"Wait now, wait now!" said Mr. Henchy, getting up quickly. "Did you ever see this little trick?"

He took two bottles from the table and, carrying them to the fire, put them on the hob. Then he sat down again by the fire and took another drink from his bottle. Mr. Lyons sat on the edge of the table, pushed his hat towards the nape of his neck and began to swing his legs.

"Which is my bottle?" he asked.

"This, lad," said Mr. Henchy.

Mr. Crofton sat down on a box and looked fixedly at the other bottle on the hob. He was silent for two reasons. The first reason, sufficient in itself, was that he had nothing to say; the second reason was that he considered his companions beneath him. He had been a canvasser for Wilkins, the Conservative, but when the Conservatives had withdrawn their man and, choosing the lesser of two evils, given their support to the Nationalist candidate, he had been engaged to work for Mr. Tierney.

In a few minutes an apologetic "Pok!" was heard as the cork flew out of Mr. Lyons' bottle. Mr. Lyons jumped off the table, went to the fire, took his bottle and carried it back to the table.

"I was just telling them, Crofton," said Mr. Henchy, "that we got a good few votes today."

"Who did you get?" asked Mr. Lyons.

"Well, I got Parkes for one, and I got Atkinson for two, and I got Ward of Dawson Street. Fine old chap he is, too—regular old toff, old Conservative! 'But isn't your candidate a Nationalist?' said he. 'He's a respectable man,' said I. 'He's in favour of whatever will benefit this country. He's a big ratepayer,' I said. 'He has extensive house property in the city and three places of business, and isn't it to his own advantage to keep down the rates? He's a prominent and respected citizen,' said I, 'and a Poor Law Guardian, and he doesn't belong to any party, good, bad, or indifferent.'" That's the way to talk to 'em."

"And what about the address to the King?" said Mr. Lyons, after drinking and smacking his lips.

"Listen to me," said Mr. Henchy. "What we want in this country, as I said to old Ward, is capital. The King's coming here will mean an influx of money into this country. The citizens of Dublin will benefit by it. Look at all the factories down by the quays there, idle! Look at all the money there is in the country if we only worked the old industries, the mills, the ship-building yards and factories. It's capital we want."

"But look here, John," said Mr. O'Connor. "Why should we welcome the King of England? Didn't Parnell himself . . ."

"Parnell," said Mr. Henchy, "is dead. Now, here's the way I look at it. Here's this chap come to the throne after his old mother keeping him out of it till the man was grey. He's a man of the world, and he means well by us. He's a jolly fine decent fellow, if you ask me, and no damn nonsense about him. He just says to himself: 'The old one never went to see these wild Irish. By Christ, I'll go myself and see what they're like.' And are we going to insult the man when he comes over here on a friendly visit? Eh? Isn't that right, Crofton?"

Mr. Crofton nodded his head.

"But after all now," said Mr. Lyons argumentatively, "King Edward's life, you know, is not the very . . ."

"Let bygones be bygones," said Mr. Henchy. "I admire the man personally. He's just an ordinary knockabout like you and me. He's fond of his glass of grog and he's a bit of a rake, perhaps, and he's a good sportsman. Damn it, can't we Irish play fair?"

"That's all very fine," said Mr. Lyons. "But look at the case of Parnell now."

"In the name of God," said Mr. Henchy, "where's the analogy between the two cases?"

"What I mean," said Mr. Lyons, "is we have our ideals. Why, now, would we welcome a man like that? Do you think now after what he did Parnell was a fit man to lead us? And why, then, would we do it for Edward the Seventh?"

"This is Parnell's anniversary," said Mr. O'Connor, "and don't let us stir up any bad blood. We all respect him now that he's dead and gone—even the Conservatives," he added, turning to Mr. Crofton.

Pok! The tardy cork flew out of Mr. Crofton's bottle. Mr. Crofton got up from his box and went to the fire. As he returned with his capture, he said in a deep voice:

"Our side of the house respects him, because he was a gentleman."

"Right you are, Crofton!" said Mr. Henchy fiercely. "He was the only man that could keep that bag of cats in order. 'Down, ye dogs! Lie down, ye curs!' That's the way he treated them. Come in, Joe! Come in!" he called out, catching sight of Mr. Hynes in the doorway.

Mr. Hynes came in slowly.

"Open another bottle of stout, Jack," said Mr. Henchy. "Oh, I forgot there's no corkscrew! Here, show me one here and I'll put it at the fire."

The old man handed him another bottle and he placed it on the hob.

"Sit down, Joe," said Mr. O'Connor; "we're just talking about the Chief."

"Ay, ay!" said Mr. Henchy.

Mr. Hynes sat on the side of the table near Mr. Lyons but said nothing.

"There's one of them anyhow," said Mr. Henchy, "that didn't renege him. By God, I'll say for you, Joe! No, by God, you stuck to him like a man!"

"Oh, Joe," said Mr. O'Connor suddenly. "Give us that thing you wrote—do you remember? Have you got it on you?"

"Oh, ay!" said Mr. Henchy. "Give us that. Did you ever hear that, Crofton? Listen to this now: splendid thing."

"Go on," said Mr. O'Connor. "Fire away, Joe."

Mr. Hynes did not seem to remember at once the piece to which they were alluding, but, after reflecting a while, he said:

"Oh, that thing, is it. . . . Sure, that's old now."

"Out with it, man!" said Mr. O'Connor.

" 'Sh, 'sh," said Mr. Henchy. "Now, Joe!"

Mr. Hynes hesitated a little longer. Then amid the silence he took off his hat, laid it on the table and stood up. He seemed to be rehearsing the piece in his mind. After a rather long pause he announced:

THE DEATH OF PARNELL
6th October 1891

He cleared his throat once or twice and then began to recite:

> He is dead. Our Uncrowned King is dead.
>   O, Erin, mourn with grief and woe
> For he lies dead whom the fell gang
>   Of modern hypocrites laid low.
>
> He lies slain by the coward hounds
>   He raised to glory from the mire;
> And Erin's hopes and Erin's dreams
>   Perish upon her monarch's pyre.

In palace, cabin or in cot
　The Irish heart where'er it be
Is bowed with woe—for he is gone
　Who would have wrought her destiny.

He would have had his Erin famed,
　The green flag gloriously unfurled,
Her statesmen, bards and warriors raised
　Before the nations of the World.

He dreamed (alas 'twas but a dream!)
　Of Liberty: but as he strove
To clutch that idol, treachery
　Sundered him from the thing he loved.

Shame on the coward, caitiff hands
　That smote their Lord or with a kiss
Betrayed him to the rabble-rout
　Of fawning priests—no friends of his.

May everlasting shame consume
　The memory of those who tried
To befoul and smear the exalted name
　Of one who spurned them in his pride.

He fell as fall the mighty ones,
　Nobly undaunted to the last,
And death has now united him
　With Erin's heroes of the past.

No sound of strife disturbs his sleep!
　Calmly he rests: no human pain
Or high ambition spurs him now
　The peaks of glory to attain.

They had their way: they laid him low.
　But Erin, list, his spirit may
Rise, like the Phoenix from the flames,
　When breaks the dawning of the day,

The day that brings us Freedom's reign
  And on that day may Erin well
Pledge in the cup she lifts to Joy
  One grief—the memory of Parnell.

Mr. Hynes sat down again on the table. When he had finished his recitation, there was a silence and then a burst of clapping: even Mr. Lyons clapped. The applause continued for a little time. When it had ceased, all the auditors drank from their bottles in silence.

Pok! The cork flew out of Mr. Hynes' bottle, but Mr. Hynes remained sitting flushed and bare-headed on the table. He did not seem to have heard the invitation.

"Good man, Joe!" said Mr. O'Connor, taking out his cigarette-papers and pouch the better to hide his emotion.

"What do you think of that, Crofton?" cried Mr. Henchy. "Isn't that fine? What?"

Mr. Crofton said that it was a very fine piece of writing.

Little Tim Brannehan

By Lord Dunsany

Either to deceive the Germans in case they should come, or some more local enemy, the people of Sheehanstown had twisted sideways the arms of the signpost that is a mile from their village; and as some years later, when I came that way in a car, the arms had not yet been put straight, I asked the way of an old man who chanced to be walking by. And one thing leading to another we got into conversation, and I asked him how things were in those parts. "Terrible, terrible," said the old man. "Sure, they're terrible. And it's the same in the whole world, too. It's all going to ruin."

"As bad as that?" I said.

"Aye," he answered. "And worse."

"And what do you think is the cause of it?" I asked.

"It's all those inventions that they make," he replied. "Sure, I can remember when bicycles were new. But that wasn't enough for them, and they must go on till they invented aeroplanes and wireless and I don't know what all. And no good came of it, and the hearts of men has corrupted. Listen now, and I'll tell you. Did you ever hear of the house and family of Blackcastle? No, well, I was thinking you came from a very long way away. And once there was no country in the world that hadn't heard of them; but they're all ruined now. And it happened like this: the estates fell into the hands of a young Lord Blackcastle, that had a hard, dry, withered heart. So that was the end of their greatness, for no man can be great with a hard heart. Aye, that was the end of them. God be with the old days."

"What did he do?" I asked.

"Do, is it?" he said. "Sure, he had a hard, withered heart. What could he do?"

"Did he commit a crime?" I asked.

"Begob, it was worse nor a crime," he said. "Sure, you wouldn't mind a bit of crime in a man. He grudged a sup of milk to a child."

"He shouldn't have done that," I said.

"It's what he did," said the old man.

"How did it happen?" I asked.

"Sure, the good Lady Blackcastle, that had been his mother, died," he said, "and there was nobody to look after him then. And he went abroad, and he went from bad to worse, and he comes home, and that's what he did. Mustn't a man have a black heart in him indeed to grudge a glass of milk to an ailing child?"

"Are you sure he did it?" I asked. "And did he mean to?"

"Did it!" he said. "And mean to! Sure the whole thing's down in writing. Look now. It's in my pocket. I have it there night and day. Can you read that?"

And he pulled out an envelope holding a half sheet of notepaper, with writing in faded ink; and crumpled and thumbed though it was, I could still read the old writing. "Let a pint of milk a day," it said, "be given to little Tim Brannehan, since he is weakly. Moira Blackcastle."

He gave me time to read it and time for the import of the note to sink in, as he stood before me, a tall, white-bearded, reproachful figure, looking at the evidence which I held in my hand of the ruin that was coming to the world.

"He comes home from abroad," he said, "and goes into his dairy, and he stops that pint of milk being given out any more. And I shows him that very letter. And it has no more effect on him than a snowflake in the face of a charging bull or a wild lion. And you have seen the letter yourself, and a man must have a hard, black heart to go against a letter like that, written by such a lady as was Lady Blackcastle, now in heaven among the blessed saints. Sure, the world's going to ruin."

"But when did all this happen?" I asked. "And who is little Tim Brannehan?"

"Sure, it happened only the other day," he said. And the old man drew himself up to his full height, straightening for a moment the limbs that the years had bent. "And do you think I don't know what I'm talking about? Sure, I'm Tim Brannehan. And I was never refused that milk for seventy years."

Homeward

BY CYRIL DALY

To give him his due, the Canon felt guilty when he told the lie. Telling a lie to an ordinary man was one thing, but telling it to a Jesuit was a different kettle of fish altogether. And he surprised himself how easy he was able to tell it. No bother at all. You'd think he'd been at it for years.

"That's all then, Canon, on the west side of Durras?" the Jesuit said, drawing a fastidious napkin across his lips.

"That's all, and you've plenty work in them five, I can tell you. They're all hard nuts."

"No one else you'd like me to see? Quite sure now?" You'd think the Jesuit knew about Connie Clinch. And he looked so eager to go, uneasy as a horse rearing for the road. He had green eyes that looked straight into your face and out the back of your skull.

"I'm quite sure. There's no one else I'm worried about," the Canon said. No cock crew, but the clock on the mantelpiece chimed, punctuating the lie. Canon Maloney tried to conduct a private disputation. Maybe it wasn't really a lie. Just a gentle deception. It'd take the Jesuit to get him out of that problem, and the Jesuit was the last man on earth he wanted to know about it.

Canon Maloney had decided he'd never again tell any mission priest about Connie Clinch. He knew what would happen, because it was the same every year. Tell any one of them—Franciscan, Dominican, Passionist, Augustinian, Carmelite or Jesuit—that you had a fellow in the parish who hadn't darkened the church door for forty years, and it was like putting a match to dynamite. They'd galvanize into action, and, armed with prayer and fasting, they'd attack the citadel of Beelzebub in the form of Connie Clinch.

The results were always the same—bleak failure. Connie would be nice to them and he'd even ask them in for a cup of tea, but they never brought him an inch nearer the church.

So the Canon was determined. God between any missionary and Connie Clinch. The order for the like of Connie hadn't been founded yet. And the Canon wasn't parish priest of Durras for twenty-five years without knowing his own stretch of river. Connie was a cute old trout, who wouldn't be played neatly in by any passing spiritual angler. Too many had tried and failed.

The Canon had his own approach to Connie. When they met, as they often did, they'd have a chat about the match last Sunday or the way the potatoes were springing up or the new tractor that John Sullivan got. The Canon never mentioned hell or heaven or death or confession. He was a shrewd old angler and a great believer in God's good time.

The first morning of the mission, Connie was in his garden watching the road from Durras. He knew the missionary would come to him first. He was letting on to be busy with his rose bushes, but in reality he was looking forward to the impending battle for his soul.

He hadn't long to wait. The Jesuit came pushing up the hill on the curate's new bike. Connie was silently marshaling his arguments which dispensed with God and explained the universe.

"Good morning," the Jesuit said. "Could you put me right for Gortnagapall?"

"Up to the yellow garage a half-mile farther on, then take the second on your right by Jer Hickey's field."

"Fine roses you have there."

"They're not bad, I suppose."

"Any trouble with greenfly?"

"I throw tea leaves on them, and divil the greenfly I see on them."

"The nicotine, I suppose. There's nicotine in tea leaves, isn't there?" the Jesuit said.

"I'm not sure what it is, but it does the trick anyway. You know a fair bit about roses yourself."

"A little. I had t.b. five years ago, and when I was convalescing, they gave me the rose garden to look after. I got to like them. We must have a chat about them sometime."

"I always enjoy a bit of a yarn about them, but there's very few in these parts knows anything about them."

"I tell you what—when you're coming to the mission tonight, bring down a few of different varieties and see if I can identify them. Mind you, no bets, but I'll have a fair try. I'll see you then."

And so the Jesuit was gone, leaving Connie in a state of utmost anguish. He had been prepared for sin, death, like a thief in the night, the last day, and Satan. He was geared up for the fact that life is short, eternity long, and here we have no resting place. In fact, he was ready to deal with all the cosmic realities. But he hadn't been quite ready for roses and greenfly.

What really worried him was the fact he had given his word about going down to the church tonight. What would everybody say? Connie was an institution in Durras, a sort of local celebrity. After all, it isn't every parish in Ireland has a man that'll fly in the face of God for forty years.

To be perfectly truthful, Connie's pride was a bit bruised too. The priest had spoken to him as if he was as innocent as an altar boy. Surely the Jesuit must have known. What was he doing, then, talking about roses and nicotine and then peddling off to see minor delinquents who hadn't been to the sacraments for a year or two?

He decided on a plan of action. He'd go down to the church as he had promised, but he'd go by the back way into the sacristy, he'd have a few words with the priest, then he'd clear off as fast as he could.

At a quarter to eight exactly—nice and early so that none of the men would see him—Connie Clinch free-wheeled down from his house into the village of Durras. As soon as he passed the barracks, he put both feet on the ground because his brakes needed a little attention. The sparks flew from the studs on his boots, and just as he reached the church, he swung round to a stop. He threw his bike against the yellow, dashed wall and crunched his way across the pebbles to the sacristy.

Holy Jamesie, the sacristan, was there with red sore eyes and no lips at all.

"Great God, Connie Clinch, what have you in here?"

"Mindin' me own business, Jamesie boy, and maybe you'd do the same. Is your man here?"

"The Canon won't be here . . ."

"Don't mind your Canon. It's the other fella I'm after."

Just then the other fella appeared at the door with the black, vestigial wings hanging from his shoulders.

"Terribly good of you to come down so early. We can have a chat in here," he said, showing Connie into the tiny committee room. As Connie walked past Jamesie, he whispered between his yellow teeth, "One word of this to anybody, Jamesie boy, an' I'll smash your brains out, so I will."

"Certainly that's Ena Harkness. No mistake about that. Right."

"You're right. Now that one."

"Super Star."

"Super Star it is. Try that."

"Perfecta. Am I right?"

"Right again. You're no fool on the road. Now the last one."

"Ah, I'd know it straight away. Vienna Charm."

"Begad, you know about roses all right and no mistake."

"That Vienna Charm is a delightful rose."

"I've only one bush of it, but it's a grand rose all right."

"We've a whole bed of them up at Rathfarnham," the Jesuit said. "I must get Brother Corrigan to send you half a dozen bushes in November."

"Ah, now, I wouldn't like to take advantage."

"He'd be delighted. What's your address?"

"Connie Clinch, Durras. That'll find me. I'm well known around here."

"Wonderful to see men like you coming to the mission—the well-known men, I mean. You see, you are observed by the other less enthusiastic parishioners, and they come along too. Don't you agree?"

"Oh, that's a fact. That's a fact."

"What's this Shakespeare says? 'So shines a good deed in a naughty world.' You see how percipient the poet was?"

"He was all that."

"But why on earth do you men stay at the back of the church? Is it shyness or what?"

"It must be shyness keeps us at the back." Connie felt the back of his head breaking out in tiny hot pin-pricks.

"On the other hand, why should we be shy in the presence of Jesus? He loved to be with sinners, and when all's said and done, aren't we all sinners?"

Connie looked at the Jesuit, at the green, brown-flecked eyes.

"If just a few men came up front, maybe the others would follow suit," the priest said.

There was a knock on the door. It was Holy Jamesie. "It's time now, Father." Connie got up like a flash, eager to make his escape.

"Do you mind if I make a suggestion?" The Jesuit's voice was soft, but there was something in it that struck Connie dumb. "Why don't you slip out through the sacristy door here and go through the altar rails and then take your place in the front bench. That'll shake them."

"Oh, holy God, that'd shake them all right," the sacristan said.

Connie looked out at the terrazzo floor of the altar and the tall gold candlesticks and the statue of the Virgin with Holy Jamesie already bustling out to place the roses in glass vases in front of it.

There was nothing for it but to go forward.

The farmers of Durras were there and the shopkeepers and the publicans and the couple of guards and the one remaining saddler. All there. And when they saw Connie Clinch appearing on the altar in front of them, the effect was devastating. Each man doubted his own eyes and his own sanity.

Connie knelt down in the front pew, beads of perspiration running along his palms. He drew both hands down along his thighs to dry them, and he was glad when the priest came out so as the eyes of the congregation would go off him, maybe, for a while.

The church had that initial strangeness of familiar but forgotten things. As the decades of the rosary followed on each other,
he was surprised to find his lips moving in involuntary response.
The words had a freshness they never had before. The fruit of the
womb. The hour of our death. Solid, fundamental, tough. They
appealed to him. Then the litany. Tower of Ivory. Ark of the
Covenant. Singular Vessel of Devotion. Refuge of Sinners. And
the murmured "Pray for us." "Pray for us." "Pray for us." The
words brought back a half-remembered world of mother, wife, and
boys. Long ago, long, long ago. Years before the loneliness closed
in.

All the same, it was funny to think he was brought into this
church nearly seventy years ago, to the huge font, where the bell-
rope hangs. And he made his First Communion there at those
wooden rails in front of him. He couldn't remember it clearly, but
there was still a vague impression of the Railway Hotel that evening, lemonade and cake, and his father in his Sunday suit. But
the Jesuit was talking.

"We'll never become saints in the big things. It's the small
things that change the world. Here, my good men, you see a statue
of the Virgin; in front of it you see those lovely roses brought here
in love by one of yourselves. Now you may say that statue is nothing but so much plaster. And, of course, you would be right. And
the flowers are simply part of the economy of nature. Right again.

"But they have been brought together with vision. Vision is the
thing. They are a way of honoring the Virgin Mother of Christ,
she whom we have just addressed as the Mystical Rose. There is a
poem called 'Rosa Mystica' which is addressed directly to her. The
man who wrote it was not only a poet but a priest also, and a
priest, I am glad to say, belonging to my own order.

Tell me the name now, tell me its name:
The heart guesses easily, is it the same?
Mary? The Virgin? Well the heart knows,
She is the mystery, she is that rose.
In the gardens of God, in the daylight divine,
I shall come home to thee, Mother of mine.

"Home, my good men, is where the heart is, where we all long for. And it is worth remembering that in order to come home, we must first wander off. Haven't we all wandered, some of us farther than others? It is good to know that she is waiting for the day we turn back.

"So no matter how far we wander, no matter how black the night of our soul, we can come home to her, Mother of mine. Those words, Mother of mine, were among the very last uttered by the great and dying Pope John. And why? Because just as the priest had the vision of the poet, so Pope John had the vision of the saint, and they knew what they would find when they found her

In the gardens of God, in the daylight divine,
I shall worship the wounds with thee, Mother of mine.

"Make no mistake, my men, having found her, we find also the fierce reality of the wounds, the reality of the cross and of the Crucified Christ."

Afterward, in Paddy Collins' public house the sermon was well discussed.

"A quare sort of sermon that."

"You'd never hear the oul Canon talkin' like that."

"Course, the Jesuits are desperate brainy men."

"Will yeh ever forget th' apparition on the altar?"

"When was he last seen in a church?"

"God only knows. I used hear my father saying it was in the trouble times it begun. A priest said from the altar that any man who took a gun in his hand against the proper government was playin' into the hands of the devil. An', of course, Connie was a mad lunatic of a rebel."

"He was at the ambush at Crossbarry, wasn't he?"

"And a fearless man they say. Never went near a church since. But a great gunman in his day."

Connie wasn't there to give his side of the story. He had slipped home, embarrassed beyond measure, as soon as Benediction was over. He looked from the porch of his cottage across the valley. A veil of mist was moving along the line of the river. This silence was a terrible thing on a summer evening.

The house was even lonelier than the valley. Kate gone from it for five years now. Five years resting out by the sea, with all belonging to her around her. And the lads. The noise of them. All gone. The world wasn't big enough for the Clinch boys. London, Boston, Providence, Perth. All the noise gone and the clatter and the dirty shoes. All reduced to a card at Christmas.

Two women, mother, and wife, had pleaded with him. But his heart was set, the memory of the clerical condemnation was still bright, and he'd bow to no priest. But the Mother of God. She was different. In the first place, she wasn't a priest. An ordinary woman cooking the tea just as Kate had done and looking across the valley with her own thoughts. Mystical Rose. A strange name that. That Jesuit fellow, too. Definitely not the worst of them. Then there was the Canon. No great harm in him. He never heard him talking about religion.

Still and all, he wouldn't be trapped. He left the porch and went into the house, and its silence bored through him. The memories of hall and stairs and kitchen. The bed was the only thing for it. He'd sleep it off, and he'd be back to himself in the morning.

But the evening was still bright, and he couldn't sleep. He tossed and turned because he was very warm. Those prayers. And the Benediction, all the lights and candles, and the altar boy swinging the golden thing with the smoke, click, click, click, back and forth, like the years swinging by. And the bright ring of metal with the Host inside and the priest holding it up and the little bells ringing. The smell of the smoke. The hymn at the end and all the men singing "I think of Thee and what Thou art. Thy majesty, Thy state . . ."

Oh, it was impossible. He was beyond the beyond. Try and work it out. No Mass of a Sunday, and there were fifty-two Sundays in the year. That was fifty-two mortal sins every year for a start. Multiply that by forty and you've enough sins to damn the world, let alone Connie Clinch. And that was still only the beginning. It was too late now; it was too late for anything. If the Canon only knew about the chat he had with the Jesuit, he'd never live it down.

But at that moment the Canon was looking absent-mindedly at the late news flashes on television, a white mug of drinking chocolate held cosily between his two hands. The Jesuit had only just gone. A shocking man for talking.

There was a sudden short ring on the doorbell.

The Canon shuffled across in his slippers to the hall and caught Betty just in time. "Hi, girl, tell them I'm gone to bed. It's that carnival crowd again wondering about the dodgems or the hobby horses. It'll keep until morning, or is it a night-club they think I have here?"

He returned to his armchair, and he sipped his drink, not noticing that the television was closed down for the night, and the blank screen flickered beside him. He heard the front door closing.

"Hi, Betty, come here."

She came in.

"Well?"

"I sent him on his way, Canon."

"Good girl. That carnival committee think I've nothing to do but stay talking all night. Who was it?"

"Connie Clinch."

"Con . . . An' you sent him off?"

"It's after half-eleven, Canon."

Something within the Canon's soul stirred, something planted a long, long time ago by the Bishop's hands, never to be stifled by routine or parish or age.

"Oh, sweet God, give me patience with you, Betty girl, or what kind of an eejit are yeh! Go out as fast as your legs will carry you and bring him back here to me. The good angler is on the river, not when most convenient, but when the hungry trout is on the rise."

Connie looked awkward in the room.

"Good-night, Connie, an' how will the Durras lads do against Kilcrohane on Sunday, do you think?"

"Is it too late in the night for confession, Canon?"

"It's a bit late all right, Connie, but they'll give us time and a half for after hours."

"Maybe it'd be better if I came back in the mornin'!"

"Please yourself, Connie boy. But they say there's no time like the present."

"It's a desperate long time, Canon. Forty years. Could you hear a confession like that, or would it have to go to the Bishop?"

"What would the Bishop know about it, Connie? Sure, that fella hasn't heard a confession this twenty years. Now let's see . . . we'll begin at the beginning."

When Connie got up from the prie-dieu, the Canon ventured asking, "You found the Jesuit a good man?" wondering how the missionary had got to the heart of the matter.

"He is a great man for the roses," was all Connie said. "But for God Almighty's sake, Canon, don't tell a word of what I told you tonight, because he thinks I'm a pillar of the church. He thinks I'm a terrible innocent man."

The following morning, the Canon and the Jesuit stood outside the church as the men filed out from Mass. Connie came out shyly, the dry taste of the sanctified Host still strange on his tongue.

"There's a great man for roses," the Jesuit said.

The Canon looked at him, but the green eyes told him nothing. The Canon gave up. He'd never understand it. Desperate clever men, these Jesuits.

Two of a Kind

By Sean O'Faolain

Max Creedon was not drunk, but he was melancholy-drunk, and he knew it and he was afraid of it.

At first he had loved being there in the jammed streets, with everybody who passed him carrying parcels wrapped in green gold, tied with big red ribbons and fixed with berried holly sprigs. Whenever he bumped into someone, parcels toppled and they both cried "Ooops!" or "Sorree!" and laughed at one another. A star of snow sank nestling into a woman's hair. He smelled pine and balsam. He saw twelve golden angels blaring silently from twelve golden trumpets in Rockefeller Plaza. He pointed out to a cop that when the traffic lights down Park Avenue changed from red to green the row of white Christmas trees away down the line changed color by reflection. The cop was very grateful to him. The haze of light on the tops of the buildings made a halo over Fifth Avenue. It was all just the way he knew it would be, and he slopping down from Halifax in that damned old tanker. Then, suddenly, he swung his right arm in a wild arc of disgust.

"To hell with 'em! To hell with everybody!"

"Oops! Hoho, there! Sorree!"

He refused to laugh back.

"Poor Creedon!" he said to himself. "All alone in New York, on Christmas-bloody-well-Eve, with nobody to talk to, and nowhere to go only back to the bloody old ship. New York all lit up. Everybody all lit up. Except poor old Creedon."

He began to cry for poor old Creedon. Crying, he reeled through the passing feet. The next thing he knew he was sitting up at the counter of an Eighth Avenue drugstore sucking black coffee, with one eye screwed up to look out at the changing traffic lights, chuckling happily over a yarn his mother used to tell him long ago about a place called Ballyroche. He had been there only once, nine years ago, for her funeral. Beaming into his coffee cup, or looking out at the changing traffic lights, he went through his favorite yarn about poor Lily:

"Ah, wisha! Poor Lily! I wonder where is she atall, atall now. Or is she dead or alive. It all happened through an Italian who used to be going from one farm to another selling painted statues. Bandello his name was, a handsome black divil o'hell! I never in all my born days saw a more handsome divil. Well, one wet, wild, windy October morning what did she do but creep out of her bed and we all sound asleep and go off with him. Often and often I heard my father say that the last seen of her was standing under the big tree at Ballyroche Cross, sheltering from the rain, at about eight o'clock in the morning. It was Mikey Clancy the postman saw her. 'Yerrah, Lily girl,' says he, 'what are you doing here at this hour of the morning?' 'I'm waiting,' says she, 'for to go into Fareens on the milk cart.' And from that day to this not a sight nor a sound of her no more than if the earth had swallowed her. Except for the one letter from a priest in America to say she was happily married in Brooklyn, New York."

Maxer chuckled again. The yarn always ended up with the count of the years. The last time he heard it, the count had reached forty-one. By this year it would have been fifty.

Maxer put down his cup. For the first time in his life it came to him that the yarn was a true story about a real woman. For as long as four traffic-light changes he fumbled with this fact. Then, like a man hearing a fog signal come again and again from an approaching ship, and at last hearing it close at hand, and then seeing an actual if dim shape wrapped in a cocoon of haze, the great idea revealed itself.

He lumbered down from his stool and went over to the telephones. His lumpish finger began to trace its way down the gray pages among the Brooklyn Ban's. His finger stopped. He read the name aloud, Bandello, Mrs. Lily. He found a dime, tinkled it home, and dialed the number slowly. On the third ring he heard an old woman's voice. Knowing that she would be very old and might be deaf, he said very loudly and with the extra-meticulous enunciations of all drunks:

"My name is Matthew Creedon. Only my friends all call me Maxer. I come from Limerick, Ireland. My mother came from the townland of Ballyroche. Are you by any chance my Aunt Lily?"

Her reply was a bark:

"What do you want?"

"Nothing at all! Only I thought, if you are the lady in question, that we might have a bit of an ould gosther. I'm a sailor. Docked this morning in the Hudson."

The voice was still hard and cold.

"Did somebody tell you to call me?"

He began to get cross with her.

"Naw! Just by a fluke I happened to look up your name in the directory. I often heard my mother talking about you. I just felt I'd like to talk to somebody. Being Christmas and all to that. And knowing nobody in New York. But if you don't like the idea, it's okay with me. I don't want to butt in on anybody. Good-by."

"Wait! You're sure nobody sent you?"

"Inspiration sent me! Father Christmas sent me!" (She could take that any way she bloody-well liked!) "Look! It seems to me I'm buttin' in. Let's skip it."

"No. Why don't you come over and see me?"

Suspiciously he said:

"This minute?"

"Right away!"

At the sudden welcome of her voice all his annoyance vanished.

"Sure, Auntie Lily! I'll be right over. But, listen, I sincerely hope you're not thinking I'm buttin' in. Because if you are—"

"It was very nice of you to call me, Matty, very nice indeed. I'll be glad to see you."

He hung up, grinning. She was just like his mother—the same old Limerick accent. After fifty years. And the same bossy voice. If she was a day, she'd be seventy. She'd be tall, and thin, and handsome, and the real lawdy-daw, doing the grand lady, and under it all she'd be as soft as mountain moss. She'd be tidying the house now like a divil. And giving jaw to ould Bandello. If he was still alive.

He got lost on the subway, so that when he came up it was dark. He paused to have another black coffee. Then he paused to buy a bottle of Jamaica rum as a present for her. And then he had to walk five blocks before he found the house where she lived. The automobiles parked under the lights were all snow-covered. She lived in a brownstone house with high steps. Six other families also had rooms in it.

The minute he saw her on top of the not brightly lit landing, looking down at him, he saw something he had completely forgotten. She had his mother's height, and slimness, and her wide mouth, but he had forgotten the pale, liquid blue of the eyes, and they stopped him dead on the stairs, his hand tight on the banister. At the sight of them he heard the soft wind sighing over the level Limerick plain and his whole body shivered. For miles and miles not a sound but that soughing wind that makes the meadows and the wheat fields flow like water. All over that plain, where a crossroads is an event, where a little, sleepy lake is an excitement. Where their streams are rivers to them. Where their villages are towns. The resting cows look at you out of owls' eyes over the greasy tips of the buttercups. The meadow grass is up to their bellies. Those two pale eyes looking down at him were bits of the pale albino sky stretched tightly over the Shannon plain.

Slowly he climbed up to meet her, but even when they stood side by side, she was still able to look down at him, searching his face with her pallid eyes. He knew what she was looking for, and he knew she had found it when she threw her bony arms around his neck and broke into a low, soft wailing just like that Shannon wind.

"Auntie! You're the living image of her!"

On the click of a finger she became bossy and cross with him, hauling him by his two hands into her room.

"You've been drinking! And what delayed you? And I suppose not a scrap of solid food in your stomach since morning?"

He smiled humbly.

"I'm sorry, Auntie. 'Twas just on account of being all alone, you know. And everybody else making whoopee." He hauled out the peace offering of the rum. "Let's have a drink!"

She was fussing all over him immediately.

"You gotta eat something first. Drinking like that all day, I'm ashamed of you! Sit down, boy. Take off your jacket. I got coffee, and cookies, and hamburgers, and a pie. I always lay in a stock for Christmas. All the neighbors visit me. Everybody knows that Lily Bandello keeps an open house for Christmas; nobody is ever going to say Lily Bandello didn't have a welcome for all her friends and relations at Christmastime—"

She bustled in and out of the kitchenette, talking back to him without stop.

It was a big, dusky room, himself looking at himself out of a tall, mirrored wardrobe piled on top with cardboard boxes. There was a divan in one corner as high as a bed, and he guessed that there was a washbasin behind the old peacock-screen. A single bulb hung in the center of the ceiling, in a fluted glass bell with pink frilly edges. The pope over the bed was Leo XIII. The snowflakes kept touching the bare windowpanes like kittens' paws trying to get in. When she began on the questions, he wished he had not come.

"How's Bid?" she called out from the kitchen.

"Bid? My mother? Oh, well, of course, I mean to say— My mother? Oh, she's grand, Auntie! Never better. For her age, of course, that is. Fine, fine out! Just like yourself. Only for the touch of the old rheumatism now and again."

"Go on, tell me about all of them. How's Uncle Matty? And how's Cis? When were you down in Ballyroche last? But, sure, it's all changed now, I suppose, with electric light and everything up to date? And I suppose the old pony and trap is gone years ago? It was only last night I was thinking of Mikey Clancy the postman." She came in, planking down the plates, an iced Christmas cake, the coffeepot. "Go on! You're telling me nothing."

She stood over him, waiting, her pale eyes wide, her mouth stretched. He said:

"My Uncle Matty? Oh, well, of course, now, he's not as young as he was. But I saw him there last year. He was looking fine. Fine out. I'd be inclined to say he'd be a bit stooped. But in great form. For his age, that is."

"Sit in. Eat up. Eat up. Don't mind me. He has a big family now, no doubt?"

"A family? Naturally! There's Tom. And there's Kitty, that's my Aunt Kitty, it is Kitty, isn't it, yes, my Auntie Kitty. And— God, I can't remember the half of them."

She shoved the hamburgers toward him. She made him pour the coffee and tell her if he liked it. She told him he was a bad reporter.

"Tell me all about the old place!"

He stuffed his mouth to give him time to think.

"They have twenty-one cows. Holsteins. The black and white chaps. And a red barn. And a shelter belt of pines. 'Tis lovely there now to see the wind in the trees, and when the night falls, the way the lighthouse starts winking at you, and—"

"What lighthouse?" She glared at him. She drew back from him. "Are ye daft? What are you dreaming about? Is it a lighthouse in the middle of the County Limerick?"

"There is a lighthouse! I saw it in the harbor!"

But he suddenly remembered that where he had seen it was in a toyshop on Eighth Avenue, with a farm beyond it and a red barn and small cows, and a train going round and round it all.

"Harbor, Matty? Are ye out of your senses?"

"I saw it with my own two eyes."

Her eyes were like marbles. Suddenly she leaned over like a willow—just the way his mother used to lean over—and laughed and laughed.

"I know what you're talking about now. The lighthouse on the Shannon! Lord save us, how many times did I see it at night from the hill of Ballingarry! But there's no harbor, Matty."

"There's the harbor at Foynes!"

"Oh, for God's sake!" she cried. "That's miles and miles and miles away. 'Tis and twenty miles away! And where could you see any train, day or night, from anywhere at all near Ballyroche?"

They argued it hither and over until she suddenly found that the coffee was gone cold and rushed away with the pot to the kitchen. Even there she kept up the argument, calling out that certainly, you could see Moneygay Castle, and the turn of the River Deel on a fine day, but no train, and then she went on about the stepping-stones over the river, and came back bubbling about Normoyle's bull that chased them across the dry river, one hot summer's day—

He said:

"Auntie! Why the hell did you never write home?"

"Not even once?" she said, with a crooked smile like a bold child.

"Not a sight nor a sound of you from the day you left Bally-roche, as my mother used to say, no more than if the earth swallowed you. You're a nice one!"

"Eat up!" she commanded him, with a little laugh and a tap on his wrist.

"Did you always live here, Auntie Lily?"

She sat down and put her face between her palms with her elbows on the table and looked at him.

"Here? Well, no— That is to say, no! My husband and me had a house of our very own over in East Fifty-eight. He did very well for himself. He was quite a rich man when he died. A big jeweler. When he was killed in an airplane crash five years ago, he left me very well off. But sure I didn't need a house of my own and I had lots of friends in Brooklyn, so I came to live here."

"Fine! What more do you want, that is for a lone woman! No family?"

"I have my son. But he's married, to a Pole, they'll be over here first thing tomorrow morning to take me off to spend Christmas with them. They have an apartment on Riverside Drive. He is the manager of a big department store, Macy's on Flatbush Avenue. But tell me about Bid's children. You must have lots of brothers and sisters. Where are you going from here? Back to Ireland? To Limerick? To Ballyroche?"

He laughed.

"Where else would I go? Our next trip we hit the port of London. I'll be back like an arrow to Ballyroche. They'll be delighted to hear I met you. They'll be asking me all sorts of questions about you. Tell me more about your son, Auntie. Has he a family?"

"My son? Well, my son's name is Thomas. His wife's name is
Catherine. She is very beautiful. She has means of her own. They
are very happy. He is very well off. He's in charge of a big store,
Sears, Roebuck on Bedford Avenue. Oh, a fine boy. Fine out! As
you say. Fine out. He has three children. There's Cissy, and Matty.
And—"

Her voice faltered. When she closed her eyes, he saw how old she
was. She rose and from the bottom drawer of a chest of drawers she
pulled out a photograph album. She laid it in front of him and sat
back opposite him.

"That is my boy."

When he said he was like her, she said he was very like his father. Maxer said that he often heard that her husband was a most
handsome man.

"Have you a picture of him?"

She drew the picture of her son towards her and looked down at
it.

"Tell me more about Ballyroche," she cried.

As he started into a long description of a harvest home, he saw
her eyes close again, and her breath came more heavily and he felt
that she was not hearing a word he said. Then, suddenly, her palm
slapped down on the picture of the young man, and he knew that
she was not heeding him any more than if he wasn't there. Her fingers closed on the pasteboard. She shied it wildly across the room,
where it struck the glass of the window flat on, hesitated, and slid
to the ground. Maxer saw snowflakes melting as often as they
touched the pane. When he looked back at her, she was leaning
across the table, one white lock down over one eye, her yellow teeth
bared.

"You spy!" She spat at him. "You came from them! To spy on
me!"

"I came from friendliness."

"Or was it for a ha'porth of look-about? Well, you can go back
to Ballyroche and tell 'em whatever you like. Tell 'em I'm starv-
ing if that'll please 'em, the mean, miserable, lousy set that never
gave a damn about me from the day I left 'em. For forty years my
own sister, your mother, never wrote one line to say—"

"You know damn well she'd have done anything for you if she

only knew where you were. Her heart was stuck in you. The two
of you were inside one another's pockets. My God, she was forever
talking and talking about you. Morning, noon, and night—"

She shouted at him across the table.

"I wrote six letters—"

"She never got them."

"I registered two of them."

"Nobody ever got a line from you, or about you, only for the
one letter from the priest that married you to say you were well
and happy."

"What he wrote was that I was down and out. I saw the letter. I
let him send it. That Wop left me flat in this city with my baby. I
wrote to everybody—my mother, my father, to Bid after she was
your mother and had a home of her own. I had to work every day
of my life. I worked today. I'll work tomorrow. If you want to
know what I do, I clean out offices. I worked to bring up my son,
and what did he do? Walked out on me with that Polack of his and
that was the last I saw of him, or her, or any human being belonging to me until I saw you. Tell them every word of it. They'll love
it!"

Maxer got up and went over slowly to the bed for his jacket. As
he buttoned it, he looked at her glaring at him across the table.
Then he looked away from her at the snowflakes feeling the win-
dowpane and dying there. He said quietly:

"They're all dead. As for Limerick—I haven't been back to Ireland for eight years. When my mum died, my father got married
again. I ran away to sea when I was sixteen."

He took his cap. When he was at the door, he heard a chair fall
and then she was at his side, holding his arm, whispering gently to
him:

"Don't go away, Matty." Her pallid eyes were flooded. "For
God's sake, don't leave me alone with them on Christmas Eve!"

Maxer stared at her. Her lips were wavering as if a wind were
blowing over them. She had the face of a frightened girl. He threw
his cap on the bed and went over and sat down beside it. While he
sat there like a big baboon, with his hands between his knees,
looking at the snowflakes, she raced into the kitchen to put on the
kettle for rum punch. It was a long while before she brought in
the two big glasses of punch, with orange sliced in them, and

brown sugar like drowned sand at the base of them. When she held them out to him, he looked first at them, and then at her, so timid, so pleading, and he began to laugh and laugh—a laugh that he choked by covering his eyes with his hands.

"Damn ye!" he groaned into his hands. "I was better off drunk."

She sat beside him on the bed. He looked up. He took one of the glasses and touched hers with it.

"Here's to poor Lily!" he smiled.

She fondled his free hand.

"Lovie, tell me this one thing and tell me true. Did she really and truly talk about me? Or was that all lies too?"

"She'd be crying rain down when she'd be talking about you. She was always and ever talking about you. She was mad about you."

She sighed a long sigh.

"For years I couldn't understand it. But when my boy left me for that Polack, I understood it. I guess Bid had a tough time bringing you all up. And there's no one more hard in all the world than a mother when she's thinking of her own. I'm glad she talked about me. It's better than nothing."

They sat there on the bed talking and talking. She made more punch, and then more, and in the end they finished the bottle between them, talking about everybody either of them had known in or within miles of the County Limerick. They fixed to spend Christmas Day together, and have Christmas dinner downtown, and maybe go to a picture, and then come back and talk some more.

Every time Maxer comes to New York, he rings her number. He can hardly breathe until he hears her voice saying, "Hello, Matty." They go on the town then and have dinner, always at some place with an Irish name, or a green neon shamrock above the door, and then they go to a movie or a show, and then come back to her room to have a drink and a talk about his last voyage, or the picture postcards he sent her, his latest bits and scraps of the news about the Shannon shore. They always get first-class service in restaurants, although Maxer never noticed it until the night a waiter said, "And what's Mom having?" at which she gave him a slow wink out of her pale Limerick eyes and a slow, wide, lover's smile.

Peasants

By Frank O'Connor

When Michael John Cronin stole the funds of the Carrick-nabreena Hurling, Football and Temperance Association, commonly called the Club, everyone said: "Devil's cure to him!" " 'Tis the price of him!" "Kind father for him!" "What did I tell you?" and the rest of the things people say when an acquaintance has got what is coming to him.

And not only Michael John but the whole Cronin family, seed, breed and generation, came in for it; there wasn't one of them for twenty miles round or a hundred years back but his deeds and sayings were remembered and examined by the light of this fresh scandal. Michael John's father (the heavens be his bed!) was a drunkard who beat his wife, and his father before him a land-grabber. Then there was an uncle or grand-uncle who had been a policeman and taken a hand in the bloody work at Mitchelstown long ago, and an unmarried sister of the same whose good name it would by all accounts have needed a regiment of husbands to restore. It was a grand shaking-up the Cronins got altogether, and anyone who had a grudge in for them, even if it was no more than a thirty-third cousin, had rare sport, dropping a friendly word about it and saying how sorry he was for the poor mother till he had the blood lighting in the Cronin eyes.

There was only one thing for them to do with Michael John; that was to send him to America and let the thing blow over, and that, no doubt, is what they would have done but for a certain unpleasant and extraordinary incident.

Father Crowley, the parish priest, was chairman of the committee. He was a remarkable man, even in appearance: tall, powerfully built, but very stooped, with shrewd, loveless eyes that rarely softened to anyone except two or three old people. He was a strange man, well on in years, noted for his strong political views, which never happened to coincide with those of any party, and as obstinate as the devil himself. Now what should Father Crowley do but try to force the committee to prosecute Michael John?

The committee were all religious men who up to this had never

as much as dared to question the judgments of a man of God: yes,
faith, and if the priest had been a bully, which to give him his due
he wasn't, he might have danced a jig on their backs and they
wouldn't have complained. But a man has principles, and the like
of this had never been heard of in the parish before. What? Put
the police on a boy and he in trouble?

One by one the committee spoke up and said so. "But he did
wrong," said Father Crowley, thumping the table. "He did wrong
and he should be punished."

"Maybe so, Father," said Con Norton, the vice-chairman, who
acted as spokesman. "Maybe you're right, but you wouldn't say his
poor mother should be punished too and she a widow-woman?"

"True for you!" chorused the others.

"Serve his mother right!" said the priest shortly. "There's none
of you but knows better than I do the way that young man was
brought up. He's a rogue and his mother is a fool. Why didn't she
beat Christian principles into him when she had him on her
knee?"

"That might be, too," Norton agreed mildly. "I wouldn't say
but you're right, but is that any reason his Uncle Peter should be
punished?"

"Or his Uncle Dan?" asked another.

"Or his cousins, the Dwyers, that keep the little shop in Lissna-
carriga, as decent a living family as there is in County Cork?"
asked a fourth.

"No, Father," said Norton, "the argument is against you."

"Is it indeed?" exclaimed the priest, growing cross. "Is it so?
What the devil has it to do with his Uncle Dan or his Uncle
James? What are ye talking about? What punishment is it to them,
will ye tell me that? Ye'll be telling me next 'tis a punishment to
me and I a child of Adam like himself."

"Wisha now, Father," asked Norton incredulously, "do you
mean 'tis no punishment to them having one of their own blood
made a public show? Is it mad you think we are? Maybe 'tis a thing
you'd like done to yourself?"

"There was none of my family ever a thief," replied Father
Crowley shortly.

"Begor, we don't know whether there was or not," snapped a
little man called Daly, a hot-tempered character from the hills.

"Easy, now! Easy, Phil!" said Norton warningly.

"What do you mean by that?" asked Father Crowley, rising and grabbing his hat and stick.

"What I mean," said Daly, blazing up, "is that I won't sit here and listen to insinuations about my native place from any foreigner. There are as many rogues and thieves and vagabonds and liars in Cullough as ever there were in Carricknabreena—ay, begod, and more, and bigger! That's what I mean."

"No, no, no, no," Norton said soothingly. "That's not what he means at all, Father. We don't want any bad blood between Cullough and Carricknabreena. What he means is that the Crowleys may be a fine substantial family in their own country, but that's fifteen long miles away, and this isn't their country, and the Cronins are neighbors of ours since the dawn of history and time, and 'twould be a very queer thing if at this hour we handed one of them over to the police. . . . And now, listen to me, Father," he went on, forgetting his role of pacificator and hitting the table as hard as the rest, "if a cow of mine got sick in the morning, 'tisn't a Cremin or a Crowley I'd be asking for help, and damn the bit of use 'twould be to me if I did. And everyone knows I'm no enemy of the Church but a respectable farmer that pays his dues and goes to his duties regularly."

"True for you! True for you!" agreed the committee.

"I don't give a snap of my finger what you are," retorted the priest. "And now listen to me, Con Norton. I bear young Cronin no grudge, which is more than some of you can say, but I know my duty and I'll do it in spite of the lot of you."

He stood at the door and looked back. They were gazing blankly at one another, not knowing what to say to such an impossible man. He shook his fist at them.

"Ye all know me," he said. "Ye know that all my life I'm fighting the long-tailed families. Now, with the help of God, I'll shorten the tail of one of them."

Father Crowley's threat frightened them. They knew he was an obstinate man and had spent his time attacking what he called the "corruption" of councils and committees, which was all very well as long as it happened outside your own parish. They dared not oppose him openly because he knew too much about all of them and, in public at least, had a lacerating tongue. The solution they favored was a tactful one. They formed themselves into a Michael John Cronin Fund Committee and canvassed the parishioners for subscriptions to pay off what Michael John had stolen. Regretfully they decided that Father Crowley would hardly countenance a football match for the purpose.

Then with the defaulting treasurer, who wore a suitably contrite air, they marched up to the presbytery. Father Cowley was at his dinner but he told the housekeeper to show them in. He looked up in astonishment as his dining room filled with the seven committeemen, pushing before them the cowed Michael John.

"Who the blazes are ye?" he asked, glaring at them over the lamp.

"We're the Club Committee, Father," replied Norton.

"Oh, are ye?"

"And this is the treasurer—the ex-treasurer, I should say."

"I won't pretend I'm glad to see him," said Father Crowley grimly.

"He came to say he's sorry, Father," went on Norton. "He is sorry, and that's as true as God, and I'll tell you no lie—" Norton made two steps forward and in a dramatic silence laid a heap of notes and silver on the table.

"What's that?" asked Father Crowley.

"The money, Father. 'Tis all paid back now and there's nothing more between us. Any little crossness there was, we'll say no more about it, in the name of God."

The priest looked at the money and then at Norton.

"Con," he said, "you'd better keep the soft word for the judge. Maybe he'll think more of it than I do."

"The judge, Father?"

"Ay, Con, the judge."

There was a long silence. The committee stood with open mouths, unable to believe it.

"And is that what you're doing to us, Father?" asked Norton in a trembling voice. "After all the years, and all we done for you, is it you're going to show us up before the whole country as a lot of robbers?"

"Ah, ye idiots, I'm not showing ye up."

"You are then, Father, and you're showing up every man, woman, and child in the parish," said Norton. "And mark my words, 'twon't be forgotten for you."

The following Sunday Father Crowley spoke of the matter from the altar. He spoke for a full half hour without a trace of emotion on his grim old face, but his sermon was one long, venomous denunciation of the "long-tailed families" who, according to him, were the ruination of the country and made a mockery of truth, justice, and charity. He was, as his congregation agreed, a shockingly obstinate old man who never knew when he was in the wrong.

After Mass he was visited in his sacristy by the committee. He gave Norton a terrible look from under his shaggy eyebrows, which made that respectable farmer flinch.

"Father," Norton said appealingly, "we only want one word with you. One word and then we'll go. You're a hard character, and you said some bitter things to us this morning; things we never deserved from you. But we're quiet, peaceable poor men and we don't want to cross you."

Father Crowley made a sound like a snort.

"We came to make a bargain with you, Father," said Norton, beginning to smile.

"A bargain?"

"We'll say no more about the whole business if you'll do one little thing—just one little thing—to oblige us."

"The bargain!" the priest said impatiently. "What's the bargain?"

"We'll leave the matter drop for good and all if you'll give the boy a character."

"Yes, Father," cried the committee in chorus. "Give him a character! Give him a character!"

"Give him a what?" cried the priest.

"Give him a character, Father, for the love of God," said Norton emotionally. "If you speak up for him, the judge will leave him off and there'll be no stain on the parish."

"Is it out of your minds you are, you half-witted angashores?" asked Father Crowley, his face suffused with blood, his head trembling. "Here am I all these years preaching to ye about decency and justice and truth and ye no more understand me than that wall there. Is it the way ye want me to perjure myself? Is it the way ye want me to tell a damned lie with the name of Almighty God on my lips? Answer me, is it?"

"Ah, what perjure!" Norton replied wearily. "Sure, can't you say a few words for the boy? No one is asking you to say much. What harm will it do you to tell the judge he's an honest, good-living, upright lad, and that he took the money without meaning any harm?"

"My God!" muttered the priest, running his hands distractedly through his grey hair. "There's no talking to ye, no talking to ye, ye lot of sheep!"

When he was gone the committeemen turned and looked at one another in bewilderment.

"That man is a terrible trial," said one.

"He's a tyrant," said Daly vindictively.

"He is, indeed," sighed Norton, scratching his head. "But in God's holy name, boys, before we do anything, we'll give him one more chance."

That evening when he was at his tea, the committeemen called again. This time they looked very spruce, businesslike, and independent. Father Crowley glared at them.

"Are ye back?" he asked bitterly. "I was thinking ye would be. I declare to my goodness, I'm sick of ye and yeer old committee."

"Oh, we're not the committee, Father," said Norton stiffly.

"Ye're not?"

"We're not."

"All I can say is, ye look mighty like it. And, if I'm not being impertinent, who the deuce are ye?"

"We're a deputation, Father."

"Oh, a deputation! Fancy that, now. And a deputation from what?"

"A deputation from the parish, Father. Now, maybe you'll listen to us."

"Oh, go on! I'm listening, I'm listening."

"Well now, 'tis like this, Father," said Norton, dropping his airs and graces and leaning against the table. " 'Tis about that little business this morning. Now, Father, maybe you don't understand us and we don't understand you. There's a lot of misunderstanding in the world today, Father. But we're quiet simple poor men that want to do the best we can for everybody, and a few words or a few pounds wouldn't stand in our way. Now, do you follow me?"

"I declare," said Father Crowley, resting his elbows on the table, "I don't know whether I do or not."

"Well, 'tis like this, Father. We don't want any blame on the parish or on the Cronins, and you're the one man that can save us. Now all we ask of you is to give the boy a character—"

"Yes, Father," interrupted the chorus, "give him a character! Give him a character!"

"Give him a character, Father, and you won't be troubled by him again. Don't say no to me now till you hear what I have to say. We won't ask you to go next, nigh or near the court. You have pen and ink beside you and one couple of lines is all you need write. When 'tis over you can hand Michael John his ticket to America and tell him not to show his face in Carricknabreena again. There's the price of his ticket, Father," he added, clapping a bundle of notes on the table. "The Cronins themselves made it up and we have his mother's word and his own word that he'll clear out the minute 'tis all over."

"He can go to pot," retorted the priest. "What is it to me where he goes?"

"Now, Father, can't you be patient?" Norton asked reproachfully. "Can't you let me finish what I'm saying? We know 'tis no advantage to you, and that's the very thing we came to talk about. Now, supposing—just supposing for the sake of argument—that you do what we say, there's a few of us here, and between us, we'd raise whatever little contribution to the parish fund you'd think would be reasonable to cover the expense and trouble to yourself. Now do you follow me?"

"Con Norton," said Father Crowley, rising and holding the edge of the table, "I follow you. This morning it was perjury, and now 'tis bribery, and the Lord knows what 'twill be next. I see I've been wasting my breath. . . . And I see too," he added savagely, leaning across the table towards them, "a pedigree bull would be more use to ye than a priest."

"What do you mean by that, Father?" asked Norton in a low voice.

"What I say."

"And that's a saying that will be remembered for you the longest day you live," hissed Norton, leaning towards him till they were glaring at one another over the table.

"A bull," gasped Father Crowley. "Not a priest."

" 'Twill be remembered."

"Will it? Then remember this too. I'm an old man now. I'm forty years a priest, and I'm not a priest for the money or power or glory of it, like others I know. I gave the best that was in me— maybe 'twasn't much but 'twas more than many a better man would give, and at the end of my days—" lowering his voice to a whisper he searched them with his terrible eyes—"at the end of my days, if I did a wrong thing, or a bad thing, or an unjust thing, there isn't man or woman in this parish that would brave me to my face and call me a villain. And isn't that a poor story for an old man that tried to be a good priest?" His voice changed again and he raised his head defiantly. "Now get out before I kick you out!"

And true to his word and character not one word did he say in Michael John's favor the day of the trial, no more than if he was a black. Three months Michael John got and by all accounts he got off light.

He was a changed man when he came out of jail, down-cast and dark in himself. Everyone was sorry for him, and people who had never spoken to him before spoke to him then. To all of them he said modestly: "I'm very grateful to you, friend, for overlooking my misfortune." As he wouldn't go to America, the committee made another whip-round and between what they had collected before and what the Cronins had made up to send him to America, he found himself with enough to open a small shop. Then he got a job in the County Council, and an agency for some shipping company, till at last he was able to buy a public house.

As for Father Crowley, till he was shifted twelve months after, he never did a day's good in the parish. The dues went down and the presents went down, and people with money to spend on Masses took it fifty miles away sooner than leave it to him. They said it broke his heart.

He has left unpleasant memories behind him. Only for him, people say, Michael John would be in America now. Only for him he would never have married a girl with money, or had it to lend to poor people in the hard times, or ever sucked the blood of Christians. For, as an old man said to me of him: "A robber he is and was, and a grabber like his grandfather before him, and an

enemy of the people like his uncle, the policeman; and though
some say he'll dip his hand where he dipped it before, for myself
I have no hope unless the mercy of God would send us another
Moses or Brian Boru to cast him down and hammer him in the
dust."

A Persian Tale

By Lynn Doyle

The wee schoolmaster, bein' inclined to a dhrop of whisky, an' not
gettin' any great encouragement from the ould sister to take it in
his own house, was in the habit of dhroppin' in til Michael
Casshidy's pub most nights; an' to keep the sister from thinkin'
long when he was away, he hit on the notion of gettin' her a pet of
some kind.

Now, though it's mortal hard to explain why, there's a sthrong
fellow feelin' between a cat an' an ould maid; an' afther goin'
round as many bastes as would ha' filled a zoo she fixed her affec-
tion on a big cat with a coat on it like a sheep, that she called a
persian, a conceited useless baste that would sit washin' an' polish-
in' at itself with the mice runnin' over it.

But ye never seen womankind yet that wasn't fond of some useless bein', cat or man; an' for many a long day Paddy Shaw, as she
called him, was the comfort of her heart.

In the end, between the laziness an' him bein' a greedy gorb of
an animal, Paddy grew to a most lamentable size an' could hardly
move about; an' Miss MacDermott got uneasy about him. The
master said the only thing for him was whisky, an', troth, himself
was well experienced in the same commodity.

"Whisky," sez the masther, "is the universal remedy for the
male kind. The female sex seems to get on without it in a most
remarkable way, but for their lords an' masters there's no medicine to be compared with it."

Now I may tell ye Miss MacDermott had no such notion of the
virtues of whisky as the wee man had—an' small wondher; for it
was him had all the fun out of what whisky was dhrunk in the

MacDermott family, an' herself all the bother. But she got terrible fond of the cat, and would ha' done near anythin' to bring it to itself again, so she give in to the masther's notion, an' even went the length of promisin' to pay for any whisky he bought while the cure was goin' on.

The wee man was terribly pleased about it. He had been what you'd know off color for a while before; but he brightened up straight away. At first I thought it was on account of him gettin' his whisky on the cheap, an', mind ye, that meant somethin'; but all the same it didn't explain why he was takin' so much intherest in the cat. At last he let out the reason himself.

"Ye'll think it strange, Pat," sez he, "comin' from a man like myself that has been singin' the praises of whisky these twenty-five years an' more; but the truth is, a kind of a doubt about the virtues of the immortal liquor has been risin' in my mind this while past."

"In the name of goodness, masther," sez I, "what has put that notion in your head?"

"It was partly put there by the doctor, that has lattherly been usin' some very alarmin' classical terms in connection with my liver, an' partly by the parish priest, a man," sez the masther, blinkin' at me a bit droll, "for whose opinion I have a great deal of respect, not only from his sacred callin', but in his capacity as manager of the Ballygullion National School.

"Now I may tell ye, Pat," went on the wee man, "that till lately any misgivin' the pair of them was able to stir up was always scatthered like mornin' mist before the third half-glass of Michael's special. But what's worst of all," sez he, "for this while past there has been a thraitor in an' about the middle button of my waistcoat basely suggestin' that the effects of our national beverage is not just as beneficent on the system as has been supposed."

"Ye're never thinkin' of givin' up the whisky altogether, masther?" sez I.

"I've been meditatin' it seriously for some time, Pat," sez he, "without gettin' much further than that. But I see some chance of comin' to a decision now that I've hit on the great an' scientific notion of thryin' the effects of a dhrop on the cat."

"How in the name of goodness is that goin' to help ye?" sez I.

"It's as simple as two-times tables," sez he. "The only difficulty i

had was in the adjustin' of what you might call the alcoholic val-
ues between me an' the animal."

"I don't quite follow ye there," sez I.

"Wait," sez he, "an' I'll explain. I suppose you're aware that the
average life of a man is generally taken to be about seventy
years?"

"I'm told they lived a deal longer in ould times, masther," sez I.
"Did they take a sup then, do ye think?"

"It's undherstood, Pat," sez the masther, "that they took a deal
of dhrink before the Flood; an' with all that they lived, some of
them, to be near a thousand. It's a very consolin' bit of history, for
if it proves anythin' at all it's that too much water is just as bad as
too much whisky; an' the case of Noah, though he made his name
by water, shows that he didn't think a heap of it as a dhrink. However, seventy years is our average these times, an' seventy years is
all a reasonable bein' need aim at.

"Now, as ye know, I'm just fifty-five. If I can stand it another
fifteen years, I've had my share, an' barrin' maybe in the matther
of whisky, I've never wanted more than my share. Well, the average life of a cat bein', say, fourteen years, it follows that the vitality
of the beast is as five to one compared with a man. Ye got the
length of proportion at school, Pat, didn't ye?"

"I did," sez I, "afther doin' a lot of damage among canes."

"Very well," sez the masther, "you'll see at once that if the cat
can stand three years' whisky, I can stand fifteen, an' that's all I
want."

"How long is he at it now?" sez I. "An' how is he doin'?"

"He's only six or eight weeks at it yet," sez the masther, "an' except in the matther of hair, where the beast is undoubtedly losin'
ground, he's doin' beyond my wildest dhreams. Instead of bein'
what he used to be, an idle useless drone of a crather, he's skippin'
about like a young one, an' killin' mice—aye, an' even rats—like a
terrier. I've noticed the same thing with myself, many a time.
There I'll be in the school as heavy as a dunce, with even vulgar
fractions a bother to me; an' before I've been in Michael's half an
hour, I can do repeatin' decimals in my head. I admit, mind ye,
that the doctor had me a bit daunted a while back; but the out-
come of this experiment has been very reassurin'. For anythin'
plain an' straightforward like colic or the worms I'll agree with

every old woman in the neighborhood that Dr. Dickson has his
points; but when he takes it upon him to lay down how far alcohol
is beneficial to the human system, the man goes clean beyond his
depth."

An' away trots the wee man up the street with the tall hat
cocked over his right eye, an' him whistlin'.

It was a month or more before I met the masther again, an'
when I did he was very serious-lookin'.

"Ye find me very low in spirits, Pat," sez he, noticin' my look.
"The truth is, I'm a bit bothered by the latest results of the inves-
tigations at present bein' conducted by myself an' that long-haired
divil of a cat. I've been observin' lately that although he's bustlin'
about fussy enough afther the mice, when ye look into results, he's
missin' a deal more than he's catchin'. An' when I came to apply
this observation to my own case, an' put down on paper the sums I
told you I could do so well in my head when I was sittin' in Michael's, I found out that though the decimals was repeatin' plenty,
the divil a very much of it was the truth. I'm still very far from
bein' convinced that whisky isn't good for the brains, mind ye,
Pat; but if the other notion should have come into the head of the
P.P. it would be no great advantage to one MacDermott."

"How could it, masther," sez I, "an' you teachin' like a professor
this half a lifetime?"

"There's a little circumstance that has given me some uneasiness
on the subject all the same," sez the masther. "The sister at home
there, though not perhaps in the same scientific way, takes near as
much intherest in Paddy as I do myself, but that hasn't kept her
from complainin' about the mice a good deal this last while; an'
here about a week ago hasn't she installed a lump of a tortoiseshell
kitten as what our friends the Presbyterians would call 'assistant
an' successor.' I never thought anythin' of it till comin' down the
road the next mornin' doesn't Father Richard stop me an' suggest
that I should appoint big Danny Burke a monitor. He put it to me
that he was thinkin' about my health, an' tryin' to make my work
a bit easier; but do you know, Pat," sez the wee man, with the ould
comical cock of his eyebrow, "I wouldn't be surprised if there was
as Presbyterian a kind of idea at the back of his head as a parish
priest could credibly be supposed to have.

"Come away on down to Michael's," sez he, "an' I'll do a bit of experimentin' on myself; for I'm in poor heart this minit."

About the third wee drop out of Michael's black bottle, he begins to revive.

"Wine, Pat," sez he, "maketh glad the heart of man. We have
the word of a very wise one on that; an' ye may swear he didn't
learn it at second hand. An' I'll go bail if he'd lived in the time of
whisky he'd ha' said the same about that too. If I was only sure it
would keep on doin' it, it's a short life an' a merry one I'd go in
for, let the docthor say what he likes. But a kind of doubt is creepin' on me even about the fun part of it. It's not lastin' with the
cat."

"Ye told me he was very lively at the first," sez I.

"At the beginnin', Pat," sez the masther, "when I'd got him to
the right mixture the noble animal used to go about the house
with a smile playin' round his whiskers like the sun on a row of
pint bottles. But lattherly his spirits has been goin' down in a way
that's not at all encouragin', an' this last week or two ye could
hardly live in the house with him."

"Ye should give him less, masther," sez I.

"I can't," sez he. "He's carnaptious enough as it is; an' if I dock
him of one spoonful of his allowance he gets clean unbearable.
He's stopped chasin' his tail, too," sez the wee man, "the only bit
of light-heartedness he had left. I've been thryin' to persuade myself that it's through him not takin' the same intherest in it now
that most of the hair is gone; but still it's a bad sign.

"In my opinion his intellect is failin'. He's beginnin' to have de-
lusions. Every now an' then he'll jump out intil the middle of the
kitchen floor as if he was killin' things. I believe it's mice he's
seein'. It's only the other night he made a wicked lepp at somethin' he thought he seen, an' near brained himself on the door of
the oven.

"The wholly all of it is, Pat, the beast is rangin' himself most
damnably on the side of the P.P. I'm beginnin' to see a melancholy prospect of spring water openin' before me. The divil take
all cats," sez he, rappin' on the table for another dhrink; "for this
long-haired curiosity is sthrikin' at the whole foundations of my
existence."

"I'll tell you what I'll do, masther," sez I; "I'll dhrop round the
morrow night an' have a look at him. Maybe I could find out

somethin' else the matter with him than the dhrink."

"If ye can, Pat," sez the wee man, shakin' me by the hand, "I'll put the whole resources of Michael's bar at your disposal, an' carry ye home myself. But I misdoubt when ye clap eyes on the dirty brute ye'll come to the same dismal conclusion about him as myself. Good night now, an' don't forget what ye said."

I was just danderin' quietly home to shire my head a bit before encountherin' the wife, when who should come up behind me but Docthor Dickson. Divil a word of a good night or anythin' else he said, but just into me like a day's work.

"I seen ye comin' out of the public house with the masther, Murphy," sez he. "Do ye know that you're assistin' that decent foolish wee body to commit suicide?"

"Bless my soul, docthor," sez I, "ye don't mean to say it's as bad as that with him."

"I do then," sez he, very short, "the man's liver is nearly rotted away with the poison he's been puttin' into him these twenty years, with you an' the like of ye eggin' him on. Ye should be ashamed of yourself, Murphy. I thought betther of ye than that."

"Ye may think betther than that of me still, docthor," sez I. "I know he's been doin' himself harm this long time. But he's in the notion of quittin' it, an' I'm goin' up the morrow night to help him in the same direction."

For I may tell ye that was what was in my head when I offered to go up. An' with that I told him all about the cat.

The docthor turned away his head as I was tellin' him; but I could see the shouldhers of him shakin.'

"There's no doubt," sez he at the last, "whether it's the whisky does it for him or not, he's a comical wee crather. An' it would be doin' a kindness to the whole counthryside as well as himself if we could bring him round again."

"An' can it be done yet, docthor?" sez I.

"If he would only stop now," sez he, "I believe I could save the liver yet, or at any rate bits of it. Let me think a minit. Do you really believe, Pat," sez he, afther a bit, "he's in earnest over this business of the cat?"

"I do," sez I. "If the liquor kills the cat, I believe he'll make a big stagger at stoppin' it himself."

"Very well," sez the docthor, "would ye take a cat's life to save a man's?"

"If the wee masther is as bad as ye say—an' I don't doubt ye over it—short of a hangin' matther I'm on for anything," sez I.

"It's well said," sez the docthor. "Then come round by my surgery the morrow night an' I'll give ye a bottle of something to dhrop in the cat's dhrink that'll make a quick an' easy end of him. And if the wee man shows no sign of takin' a lesson by it, ye might near as well give him the rest of the bottle himself; for to be plain with ye," sez the docthor, very serious-lookin', "if he doesn't soon alther his way of goin', he's likely to make a poor enough end of it."

When I looked at the cat the next night, the docthor's words came into my mind, an' troth they were true. The divil a more miserable anatomy of a bein' ye ever looked at in your life. From a big, lazy, sonsy-looking animal with a fleece on him like a Shrop ram he was gathered into a wee miserable dwinlin' crather with not as much hair on him as would ha' made a shavin' brush. I don't mind tellin' ye that the look of him gave my own thoughts a twist in the direction of spring water. For it come into my head that bad an' all as it was for the cat himself, it would ha' been a deal worse if he'd had a wife an' family dependin' on him.

"If the whisky has done that on him, masther," sez I, "he's no great advertisement for it."

"There's no denyin' that he's gettin' to be a very uncomfortable-lookin' crony to take a dhrink along with," sez the masther, blinkin' at him very sober. "If ye can find nothing' else the matther with him, I misdoubt the takin's of Michael Casshidy's bar is goin' down one of these days with a wallop. But wait till ye see the change on him when he gets a sup. Here, Paddy, Paddy," sez he, an' reaches down a saucer.

Sure enough there was a wondherful change come on the brute the minit he seen it. Up went the ould motheaten tail over his back as if he was a kitten again; and though ye'd ha' thought by the look of him a minit before he wouldn't have budged from where he was lyin' if the house was on fire, he was at the saucer in two lepps an' over the whiskers in it before it was well on the floor.

"It's a horrid pity, Pat," sez the masther, "that any doubt of the virtues of the stuff should be creepin' on the cowld stomachs of the present generation; for there's no denyin' it's the great medicine.

Look at the poor benighted crather that hasn't near the intelligence an' none of the book learnin' of a man like me, an' even himself would hardly lift his head from the saucer if ye tould him the next minit was to be his last."

There was more truth in the wee man's words than he knowed. As he went into the panthry for two glasses, I emptied the doctor's bottle into the saucer. The cat took about three more laps at it, shook his head, give back a step, an' rolled on the floor.

"Masther," I shouts, "masther! come here quick. The cat's gone."

An' sure enough before the masther got the length of where he was lyin', poor Paddy was as dead as Hecthor.

The masther straightened himself up afther a long look at him, went over to the dhresser where he had a gallon jar sittin', an' poured himself out a rozener that if the cat had got it would ha' saved Doctor Dickson the expense of a bottle. I could hear the tumbler rattlin' again his teeth as the stuff went down. When he turned round, he was very white an' washy-lookin'.

"I'm sorry about the brute, Pat," sez he, afther a minit or two. "Not because he's dead; for the way things was goin' with him, it was in my mind to step down to the docthor's one of these nights an' give him a speedy release; but it's at the back of my head that maybe I didn't give him fair play. Well, it's past prayin' for now, like many another thing, an' we'll let it go. First of all, by way of carryin' out the funeral customs of this island, an' next, to celebrate his memory, we'll just have a thimbleful apiece."

"I'll put this stuff out of the road first," thinks I to myself, liftin' the saucer an' throwin' the contents of it in the fire.

When I looked at the wee masther, he was layin' down his glass. There was just what ye'd know of color come into his face, an' when he spoke it was the ould masther again.

"It's three months, Pat," sez he, "since the late lamented an' myself embarked on this experiment, an' five times three is fifteen. That gives me till October is a year. I'll turn it over in my mind for a minit or two, an' in the meantime we'll carry out a great an' appropriate notion that came into my head as I watched ye there pourin' that saucerful of good dhrink on the fire.

"When I had made up my accounts to finish off my deceased unfortunate colleague, I was greatly bothered about the question of his last rites. To give him Christian burial was clean out of the question; for as far as I could see there was no hope of him dyin' in a state of grace. Then takin' into account that the ould Egyptians considhered the cat a sacred animal, I thought of thryin' their way of it; but the divil a thing I knowed about embalmin'—which was the way they done it—no more than my grandmother; an' to pickle the beast would be to make a very scaresome-lookin' corpse of him. But watchin' ye just now, as I said, it come on me like a flash that we'd pay him our last respects in the ancient Roman manner."

"An' what else would that be but Christian burial, masther?" sez I.

"It's another kind of Romans that's in my mind, Pat," sez he, "an older branch of the family. Away out to the coal-hole an' bring a good armful of sticks an' shavin's to the foot of the garden, an' I'll show ye how it's done.

"Now, Pat," sez the wee man, layin' the cat on the top of the sticks, "put a match to the shavin's, till I go back for the rest of the materials."

By the time I heard him behind me, there was nothin' left of poor Paddy but the bones; an' when I looked round, the masther was comin' down the garden with the gallon jar in one hand an' two tumblers in the other.

"It was the practice of the same Romans, Pat," sez he, "when they had burned the corpse of the deceased, to put out the fire with a drop of the very best—or rather, Misther Murphy," sez he, blinkin' in the firelight, "with the best the poor benighted heathen knew about, havin' in those days nothin' more satisfactory to dhrink than a cowld splash of wine. An' though I don't find it in the books, there's no manner of doubt that, such as it was, they took a jorum at the same time just to dhrive away sorrow. So we'll do the full rites by poor Paddy." With that he sets the tumblers on the ground an' pours out two stiff ones.

"Stand back now, Pat," sez he; an' before I knowed what he was afther, he had cowped the gallon jar on the fire. The flames went up with a woof! would ha' frightened ye, an' for a minit I thought the masther was desthroyed; but when I thrailed him back, barrin' the nap on his tall hat, he wasn't a thraneen the worse.

"Didn't I tell ye," sez he. "The divil an ancient Roman ever seen a flame like that in his life. It's the great stuff—gimme my glass—an here's Paddy Shaw's memory in the last dhrop—worse luck—I'll ever taste of it."

Epigrams

By Oscar Wilde

An engagement is hardly a serious one that has not been broken off at least once.

The truth is rarely pure and never simple. Modern life would be very tedious if it were either, and modern literature an impossibility.

Women only call each other sister after they have called each other a lot of other things first.

The good end happily, the bad unhappily. That is what fiction means.

Relations are simply a tedious pack of people who haven't got the remotest knowledge of how to live, nor the smallest instinct about when to die.

Long engagements give people the opportunity of finding out each other's character before marriage, which is never advisable.

Life is far too important a thing ever to talk seriously about.

What with the duties expected of one during one's lifetime, and the duties exacted from one after one's death, land has ceased to be either a profit or pleasure. It gives one position and prevents one from keeping it up.

We are all of us so hard-up nowadays that the only pleasant things to pay are compliments. They're the only things we *can* pay.

A cynic is a man who knows the price of everything, and the value of nothing.

A sentimentalist is a man who sees an absurd value in everything and doesn't know the market price of a single thing.

My own business always bores me to death. I prefer other people's.

Women always want one to be good. And if we are good when they meet us, they don't love us at all. They like to find us quite irretrievably bad and to leave us quite unattractively good.

It is an awfully dangerous thing to come across a woman who thoroughly understands one. They always end by marrying one.

Misfortunes one can endure—they come from outside, they are accidents. But to suffer for one's own faults—Ah! there is the sting of life.

My experience is that as soon as people are old enough to know better, they don't know anything at all.

If one could only teach the English how to talk and the Irish how to listen, society would be quite civilized.

No woman, plain or pretty, has any common-sense at all. Common-sense is the privilege of our sex and we men are so self-sacrificing that we never use it.

The only thing to do with good advice is to pass it on. It is never of any use to oneself.

Questions are never indiscreet, answers sometimes are.

The reason we are so pleased to find out other people's secrets is that it distracts public attention from our own.

To get into the best society nowadays, one has either to feed people, amuse people, or shock people.

One should never trust a woman who tells one her real age. A woman who would tell that would tell anything.

When a man says he has exhausted life, one always knows life has exhausted him.

The only difference between a saint and a sinner is that every saint has a past, and every sinner has a future.

I can't help detesting my relations. I suppose it comes from the fact that we can't stand other people having the same faults as ourselves.

There is only one thing in the world worse than being talked about, and that is not being talked about.

Nothing makes one so vain as being told that one is a sinner.

I can believe anything, provided it is incredible.

There is hardly a person in the House of Commons worth painting, though many of them would be better for a little whitewashing.

Every great man nowadays has his disciples, and it is always Judas who writes the biography.

It is only an auctioneer who can equally and impartially admire all schools of art.

Spies are of no use nowadays. Their profession is over. The newspapers do their work instead.

Erin Go Bragh!

BY FRANK SULLIVAN

When March seventeenth rolls around each year, your correspondent stirs with an impulse to stick a reporter's card in his hat brim and hurry over to Fifth Avenue to help his fellow newshawks cover the St. Patrick's Day parade. For many years when I was a chronicler of small beer and big parades in Manhattan, I used to get that assignment regularly, and a pleasant assignment it was.

Possibly my name had something to do with my getting it, or possibly it was the fact that the *New York World* city desk found out that I did not mind traveling considerable distances on foot. This was a quirk that caused more than one of my colleagues to regard me with puzzled brows. Why should anyone in his right sense like to walk? I had been a practicing reporter for only a few months when I drew an assignment to walk with the 27th Division in the welcome-home parade celebrating its return from That Other War, in March of 1919. The division marched from Washington Square up Fifth Avenue to 110th Street, a hike of five miles. I was recently out of the infantry myself, so a hike of five miles was a mere trifle. But the assignment was not one that seasoned and sedentary reporters clamored for, and when I expressed pleasure at getting it, even the day city editor recoiled in suspicion and inquired anxiously if I felt quite well. Why, in those days I could have paced Eleanora Sears in one of those famous hikes she took periodically from Beacon Street to Newport.

At any rate I profited by drawing the assignment to accompany the 27th Division up Fifth Avenue that spring day, for during the afternoon I met for the first time two sterling lads whose friendship I treasured in the years that followed. I refer to Donald Henderson Clark and Gene Fowler, two of the greatest reporters ever to hit New York and two of the wiliest experts in making out expense accounts. I found this out soon after the parade assignment, when I met the two boys again in New Haven, where we had assembled to get the details of a Town and Gown riot.

On our way back to New York we were making out our expense accounts and my two mentors, suspicious that I was perhaps a bit innocent in that art, demanded to see my expense sheet. I shall never forget the shocked cry of horror that escaped them when they saw its modesty. They told me sternly that such a piddling little swindle sheet would create the worst precedent possible.

"Do you want to spoil these publishers, pampering them like this?" they asked, and they rewrote my expense account. It was a work of art when they finished with it. I presented it at the cashier's window of my newspaper. He gave a low whistle of admiration, and said, "How long you been working here, Bub?" I told him a few months. "You're learning fast; you'll go far," he said, and paid the account without a murmur. That expense account was the basis of the fortune which I later lost in the crash of 1929.

But, I digress, and that will probably surprise nobody. The St. Patrick's Day parade was a congenial assignment, provided you were well protected from cold—and the marchers were in those days. It was before the invention of the drum majorette with the bare knees. For weather, St. Patrick's Day is a notoriously unpredictable holiday. You would think that no weather would have the temerity to be other than sunny and mild on the feast day of the great Irish Bishop (who, by the way, was a Roman), but it does. Once in a while you get a balmy, warm St. Patrick's Day, but more often you get one calculated to congeal the hardiest Irishman. Icy winds may nip the ears and noses of the marchers and stiffen the fingers of the bandsmen so they can hardly manage to play "Killarney" or "The Wearing of the Green." In recent years, no longer a chronicler of the parade but an observer, I have stood at the curb watching many of the parades and no matter how warmly wrapped I am, I always shiver at the sight of the drum majorettes in their knee-length skirts, their bare legs blue with cold.

I wonder what happened to the little girl who committed the awful gaffe in a St. Patrick's Day parade a few years ago. She must have been drummed out of her fife and drum corps in disgrace, at the very least. I wouldn't be surprised if she became a pariah and went about her studies at school shunned by her classmates.

It was in front of St. Patrick's Cathedral the poor lass came a cropper. Traditionally, the Cardinal and his staff seat themselves before the Cathedral entrance and watch the parade from that coign. When they are passing the Cathedral, the marchers put out their best efforts. The bands play their lustiest, the pipes give an extra skirl, and the grand marshal of the parade steps out of line to pay his respects to the Cardinal Archbishop.

On the afternoon the poor little girl met her Waterloo (Waterloo is a famous decisive battle lost by Napoleon because he had too few Irishmen in his army) she and her corps prepared to give of their best as they approached the Cathedral. Her stride smartened. The knees came up with extra zest, and she made ready with her most intricate baton twirlings for the benefit of the distinguished and reverend reviewers. She was doing good, too, when the awful thing happened, the horror that must haunt the nightmares of all drum majorettes—and of all drum majors, too, if there be any males left in the profession. Just at the moment when she was passing the Cathedral, she sent her baton soaring into the air in a daring salute. And when it came down she failed to catch it!

The unfortunate colleen retrieved the baton after it had clattered to the ground and stepped off as though nothing had happened, but she couldn't fool me. I knew she was a broken woman; broken at the very threshold of a promising career as a twirler of batons. I wonder what became of her. I suppose there was only one course left for her. She must have married the boy who dropped the punt that lost the Ivy League football championship for deal old Siwash. They probably went to live in Kamchatka, where no one ever would know of their blighted lives.

I trust the same pleasant arrangements as of yore still are made for the comfort of the honored guests and the press at the parade. The grand marshal, with hospitality befitting the occasion, always set up a parade headquarters in one of the hotels near the official reviewing stand: the Plaza, or the Sherry Netherlands, or the Savoy-Plaza. Distinguished guests could repair to the headquarters to get warm, and the press could go there to get information. There was always a first-aid room at headquarters, stocked with an abundance and variety of the very best brands of anti-freeze mixtures. It was remarkable to see a reporter blue from the cold enter that first-aid room and emerge in an hour or two, or three, his visage ruddy with the glow of health. Who says it's healthier to be out in the fresh air?

"Cead Mile Failte" was the word at the grand marshal's headquarters and wasn't I the gossoon who knew that that bit of Gaelic means "A Hundred Thousand Welcomes," for hadn't my father told me so many years before?

I was too small to remember a unique St. Patrick's Day parade that once took place in Saratoga, but I have heard tell about it in the family. It was the year that my father was head of Division Number 4, Ancient Order of Hibernians, and, ex-officio, slated to head the parade on the great day. He was looking forward to it, too, for it was an honor and a pleasure. He had a badge of office which I do remember and which I admired greatly. It was about a foot long and so expansive that in itself it constituted a chest protector not to be sneered at. One side was green, with a harp embroidered in gold. That side was for wear on March seventeenth and other joyful Hibernian occasions. The reverse was black and there was a silver cross embroidered on it. That side was for wear at the funerals of comrades.

Several days before St. Patrick's Day, my father became ill. What made him madder was that the malady was not a proper disease that a man could respect, but a child's ailment that he had caught from his progeny, namely, the mumps! He said he would go out and lead the parade anyhow, come hell or high water, but the doctor vetoed that. My father told the doctor what he could do, but then my mother stepped in and sided with the doctor. So they mowed my poor father down, between the two of them, but not until they knew they had been in a battle.

We lived on a sequestered street which in those years, when winter was winter, was apt to be well equipped with slush even as late as March seventeenth and was indeed covered with it that year. My father's friends in Division Number 4 decided that it was a thing not to be borne that Dennis Sullivan should have no part in the parade. So they alerted the line of march, made a slight detour of a couple of miles, and waded past our house in review, shouting the greetings of the day to my father, seated at an upstairs front window in a considerable state of emotion. It was a great day for him and it was a great day for my brothers and sister. Not many kids have a parade go two miles out of its way just to pass by their house.

Bird Milligan

BY OLIVER ST. JOHN GOGARTY

This is how he got his nickname, the Bird. He went to a fancy-dress ball at a roller-skating rink dressed in a kind of loose garment or robe. He was supported by two holy women. When the dancing was in full swing, he laid an egg as big as a football, flapped his

wings, and chortled. The manager threw him out and the holy
women with him. But he was Bird Milligan from that day. He was
called the Bird by so many people that his other name was forgotten.

Dublin is not like Paris, where they say that in the garden of the
Tuileries knights in armor are to be seen sitting with one-eyed
pirates, and nobody takes any notice even of the man with the
crossbow who assures everyone that he was the man who killed
King Richard Lion-Heart. Nevertheless Dublin has, if not para-
noiacs, eccentrics surely. It was Boyle Tisdall Stewart Fitzgerald
Farrell, who was called Endymion because he was touched by the
moon. He caricatured in his own person anything of which he dis-
approved. He carried two sabers and wore starched cuffs on his
ankles to show that the world was upside-down. Sometimes he
made a nuisance of himself by going into the public library and
entering all his names in the book. That done, he left muttering.
Then there was Professor Maginni, Professor of Deportment. His
idea of deportment caused him to dress in a dark brown frock coat,
striped trousers, brown shoes, top hat, and waxed mustache. He
walked mincingly. He walked about for business purposes. His real
name was Maginnis. Evidently he thought that Maginni gave his
name an Italian flourish all the more useful for business. No one
could accuse the Bird of acting for business purposes. It would be
very hard to see anything faintly resembling business in the laying
of an egg.

The Bird retired for a month to his farm near Dublin. People
said that he was engaged in breaking in young horses. He had the
reputation of being a good horseman. It is hard to say how these
rumors got about. Perhaps because his nose was broken by a horse
throwing his head back suddenly. To suffer such an accident he
must have spent his time among young horses, and hostlers' talk in
the taverns did the rest. He certainly had a buggy with a fine horse
in the shafts when he appeared in town. By that two-wheeler hangs
a tale. He and a young woman were seen driving up the slope of
Portbello Bridge. They were evidently quarreling, for the Bird's
voice was raised so that anything the lady said could not be heard.
But the Bird's voice was distinctly heard when the buggy reached
the crest of the bridge, because it halted for a moment there. "You
have been the pest of my life," the Bird shouted, "and it's time it

ended." With that he threw her bodily into the canal. A policeman in full uniform plunged, helmet and all, into the water. He
swam to the rescue, only to find a dummy from a shop window in a
fashionable part of the town in his arms. By the time he came out
and looked for the Bird, the Bird had flown.

A complaint was laid, not by the police, but by some busybody,
with the father of the Bird. The Bird's father was an alderman of
the city and a most respectable man. He should curb his son. Perhaps his father had not looked after the Bird with due care. It was
known the alderman was a widower, so the busybody argued. His
father at last reluctantly consented. He spoke to the Bird, and
whatever he said to him, the Bird went to Canada for a while. But
the Bird came back.

If you want to look for the counterpart of the merrie men of
Dublin, you will have to look at some of the characters in Russian
novels—Turgenev, for example. But the characters in these novels
tend to do dangerous feats which are meaningless. A young man
jumps his horse over a precipice where failure means loss of life.
They are not truly counterparts.

The Bird was within his right, and he should not have been
thrown out of the skating rink ball. After all, it was a fancy-dress
affair. If the fancy dress represented a bird, it was quite in order to
lay an egg. And the manager was in no position to decide how big
the egg should be.

During the Bird's absence in Canada, the town depended for its
merriment on Endymion; and he did his best. That is doubtless
why the Bird's exploits and Endymion's tend to merge, so it is better to know the authors of the different actions that kept the old
town amused. Endymion must be credited with the fishing incident. It took place in this way. Dublin has two-decker buses, some
of them open at the top. On one of these Endymion stood fishing.
He had a salmon rod and a line at the end of which was a fly as
large as a sparrow. Solemnly he cast the fly onto the cement sidewalk. He waited until some passenger would try to humor him by
asking if he had caught anything. Then Endymion would come
into his own. "What, on that?" he would say, pointing to the
cement sidewalk. "You must be mad!" So that helps us to differen-
tiate between Endymion and the Bird. A further source of confusion comes from the two sabers Endymion carried on occasion to

show his disapproval of warfare. The Bird may have borrowed one or provided one himself. After his return from Canada, he went to an Italian warehouse, as the delicatessens were called in Dublin. Hams and flitches of bacon hung suspended from an iron bar high in the air outside the store. One morning before the rush hour the Bird approached the owner of the delicatessen and bought a ham. He got a receipt. After the transaction he asked the proprietor to let the ham hang where it was for a few hours. The Bird had other things to do, and he did not wish to cart the ham around with him. To this the owner consented. At the rush hour the Bird returned. He had a saber in his hand with which he *addressed* the ham, inviting it to a duel. After a few flourishes he transfixed the ham and, putting it over his shoulder, ran off. He was closely pursued by two policemen. Cornered at last, the Bird produced the receipt for the ham and asked was there no liberty left in the country when a man couldn't buy a ham without being arrested?

As a result of this exploit, and probably because of a few others, the Bird was sent to Australia. He pretended that he went willingly, that it was a country that delighted in horses and it was just the place for him. But after a few months the Bird proved to be a homing pigeon. He returned.

Dublin is possessed of a Ballast Office, over the door of which is a clock which tells sidereal time. Promptly at noon the Bird took up his station before the clock. When the clock's hands pointed to the hours, two alarm clocks which the Bird had in his tail pocket went off together. Much mirth attended the Bird. He smiled and went off satisfied. He had the exact time.

All the aldermen of the city, headed by the Lord Mayor, planned to hold a World's Fair. It would be like nothing on earth. It was.

Nations from all parts of the globe were invited to show their wares and to be sure that their national costumes were represented. The Americas were in it; South Africa and the Far East, which meant Japan. It was Japan that caused the most interest. This was largely if not altogether due to a tribe that were never before beheld by Western eyes. They were the hairy Ainus, a very primitive tribe who were reputed to go into dark caves and to fight with bears with nothing but a knife and a bearskin thrown loosely over their shoulders. The bear would grapple with the Ainu only to find that the bearskin came off in the fight, during which he was disemboweled. A whole family of hairy Ainus was displayed, children and all. They were copper-colored, even to the baby in arms. The baby was not long in arms, for it disappeared mysteriously. Whereupon a truly frightful uproar broke out. Nobody knew what the mother was saying. She was pointing to her breasts; but nobody understood. The man of the tribe was desperate. He would have broken loose but for the iron bars behind which the family was ensconced. At last someone, probably a member of the Japanese government, said that the baby had disappeared and that, naturally, the parents were frantic. Would no one search for it? If the Ainus broke out . . .

At last the baby was found in the French pavilion. It was at long last, for nobody thought of searching there. The baby was found smiling, for it was interested in a bottle of warm milk the like of which it had never seen.

The aldermen held a special meeting. Eyes, unfriendly for the most part, were turned on Alderman Milligan. Was he not directly responsible for getting the corporation of the city in such a jam? Had the baby been found anywhere but in the French pavilion, it might have been a different matter. As it was, the French took the placing of the baby there as a direct insult. Obviously, the reference intended was a reference to their falling birth rate, as well as the fact that the French nation was very high in the scale of infant mortality. An international incident could be made of such an insult. The French consul attended and he took a lot of placating. He forgave the aldermen because it was proved to his satisfaction that none of them was responsible.

The Bird was banished.

Months later, a friend was strolling down a street in Buenos Aires. There was a large hole in the street, at the bottom of which a man was working with a pick. The friend chanced to look down. He thought he recognized the broad shoulders and the red neck, which were out of keeping with the local workmen. "Good Heavens, Bird, is that you?" The Bird looked up. "Get to hell out of that! It took a mighty lot of influence to get me this job!"

He was through with bad companions. It may have been due to the difficulty of securing a job or it may not. But there were no more "incidents" in Dublin.

The first and last I saw of the Bird was in the Phoenix Park, which is said to be the largest park enclosed by a wall in Europe. He must have been pointed out to me, for I never remember meeting him. I saw the nose across his face, the red face and neck, and the well-dressed setup of the man as he came prancing by on a big bay horse. I saw his light brown waistcoat, his riding gloves, one of which fell over his left wrist, the bowler hat, the riding trousers and boots. He raised his whip in an exaggerated salute and cantered off.

That was long after the changing of the Ainu baby: you cannot call it stealing, for it never left the Fair.

The Bird was of a generous nature; he harmed nobody. Dublin is a lesser place since it lost its men of mirth.

The Miraculous Revenge

BY BERNARD SHAW

I arrived in Dublin on the evening of the 5th of August, and drove to the residence of my uncle, the Cardinal Archbishop. He is, like most of my family, deficient in feeling, and consequently cold to me personally. He lives in a dingy house, with a side-long view of the portico of his cathedral from the front windows, and of a monster national school from the back. My uncle maintains no retinue. The people believe that he is waited upon by angels. When I knocked at the door, an old woman, his only servant, opened it, and informed me that her master was then officiating in the cathedral, and that he had directed her to prepare dinner for me in his absence. An unpleasant smell of salt fish made me ask her what the dinner consisted of. She assured me that she had cooked all that could be permitted in His Holiness's house on a Friday. On my asking her further why on a Friday, she replied that Friday was a fast day. I bade her tell His Holiness that I had hoped to have the pleasure of calling on him shortly, and drove to a hotel in Sackville Street, where I engaged apartments and dined.

After dinner I resumed my eternal search—I know not for what; it drives me to and fro like another Cain. I sought in the streets without success. I went to the theatre. The music was execrable, the scenery poor. I had seen the play a month before in London, with the same beautiful artist in the chief part. Two years had passed since, seeing her for the first time, I had hoped that she, perhaps, might be the long-sought mystery. It had proved otherwise. On this night I looked at her and listened to her for the sake of that by-gone hope, and applauded her generously when the curtain fell. But I went out lonely still. When I had supped at a restaurant, I returned to my hotel, and tried to read. In vain. The sound of feet in the corridors as the other occupants of the hotel went to bed distracted my attention from my book. Suddenly it occurred to me that I had never quite understood my uncle's character. He, father to a great flock of poor and ignorant Irish; an austere and saintly man, to whom livers of hopeless lives daily appealed for help heavenward; who was reputed never to have sent away a troubled peasant without relieving him of his burden by sharing it; whose knees were worn less by the altar steps than by the tears and em-braces of the guilty and wretched; he had refused to humour my light extravagances, or to find time to talk with me of books, flow-ers, and music. Had I not been made to expect it? Now that I needed sympathy myself, I did him justice. I desired to be with a true-hearted man, and to mingle my tears with his.

I looked at my watch. It was nearly an hour past midnight. In the corridor the lights were out, except one jet at the end. I threw a cloak upon my shoulders, put on a Spanish hat, and left my apartment, listening to the echoes of my measured steps retreating through the deserted passages. A strange sight arrested me on the landing of the grand staircase. Through an open door I saw the moonlight shining through the windows of a saloon in which some entertainment had recently taken place. I looked at my watch again. It was but one o'clock; and yet the guests had departed. I entered the room, my boots ringing loudly on the waxed boards. On a chair lay a child's clock and a broken toy. The entertainment had been a children's party. I stood for a time looking at the sha-dow of my cloaked figure upon the floor, and at the disordered decorations, ghostly in the white light. Then I saw that there was a grand piano, still open, in the middle of the room. My fingers throbbed as I sat down before it, and expressed all that I felt in a grand hymn which seemed to thrill the cold stillness of the

shadows into a deep hum of approbation, and to people the radiance of the moon with angels. Soon there was a stir without too, as
if the rapture was spreading abroad. I took up the chant triumphantly with my voice, and the empty saloon resounded as though
to the thunder of an orchestra.

"Hallo, sir!" "Confound you, sir—" "Do you suppose that
this—" "What the deuce—?"

I turned, and silence followed. Six men, partially dressed, and
with dishevelled hair, stood regarding me angrily. They all carried
candles. One of them had a bootjack, which he held like a trun-
cheon. Another, the foremost, had a pistol. The night porter was
behind trembling.

"Sir," said the man with the revolver, coarsely, "may I ask
whether you are mad, that you disturb people at this hour with
such an unearthly noise?"

"Is it possible that you dislike it?" I replied, courteously.

"Dislike it!" said he, stamping with rage. "Why—damn everything—do you suppose we were enjoying it?"

"Take care. He's mad," whispered the man with the bootjack.

I began to laugh. Evidently they did think me mad. Unaccus-
tomed to my habits, and ignorant of music as they probably were,
the mistake, however absurd, was not unnatural. I rose. They
came closer to one another; and the night porter ran away.

"Gentlemen," I said, "I am sorry for you. Had you lain still and
listened, we should all have been the better and happier. But what
you have done, you cannot undo. Kindly inform the night porter
that I am gone to visit my uncle, the Cardinal Archbishop. Adieu!"

I strode past them, and left them whispering among themselves.
Some minutes later I knocked at the door of the Cardinal's house.
Presently a window on the first floor was opened; and the moon-
beams fell on a grey head, with a black cap that seemed ashy pale
against the unfathomable gloom of the shadow beneath the stone
sill.

"Who are you?"

"I am Zeno Legge."

"What do you want at this hour?"

The question wounded me. "My dear uncle," I exclaimed, "I
know you do not intend it, but you make me feel unwelcome.

Come down and let me in, I beg."

"Go to your hotel," he said sternly. "I will see you in the morning. Good night." He disappeared and closed the window.

I felt that if I let this rebuff pass, I should not feel kindly towards my uncle in the morning, nor, indeed, at any future time. I therefore plied the knocker with my right hand, and kept the bell ringing with my left until I heard the doorchain rattle within. The Cardinal's expression was grave nearly to moroseness as he confronted me on the threshold.

"Uncle," I cried, grasping his hand, "do not reproach me. Your door is never shut against the wretched. I am wretched. Let us sit up all night and talk."

"You may thank my position and not my charity for your admission, Zeno," he said. "For the sake of the neighbours, I had rather you played the fool in my study than upon my doorstep at this hour. Walk upstairs quietly, if you please. My housekeeper is a hard-working woman: the little sleep she allows herself must not be disturbed."

"You have a noble heart, uncle. I shall creep like a mouse."

"This is my study," he said, as we entered an ill-furnished den on the second floor. "The only refreshment I can offer you, if you desire any, is a bunch of raisins. The doctors have forbidden you to touch stimulants, I believe."

"By heaven—!" He raised his finger. "Pardon me; I was wrong to swear. But I had totally forgotten the doctors. At dinner I had a bottle of *Grave*."

"Humph! You have no business to be travelling alone. Your mother promised me that Bushy should come over here with you."

"Pshaw! Bushy is not a man of feeling. Besides, he is a coward. He refused to come with me because I purchased a revolver."

"He should have taken the revolver from you, and kept to his post."

"Why will you persist in treating me like a child, uncle? I am very impressionable, I grant you; but I have gone round the world alone, and do not need to be dry-nursed through a tour in Ireland."

"What do you intend to do during your stay here?"

I had no plans; and instead of answering I shrugged my shoulders and looked round the apartment. There was a statuette of the Virgin upon my uncle's desk. I looked at its face, as he was wont to look in the midst of his labours. I saw there eternal peace. The air became luminous with an infinite network of the jewelled rings of Paradise descending in roseate clouds upon us.

"Uncle," I said, bursting into the sweetest tears I had ever shed, "my wanderings are over. I will enter the Church, if you will help me. Let us read together the third part of *Faust*; for I understand it at last."

"Hush, man," he said, half rising with an expression of alarm. "Control yourself."

"Do not let my tears mislead you. I am calm and strong. Quick, let us have Goethe:

> Das Unbeschreibliche,
> Hier ist gethan;
> Das Ewig-Weibliche,
> Zieht uns hinan."

"Come, come. Dry your eyes and be quiet. I have no library here."

"But I have—in my portmanteau at the hotel," I said, rising. "Let me go for it, I will return in fifteen minutes."

"The devil is in you, I believe. Cannot—"

I interrupted him with a shout of laughter. "Cardinal," I said noisily, "you have become profane; and a profane priest is always the best of good fellows. Let us have some wine; and I will sing you a German beer song."

"Heaven forgive me if I do you wrong," he said; "but I believe God has laid the expiation of some sin on your unhappy head. Will you favor me with your attention for a while? I have something to say to you, and I have also to get some sleep before my hour for rising, which is half-past five."

"My usual hour for retiring—when I retire at all. But proceed. My fault is not inattention, but over-susceptibility."

"Well, then, I want you to go to Wicklow. My reasons—"

"No matter what they may be," said I, rising again. "It is enough that you desire me to go. I shall start forthwith."

"Zeno! Will you sit down and listen to me?"

I sank upon my chair reluctantly. "Ardor is a crime in your

eyes, even when it is shown in your service," I said. "May I turn down the light?"

"Why?"

"To bring on my sombre mood, in which I am able to listen with tireless patience."

"I will turn it down myself. Will that do?"

"I thanked him, and composed myself to listen in the shadow. My eyes, I felt, glittered. I was like Poe's raven.

"Now for my reasons for sending you to Wicklow. First, for your own sake. If you stay in town, or in any place where excitement can be obtained by any means, you will be in Swift's Hospital in a week. You must live in the country, under the eye of one upon whom I can depend. And you must have something to do to keep you out of mischief, and away from your music and painting and poetry, which, Sir John Richards writes to me, are dangerous for you in your present morbid state. Second, because I can entrust you with a task which, in the hands of a sensible man, might bring discredit on the Church. In short, I want you to investigate a miracle."

He looked attentively at me. I sat like a statue.

"You understand me?" he said.

"Nevermore," I replied, hoarsely. "Pardon me," I added, amused at the trick my imagination had played me, "I understand you perfectly. Proceed."

"I hope you do. Well, four miles distant from the town of Wicklow is a village called Four Mile Water. The resident priest is Father Hickey. You have heard of the miracles at Knock?"

I winked.

"I did not ask you what you think of them, but whether you have heard of them. I see you have. I need not tell you that even a miracle may do more harm than good to the Church in this country, unless it can be proved so thoroughly that her powerful and jealous enemies are silenced by the testimony of followers of their heresy. Therefore, when I saw in a Wexford newspaper last week a description of a strange manifestation of the Divine Power which was said to have taken place at Four Mile Water, I was troubled in my mind about it. So I wrote to Father Hickey, bidding him give me an account of the matter if it were true, and if not, to denounce from the altar the author of the report, and to contradict it

in the paper at once. This is his reply. He says—well, the first part
is about Church matters: I need not trouble you with it. He goes
on to say—"

"One moment. Is that his own handwriting? It does not look
like a man's."

"He suffers from rheumatism in the fingers of his right hand,
and his niece, who is an orphan, and lives with him, acts as his
amanuensis. Well—"

"Stay. What is her name?"

"Her name? Kate Hickey."

"How old is she?"

"Tush, man, she is only a little girl. If she were old enough to
concern you, I should not send you into her way. Have you any
more questions to ask about her?"

"None. I can fancy her in a white veil at the rite of confirma-
tion, a type of faith and innocence. Enough of her. What says the
Reverend Hickey of the apparitions?"

"They are not apparitions. I will read you what he says. Ahem!

"In reply to your inquiries concerning the late miraculous
event in this parish, I have to inform you that I can vouch for
its truth, and that I can be confirmed not only by the inhabitants of the place, who are all Catholics, but be every person
acquainted with the former situation of the graveyard referred to, including the Protestant Archdeacon of Baltinglass,
who spends six weeks annually in the neighbourhood. The
newspaper account is incomplete and inaccurate. The following are the facts: About four years ago, a man named
Wolfe Tone Fitzgerald settled in this village as a farrier. His
antecedents did not transpire, and he had no family. He lived
by himself, was very careless of his person; and when in his
cups, as he often was, regarded the honour neither of God nor
man in his conversation. Indeed if it were not speaking ill of
the dead, one might say that he was a dirty, drunken, blasphemous black-guard. Worse again, he was, I fear, an atheist,
for he never attended Mass, and gave his Holiness worse language even than he gave the Queen. I should have mentioned
that he was a bitter rebel, and boasted that his grandfather
had been out in '08, and his father with Smith O'Brien. At

last he went by the name of Brimstone Billy, and was held up
in the village as he type of all wickedness.

"You are aware that our graveyard, situated on the north
side of the water, is famous throughout the country as the
burial place of the nuns of St. Ursula, the hermit of Four
Mile Water, and many other holy people. No Protestant has
ever ventured to enforce his legal right of interment there,
though two have died in the parish within my own recollection. Three weeks ago, this Fitzgerald died in a fit brought on
by drink, and a great hullabaloo was raised in the village
when it became known that he would be buried in the graveyard. The body had to be watched to prevent its being stolen
and buried at the cross-roads. My people were greatly disappointed when they were told I could do nothing to stop the
burial, particularly as I of course refused to read any service
on the occasion. However, I bade them not interfere; and the
interment was effected on the 14th of July, late in the evening, and long after the legal hour. There was no disturbance. Next morning, the graveyard was found moved to the
south side of the water, with the one newly-filled grave left
behind on the north side; and thus they both remain. The
departed saints would not lie with the reprobate. I can testify
to it on the oath of a Christian priest; and if this will not
satisfy those outside the Church, everyone, as I said before,
who remembers where the graveyard was two months ago,
can confirm me.

"I respectfully suggest that a thorough investigation into
the truth of this miracle be proposed to a committee of Protestant gentlemen. They shall not be asked to accept a single
fact on hearsay from my people. The ordnance maps show
where the graveyard was; and anyone can see for himself
where it is. I need not tell your Eminence what a rebuke this
would be to those enemies of the holy Church that have
sought to put a stain on her by discrediting the late wonderful
manifestations at Knock Chapel. If they come to Four Mile
Water, they need cross-examine no one. They will be asked to
believe nothing but their own senses.

"Awaiting your Eminence's counsel to guide me further in the matter,

"I am, etc.

"Well, Zeno," said my uncle, "what do you think of Father Hickey now?"

"Uncle, do not ask me. Beneath this roof I desire to believe everything. The Reverend Hickey has appealed strongly to my love of legend. Let us admire the poetry of his narrative and ignore the balance of probability between a Christian priest telling a lie on his oath and a graveyard swimming across a river in the middle of the night and forgetting to return.'

"Tom Hickey is not telling a lie, sir. You may take my word for that. But he may be mistaken."

"Such a mistake amounts to insanity. It is true that I myself, awaking suddenly in the depth of night, have found myself convinced that the position of my bed had been reversed. But on opening my eyes the illusion ceased. I fear Mr. Hickey is mad. Your best course is this. Send down to Four Mile Water a perfectly sane investigator; an acute observer; one whose perceptive faculties, at once healthy and subtle, are absolutely unclouded by religious prejudice. In a word, send me. I will report to you the true state of affairs in a few days, and you can then make arrangements for transferring Hickey from the altar to the asylum."

"Yes, I had intended to send you. You are wonderfully sharp and you would make a capital detective if you could only keep your mind to one point. But your chief qualification for this business is that you are too crazy to excite the suspicion of those whom you may have to watch. For the affair may be a trick. If so, I hope and believe that Hickey has no hand in it. Still, it is my duty to take every precaution."

"Cardinal may I ask whether traces of insanity have ever appeared in our family?"

"Except in you and in my grandmother, no. She was a Pole; and you resemble her personally. Why do you ask?"

"Because it has often occurred to me that you are, perhaps, a little cracked. Excuse my candour, but a man who has devoted his life to the pursuit of a red hat, who accuses everyone else besides himself of being mad, and who is disposed to listen seriously to a tale of a peripatetic graveyard, can hardly be quite sane. Depend upon it, uncle, you want rest and change. The blood of your Polish grandmother is in your veins."

"I hope I may not be committing a sin in sending a ribald on the Church's affairs," he replied, fervently. "However, we must use the instruments put into our hands. Is it agreed that you go?"

"Had you not delayed me with this story, which I might as well have learned on the spot, I should have been there already."

"There is no occasion for impatience, Zeno. I must first send to Hickey to find a place for you. I shall tell him that you are going to recover your health, as, in fact, you are. And, Zeno, in Heaven's name be discreet. Try to act like a man of sense. Do not dispute with Hickey on matters of religion. Since you are my nephew, you had better not disgrace me."

"I shall become an ardent Catholic, and do you infinite credit, uncle."

"I wish you would, although you would hardly be an acquisition to the Church. And now I must turn you out. It is nearly three o'clock, and I need some sleep. Do you know your way back to your hotel?"

"I need not stir. I can sleep in this chair. Go to bed, and never mind me."

"I shall not close my eyes until you are safely out of the house. Come, rouse yourself, and say good night."

The following is a copy of my first report to the Cardinal:

Four Mile Water, County Wicklow,
10th August

My Dear Uncle,

The miracle is genuine. I have affected perfect credulity in order to throw the Hickeys and the countryfolk off their guard with me. I have listened to their method of convincing sceptical strangers. I have examined the ordnance maps, and cross-examined the neighbouring Protestant gentlefolk. I have spent a day upon the ground on each side of the water, and have visited it at midnight. I have considered the upheaval theories, subsidence theories, volcanic theories, and tidal wave theories which the provincial *savants* have suggested. They are all untenable. There is only one scoffer in

the district, an Orangeman; and he admits the removal of the
cemetery, but says it was dug and transplanted in the night by
a body of men under the command of Father Tom. This also
is out of the question. The interment of Brimstone Billy was
the first which had taken place for four years; and his is the
only grave which bears a trace of recent digging. It is alone on
the north bank, and the inhabitants shun it after nightfall. As
each passer-by during the day throws a stone upon it, it will
soon be marked by a large cairn. The graveyard, with a ruined
stone chapel still standing in its midst, is on the south side.
You may send down a committee to investigate the matter as
soon as you please. There can be no doubt as to the miracle
having actually taken place, as recorded by Hickey. As for me,
I have grown so accustomed to it that if the county Wicklow
were to waltz off with me to Middlesex, I should be quite impatient of any expressions of surprise from my friends in London.

Is not the above a businesslike statement? Away, then, with
this stale miracle. If you would see for yourself a miracle
which can never pall, a vision of youth and health to be
crowned with garlands for ever, come down and see Kate
Hickey, whom you suppose to be a little girl. Illusion, my lord
cardinal, illusion! She is seventeen, with a bloom and a brogue
that would lay your asceticism in ashes at a flash. To her I am
an object of wonder, a strange man bred in wicked cities. She
is courted by six feet of farming material, chopped off a spare
length of coarse humanity by the Almighty, and flung into
Wicklow to plough the fields. His name is Phil Langan; and
he hates me. I have to consort with him for the sake of Father
Tom, whom I entertain vastly by stories of your wild oats
sown at Salamanca. I exhausted all my authentic anecdotes
the first day; and now I invent gallent escapades with Spanish
donnas, in which you figure as a youth of unstable morals.
This delights Father Tom infinitely. I feel that I have done
you a service by thus casting on the cold sacerdotal abstraction
which formerly represented you in Kate's imagination a ray
of vivifying passion.

What a country this is! A Hesperidean garden: such skies!
Adieu, uncle.

                                        Zeno Legge.

Behold me, then, at Four Mile Water, in love. I had been in love frequently; but not oftener than once a year had I encountered a woman who affected me as seriously as Kate Hickey. She was so shrewd, and yet so flippant! When I spoke of art she yawned. When I deplored the sordidness of the world she laughed, and called me "poor fellow!" When I told her what a treasure of beauty and freshness she had she ridiculed me. When I reproached her with her brutality she became angry, and sneered at me for being what she called a fine gentleman. One sunny afternoon we were standing at the gate of her uncle's house, she looking down the dusty road for the detestable Langan, I watching the spotless azure sky, when she said:

"How soon are you going back to London?"

"I am not going back to London, Miss Hickey. I am not yet tired of Four Mile Water."

"I'm sure Four Mile Water ought to be proud of your approbation."

"You disapprove of my liking it, then? Or is it that you grudge me the happiness I have found there? I think Irish ladies grudge a man a moment's peace."

"I wonder you have ever prevailed on yourself to associate with Irish ladies, since they are so far beneath you."

"Did I say they were beneath me, Miss Hickey? I feel that I have made a deep impression on you."

"Indeed! Yes, you're quite right. I assure you I can't sleep at night for thinking of you, Mr. Legge. It's the best a Christian can do, seeing you think so mighty little of yourslf."

"You are triply wrong, Miss Hickey: wrong to be sarcastic with me, wrong to pretend that there is anything unreasonable in my belief that you think of me sometimes, and wrong to discourage the candour with which I always avow that I think constantly of myself."

"Then you had better not speak to me, since I have no manners."

"Again! Did I say you had no manners? The warmest expressions of regard from my mouth seem to reach your ears transformed into insults. Were I to repeat the Litany of the Blessed Virgin, you would retort as though I had been reproaching you. This is because you hate me. You never misunderstand Langan, whom you love."

"I don't know what London manners are, Mr. Leggs; but in Ireland gentlemen are expected to mind their own business. How dare you say I love Mr. Langan?"

"Then you do not love him?"

"It is nothing to you whether I love him or not."

"Nothing to me that you hate me and love another?'

"I did not say that I hated you. You are not so very clever yourself at understanding what people say, though you make such a fuss because they don't understand you." Here, as she glanced down the road again, she suddenly looked glad.

"Aha!" I said.

"What do you mean by 'Aha'?"

"No matter. I will now show you what a man's sympathy is. As you perceived just then, Langan—who is too tall for his age, by-the-by—is coming to pay you a visit. Well, instead of staying with you, as a jealous woman would, I will withdraw."

"I don't care whether you go or stay, I'm sure. I wonder what you would give to be as fine a man as Mr. Langan."

"All I possess: I swear it! But solely because you admire tall men more than broad views. Mr. Langan may be defined geometrically as length without breadth; altitude without position; a line on the landscape, not a point in it."

"How very clever you are!"

"You do not understand me, I see. Here comes your lover, stepping over the wall like a camel. And here go I, out through the gate like a Christian. Good afternoon, Mr. Langan. I am going because Miss Hickey has something to say to you about me which she would rather not say in my presence. You will excuse me?

"Oh, I'll excuse you," said he boorishly. I smiled, and went out. Before I was quite out of hearing, Kate whispered vehemently to him, "I hate that fellow."

I smiled again; but I had scarcely done so when my spirits fell. I walked hastily away with a coarse threatening sound in my ears like that of the clarionets whose sustained low notes darken the woodland in "Der Freischütz." I found myself presently at the graveyard. It was a barren place, enclosed by a mud wall with a gate to admit funerals, and numerous gaps to admit the peasantry, who made short cuts across it as they went to and fro between Four Mile Water and the market town. The graves were mounds overgrown with grass: there was no keeper; nor were there flowers, railings or any of the conventionalities that make an English grave-yard repulsive. A great thornbush, near what was called the grave of the holy sisters, was covered with scraps of cloth and flannel, attached by peasant women who had prayed before it. There were three kneeling there as I entered, for the reputation of the place had been revived of late by the miracle, and a ferry had been estab-lished close by, to conduct visitors over the route taken by the graveyard. From where I stood I could see on the opposite bank the heap of stones, perceptibly increased since my last visit, marking the deserted grave of Brimstone Billy. I strained my eyes broodingly at it for some minutes, and then descended the river bank and en-tered the boat.

"Good evenin' t' your honour," said the ferryman, and set to work to draw the boat hand-over-hand by a rope stretched across the water.

"Good evening. Is your business beginning to fall off yet?"

"Faith, it never was as good as it might ha' been. The people that comes from the south side can see Billy's grave—Lord have mercy on him—across the wather; and they think bad of payin' a penny to put a stone over him. It's them that lives tow'rst Dublin that makes the journey. Your honour is the third I've brought from south to north this blessed day."

"When do most people come? In the afternoon, I suppose?"

"All hours, sur, except afther dusk. There isn't a sowl in the counthry ud come within sight of that grave wanst the sun goes down."

"And you! Do you stay here all night by yourself?"

"The holy heavens forbid! Is it me stay here all night? No, your honour; I tether the boat at siven o'hlyock, and lave Brimstone Billy—God forgimme!—to take care of it t'll mornin'."

"It will be stolen some night, I'm afraid."

"Arra, who'd dar come next or near it, let alone stale it? Faith, I'd think twice before lookin' at it meself in the dark. God bless your honour, and gran'che long life."

I had given him sixpence. I went to the reprobate's grave and stood at the feet of it, looking at the sky, gorgeous with the descent of the sun. To my English eyes, accustomed to giant trees, broad lawns, and stately mansions, the landscape was wild and inhospitable. The ferryman was already tugging at the rope on his way back (I had told him I did not intend to return that way), and presently I saw him make the painter fast to the south bank; put on his coat; and trudge homeward. I turned towards the grave at my feet. Those who had interred Brimstone Billy, working hastily at an unlawful hour, and in fear of molestation by the people, had hardly dug a grave. They had scooped out earth enough to hide their burden, and no more. A stray goat had kicked away a corner of the mound and exposed the coffin. It occurred to me, as I took some of the stones from the cairn, and heaped them so as to repair the breach, that had the miracle been the work of a body of men, they would have moved the one grave instead of the many. Even from a supernatural point of view, it seemed strange that the sinner should have banished the elect, when, by their superior numbers, they might so much more easily have banished him.

It was almost dark when I left the spot. After a walk of half a mile, I recrossed the water by a bridge, and returned to the farmhouse in which I lodged. Here, finding that I had had enough of solitude, I only stayed to take a cup of tea. Then I went to Father Hickey's cottage.

Kate was alone when I entered. She looked up quickly as I opened the door, and turned away disappointed when she recognized me.

"Be generous for once," I said. "I have walked about aimlessly for hours in order to avoid spoiling the beautiful afternoon for you by my presence. When the sun was up I withdrew my shadow from your path. Now that darkness has fallen, shed some light on mine. May I stay half an hour?"

"You may stay as long as you like, of course. My uncle will soon be home. He is clever enough to talk to you."

"What! More sarcasms! Come, Miss Hickey, help me to spend a pleasant evening. It will only cost you a smile. I am somewhat cast down. Four Mile Water is a paradise; but without you, it would be a little lonely."

"It must be very lonely for you. I wonder why you came here."

"Because I heard that the women here were all Zerlinas, like you, and the men Masettos, like Mr. Phil—where are you going to?"

"Let me pass, Mr. Legge. I had intended never speaking to you

again after the way you went on about Mr. Langan today; and I
wouldn't either, only my uncle made me promise not to take any
notice of you, because you were—no matter; but I won't listen to
you any more on the subject."

"Do not go. I swear never to mention his name again. I beg your
pardon for what I said: you shall have no further cause for complaint. Will you forgive me?"

She sat down, evidently disappointed by my submission. I took a
chair, and placed myself near her. She tapped the floor impatiently
with her foot. I saw that there was not a movement I could make
not a look, not a tone of my voice, which did not irritate her.

"You were remarking," I said, "that your uncle desired you to
take no notice of me because—"

She closed her lips, and did not answer.

"I fear I have offended you again by my curiosity. But indeed, I
had no idea that he had forbidden you to tell me the reason."

"He did not forbid me. Since you are so determined to find
out—"

"No, excuse me. I do not wish to know, I am sorry I asked."

"Indeed! Perhaps you would be sorrier still to be told. I only
made a secret of it out of consideration for you."

"Then your uncle has spoken ill of me behind my back. If that
be so, there is no such thing as a true man in Ireland. I would not
have believed it on the word of any woman alive save yourself."

"I never said my uncle was a backbiter. Just to show you what
he thinks of you, I will tell you, whether you want to know it or
not, that he bid me not mind you because you were only a poor
mad creature, sent down here by your family to be out of harm's
way."

"Oh, Miss Hickey!"

"There now! You have got it out of me; and I wish I had bit my
tongue out first. I sometimes think—that I mayn't sin!—that you
have a bad angel in you."

"I am glad you told me this," I said gently. "Do not reproach
yourself for having done so, I beg. Your uncle has been misled by
what he has heard of my family, who are all more or less insane.
Far from being mad, I am actually the only rational man named
Legge in the three kingdoms. I will prove this to you, and at the
same time keep your indiscretion in countenance, by telling you

something I ought not to tell you. It is this. I am not here as an invalid or a chance tourist. I am here to investigate the miracle. The Cardinal, a shrewd if somewhat erratic man, selected mine from all the long heads at his disposal to come down here, and find out the truth of Father Hickey's story. Would he have entrusted such a task to a madman, think you?"

"The truth of—who dared to doubt my uncle's word? And so you are a spy, a dirty informer."

I started. The adjective she had used, though probably the commonest expression of contempt in Ireland, is revolting to an Englishman.

"Miss Hickey," I said, "there is in me, as you have said, a bad angel. Do not shock my good angel—who is a person of taste—quite away from my heart, lest the other be left undisputed monarch of it. Hark! The chapel bell is ringing the angelus. Can you, with that sound softening the darkness of the village night, cherish a feeling of spite against one who admires you?"

"You come between me and my prayers," she said hysterically, and began to sob. She had scarcely done so, when I heard voices without. Then Langan and the priest entered.

"Oh, Phil," she cried, running to him, "take me away from him: I can't bear—" I turned towards him, and showed him my dog-tooth in a false smile. He felled me at one stroke, as he might have felled a poplar tree.

"Murdher!" exclaimed the priest. "What are you doin, Phil?"

"He's an informer," sobbed Kate. "He came down here to spy on you, uncle, and to try and show that the blessed miracle was a make-up. I knew it long before he told me, by his insulting ways. He wanted to make love to me."

I rose with difficulty from beneath the table, where I had lain motionless for a moment.

"Sir," I said, "I am somewhat dazed by the recent action of Mr. Langan, whom I beg, the next time he converts himself into a fulling-mill, to do so at the expense of a man more nearly his equal in strength than I. What your niece has told you is partly true. I am indeed the Cardinal's spy; and I have already reported to him that the miracle is a genuine one. A committee of gentlemen will wait on you tomorrow to verify it, at my suggestion. I have thought that the proof might be regarded by them as more complete if you were taken by surprise. Miss Hickey, that I admire all that is admirable in you is but to say that I have a sense of the beautiful. To say that I love you would be mere profanity. Mr. Langan, I have in my pocket a loaded pistol, which I carry from a silly English prejudice against your country-men. Had I been the Hercules of the ploughtail, and you in my place, I should have been a dead man now. Do not redden; you are safe as far as I am concerned."

"Let me tell you before you leave my house for good," said Father Hickey, who seemed to have become unreasonably angry, "that you should never have crossed my threshold if I had known you were a spy; no, not if your uncle were his Holiness the Pope himself."

Here a frightful thing happened to me. I felt giddy, and put my hand to my head. Three warm drops trickled over it. Instantly I became murderous. My mouth filled with blood, my eyes were blinded with it; I seemed to drown in it. My hand went involuntarily to the pistol. It is my habit to obey my impulses instantaneously. Fortunately, the impulse to kill vanished before a sudden perception of how I might miraculously humble the mad vanity which these foolish people had turned up in me. The blood receded from my ears; and I again heard and saw distinctly.

"And let *me* tell you," Langan was saying, "that if you think yourself handier with cold lead than you are with your fists, I'll exchange shots with you, and welcome, whenever you please. Father Tom's credit is the same to me as my own, and if you say a word against it, you lie."

"His credit is in my hands," I said. "I am the Cardinal's witness. Do you defy me?"

"There is the door," said the priest, holding it open before me. "Until you can undo the visible work of God's hand your testimony can do no harm to me."

"Father Hickey," I replied, "before the sun rises again upon Four Mile Water, I will undo the visible work of God's hand, and bring the pointing finger of the scoffer upon your altar."

I bowed to Kate, and walked out. It was so dark that I could not at first see the garden-gate. Before I found it, I heard through the window Father Hickey's voice, saying, "I wouldn't for ten pound that this had happened, Phil. He's as mad as a March hare. The Cardinal told me so."

I returned to my lodging, and took a cold bath to cleanse the blood from my neck and shoulder. The effect of the blow I had received was so severe, that even after the bath and a light meal I felt giddy and languid. There was an alarum-clock on the mantel piece. I wound it; set the alarum for half-past twelve; muffled it so that it should not disturb the people in the adjoining room; and went to bed, where I slept soundly for an hour and a quarter. Then the alarum roused me, and I sprang up before I was thoroughly awake. Had I hesitated, the desire to relapse into perfect sleep would have overpowered me. Although the muscles of my neck were painfully stiff, and my hands unsteady from my nervous disturbance, produced by the interruption of my first slumber, I dressed myself resolutely, and after taking a draught of cold water, stole out of the house. It was exceedingly dark and I had some difficulty in finding the cow-house, whence I borrowed a spade, and a truck with wheels, ordinarily used for moving sacks of pota-toes. These I carried in my hands until I was beyond earshot of the house, when I put the spade on the truck, and wheeled it along the road to the cemetery. When I approached the water, knowing that no one would dare to come thereabout at such an hour, I made greater haste, no longer concerning myself about the rattling of the wheels. Looking across to the opposite bank, I could see a phosphorescent glow, marking the lonely grave of Brimstone Billy. This helped me to find the ferry station, where, after wandering a little and stumbling often, I found the boat, and embarked with my implements. Guided by the rope, I crossed the water without difficulty; landed; made fast the boat; dragged the truck up the bank; and sat down to rest on the cairn at the grave. For nearly a quarter of an hour I sat watching the patches of jack-o'-lantern fire, and collecting my strength for the work before me. Then the distant bell of the chapel clock tolled one. I rose, took the spade, and in about ten minutes uncovered the coffin, which smelt horribly. Keeping to windward of it, and using the spade as a lever, I contrived with great labour to place it on the truck. I wheeled it without accident to the landing-place, where, by placing the shafts of the truck upon the stern of the boat and lifting the foot by main strength, I succeeded in embarking my load after twenty minutes' toil, during which I got covered with clay and perspiration, and several times all but upset the boat. At the southern bank I had less difficulty in getting truck and coffin ashore, and dragging them up the graveyard.

It was now past two o'clock, and the dawn had begun, so that I had no further trouble from want of light. I wheeled the coffin to a patch of loamy soil which I had noticed in the afternoon near the grave of the holy sisters. I had warmed to my work; my neck no longer pained me; and I began to dig vigorously, soon making a shallow trench, deep enough to hide the coffin with the addition of a mound. The chill pearl-coloured morning had by this time quite dissipated the darkness. I could see, and was myself visible, for miles around. This alarmed me, and made me impatient to finish my task. Nevertheless, I was forced to rest for a moment before placing the coffin in the trench. I wiped my brow and wrists, and again looked about me. The tomb of the holy women, a massive slab supported on four stone spheres, was grey and wet with dew. Near it was the thornbush covered with rags, the newest of which were growing gaudy in the radiance which was stretching up from the coast on the east. It was time to finish my work. I seized the truck; laid it alongside the grave; and gradually prized the coffin off with the spade until it rolled over into the trench with a hollow sound like a drunken remonstrance from the sleeper within. I shovelled the earth round and over it, working as fast as possible. In less than a quarter of an hour it was buried. Ten minutes more sufficed to make the mound symmetrical, and to clear the traces of my work from the adjacent sward. Then I flung down the spade; threw up my arms; and vented a sign of relief and triumph. But I recoiled as I saw that I was standing on a barren common, covered with furze. No product of man's handiwork was near me except my truck and spade and the grave of Brimstone Billy, now as lonely as before. I turned towards the water. On the opposite bank was the cemetery, with the tomb of the holy women, the thornbush with its rags stirring in the morning breeze, and the broken mud wall. The ruined chapel was there too, not a stone shaken from its crumbling walls, not a sign to show that it and its precinct were less rooted in their place than the eternal hills around.

I looked down at the grave with a pang of compassion for the unfortunate Wolfe Tone Fitzgerald, with whom the blessed would not rest. I was even astonished, though I had worked expressly to this end. But the birds were astir, and the cocks crowing. My land-

lord was an early riser. I put the spade on the truck again, and
hastened back to the farm, where I replaced them in the cowhouse.
Then I stole into the house, and took a clean pair of boots, an
overcoat, and a silk hat. These, with a change of linen, were sufficient to make my appearance respectable. I went out again, bathed
in the Four Mile Water, took a last look at the cemetery, and
walked to Wicklow, whence I travelled by the first train to Dublin.

Some months later, at Cairo, I received a packet of Irish newspapers and a leading article, cut from the *Times,* on the subject of
the miracle. Father Hickey had suffered the meed of his inhospitable conduct. The committee, arriving at Four Mile Water the
day after I left, had found the graveyard exactly where it had formerly stood. Father Hickey, taken by surprise, had attempted to
defend himslef by a confused statement, which led the committee
to declare finally that the miracle was a gross imposture. The
Times, commenting on this after adducing a number of examples
of priestly craft, remarked, "We are glad to learn that the Rev.
Mr. Hickey has been permanently relieved of his duties as the parish priest of Four Mile Water by his ecclesiastical superior. It is
less gratifying to have to record that it has been found possible to
obtain two hundred signatures to a memorial embodying the absurd defense offered to the committee, and expressing unabated
confidence in the integrity of Mr. Hickey."

For the Bend
in the Road

For the Bend in the Road

In the average jovial gathering, the "One for the road" usually ends the evening. Not so in Irish circles. With their innate love for laughter and prolonging the talks, they like to extend the end. Hence, in an average Celtic get-together, somehow, after somebody has proposed one for the road, another celebrant invariably will follow with "One for the bend in the road."

Once in the lone snug pub in little Maghery, Donegal, we heard a lad follow even the "One for the bend in the road" with one for "the poor souls in Purgatory."

Naturally, with these post and late toasts, a story usually follows. Sometimes, the story may be short but just as easily it could be long—any excuse for not breaking up the party too early.

A warning to Irish-Americans to have a care when they go to Ireland to look up the relatives, especially those far removed, was given by Bob Considine, the famed roving correspondent. Bob pointed out that to your fifth cousin Padraic, once removed, you may be just another blustering Yank who happens to have the same name and who wants, tacitly or openly, to tell Padraic how well you are doing in the States.

"Cousin Jack, may the good Lord bechune ya and all harm," Considine once exclaimed as he plunged into J. Considine's Butcher Shoppe on O'Connell Street in Ennis, Clare, to renew their acquaintance. The butcher posed his cleaver in mid-stroke, looked at Bob and said, "You're getting fat."

Actor Pat O'Brien tells the story of the priest preaching a mission sermon, who warned his listeners about the suddenness of death. "Before another day is ended," he thundered, "somebody in this parish will die."

Seated in the front row was a little old Irisher who laughed out loud at this statement. Very angry, the priest said to the jovial old man, "What's so funny?" "Oh!" spoke up the oldster, "I'm not a member of this parish."

Playwright Marc Connelly tells of the Saturday afternoon he spent in his room at the Hotel Gresham, Dublin. Connelly had arrived earlier that morning and called Lennox Robinson, the Abbey playwright, as to whether two tickets were available that evening for one of Robinson's plays. Robinson explained that the Abbey, being a small theater, was already sold out, but that he would endeavor to get a pair of tickets, and would call Connelly back.

Not to miss Robinson's call, Connelly remained in his room all afternoon at the Gresham. Finally, he decided he would leave his room. When he went down to the lobby, the telephone operator called, "Oh, Mr. Connelly, I've been trying to get you all day. Mr. Lennox Robinson has two tickets for you. I paged you in every one of the man's bars and I even sent Hughie, the doorman, to look in and see if you were in Mooney's across the street."

"I've been in my room all afternoon," explained Connelly, "because I've been waiting for this call. Why didn't you call my room?"

"Ring your room!" exclaimed the colleen. "Now what would you be doing in your room on a nice Saturday holiday. Naturally, I thought you would be in one of the bars. Where else would a foine man like yourself be on a Saturday?"

Once we registered at the Shelbourne in Dublin. My wife took a trip up to the North and phoned me from there. The operator told her that I wasn't registered. It so happened that a friend who was waiting to see me was standing at the phone exchange and told the operator that I was in room 607.

Later, when I protested at the desk that the operator hadn't registered me in yet, the clerk look a bit astounded.

"But, sir, you arrived on Saturday; this happens to be only Tuesday. Naturally the telephone operator hasn't got her records straight yet."

In the railroad station at Cork, there's a sign on the train going to

Dublin. I asked a railroad employee whether the train was a local or express. He didn't seem to understand my question, so I proceeded to explain.

"Well," I said. "If it's a local it will be a slow train."

"Oh," he said, "this train is not so slow."

"Then," I said, "it must be an express."

"No," he said, "it's not so fast either."

In our parish of St. Michael's, in the early days, a saloonkeeper by the name of Kelly lost his license. This was quite disgraceful and everywhere Kelly went people commented that Kelly lost his license. To lose a license in those days, a saloon had to be pretty bad. Kelly was disgusted to hear "Kelly lost his license" everywhere he went.

One Sunday when setting out for Mass, he pondered, "When I go to church, I won't be hearing 'Kelly lost his license.' "

However, he was a few minutes late for Mass and when he came in, the priest was turning to the congregation and singing the Latin Kyrie Eleison and repeating it. To Kelly's ear he was singing "Kelly lost his license," so he departed and never returned to the church.

It was the same saloonkeeper, Kelly, who had generously offered to put in a new stained-glass window in the parish church in Philadelphia. The pastor suggested he put a brass plaque on it commemorating Kelly's parents.

"Oh, no," said Kelly, "just put 'After Mass, visit Kelly's!' "

The Jews and Irish have always had a close affinity. Some crude cynics have said they are both lost tribes. Anyway, in Ireland, the Jewish colony has existed for centuries and developed many leaders in the nation. In recent years, Dublin has had a Jewish mayor, Robert C. Briscoe, a very personable Irisher who played a part in the Rebellion.

The late Rabbi Herzog, who was a leader in Israel, originally came from Dublin. We remember first meeting him back in the 1930's, when he was a great friend of Dr. Oliver Gogarty, Brinsley McNamara and other Irish wits. Later, we met him in Jerusalem, where his Hebraic speech was delivered in that wonderful, musical Dublin accent with the faint touch of a brogue. We remember full

well Rabbi Herzog introducing us to a delegation of visitors with a
short speech in which, in true Irish fashion, he built us up, away
up, and then tore us down again.

Rabbi's beginning gave us quite a glow, for he said: "John
McCarthy has brought here something cultural which Israel needs
and can use." As we beamed, thinking how could we bring to this
great ancient land anything new culturally, Rabbi Herzog quickly
added: "McCarthy brings us Irish jokes."

In New York today, there is the Loyal League of Yiddish Sons of
Erin. To belong, you must be a Jew born in Ireland. Annually,
the League holds a celebration called "Erev St. Patrick's Day Banquet." "Erev" in Hebrew means "holiday eve." What the League
does is to combine March 17th, St. Patrick's Feast Day, with March
26th, Purim, most festive of Hebrew holidays commemorating
Queen Esther's success in preventing a Persian tyrant from wiping
out her people.

So on Erev St. Patrick's Day celebration, the League selects a
colleen Queen Esther. In 1967, Rosalyn Finkelstein from the
Bronx, New York, was the lucky colleen to be chosen Queen. At
the Banquet, green matzoballs and green bagels are served.

"Green bagels," assures Michael Mann, president of the Loyal
League of Yiddish Sons of Erin. "They're good if you acquire a
taste for them. We're kosher Irish."

What's more, there is prime beef O'Malley, litvak chopped liver
and kishka à la Killarney on the menu at the annual "gathering of
the clan"—the Irish-Jewish clan in Manhattan.

"It's pretty much a sort of celebration for the common heritage
of the two ancient civilizations—Irish and Jewish," explains Mann,
a Jew whose father was a harnessmaker in Dublin.

"Now in our adopted land, we celebrate the fruits of our friendship," said Mann.

Robert Winternitz, well-known in advertising and theatrical circles, likes to repeat a comment that he once heard in McDaid's
Pub in Dublin. There Bob overheard several Irish intellectuals
discussing men and women. One intellectual stopped talking, laid
down his pint on the bar and asked the assembled group whether
or not they knew what was behind every successful man. A couple
brought forth the usual answer of the wife, another the parents,

etc. However, the Irish intellectual waved such conjectures aside and said, "Behind every successful man is an astonished mother-in-law."

A long-time stage and screen star, Frank McHugh, was a great friend of the late Frank Fay, who achieved great success in the Broadway play "Harvey." McHugh tells this one about Frank Fay's car.

When Frank Fay and actress Barbara Stanwyck were divorced, Fay received Barbara's car as part of the community property settlement. This was an expensive foreign car with all kinds of gadgets. It was widely known and envied in Hollywood and Beverly Hills. Fay was very friendly with his pastor, the late Mgsr. Kenneally. So Fay suggested to the Monsignor that he take the car and raffle it off.

"Everybody knows my wife's car," said Fay, "so why don't you announce a raffle, but by all means be sure and emphasize that it was Barbara Stanwyck's car. That will immediately identify it to everyone in your congregation. Most of your parishioners would like to own it, so they should take five or ten chances. Don't mention my name. But, Monsignor, emphasize it is Barbara Stanwyck's car."

On Sunday, Mgsr. Kenneally made his announcement. When he came to say who owned the car, he began to hem and haw and said, "The car you all know belongs to ——" he paused again, "——," and then said, "The car belongs to Mrs. Fay." He stopped again. "As I was telling you, this car—as you all know and have seen around Beverly Hills and Hollywood—you have seen it around. Many of you say 'There goes the car that belongs to —— (pause) —— belongs to Mrs. Fay.' "

Finishing the announcement, the Monsignor took up the Gospel and started to read about how the Lord went down to the temple. He stopped abruptly, shot his hand up and shouted: "Belongs to Barbara Stanwyck!"

The same Frank McHugh comes from a long line of actors. In the early days in the theater, the entire McHugh family played together. There was his father, Cutie McHugh; Mother McHugh; Kitty McHugh; and his brothers, Jim, Eddie, and Matt. Frank's father played in "Of Human Hearts" longer than any other actor in any other Irish production, including Eugene O'Neill's father in "The Count of Monte Cristo" and Frank Bacon in "Lightnin'."

Before going into "Of Human Hearts," Frank relates how his father used to play in a special road show built around a trip to Ireland. All the scenes were on a big revolving stage: Killarney, the Giants' Causeway, Dublin, et al. As the stage revolved, Frank's father would change costumes, make comments, do an Irish jig or sing a ballad.

While playing with his two brothers, Eddie and Matt, in vaudeville, Frank recalls that they always made it a point to borrow half their salary by Wednesday night. Hence, in case they were fired or the house went broke, at least they had half their pay. Frank said that on one tour their grandmother died sixty-two times and their parents were near death some fifty times—any story just to get their money.

Speaking of the old days, Frank comments that "Old actors never died. They just got lost looking for a friendly saloon and were never heard from again."

Returning to New York on an airplane, and dressed in simple black street attire, Cardinal Francis Spellman was seated next to a man who, not recognizing him, asked:

"Where are you stationed, Father?"

"In New York," the prelate replied.

"Where in New York?"

"At the Cathedral."

"Say," said the traveler, "that must be a good job."

"You're telling me," said the Cardinal.

"It's bad taste," once remarked novelist Sean O'Faolain, "to be serious in Ireland. You have no heroes in Ireland, and were you to have one, you must laugh at him, too." This dictum is carried out to the letter, especially by the Irish cabbies or "jarveys," as they are called there. No respectors of persons or reputations. That makes them delightful conversationalists.

I carry in my wallet a card given me in Portmarnock by jarvey Purcell. As I was getting out of his cab to go to the golf course there, Purcell asked: "Will ye be staying in town tonight? If so, you better have my card." I did. Later I glanced at the card and read: "Ring Purcell's Garage for Taxi. Drunk or sober, we will see you home."

Another time I took a cab to the General Post Office in Dublin. This old Victorian edifice was the scene of the 1916 Irish Rebellion which eventually led to Ireland's freedom. When we arrived at the post office, I commented: "Well, here's where it all began."

"How right you are, sir," politely replied the jarvey. " 'Twas here on Easter Sunday 1916 when thirty-three brave lads—be sure and mark the number, sir—went into that post office. For three whole days these brave lads held the entire British army and British navy too, sir, at bay."

"Now, sir, do you believe in paradoxes?" continued the jarvey. I admitted I did.

"Well, sir, do you know that today the Irish Government is paying full army pensions to some 9,183 brave lads who claimed that they too went into that post office on that Easter Sunday in 1916 and fought for Ireland."

Then, as if an afterthought, the jarvey added: "When you are in there, sir, see if the post office could hold 9,183."

Mark Twain once observed: "Give an Irishman lager for a month, and he's a dead man. An Irishman is lined with copper, and the beer corrodes it. But whiskey polishes the copper and is the saving of him."

"George," said the Mayo wife on the way home from Sunday church service, "did you notice the beautiful fur coat Mrs. Armstrong was wearing today?"

"No," replied her husband, "I'm afraid I didn't. In fact, I was dozing most of the time."

"Oh, George! A lot of good it does you to go to church."

An enthusiastic devotee of fishing, Basil Burton, the London publisher, has been going for years to Ireland to indulge in his favorite sport.

During World War II, Burton was not able to get to Ireland regularly. However, after a long absence, he managed a trip there.

The first thing Burton did was to look up his regular guide, Brendon. However, Brendon begged off escorting him because, as he confided, he was gainfully employed by some German agents to lay mines about the Irish shores. That Burton was British did not deter Brendon from telling him about his connection with the enemy. After all, wasn't Mister Burton an old pal who would not begrudge a friend making a few extra bob?

So Burton then approached Brendon's brother Sean, who had occasionally come along on past fishing trips. However, Sean was sorry, but he, too, would not guide Burton on account of having a full-time job. Sean, too, frankly told what it was. Sean had been engaged by the British Admiralty to pick up the German mines which his brother Brendon would lay.

An Irish beggar sat on a bridge urging his appeal to the charity of passers-by with all the eager and versatile eloquence of his countrymen. As one couple passed, he exlaimed: "May the blessings of the Lord which brings love and joy and wealth and a fine family follow you all the days of your life." A pause. When the couple passed the Irisher by without contributing, he hollered after them, "And never overtake you."

Some years ago I was stranded in a downpour outside Glasnevin Cemetery, Dublin, when a top-hatted jarvey in an old-fashioned hansom cab with an almost lifeless nag drove up. Of course, he had no meter albeit I was very happy to engage him.

As the spiritless horse clip-clopped leisurely in from the cemetery to the Gresham Hotel, the jarvey sparked the conversation which consisted mainly of questions about my travels on the European continent and to the various cities in the United States.

When we arrived at the Gresham and I asked what the fare was, the jarvey was seemingly insulted. "The very idea, sir," he admonished me paternally, "of a cosmopolitan gentleman like your good self who has been to London, Paris, Rome, Chicago and other far-off places asking me, a poor ignorant jarvey who has never been outside of Dublin, the fare. Why, sir, you should know full well what it's worth, for you have taken many such joyous journeys." "Lay off the blarney," I answered. "Unless you tell what the fare is, I will go in and check with Hughie, the doorman here at the

Gresham, as to what the jarvey fare from Glasnevin should be."

"Well, I'll tell ye, sir," said he with a sly wink, "the meanest man I ever drove in from Glasnevin to the Gresham—aye, sir, the meanest man—gave me twenty shillin's." In those days, 20 shillings was almost $4. Not wanting to be his meanest fare, I gave him 25 shillings, or about $5.

Out of curiosity, I did ask Hughie, the doorman at the Gresham, what was the average jarvey fare in from Glasnevin. "Have you paid him yet?" cautiously inquired Hughie before committing himself. I replied that I had already paid. Relieved, Hughie said: "It averages about ten shillings or two dollars, sir."

My good wife Evelyn, who knows Ireland far better than her husband does, always asks a jarvey first for an estimate of what the fare will be before engaging him. Once, coming out of Trinity College, she hailed a jarvey and inquired what his fare would be to take her to the Gresham Hotel.

"Four shillings, miss."

"Go on," said my wife, "the Gresham is really only a few blocks up the street. Two shillings is plenty for that trip."

Came back the jarvey pronto with: "Two shillings is what I said, miss."

The local District Judge had given the defendant a lecture on the evils of drink. But in view of the fact that this was the first time the man had been drunk and incapable, the case was dismissed on payment of ten shillings costs.

"Now don't let me ever see your face again," said the Justice sternly as the defendant turned to go.

"I'm afraid I can't promise that, sir," said the released man.

"And why not?"

"Because I'm the barman at your regular pub, The Shamrock."

The good Donegal Sister had her class studying their cathechism. When she asked one little boy if he had progressed in his studies as far as original sin, he replied proudly:

"Oh, yes, Sister. I'm beyond redemption."

During one of the not infrequent economic crises in Dublin, a prominent Irish tycoon said, "Our economy's rotten, we have no proper industry, the bottom's fallen out of agriculture, the weather's desperate and our politicians idiots, but it's a damn fine country to live in, just the same."

Norton Mockridge, the very personable, talented newspaper columnist, heard this Irish tale from Arthur B. Kane of Dobbs Ferry, New York, who is a good friend of the Irish gentleman involved.

A short but strongly built, square-jawed man was known to his buddies as a man who's fast with his fists. He's also known for the pipe that's always clenched between his teeth, emitting dense clouds of smoke and showers of sparks.

On the day of the sail, Mac and his wife boarded the Hudson River Day Liner and set up two folding chairs next to the railing. Scores of other people, attracted by the sunny autumn weather, gathered around them and soon all the chairs were taken.

When Mrs. Mac started to unwrap their sandwiches, Mac got up and went to the bar to get some drinks. But when he returned, drinks in hand, he found his chair was gone.

"Where's me chair?" he sputtered, as he set down the drinks. His wife pointed and said: "That man over there took it before I could stop him."

"Ah, hah!" roared Mac. And he strode over, fixed this husky, dark-haired man with a terrible stare, tapped him on the shoulder and said: "Ye'll stand up!"

The man stood up and Mac grabbed the chair and whisked it out from beneath him. But the man, startled as he was, grabbed it, too. The two men wrestled for the chair for a moment or so and Mac, getting purple in the face and puffing so hard on his pipe that it looked like a locomotive belching fire, finally gave a great heave and twisted it out of the other fellow's hands.

Triumphantly, he marched back to his wife's side, plunked the chair on the deck and dropped into it. Mrs. Mac reached over and gently patted his head.

"But, dear," she said. "That wasn't the man."

Our good friend in Rye, New York, James M. Voss, president of Caltex, suggested that the next time we went to Ireland we take a look at the group of attractive service stations which his petroleum company has placed there on the highways. We did. Stopping at one small station in a remote spot in Sligo, we told the attendant that there was something wrong with our car. It had a peculiar sound as if it were singing. Replied the attendant, "Aye, you're lucky, sir, your car obviously has talent."

As the attendant started to work on our car, we told him how in the States, Texaco, part of his firm, was well-known for their rest rooms and lavatory facilities. So jokingly we said, "You Irish would not let the Yanks top you in that service, so we would like to see yours." "Indade not," replied the attendant. "Come along with me." With that he took us to a wide-open field behind the gas pumps, and with a wide sweep of his arm said: "Here are your rest rooms—as far as you see, sir!"

When a neighbor remarked to Pat Morrissey, 79, "What a beautiful autumn day it is," Pat replied, "I'll tell you how beautiful it is. It's so pretty today that I wish I was working again so that I could take the day off."

Following his readings of selections from Oscar Wilde's works in a Manhattan theatre, Micheál MacLiammóir, Ireland's superb performer, confided to the press: "In my one-man show, I expect to have nothing but the most harmonious relationship with the cast."

Speaking of Guinness, this internationally famous stout is brewed in the largest brewery in the world at St. James's Gate, Dublin. Tours through the brewery are conducted daily. On one of these, two Irishers were gazing in awe at the vast vats containing the foamy black brew when one observed: "If ye fell into that, you'd be drowned." "But, oh," said the other, "what a happy death!"

Dan Keefe, vice-president of McCann-Erickson, tells of his encounter of a morning on Third Avenue, New York, with an Irishman who was just coming out of Tim Costello's saloon. The Irishman stopped Keefe and asked for a quarter. Endeavoring to have some fun, Keefe pompously replied: "My good man, I never dispense alms on the street." This stopped the Irisher, but just for an instant. His Celtic comeback was: "What do you want me to do? Open an office just to handle your business?" Keefe paid because he thought the answer was worth at least a half-dollar.

Bishop Fulton J. Sheen, head of the diocese of Rochester, New York, relates that shortly after his elevation to the rank of Bishop he made the first of his many appearances on television, and stopped for a cup of coffee at the drugstore in the building where the studio was located, with his red cape already in place. The girl at the counter, obviously used to serving actors in every kind of costume, took the red cape very much in stride and asked blithely, "What's yours, Cock Robin?"

According to John Ryan, the well-known New York antique dealer, there is an old Irish lady who sells shoelaces on Lexington Avenue and has been doing same for years. In fact, Ryan claims she has the original stock of shoelaces with which she started in business because people, to get rid of her, give her a quarter and never take a pair of shoelaces. For some months, Ryan was able to avoid her, but one recent morning, she fenced him in. Ryan proffered his usual quarter and started off without taking any shoelaces. "Just a minute, sir," called the Celtic crone, "since you been away, the price has gone up to thirty-five cents."

"Give us Irish a miserable thought," said famed actress Laurette Taylor, "and we create an Ibsen drama."

A priest in Cork was summoned to a house where a woman, a devoted parish worker, had been taken seriously ill. It so happened that the woman was not of his parish; but as he had been urgently summoned and lived quite near, he decided to call.

While waiting to be shown to the sickroom, he struck up a conversation with the little girl of the house.

"I hope your mother isn't too bad," he ventured. "By the way, are there no priests available in your own parish?"

"Oh, yes, Father," she said in a matter-of-fact tone. "Father X is on duty. But we thought it might be something contagious and we didn't want to take any risks."

The parish priest in Dublin was plainly shocked by the harrowing tale that was being told him by the prosperous-looking caller. And it concerned a family in his parish.

"Yes," the visitor assured the parish priest, "the Murphy family are in desperate straits. Not only are they on the borderline of starvation, but they will certainly be evicted—imagine, in this terrible weather—and their furniture thrown out into the street unless 15 pounds is immediately collected for the rent."

"Shocking," agreed the now distressed parish priest. "Something will have to be done about it. . . . By the way, I don't think you are a parishioner. May I ask who you are?"

The visitor wiped away his tears, blew his nose and, managing to compose himself, replied: "Me? . . . I'm the landlord."

In a New York restaurant a rather pompous-looking Englishman sat at a table next to an Irishman. In a very definite English accent he gave an order to the waiter for English beef, English mustard and some English muffins. Also some English tea. He emphasized the English bit in every case.

When the waiter asked the Irishman what he wanted—he ordered Irish stew, some Irish bacon and eggs, some Irish pudding and "by all means, Irish tea."

"Anything more?" asked the waiter.

"Yes," said the Irishman. "I wish that man there would say something."

The Irish in Ireland don't put much stand by time. It's their feeling that one gift that God has given them is time.

One day, while walking down O'Connell Street, I found that my watch had stopped so I asked several people what the time was. None had any watches on them and they stared at this curious Yank who had an interest in time. Of course, I couldn't find a public clock and those in the jewelry stores were not running. As I was crossing O'Connell at Middle Abbey Street, I spotted a traffic officer and thought surely he would have a watch. So I stepped up to him and said,

"Officer, do you know the exact time?"

And he said, "The exact time, sir?"

"Yes, the exact time."

The officer pondered a minute, looked skyward and asked, "Was it the exact time you wanted?"

I replied that it was.

"Well, sir," he replied, "it's exactly between one and two."

On the Irish army rifle range, the sergeant asked the corporal,

"I wonder what Private Kelly did before he enlisted?"

"Why?" the corporal asked.

"Every time he fires a shot," the sergeant replied, "he takes out his handkerchief and wipes his fingerprints off the rifle."

A sculptor in Clare told of his failure to persuade the youthful Widow Crowley to put up a monument to her departed husband.

"Yerra, Mr. Johnson," she said, "what's the good of putting up a monument to Martin's memory? He hadn't memory enough to remember where he left his hat while he was eating his dinner."

During a school assembly in Chicago, the glee club began to warble out "When Irish Eyes Are Smiling." In the middle of the song, a woman in the audience began to cry softly.

"Why, I didn't know you were Irish," a nearby woman said to her in comforting tones.

"I'm not," the woman sobbed. "I'm a music teacher."

John McCormack, famed Irish tenor, once was in a motorcar accident. A certain Cork paper that recorded the accident added: "We are happy to state that he was able to appear the following evening in four pieces."

The Donegal definition of a hangover: "Something occupying a head that wasn't used the night before."

"I am allergic to all Irish wit, charm and humour not provided by myself," remarked historian D. W. Brogan.

John Dillon once told a story about himself. He lived outside Dublin in the suburbs and he commuted daily. Dillon didn't smoke and couldn't stand any of the people who did. One morning as he was seated in the train carriage, an elderly Irishman sat opposite him and lit up his pipe. Immediately, Dillon said, "Look, my good man, this is a nonsmoking carriage and I wish that you would put that pipe away. Here is my card so that you know the important source from which this comes."

The elderly man looked at the card and put it in his pocket. However, he kept on smoking. This infuriated Dillon no end; hence, when the train stopped at a junction, Dillon got out from the carriage and began to look for a guard. It was one of the old-fashioned carriages with single compartments, with no connecting corridors, and the passengers locked in. When Dillon found the guard, he complained loudly and demanded that he oust the old man. The train guard went into the carriage and informed the old man that he must stop smoking. With that, the old man reached in his pocket and pulled out Dillon's card.

"Oh, okay, your Lordship," and the guard tipped his hat and went on. When he came back to the platform, he said, "I'd like to stop him, but I don't dare. That's that old crazy politician Dillon with the blabber mouth. If I crossed him, it might cost me my job. You know what a revengeful ass he is."

Brendan Behan, late Irish author, was the soul of courtesy, but there were times when he could give back as good as he got.

Brendan and a friend were emerging from the Long Hall in Dublin during the Christmas season, and Brendan had the misfortune to bump into a lady laden with parcels, the result being to scatter her parcels all over the pavement.

Brendan promptly swooped to recover them from among the feet of the passers-by and restore them to her arms, but her ladyship's temper was not thereby placated.

"I'd have you know," she declared angrily, "that my husband's a detective, and, if he was here, he'd take ye!"

This was too much for Brendan, who after all had done his best. "Ma'am," said he, "I don't doubt it. If he took you, he'd take anything."

In West Kerry, the wife commented, "When we were first married, you took the small piece of steak and gave me the larger.

You don't love me any more."

"Nonsense, darling," replied hubby, "you cook better now."

Fishmonger in Sligo, wrapping up salmon: "Fine colour, ma'am, isn't it?"

Customer: "Yes, I imagine it's blushing at the price."

Irish intellectual: One who goes to an art gallery even when it's not raining.

Patrick Cannon, the editor of the Irish edition of the *Catholic Digest*, is a great milk drinker and he's rather particular that the milk be perfect when served. Recently, while in a Dublin restaurant, he asked the young girl waitress whether or not the milk that she served him was fresh. "If it was any fresher, it would be grass," she replied.

At the International Catholic Press Convention held in New York a few years ago, there was a delegate from Ireland who was a priest from an obscure order unknown in America. The editor of a Catholic magazine, in a conversation with the Irish delegate, politely asked what the delegate's order was noted for. "Well, I tell you," replied the Irish priest. "Our order is not as scholarly as the Jesuits nor as large as the Dominicans. Neither are we as silent as the Trappists. However, when it comes to humility, we are tops."

The *Irish Digest* reprinted a selection of statements in insurance claims made recently in Ireland.

"I knocked over a man. He admitted it was his fault, as he had been run over before."

"The accident was due to the other man narrowly missing me."

"I collided with a stationary bus coming the other way."

"A cow wandered into my car. I was afterwards informed that the cow was half-witted."

"She suddenly saw me, lost her head, and we met."

"A truck backed through my windscreen into my wife's face."

"I bumped a lamppost which was obscured by pedestrians."

"I ran into a shop window and sustained injuries to my wife."
"I collided with a stationary tree."
"Dog on the road applied brakes, causing a skid."
"The other man altered his mind, so I had to run into him."
"I misjudged a lady crossing the street."
"Coming home, I drove into the wrong house and collided with a tree I haven't got."
"I told the other idiot what he was and went on."

"Has anybody here dropped a shilling?" asked the Dublin bus conductor after he had picked up a halfpenny.
"Yes—I'm certain it is mine," said a smart woman passenger.
"Well, ma'am," said the conductor, "here's a halfpenny on account. If we find the other eleven and a half pence, the Company will let you know."

That gay companion, Frank Sullivan, one-time newspaper columnist and *New Yorker* contributor, now the Sage of Saratoga, New York, has a hobby of collecting reupholstered proverbs. Here are a choice few:
"A man is known by the Russian he scratches."
"An apple a day is the evil thereof.
"He that keeps the doctor away will live to fight another day."
"A penny saved is a pound foolish."
"Beauty is only the spice of life."
"A fool and his money rush in where angels fear to tread."
"A word to the wise is resented."
"Sleeping dogs make strange bedfellows."
"A woman's work is all play."

Irish lass to her host of the evening, "Gosh, Seamus, I had enough fun tonight to last me ten years."
"See you then!"

From a Belfast travel agent's advertisement: "If you went abroad at a cheaper price than ours, you were deported."

Bernard Shaw wrote novels before writing plays. They weren't successful and one rejected manuscript was thrown into a corner of his London digs where rodents nibbled at it. Later Shaw commented, "Even the mice couldn't finish it."

After months of industrious searching, a young Cork actor at long last got his first part in a Dublin show. He was so happy and excited he phoned his father, broke the good news and explained: "I play a man who's been married for twenty years."

"Good for you," replied his dad. "Keep up the good work and eventually you may get a speaking part."

Every Irishman needs a wife, because many things go wrong that he can't blame on the government.

Annually in Galway, they used to have what was known as "The Flapper Races," in which anything went. Oft, the jockeys decided among themselves in advance which one would win. The late Joe McGrath, one of the founders of the Irish Sweepstakes, had a favorite story about these Galway Flapper Races.

It seemed that the neighbor of an owner who had an entry in one of these Flapper meetings asked him how his horse was going to make out.

"How should I know?" replied the owner. "Why don't you go down to the paddock and ask Paddy, my jockey."

"I'll not do that," retorted the neighbor. "I'm no tout. I know you, the owner, so why should I have to ask your hireling for information?"

"Okay," said the owner, "come along with me and I'll ask Paddy meself, personally." So owner and neighbor headed toward the paddock. When they arrived, Paddy, short, stumpy, sullen and snobby, was already mounted.

"Hello, Paddy," greeted the owner. "How are we making out today?"

"We are not making out today," snarled Jockey Paddy, "for I'm not even going to try to do anything."

"So," said the owner, turning to the neighbor, "there is your answer." With that the owner slapped his racehorse on the flank, saying, "Okay, Paddy, good luck anyway."

The neighbor was flabbergasted. At once he began berating Paddy violently, calling him every possible infamous name.

"Aye," commented the owner, "Paddy is not such a bad lad.

Indade, a good many jockeys wouldn't have told you that much."

Displayed in the window of a Belfast beauty parlor is the sign: "Men! Please do not whistle when a gorgeous girl emerges—it may be your grandmother."

"A learned man is an idler who kills time by study."—Bernard Shaw

A judge in Cork asked: "Were you present at the beginning of the trouble between your friend and his wife?"
Witness: "Sure, wasn't I best man at their wedding!"

An old railway signalman in Donegal was an important witness in action for damages brought by a man who had been knocked down at a level crossing. He insisted that he had waved his lantern frantically, but vainly, and a stiff cross-examination failed to shake his story.
"Congratulations, Mick," said the superintendent after the case was settled. "I was afraid you might break down."
"No fear," replied Mick. "But I don't mind admitting now that I was scared that fellow was going to ask me if my lantern was lit."

During the troublesome times of the early 1920's, an Irish landlord told his steward, "Tell the tenants that any threats to shoot you instantly will not intimidate me."

Cyril Cusack, the well-known Irish actor, is an old friend of ours and on our last visit to Dublin, he invited me out to his house for dinner and asked me to come out early. I asked instructions on how to get there and he said,
"Now I'll tell you—you go down near where Nelson's Pillar is and you'll catch a bus marked Dalkey, which arrives there usually on the hour. However, Tim, who drives this bus, is a temperamental lad. Sometimes he waits for five or ten minutes and sometimes he won't wait at all and drives back. So I suggest you go down there early, otherwise you'll have an hour's wait."
Since I was invited to dinner and Cyril's favorite drink is

Guinness, I bought a goodly supply of pints and proceeded to follow instructions. However, down around Nelson's Pillar traffic was almost like 42nd Street and Fifth Avenue in New York City, with cars and busses going this way and that. I took a chance and followed his instructions and was standing there with my arms laden with Guiness when I spotted a traffic officer looking daggers at me. To appease him, I said,

"Officer, if I stand exactly where I am, will I get the bus for Dalkey?"

Very politely he replied, "If you stand exactly where you are, you'll get the bus for Dalkey right in the middle of your arse!"

In front of Trinity College, Dublin, I asked a civic guard who was directing traffic how I could get from there to Bray.

"Bray was it you want to go to?" he said.

"Yes," I replied. "Bray."

He turned to me and asked, "You're sure it's Bray?"

"Yes."

"And you want to go there from here?"

"Yes."

"I'm telling you, sir," responded the civic guard. "If it's Bray you want to go to from here, you'll have to start from somewhere else."

Regardless of what country they happen to be born in, Irishmen, nigh on to every generation, are supposedly blessed with blarney. The word itself derives from Blarney Castle, near Cork, Ireland, which was built in 1446 by Cormac McCarthy. In the Blarney Castle rests the famous Blarney Stone, reputed to confer eloquence on those who kiss it.

However, it takes some doing to kiss the Blarney Stone , for it is placed in an almost inaccessible position near the top of the castle's eighteen-foot thick wall. Evidently it is worth the effort. For instance, an anonymous poem, quoted in John Gibson Lockhart's *Life of Sir Walter Scott,* pledges:

> The Stone this is
> Whoever kisses
> He never misses
> To grow eloquent.

'Tis he may clamber
To my lady's chamber
Or be a member
of Parliament.

In Webster's Dictionary, blarney is defined as "smooth, whee-dling talk, cajoling flattery." However, Irishmen much prefer the definition of blarney as aptly given by one of their own, namely, Bishop Fulton J. Sheen. Says the good Bishop: "Baloney is flat-tery so thick it cannot be true, and blarney is flattery so thin we like it."

Actually, the term "blarney" originated in the dealings of Queen Elizabeth I with the then Lord of Blarney, Cormac MacDermott McCarthy, a direct descendant of the great Cormac. Repeatedly, the Lord of Blarney was asked by the Queen's deputy, Carew, to renounce the traditional system by which Irish clans elected their chiefs, and to take tenure of his lands from the Crown.

While seeming to agree to this proposal, the politic Lord of Blarney put off the fulfillment of his promise from day to day with "fair words and soft speech" until the annoyed Queen Eliza-beth snorted: "This is all Blarney. What he says he never means."

That amusing colleen, Peg Bracken, observes: "Someone once remarked that he didn't really like to drink—it was just some-thing to do while getting drunk. I've often felt the same way about travel. It's just something to do while getting somewhere. Or in order to have been somewhere."

Lovely Loretta McSweeney fell in love with Irving Marks. How-ever, because of the difference in their respective religions, their romance seemed doomed to failure. Loretta, an ardent Catholic, was adamant in being married in the Church, whereas, Irving would not agree to a Catholic marriage. Loretta discussed her dilemma with her parents. Her father pointed out that, since Irving was a salesman, he would likely be easy to sell and sug-gested that Loretta study up on her religion and give a con-vincing Catholic presentation to Irving. Loretta did. Soon, she was able to tell her parents that Irving had liked her presentation very much, and she thought he would become a Catholic. Elated, her parents congratulated her on her sales ability.

It turned out that Loretta certainly did make a good sale. Several days later, she came home in tears. Her parents asked what was the matter, "Is Irving reneging on becoming a Catholic?" "No," said Loretta, "now Irving wants to become a priest!"

In one of many interesting pieces about New York, Irish authority Jimmy Breslin tells about Mrs. Ryan, a mean-looking blonde, who claimed her husband was not thoughtful.

"In this," says Jimmy, "she was wrong; her husband thought about her too much. One morning on his way to work, he thought about her so much that he got off the subway at 34th Street and went to the Greyhound Terminal and took a bus to Yuma, Arizona."

As an altar boy in his home town of St. Louis, publicist Henry Woods remembers one time when he was en route to serve the 6 A.M Mass. As he was passing a dark alley, a rat ran out. Suddenly Henry was seized on the shoulder by an old Irisher apparently en route home after a hard night out. As the Irisher grabbed Henry, he cried out: "Lad, what did you just see what came out of that alley?" "A rat," replied Henry. "Thank God for that!" said the Irisher as he lurched away.

Due to the changes to one-way avenues in New York City, the drivers, a number of whom are lads not too long from Mayo, Cavan, and other counties in Ireland, are continuously asked questions about which bus is going where. Recently, our Mayo man was asked if a Madison Ave. bus at 57th Street went to 96th Street.

"I'm tired of answering questions," he growled. "Ask the starter."

"Where is he?"

"On 23rd Street."

Coming down to New York on the New Haven Railroad from his home in Rye, N.Y., adman Richard McShane Kelly reports the incident of a lovely model in a miniskirt getting on at New Rochelle.

Ignoring the ogling Madison Avenue passengers en route to work, she sashayed down the smoking compartment to a chair next to an old pipe-smoking Irisher.

As the model eased herself into the car chair, her miniskirt, much to the enjoyment of the Madison Avenuers, went up. As she started to pull it down, the Irish ancient turned to her, tapped her on the knee with his pipe, and said, "Don't go to any bother for me, lass. My hobby is smoking."

Margery Boland, the well-known Dublin modiste, and her lady associate crossed over to London to an international fashion show. All around them in the Savoy Grill people were speaking French, German or Italian. Not wanting to be out of it, and to impress those around them, particularly the stately Savoy waiter, Margery and associate began reciting the Lord's Prayer in Gaelic. The ladies thought that they were making quite an impression, especially upon the waiter. When they had finished, the waiter said in a thick Irish brogue, "Do you girls also know the Hail Mary?"

Bishop Fulton J. Sheen tells this one on himself. The late Grace Moore was a fan of Bishop Sheen's speaking style, as who isn't, and refused to believe his story that "I'm the worst singer in the world." Miss Moore summoned a pianist and coaxed the good Bishop into singing a few bars—at which point the late great diva stopped the music, threw up her hands and sighed, "You're right, you are the worst singer in the world!"

Patrick only intended to put a dollar in the collection plate at Mass, but somehow he got mixed up and put in a ten-dollar bill instead. After Mass he was lamenting his mistake to a friend.

"Sure, Pat—Father Dugan is a nice man. Why don't you go over to the rectory and tell him your mistake? I know he'll refund you nine dollars. I'll go with you, too."

As the pair got up the steps of the rectory, Pat hesitated, then came down the steps commenting,

"Ah—I gave it to heaven—the hell with it!"

Some years ago Michael J. Flanagan, a successful New York contractor, was standing on the deck of the Staten Island Ferry when a car got loose and sent him into the river and he drowned.

The following Sunday his widow, all decked out in deepest black, was standing on the church steps after Mass receiving condolences and enjoying every minute of it, when an old friend of the contractor came up.

"I'm sorry, Mary, for your trouble," offered the friend. "Did Mike leave you well fixed?"

"Oh, he did!" she said. "He left me almost a half million dollars."

"Well now, that's not bad for a man who couldn't read or write."

"Nor swim either," added the widow.

Once, while visiting relatives in Donegal, our Uncle Barney suggested we go for a ride one Sunday afternoon. He suggested we might find a place for tea. However, we were rather cold and suggested a drink might be better. Our uncle explained to us that there were legal closing hours on Sunday afternoon and the pubs thereabout would not be open until around 4:30. It was then only 2 P.M.

Being American, we didn't think everyone would be observing the law, so we said to Uncle Barney,

"Look. You've been in these hills for a number of years. Surely you must know one place where we can get a drink."

With that Barney drove down into the center of town and pulled up short in front of a police sergeant directing a small amount of Sunday traffic and said,

"Officer, do you know where we can get a drink here in town?"

"You know full well," responded the officer, "that it's closing hours and there are no places open." However, spotting me, he remarked, "I suppose your Yankee friend is sick and needs medicine. Is that the answer?"

"No," replied Barney, "he's not sick, but his failure to get a drink on a Sunday afternoon could be almost fatal to the economic future of Ireland."

"Just how could it be?" asked the officer.

My uncle then proceeded to point out to the officer that he, being a discerning man, should realize the future of Ireland depends on the tourist industry, with the bulk of tourists coming from America, and arguing that "If I had a long tongue and should go back to America and tell everybody that I couldn't get a drink on Sunday in Ireland, few Americans would want to come here." The officer agreed that this could be a catastrophe and finally said,

"Do you know Mullins' Place? It's right down the road and turn left on one block. Now Mullins is a crusty man, but thrifty, and is the kind who will never let a shilling get by him without grabbing it. However, if you will go down there, I think he'll open up and serve you a drink, if you mention my name, which is Sergeant Emmet O'Laughlin."

So we drove down to Mullins' Place. It was locked up tight, so we hammered long enough until Mullins opened the door just on a slant. He was not only crusty but very curt and told us pronto that it was closing hours and against the law to serve. We played our trump card and said that Sergeant O'Laughlin had sent us.

"Oh, he did, did he?" With that Mullins slammed the door in our faces and bolted it. When we got to the highway, we saw Sergeant O'Laughlin doing a double directly to Mullins' Place when he saw us and hailed us with the remark,

"Oh, you Yanks don't know how to drink. You throw one drink down and run without savoring it. We Irish like to have several and take our time. Indeed, I was just on my way to join you for a sociable drink and here you are on your way."

I explained to the sergeant that Mullins didn't open up and sell or give us a drink.

"Did you mention my name—Sergeant Emmet O'Laughlin?"

"As a matter of fact, sergeant," I said, "we did mention your name and that was the clincher, because Mullins immediately slammed the door in our faces and bolted and locked it."

The look that came over Sergeant Emmet O'Laughlin's face was that as though I had given him a long hand slash, and, after flinching and shaking his head for a long time he threw out his arms and said in very dramatic fashion,

"That's Ireland for you! That's Ireland all over! No respect for the law whatsoever!"

Gourmet Harry Johnson heard this in Sligo. During the time

of the "Trouble" back in the early twenties, the British had sent over a special constabulary who, because of their black jackets and tan leather belts, were known as the "Black and Tans" and The Irish didn't hesitate to take reprisals against them.

One afternoon Father Morrissey had just come out from hearing confessions when the door opened and a lad came in with cap in hand and said he had to go to confession.

"Don't you see, lad," said Father Morrissey, "I have just finished hearing confessions and I'm on my way over to Terry McKenna's for a wee drop of Guinness before my supper. Go away and come back tomorrow."

"No, Father," said the lad, almost shouting. "I've committed a sin and I've got to tell you."

Patiently the good Father explained that he was all finished hearing confessions and had to get his drop of Guinness at McKenna's. With that, the lad became almost hysterical.

"You've got to hear my confession because the sin is preying on my mind and I've been unable to sleep a wink for a week."

"Now there, lad," said the good Father, "don't get hysterical. I tell you what I'll do. I'll hear your confession on one condition— that you make it quick and get it over with because I'm due over to McKenna's for my wee drop of Guinness before my supper."

"Bless me, Father," said the lad. "Do you know about the dynamiting of the Black and Tan barracks in which seven British Black and Tans were killed? Well, it was I, Father, who lit the dynamite that blew those souls to eternity. It was me, Father. Can I be forgiven?"

Father Morrissey said nothing and waited for the lad to proceed further. When he didn't, he said,

"Look, lad, stop talking politics and get on with your confession because I'm due over at McKenna's for a wee drop of Guiness."

The counter-story to the Sligo one of the confession is another one of the "Trouble" they tell in County Meath and concerns the man who came into the confessional and told the priest that he had two sins to confess—one was a wee sin and one was a big sin. Then asked the priest which one should he tell first.

"Look, man," the priest said. "It makes no difference to me

which one you tell first—the wee one or the large one—but I do want you to start your confession."

"Well, Father, I'll start with the wee one. The wee one is that I shot and killed a policeman."

The priest roared. "Man, do you call murdering a police officer in cold blood a wee sin? I fear to know what the big sin is."

"Oh, Father, I missed the sergeant."

Two oldsters living on their pension in Donegal would meet every day and walk to every saloon in town.

One day, one of them said, "I read in the papers that if all the saloons in Ireland were set end to end, they'd reach from Belfast to London."

"Oh," says the other, "what a walk."

Dr. Oliver Gogarty had a way of testing his patients about his diagnoses.

When he was once consulted by a man who thought he was going deaf, the good doctor told him, "This is a case of excessive nervousness showing its psychosomatic form of deafness. Now I happen to know that gambling, alcohol and sex stimulate a majority of people."

"Ah, now, what are you drivin' at, doc?"

"You'll have to," said Dr. Gogarty, "give up poker, whiskey and sex."

"Are you crazy, doctor," bellowed the patient. "Just for a little hearing?"

An Irish prisoner about to go on trial was being consoled by his parish priest.

"Now, Dennis," said the priest confidently, "you'll get justice in this court."

"Truth, yer rivirence," replied Dennis, "that's jist what I'm afraid of."

A parish priest ran into one of his parishioners who was a bit under the weather and upbraided him by saying that drink was his enemy.

"Ah, but, Father, didn't you only last Sunday tell us that we should love our enemies!"

"I did," replied the priest, "but I didn't tell you to swallow them."

Frank Vos, the Manhattan ad agent, recently went to Ireland with his Irish wife to visit her relatives. While in a Dublin pub there, he heard the tale about one man advising another how to get winners on the track.

"What you do," Collins advised his friend Cullen, "is to take your card of selections for the day's race to the little Chapel on Upper O'Connell Street, opposite the Parnell Statue. When there, light a candle for each one of your selections. Then, boy, every one will be a winner."

The next day when Cullen met Collins, he said, "That was fine advice. I picked seven horses and all came in last."

"Did you go to the Chapel I told you about?"

"I did."

"And you lit seven candles?"

"I did."

"Were they large or small candles?" asked Collins.

"Small ones," replied Cullen.

"Oh," said Collins with disgust. "The small ones are for the dogs."

Rev. Luke Missett, C.P., the business manager of *Sign Magazine*, remembers a sermon he heard once in his youth by an irascible old Irish pastor in Baltimore. It seems that the pastor wanted to organize the parish to participate in a temperance parade. Baltimore being the home of the finest rye in America and good beer too, few of the parishioners were interested in becoming teetotalers. Consequently, nobody showed for the parade.

The next Sunday, the Irish pastor lashed out at his congregation and told them in plain words that "They were not fit to drive the manure wagon."

Some of the congregation complained to Cardinal Gibbons, his superior, who told the pastor to apologize. He did the following Sunday.

"Last Sunday," said he, "I said you were not fit to drive the manure wagon. I apologize to one and all of ye. Every last one of ye are fit to drive the manure wagon."

Back in the old days in Kansas City, Mo., dentist John Devaney recalls that there was an old Irishman who distributed stout. He had a unique way of advertising same. He would hang bottles on cemetery railings with an accompanying sign—"If You Want to Keep Out, Drink Our Stout."

The urbane publisher of *The Critic,* Dan Herr, tells of a mythical Irish saint named "St. Fidgeta" who disturbed her pagan Druid teachers so much with her fidgeting that she was slapped to death, eventually becoming the "patroness of nervous and unmanageable children."

Robert Gibbings, well-known British author and illustrator, who did several books on Ireland, tells in one, "Lovely is the Lee," how the Irish love to talk and describes how even to get a phone call through may entail a conversation. When asking a number on a Cork telephone, here is what Gibbings got from the operator:

"Hold on a while now and I'll see if I can get him for you. I have an idea he was away shooting for the weekend, but I'll see if I can get him. Isn't it a grand day? Yerra, 'tis like summer. Another fortnight now and we'll be into spring. Tell me, who am I speaking to? Oh, to be sure, I know you well. I saw you the other night. 'Who's that?' said I to Paddy Riordan. 'Sure, that's Bob Gibbings,' says he, 'the fellow is writing a book about Cork.' Hold on a while, I think you're through. Ah, you're not. I'm Mick Ahern that lived at Curraheen. You wouldn't remember me but —hold on a while—'tis wonderful weather. Did you see any widgen when you were down at Imokilly? They tell me the place is full of them. Oh, indeed, yes, I saw you on the bus. 'Tis a grand spot down there. Hold on a while, you're through. Good-by now and good luck, you're through."

Some of the many Irish bus drivers in Manhattan are very pleasant and accommodating. Some can be quite crusty at times. Recently, on Madison Avenue, an elderly gent was getting on the bus, and the driver, anxious to get going before the light turned red, started to close the door on him. Although the door crushed his hat, the oldster persisted and the bus driver relented and finally let him in, thereby missing the light. The passenger was furious. "I suppose," roared he, "it would be expecting too much for you to apologize. However, at least, you can say you're sorry." The Irisher turned in his seat, looked the passenger over contemptuously from head to toe and replied, "That will be the day!"

An American and an Irishman were enjoying a ride in the country, when they came upon an unusual sight—an old gallows, or gibbet. The American thought he would have a joke on his Irish companion.

"You see that, I reckon," said he to the Irishman, pointing to the gallows. "And now where would you be if the gallows had its due?"

"Riding alone," coolly replied Paddy.

Outside the New York building where Karl Kaiser, the oil magnate, works is an Irisher lady who sells newspapers. She is a sharp-tongued person and only pleasant when she wants to be. Foolish questions annoy her no end, or at least what she thinks are foolish questions. The other day, Karl overheard a conversation she was having with a tall Texan who had apparently asked directions of her. "Look, mister," the Irisher lady said, "this town of New York has an uptown and downtown and an East side and a West side, that's all. So how in the hell should I know which way is North?"

North of the Border and Down Under

Canadian Celts

As in the United States and Australia, the Irish have been in Canada for a long time and in goodly numbers, too.

With Montcalm, the French commander, at the Battle of Quebec in 1759, there were several Irish brigades. Following the defeat of Montcalm by the British at Quebec, the French Army retired to Montreal where, a year later, the French surrendered.

With this capitulation, the several hundred survivors of the Irish brigades realized that since they were British subjects, they could be shot for treason. Hence, the Irish soldiers quickly faded into French-Canadian settlements. To escape detection, they changed their names into French. For instance, Captain McCarthy of the Irish brigade became Citizen Macarti, while Sergeant Boyle was henceforth known as Citizen Boylieu. Few ever returned to Ireland. Nearly all intermarried with the Canadian French and became permanent residents. Their influence was felt, too. For example, the one day of the year in the Province of Quebec on which the $25 fine for drunkenness is waived is St. Patrick's Day.

Some current carping critics even have the audacity to claim that the belligerent Canadian French separatists who are now vociferously striving to take the Province of Quebec out of the Dominion are the direct descendants of those members of Montcalm's Irish brigades.

Actually, twice, Irishmen attempted to take over Canada and hold it in ransom until Ireland was freed by the British. In 1866, a group of 800 Irishers, known as the Fenians, a name taken from the legendary band of warriors in Ireland headed by Finn Mac-Cumhaill, crossed the Niagara River and captured Fort Erie. Nearly all of the Fenians were veterans of the Union and Confederate armies in the Civil War who had united in a common cause to lick the British. However, they were defeated. The Fenians tried another Canadian invasion a year later. This, too, was thwarted.

The first Irish who came to settle rather than to fight went mainly to the Maritime Provinces on the East Coast. The Charitable Irish Society of Halifax was founded in 1786. The Great Famine in Ireland in the 1840's brought thousands to Canada. These settled all over the country. The Catholic Cathedral in Toronto is St. Michael's and a major church in Montreal is St. Patrick's. Thanks to the early British treaties with the French, the Irish Catholics were granted religious freedom as well as state support for their schools.

Despite this religious toleration, the Irish immigrants did not flourish as well in Canada as their fellow compatriots did in the United States and in Australia. In Canada, the Irish were up against the entrenched Establishment, which did not look too favorably upon them. The ruling Canadian Establishment was and still is to an extent made up of the descendants of the original English settlers, along with those of the loyalists who fled the American Colonies during the Revolution, the Scots and the North of Ireland Irish who are, as it is well-known, just some Scots who got hung up for a couple of centuries on their way to Canada.

With the North of Ireland Irish, there were many Orangemen organizations. As in the United States and Australia, there were the traditional fights on the anniversary of the Battle of Boyne on July 12th and on March 17th, St. Patrick's Day.

Nevertheless, the Irish persevered. Many rose to high places. Among them were Thomas D'Arcy McGee, Nicholas Floyd Gavin, Eugene James Cummings, Lawrence O'Connor Boyle, Richard John Uniache, and Charles McCrea.

Top Canadian writers with a Celtic background are F. B. Tracy, Thomas Chandler Haliburton, J. M. McMullin, W. P. M. Kennedy, Morley Callaghan, Gregory Clark, Peter Donovan, and Marshall McLuhan.

Few writers anywhere recently have caused as much furor as McLuhan. His *The Medium Is the Massage* has been discussed around the world. Very elegant and eloquent, Professor McLuhan on the platform recalls the early George Bernard Shaw in the

manner in which his Celtic sparkling torrent of language con-
founds audiences. Again, as with Shaw, the audience reaction is
invariably mixed.

Advice to Youth

An enterprising young Irish journalist from Dublin was Terrence
Murphy, who made a name for himself covering the Canadian
Parliament in the great days of Prime Minister Sir John Alex-
ander Macdonald.

An admirer of Macdonald, Murphy was always careful to quote
him correctly. He knew that the Prime Minister took pains in
preparing his speeches in advance and what he had to say was
usually worthwhile.

One evening at a banquet, where the wine flowed freely, Macdonald was at the bottom of a long list of speakers. While waiting
for his turn, the Prime Minister had plenty to drink. So much so,
in fact, that when he got up to speak, his talk did not make much
sense.

Murphy, being a true Irish gentleman, would not criticize any
man in his cups. The morning after the banquet, Murphy went
to see the Prime Minister and told him that he had missed most
of his speech and asked if he would repeat some parts of it.

Instead, the agreeable Macdonald gave forth for an hour or
more the splendid speech which he had prepared in advance and
which, because of the wine, he had forgotten to deliver. Journalist Murphy was deeply grateful to the Prime Minister and expressed his appreciation.

However, the Prime Minister gruffly shut off Murphy's words
of thanks with "Look, young man, Canada is not Ireland. If you
are going to get anywhere in this country as a journalist, never
cover any assignment when you are drunk."

Correct Count

Newman Mallon, the engaging librarian of the Toronto Public
Library, tells of the local Irisher boasting about the grand party

he and his pals had the night before.

"Aye," sez he, "Wasn't it a great night the five of us had."

"Who were the five?" asked a listener.

"Well," said the Irisher as he began counting on his fingers. "There was one, that's me. There was Clancy, that's two. There was the Quigley twins, that's three, and there was Sullivan, that's four."

"But you said there were five and you count only four."

"Jist a minute, let me count again," replied the Irisher as he again began to pick off the number on his fingers. "There was one, that was me. Two, there was Clancy. Three, there was the Quigley twins, and four, there was Sullivan. Shure, I must have taken a wee drop too many, because last night I thought there was five of us at the party. Now I know there's only four."

A Secret Union

By Gregory Clark

You do not ordinarily rassle with a clergyman, unless he happens to be either your brother, cousin, son or nephew. A chaplain in the army comes close to those categories among his young fellow-officers—especially if he is a young chaplain.

Capt. William Henry Davis, M.C., was a young chaplain. And I was rassling with him because I had caught him red-handed, rifling my kit. I owned a copy of George Moore's blasphemous novel, *The Brook Kerith*. And it was Padre Davis's avowed intention to steal the book from me and burn it, in order to save my soul. Padre Davis was an Anglican, and he could not comprehend my fine, subtle, Presbyterian attitude that I was ordained to salvation or damnation, regardless of whether I read the book or not. As a matter of fact, it turned out to be a very dull book, the poorest of the great Irish novelist's showy enterprises.

But when I saw a candle lit in my billet, I sneaked in, tippy-toe, to find the reverend chaplain in the very act of rifling my kit. I pounced on him.

We wrestled and rolled around the room, and I tripped him backwards over a camp cot. I got him by the throat and was threatening him with dire punishments of an earthly kind when, in the candlelight, I saw, to my complete consternation, a black string of beads come snaking out of his tunic breast pocket. A string of beads, and then a glittering silver crucifix.

I snatched it, leaped up and stood back.

"Church of *England*, hey?" I shouted, waving the rosary in the air. "Wait till I spread the news among our fine Grey County Orangemen! Our wild-eyed Frontenac County Orangemen!"

Our regiment had an overwhelming Protestant membership.

Padre Davis leaped. I dodged. He chased me around the billet, breathlessly begging me to give him the rosary. He halted.

"Clarkie! Clarkie!" he pleaded, in a low voice. "Please. Give me the rosary. And don't mention it to a living soul."

"Oh, no?" I gloated. "The regiment will eat you alive. Church of England, indeed!"

"Clarkie, listen," he hissed. "You were there last week when Bruneau died."

"I was," I admitted, sobering.

"Bruneau thought I was a priest. It was too late to send for another chaplain. He was dying, you remember?"

I remembered. Bruneau was one of the greatest young men I ever knew. We carried him into a dugout, terribly wounded, and out of his head. Padre Davis had come magically out of the night, and knelt by Bruneau and the medical officer.

"Clarkie, when Bruneau mistook me for a priest, when he called me Father, I pretended I was a priest. To comfort him. I took my jackknife from my pocket, Clarkie, and opened it halfway, see, to make a half of a cross. I touched his brow and his lips with it, Clarkie, and I said the Lord's Prayer in Latin—a thing I learned as a student—and I recited some Horace, and pretended that I was giving him absolution. And he died, Clarkie, and I was pressing my half-open jackknife to his lips. . . ."

I tossed the rosary back to Padre Davis.

"The next morning," he said, "I went to the Catholic chaplain of the brigade and confessed what I had done. We thought about it for a while, remembering the way the men die, some of his faith, some of mine.

"So I handed him my prayer book, and he handed me his. And in the back pages, see, he has written the phrases of extreme unction of the Catholic faith, and I wrote the prayers for the dying, of the Anglican faith, in the back of his prayer book. And we have a little private arrangement that he will be chaplain to my boys, and I will be priest to his, whenever it is too late."

You could hear the candle burning, such was the stillness of my billet.

"He gave me," said Padre Davis, "this rosary to carry, in case."

I kept looking at the Padre.

"Clarkie, you will not mention this? To anyone?"

I shook my head. It was not safe to speak.

Six weeks later, Padre Davis, at Amiens, was buried along with one officer and twelve men of the regiment in adjoining graves. The whole regiment was on parade. I was Adjutant.

When they placed Padre Davis in his grave, before extending the blanket over him, the rosary slid half out of his tunic pocket.

"Tuck that back in!" I ordered.

Bumps and a Brogue

BY PETER DONOVAN

As we were combing our hair somewhat hurriedly in our boudoir at 8:58 the other morning—we are supposed to be down at the office at nine—it was suddenly borne in upon us that we had a remarkable set of bumps on our head. We made this discovery by the simple and painful process of running into several of them with a large, sharp comb. We thereupon decided that a set of protuberances like ours should be measured at once by a competent phrenologist.

We had seen the Professor's notices in the "want-ad" departments of the local dailies; and our attention had been drawn to them by their diagrams of extraordinarily bumpy heads, and the peculiar line of language in which the Professor advanced his modest claims to be regarded as a benefactor of the human race and one of the greatest phrenologists of all time. Besides, the Professor's protuberance-parlors were on our way down to the office. They have a central location, so that phrenological patients can run in every now and then and have a new bump examined, we presume.

We read the handsome and dignified brass plate on the door, and we knocked a respectful knock. After two or three minutes of waiting we knocked again—less respectfully. After we had knocked several more times, with constantly diminishing respect and constantly increasing force, the door was opened by a blond and comely young woman who explained that the Professor's hours were from three to five in the afternoon, and from seven to eight in the evening—to accommodate people who might drop in on their way to the theatre, no doubt. Did we want a chart as well as a reading?

"How much does the Professor set one back for a chart?" we inquired, as we toyed with the forty cents left out of our weekly envelope of the Saturday before. Two dollars for a reading and five dollars for a chart.

We stated firmly that we would have two dollars' worth, and that we would come for it at three o'clock in the afternoon. We were going to see this thing through if we had to hock something. As we bowed our adieu smilingly, the young lady pressed upon us one of the Professor's cards, in which we were advised to "get my new great chart and be helped—as many also numerous worried, etc., have—for life." On the back of the card there was more of the Prof's best phrenological English, which promised among much else that "marriage adaptions" would be explained. Immediately we resolved that we would see him that very day or expire in the effort.

We got there at three. The same blond and comely young woman let us in. Would we take off our hat and coat and sit in the parlor till the Professor got through examining the bumps on someone else's cranial arch? We would and we did. We sat down by a table on which there was a pile of calling cards—presumably left by grateful persons whose protuberances had been explained—and also a bound copy of the Professor's famous chart. We opened it and glanced through a few long passages on amativeness and combativeness and philoprogenitiveness and other polysyllabic characteristics, as indicated by convexities on the skull.

While we read there floated down to us from the mysterious regions above a rich Hibernian voice and the most superb brogue we had heard in many a long day. It was one of those thick, mashed-potatoes-and-buttermilk brogues which usually go with a semicircular rim of reddish whiskers and a prehensile upper lip. We dropped the book and listened. We didn't pay any particular attention to what was being said—far be it from us to display an ungentlemanly curiosity as to the meaning of anyone else's bumps! We just listened to the voice. It made us think of St. Patrick ordering the snakes out of Ireland.

The voice came downstairs and accompanied someone to the front door. "Goodboy and good luck to yez both," said the voice —perhaps some cautious young man was having his financée's head studied—and then we were told that the Professor awaited us in his sanctum. We hastened out just in time to see a pair of short, thick legs scurrying upstairs ahead of us. We joined them in a neat little office at the top—where legs are usually joined— and found that they and the voice belonged to the Professor, in whose hands we had come prepared to place our head and a two-dollar bill.

The Professor looked us over, and we in turn gazed at him with the respectful and somewhat timid interest due to his professional insight into human character and destiny. But we must confess to a distinct disappointment. We had expected to see a large and impressive personage, with the face of a seer, piercing eyes, flowing locks—also a flowing robe, covered with cabalistic signs. We had expected him to be a sort of cross between a medicine man and an ancient alchemist. Instead we saw a round-faced, plump little Irishman, with close-cropped hair, a bristling mustache, and a decided leaning towards rotundity in the abdominal profile.

"Well, young man, and what can Oi do for ye?" asked the Professor, as though we might have come to get a tooth filled, or be measured for a new pair of pants.

We explained that we had come to have our head read, with a view to finding out what business in life we were best fitted for, and also to have our "marriage adaption" explained.

Without a word the Professor sat us in a chair in the middle of the room. Still without a word he seized a pair of callipers that

were unpleasantly suggestive of ice-tongs. Then in ominous silence he proceeded to pick up our head by the ends, by the sides,
by the front, by the back, under the ears, and in several other
painful places where heads are not usually picked up. We felt as
though our head were a block of ice, which was being carried up
several long flights of stairs. And each time the Professor seized it
in the tongs, he carefully scrutinized the scale at the top of them.
Some measurements he took several times, either to verify them,
or to make it plain that he was working hard on our case.

Having finished with the callipers, he drew out a tape and measured our head in more ways than we had ever thought possible
—around the rim, over the dome, back of the ears, till we must
have resembled a new real-estate subdivision. Only he didn't
drive in any stakes. Finally he tilted our head back as far as it
would go, and very solemnly measured us over the eyes to the
point of the jaw on each side. This he did four or five times, gazing sternly at the tape each time like a judge warning a backward
witness.

Then he gave us the third round. He grasped our head firmly in
his hands, and pressed our various bumps with fingers that
seemed to be about the size and shape of chocolate éclairs. But
they were not soft. On the contrary, they were very hard indeed.
Just when we felt sure that our last bump had given way under
the pressure, he rocked our head violently from side to side, backwards and forwards. Reducing us to a momentary condition of
coma by gouging his thumbs into us at that sensitive point
where one's spinal column joins one's cerebellum—or is it one's
medulla oblongata?—he seized us by the hands, each in turn,
wobbled our wrists, twisted our fingers, and finally did his best to
remove our thumbs completely. This, we believe, is what alien-
ists call the "thumb test."

The Professor sat down. All this time he had preserved an ab-
solute and ominous silence. Now he gazed at us with melancholy
interest, and we nerved ourself to hear the worst. Immediately he
plunged into an abyss of statistics. We can recall only a few of
them, and probably these few are not altogether correct. We
never were much good at arithmetic. Besides, the Professor reeled
them off at breathless speed.

"The average head is twenty-wan to twenty-wan and a half

inches in circumference," he roared in a voice that would easily
carry a block in all directions, "and your head is twenty-three and
a half. Over the dome the average head is twilve to twilve and a
half inches; yours is fourteen. In len'th the average head is siven
to siven and a half inches; yours is eight and a half. And your
head is six and three quarter inches woide, while the average is
only foive and a half."

We asked if he had any objections to our jotting down a few of
those figures. He had.

"Niver you mind, niver you mind," said the Professor impatiently waving our question aside, "ye don't need them. You listen to me and to what Oi'm tellin' ye. It doesn't matter if ye forgit thim misurements. But here is wan Oi don't want ye to forgit.
This is the most important of thim all. Oi misured ye over the
oiyes to the temporo-mandible j'int. Well, the average woman
misures there from tin and a half to ilivin inches; and the average
man from ilivin to ilivin and a half. And many a foine, dacent,
respectable man comes in to me that doesn't misure over tin and
a half. But you, me young man, you misure twilve and wan-
eighth inches."

The Professor leaned back to let it soak in. We gasped in delighted amazement. What do you know about that?—"twilve and
wan-eighth" inches to our temporo-mandibles! Nothing cheap
about our mandibles, eh, what?

"Av coorse," said the Professor deprecatingly, "Napoleon misured fourteen inches; the Duke of Wellington misured thirteen;
and Timothy Eaton—gawd rest his soul!—misured twilve and
three-quarters."

We were out-classed! There could be no doubt of it. But then
who are we that we should compete with the great immortals,
with Bonaparte and the Iron Duke and the founder of a department store? Besides, we were in good company with our "twilve
and wan-eighth." So we plucked up heart of grace and listened
cheerfully to the Professor as he continued.

"You have a foine head," said he, "one of the foinest that has
come to me in a year or more. But it's a head that requoires special attintion. In fact, it requoires moy thurd course, which is tin
dollars. Me terms is always the same. There is no change and no
reduction. It is two dollars for a plain readin', foive dollars for a

chart, and foive dollars extry for me thurd course of special attintion and secret advoice. Just that, tin dollars, no more and no
less!"

The Professor said it with great solemnity and impressive slow-
ness, especially the last phrase, presumably with a view to fore-
stalling any endeavor on our part to obtain this wonderful
"thurd" course for nine dollars and a half or eight-ninety-eight.
We dismissed the whole subject, and asked him what calling in
life we seemed best fitted for—if any.

"Oi'm comin' to that, Oi'm comin' to it," said the Professor in
a very testy tone of voice. "But furst Oi want ye to understand
the advantages of havin' a chart. No man can possibly remimber
all the things Oi'm goin' to tell ye, and it is quoite essintial ye
should have a chart. It will be worth thousands to ye."

Suddenly we saw the reason why he had been so very peremp-
tory in his refusal to let us take notes. He wanted to reduce us to
helpless amazement by the flow of his statistics. We were amazed,
all right, but still firm in our resolve to spend no more than two
dollars—it was all we had been able to raise at the office.

The Professor returned to that magnificent head of ours, intimating that it stood out like the rock of Gibraltar from amid the
ordinary run of heads that came to him for inspection. But this
did not make us so conceited as the reader might imagine. It occurred to us that the average head that comes to a phrenologist
may be rather small and thick, possessors of such heads having
naturally most reason to wonder what they are fitted for in life.

"You have a big head," said the Professor, "a head quoite large
enough for almost anny purpose known to man. And it is a well-
shaped head. Some heads that have a big dome have a depression
in the top. But you've a ridge on yer skull that ye could balance a
lead pencil on. That shows great stren'th of character. But you
have one fault. On oither soide of that ridge, where the bumps of
hope ought to be, you've a hollow. Ye lack confidence in yerself.
Y're nervous and diffident. And that is where moy chart would be
worth untold wealth to ye. It would show ye how to develop yer
hopefulness, and also yer chest—the chest havin' a great deal to do
with yer hopefulness. Whoy, with a head loike yours ye could do
almost annythin'!"

Instinctively, we sat very erect, feeling that the Professor was about to enter on a list of the splendid careers from which we had only to choose. We were confident that he was about to proclaim the magnificent position we would one day occupy in the literary hall of fame. After what he had said about our peerless set of protuberances, we felt that no forecast could be too rosy. So we straightened up in eager expectation.

"With a head loike yours," said the Professor in his loudest and most impressive tone, "ye'd have no difficulty in takin' a very liberal eddication if ye'd only lay yer moind to it. Ye moight roise to be a bookkeeper or a commercial thraveller. Ye moight even become a lawyer or a doctor or a profissional man, if ye only had confidence in yerself. Ye could be a foine piano-player and an iligant parlor singer. Ye could also be a fluent and graceful public speaker. Ye have a good deal of real-estate ability and consid'rable speculatin' capacity and quoite a bit of organizin' talent. Ye could be a furst-rate draughtsman; and ye have a genius for inventin'. In fact, ye could be almost annythin' ye made up yer moind to be—and there ye are!"

Yes, there we were! We could take a "liberal eddication," if only—and all the time a big parchment with a huge red seal lay carefully rolled up in our trunk as evidence of our scholastic attainments! It is the only evidence we possess. We could "roise" to be a bookkeeper or a commercial "thraveller"—but never a word to the effect that we might someday be able to write or might ever aspire to journalistic eminence. Not that the Professor was necessarily so far astray at that. He may have been quite right. We admit it humbly. But it was a sad blow to have such a commonplace future outlined for us, after the way he had raised our hopes. And real-estate ability!—it sounded like an attack on our moral character.

"Moreover, ye could become a foine boxer," he continued, "or a beautiful fencer. Ye have such soople movements. Ye could learn to fence in half the toime it takes an ordinary man. And a useful thing it is, too. Suppose ye were attacked on the street, fer instance."

All we would have to do in such a case, we presume, would be to draw our flashing rapier, throw ourself on guard, and "have at you, varlets!" Or perhaps the Professor intended that we should do this with our walking-stick or rolled-up umbrella. Somehow

the idea did not appeal much to us—spitting a man with your umbrella musses it up so dreadfully.

A bright idea suddenly occurred to us to relieve our deep de-
jection. Our "marriage adaptions" still remained to be explained.
Timidly we broached the subject, for ours is a tender and shrinking nature, and we are not in the habit of speaking out in meeting about our dearest hopes. Our voice sank to a whisper as we
asked if he thought we ought to get married.

"Would Oi advoise ye to git marrud?" roared the Professor,
possibly for the benefit of some new patients who were just being
let in—he had stopped to listen to the door-bell a few moments
previously. "Av coorse Oi would. There are physiol'gical reasons
for it. Ye know what they say, don't ye?"

Here the Professor smiled and winked in a distinctly doggish
manner. We felt that he was about to say something decidedly
improper in connection with those same "physiol'gical" reasons.
We blushed violently.

"Ye know, they say that single min go insane much oftener
than marrud min. And it is explained on physiol'gical grounds.
Take the Turks, fer instance. Look at the foine, upstandin',
healthy min they are, with their harems and their Circassian
slaves and all the rist of it. And Oi remimber when Oi was in the
heart of Africa forty years ago . . ."

"What part of Africa were you in?" we asked, expecting to be
told that he had acted as a guide for David Livingstone.

"Oi was at Cape Town—no, no, Oi was two thousand moiles
north of Cape Town, up in a country they call Nay-tawl. The
whole district was filled with magnificent fellas, great, big, deep-
chested, two-fisted, up-standin' six-footers, ivry wan of thim with
their six or sivin woives—and divil a bit of immorality in the
whole country!"

Under the circumstances we could easily believe in the high
moral status of the inhabitants of Natal. But we didn't see how it
helped our particular case. Whatever may be our personal opin-
ions on the subject of polygamy, police magistrates have been
known to cherish prejudices against people who carry "physiol'gy" as far as that.

The Professor went back to his chart. He dragged one out of a
drawer and insisted that we should gaze upon the picture of a

hairless gentleman with his head neatly divided into choice building lots, each containing a little sketch suggestive of the characteristic represented by a bump at that point. For instance, in the section allotted to "amativeness"—lovely word!—there was a picture
of a young man and young woman kissing. In the section labelled
"combativeness" two prize-fighters faced one another; while in
the "love of home" department a gentleman sat under a large
stump and gazed wistfully at a barn in the distance.

We still refused to be won over, even by these allurements of
graphic art. Thereupon the Professor read out several extracts of
a nature to help us in the development of hopefulness and our
chest.

"Ye must practice self-confidence and hopefulness," said he.
"That's the only way ye can develop yer faculty of hope. And the
chart shows ye how ye can do it."

Presumably the chart contained directions for fifteen-minute
hoping exercises to be gone through morning and night. In the
course of time, no doubt, we would develop into one of the best
little hopers in town. But for the time being we were still somewhat dejected. We couldn't get our mind off those "foine, up-
standing' min in Nay-tawl."

As a final inducement, the Professor took a five-cent piece out
of his pocket, and bent it to show the strength of his fingers. He
said he didn't do it for everyone—whether on account of the wear
and tear on his fingers or on five-cent pieces, he left to the imagination. He also made us feel his biceps and watch the expansion
of his chest, all acquired by carefully following out the directions
on the chart—five dollars!—and also the third course and secret
advice, which we would have to swear not to communicate—ten
dollars!

"Oi'll tell ye the secret soign possessed by all the strongest min
in the world," he assured us, "not only proize-foighters and wras-
tlers, but great doctors and artists as well. Oi'll tell it to ye so ye
can pick thim out on the street. That's part of the secret advoice.

But we refused to rise to the bait. As a result we are still unable
to tell a "wrastler" on the street from a drug-clerk, or a "proize-
foighter" from a country curate.

We entrusted a two-dollar bill to the Professor's care. We
thanked him for the information he had given us. Then we

came sadly away, wondering vaguely how much was the fare to Nay-tawl.

A Very Merry Christmas

By Morley Callaghan

After midnight on Christmas Eve hundreds of people prayed at the crib of the Infant Jesus which was to the right of the altar under the evergreen-tree branches in St. Malachi's Church. That night there had been a heavy fall of wet snow, and there was a muddy path up to the crib. Both Sylvanus O'Meara, the old care-taker who had helped to prepare the crib, and Father Gorman, the stout, red-faced, excitable parish priest, had agreed it was the most lifelike tableau of the Child Jesus in a corner of the stable at Bethlehem they had ever had in the church.

But early on Christmas morning Father Gorman came running to see O'Meara, the blood all drained out of his face and his hands pumping up and down at the sides and he shouted, "A ter-rible thing has happened. Where is the Infant Jesus? The crib's empty."

O'Meara, who was a devout, innocent, wondering old man, who prayed a lot and always felt very close to God in the church, was bewildered and he whispered, "Who could have taken it? Taken it where?"

"Take a look in the crib yourself, man, if you don't believe me," the priest said, and he grabbed the caretaker by the arm, marched him into the church and over to the crib and showed him that the figure of the Infant Jesus was gone.

"Someone took it, of course. It didn't fly away. But who took it, that's the question?" the priest said. "When was the last time you saw it?"

"I know it was here last night," O'Meara said, "because after the midnight Mass when everybody else had gone home I saw Mrs. Farrel and her little boy kneeling up here, and when they stood up I wished them a merry Christmas. You don't think she'd touch it, do you?"

"What nonsense, O'Meara. There's not a finer woman in the parish. I'm going over to her house for dinner tonight."

"I noticed that she wanted to go home, but the little boy wanted to stay there and keep praying by the crib; but after they went home I said a few prayers myself and the Infant Jesus was still there."

Grabbing O'Meara by the arm the priest whispered excitedly, "It must be the work of communists or atheists." There was a sudden rush of blood to his face. "This isn't the first time they've struck at us," he said.

"What would communists want with the figure of the infant Jesus?" O'Meara asked innocently. "They wouldn't want to have it to be reminded that God was with them. I didn't think they could bear to have Him with them."

"They'd take it to mock us, of course, and to desecrate the church. O'Meara, you don't seem to know much about the times we live in. Why did they set fire to the church?"

O'Meara said nothing because he was very loyal and he didn't like to remind the priest that the little fire they had in the church a few months ago was caused by a cigarette butt the priest had left in his pocket when he was changing into his vestments, so he was puzzled and silent for a while and then whispered, "Maybe someone really wanted to take God away, do you think so?"

"Take Him out of the church?"

"Yes. Take Him away."

"How could you take God out of the church, man? Don't be stupid."

"But maybe someone thought you could, don't you see?"

"O'Meara, you talk like an old idiot. Don't you realize you play right into the hands of the atheists, saying such things? Do we believe an image is God? Do we worship idols? We do not. No more of that, then. If communists and atheists tried to burn this church once, they'll not stop till they desecrate it. God help us, why is my church marked out for this?" He got terribly excited and rushed away shouting, "I'm going to phone the police."

It looked like the beginning of a terrible Christmas Day for the parish. The police came, and were puzzled, and talked to everybody. Newspapermen came. They took pictures of the church and of Father Gorman, who had just preached a sermon that startled the congregation because he grew very eloquent on the subject of vandal outrages to the house of God. Men and women stood outside the church in their best clothes and talked very gravely. Everybody wanted to know what the thief would do with the image of the Infant Jesus. They all were wounded, stirred and wondering. There certainly was going to be something worth talking about at a great many Christmas dinners in the neighbourhood.

But Sylvanus O'Meara went off by himself and was very sad. From time to time he went into the church and looked at the empty crib. He had all kinds of strange thoughts. He told himself that if someone really wanted to hurt God, then just wishing harm to Him really hurt Him, for what other way was there of hurting Him? Last night he had had the feeling that God was all around the crib, and now it felt as if God wasn't there at all. It wasn't just that the image of the Infant Jesus was gone, but someone had done violence to that spot and had driven God away from it. He told himself that things could be done that would make God want to leave a place. It was very hard to know where God was. Of course, He would always be in the church, but where had that part of Him that had seemed to be all around the crib gone?

It wasn't a question he could ask the little groups of astounded parishioners who stood on the sidewalk outside the church, because they felt like wagging their fingers and puffing their cheeks out and talking about what was happening to God in Mexico and Spain.

But when they had all gone home to eat their Christmas dinners, O'Meara, himself, began to feel a little hungry. He went out and stood in front of the church and was feeling thankful that there was so much snow for the children on Christmas Day when he saw that splendid and prominent woman, Mrs. Farrel, coming along the street with her little boy. On Mrs. Farrel's face there was a grim and desperate expression and she was taking such long fierce strides that the five-year-old boy, whose hand she held so tight, could hardly keep up with her and pull his big red sleigh. Sometimes the little boy tried to lean back and was a dead weight and then she pulled his feet off the ground while he whimpered, "Oh, gee, oh, gee, let me go." His red snowsuit was all covered with snow as if he had been rolling on the road.

"Merry Christmas, Mrs. Farrel," O'Meara said. And he called to the boy. "Not happy on Christmas Day? What's the matter, son?"

"Merry Christmas, indeed, Mr. O'Meara," the woman snapped to him. She was not accustomed to paying much attention to the caretaker. A curt nod was all she ever gave him, and now she was furiously angry and mortified to bother with him. "Where's Father Gorman?" she demanded.

"Still at the police station, I think."

"At the police station! God help us, did you hear that, Jimmie?" she said, and she gave such a sharp tug at the boy's arm that she spun him around in the snow behind her skirts where he cowered, watching O'Meara with a curiously steady pair of fine blue eyes. He wiped away a mat of hair from his forehead as he watched and waited. "Oh, Lord, this is terrible," Mrs. Farrel said. "What will I do?"

"What's the matter, Mrs. Farrel?"

"I didn't do anything," the child said. "I was coming back here. Honest I was, mister."

"Mr. O'Meara," the woman began, as if coming down from a great height to the level of an unimportant and simple-minded old man, "maybe you could do something for us. Look on the sleigh."

O'Meara saw that an old coat was wrapped around something on the sleigh, and stooping to lift it, he saw the figure of the Infant Jesus there. He was so delighted he only looked up at Mrs. Farrel and shook his head in wonder and said, "It's back and nobody harmed it at all."

"I'm ashamed, I'm terribly ashamed, Mr. O'Meara. You don't know how mortified I am," she said, "but the child really didn't know what he was doing. It's a disgrace to us, I know. It's my fault that I haven't trained him better, though God knows I've tried to drum respect for the church into him." She gave such a jerk at the child's hand he slid on his knee in the snow, keeping his eyes on O'Meara.

Still unbelieving, O'Meara asked, "You mean he really took it from the church?"

"He did, he really did."

"Fancy that. Why, child, that was a terrible thing to do," O'Meara said. "Whatever got into you?" Completely mystified, he turned to Mrs. Farrel, but he was so relieved to have the figure of the Infant Jesus back without there having been any great scandal that he couldn't help putting his hand gently on the child's head.

"It's all right, and you don't need to say anything," the child said, pulling away angrily from his mother, and yet he never took his eyes off O'Meara, as if he felt there was some bond between them. Then he looked down at his mitts, fumbled with them and looked up steadily and said, "It's all right, isn't it, mister?"

"It was early this morning, right after he got up, almost the first thing he must have done on Christmas Day," Mrs. Farrel said. "He must have walked right in and picked it up and taken it out to the street."

"But what got into him?"

"He makes no sense about it. He says he had to do it."

"And so I did, 'cause it was a promise," the child said. "I promised last night, I promised God that if He would make Mother bring me a big red sleigh for Christmas I would give Him the first ride on it."

"Don't think I've taught the child foolish things," Mrs. Farrel said. "I'm sure he meant no harm. He didn't understand at all what he was doing."

"Yes, I did," the child said stubbornly.

"Shut up, child," she said, shaking him.

O'Meara knelt down till his eyes were on a level with the child's and they looked at each other till they felt close together and he said, "But why did you want to do that for God?"

" 'Cause it's a swell sleigh, and I thought God would like it."

Mrs. Farrel, fussing and red-faced, said, "Don't you worry. I'll see he's punished by having the sleigh taken away from him."

But O'Meara, who had picked up the figure of the Infant Jesus, was staring down at the red sleigh; and suddenly he had a feeling of great joy, of the illumination of strange good tidings, a feeling that this might be the most marvellous Christmas Day in the whole history of the city, for God must surely have been with the child, with him on a joyous, carefree holiday sleigh ride, as he ran along those streets and pulled the sleigh. And O'Meara turned to

Mrs. Farrel, his face bright with joy, and said, commandingly, with a look in his eyes that awed her, "Don't you dare say a word to him, and don't you dare touch that sleigh, do you hear? I think God did like it."

The Irish Down Under

Australia was first settled in 1788 as a penal station. This was in New South Wales. The Irish were among the first colonists because after the 1798 Rebellion in Ireland, shiploads of Irish political prisoners were sent there. Later Irish uprisings, particularly the one in 1848, brought more Irish prisoners, including a number who later became celebrated citizens not only in Australia but also in the United States.

Of course, those Irishmen from Australia who made names for themselves in America were ones who had managed to escape from Down Under as prisoners.

Though many Irish arrived in Australia as prisoners, they were freed in due course to stake land claims and become permanent residents and citizens. Many did. Before long, as Irishmen usually do everywhere, they became a colorful, strong segment of Australian activities.

Actually, those Irishmen who were sent to Australia really had no stigma attached to their names. The fact is that many were dispatched there by the British authorities without even a trial. Then as today, these Irish prisoners were hailed as heroes. True or not, reports persist that some of Australia's first families, because of their relation to these early Irish prisoners, regard themselves in the same category as those Americans who belong to Daughters of the Revolution, Sons of the Revolution and the Society of Cincinnatus. After all, prisoners or not, historically, the Irish were among the first settlers of Australia and helped in making it the great nation it is today.

There are even tales that some Australian aristocrats of Irish ancestry now proudly display in their drawing rooms the leg-arms, the balls and chains which their Irish forebears wore upon arrival in Australia. These family heirlooms are cherished much as the possession of portraits by Copley, Stuart or Peale is treasured by Americans of Colonial lineage.

The discovery of gold in Australia in 1851 lured many free Irish there. The stories of these Irish miners much resemble those told about the Irish miners in the Colorado, California and Alaskan gold rushes.

To Australia, the Irish furnished many premiers and governors, just as in the U.S.A. they produced innumerable political and labor leaders, top journalists and theatrical stars. Among the Irish who made names for themselves in Australia were Sir Charles Gavan Duffy, James Darragh, Martin Hogan, Sir James Martin, Michael Harrington and Thomas Hasselt Cranston.

Among the celebrated political Irish prisoners sent to Australia were William Smith O'Brien, John Mitchel, Thomas Francis Meagher and John Boyle O'Reilly. The first three named took part in the 1848 Irish insurrection, right after the terrible famine in Ireland. 'O'Reilly joined the British army in 1863 with the intention of inciting a revolt in conjunction with a Fenian uprising.

O'Brien was finally pardoned. However, Mitchel, Meagher and O'Reilly made thrilling escapes from Australia to the United States. All three settled here. Mitchel and O'Reilly became successful newspaper editors. O'Reilly was the publisher and owner of the *Boston Pilot*. Mitchel's grandson, John Purroy Mitchel, became Mayor of New York (1914–1918).

During the Civil War, Meagher was made a captain of a company of volunteers which he had raised for the famous Fighting 69th Regiment of New York. He rose to the rank of a general and fought at Bull Run, Antietam, Chancellorsville and Fredericksburg. Later, he served as governor of the Montana territory.

Incidentally, the British government requested of the American authorities respectively the return of Mitchel, Meagher and O'Reilly to Australia as fugitives. However, the Irish influence and vote in those times as now was sizable enough in America for the authorities to safely ignore the request of the British to return these Irish heroes to captivity.

Down through Australian history, the activities of the Irish are very similar to those in America. As in America, there are Irish ballads, bulls, political tales and many anecdotes emitting, of course, from the pubs. There are, too, the traditional clashes with Orangemen on the anniversary of the Battle of the Boyne, on July 12th, and on St. Patrick's Day, March 17th. As always, the Irish are always, Irish, whether they settle in America or the Antipodes.

Late Licenses

An Irish-Australian addressed his employees on absenteeism with, "Looking about, me, I see a number of faces that are not here; what I have to say applies particularly to those who are absent, and I hope they will listen attentively and make a note of every word."

Traveler: "Could you direct me to Hogan's pub, mate?"

Irish settler: "Go as far as the Methodist Church, over there by them pine trees. Turn to the right down towards Dingo Gully until you come to the school, then turn left and follow the track as far as Pat Ryan's shack. That will bring you on the main road, turn left and keep going for another three miles."

Traveler: "That's clear enough. Where will that bring me to?"

Irish settler: "Right back here."

Traveler (perplexed) : "But what in the name of Larry do I come back here for?"

Irish settler: "Shure, so I can give you the rest of the directions. If I tried to tell them all at once, aye, you'd only get real confused."

When the Salvation Army opened in Clare, South Australia, the inhabitants tolerated singing of hymns to tunes such as "Clementine" and "Two Little Girls in Blue," but when a hymn was sung to "The Wearing of the Green," an Irishman remarked, "Hasn't Ireland enough throubles without that sort of thing?"

The cemetery at Norfolk Island, the "Ocean Hell" of Australia, is full of poignant reminders of their convict days. Occasionally, there is a touch of grim humor, as one stone which is inscribed:

"Here's the body of Patrick O'Rourke who died suddenly." (He was hanged.)

Father Cleary was a good, charitable, kind-hearted priest. His heart was always very much in his profession. For instance, the good Father was attending a criminal who had been condemned to death for a capital offense. At the last moment, the prisoner's sentence was commuted to imprisonment.

In speaking of the affair, Father Cleary commented: "Sure it was the greatest pity in the world he was not hanged. I never saw a sinner so truly penitent as he was. Faith, he'll never have such another chance for salvation."

Sir Thomas Bent, the Premier of Victoria from 1904 to 1909, was widely known as Tommy. He was a rugged politician of the frontier school and had friends from all classes. When Bent died, his panegyric was uttered by Paddy Reynold, mine Irish host of the Cathedral Hotel, Melbourne. Stated Paddy: "Say what you like about Sir Thomas Bent, but he was a man. He mightn't have much honesty if there was big money to be got, and he liked his gin and tonic strong an' fraquint, an' a roving eye for wimmen, but outside them matters, he was as pure as the drivveling snow."

In the 1850's things were done, in Victoria, in a free-and-easy, unconventional way. At Murphy's Castlemaine Hotel when the sessions were on, and at the dinner-table, along with the judge on circuit, his associate, the Crown prosecutor, and a number of barristers, were several persons charged with criminal offenses, but out on bail. Among these were two young men from Smythesdale, who were to take their trial for tarring and feathering a man. After dinner, at the suggestion of bibulous little barrister McDonough (known as John Phillpott Curran), the table was removed. Quinn, a surveyor, produced his fiddle, and soon was presented an astonishing spectacle, judge, men on the jury list, solicitors, barristers and offenders, whooping around in a jig, and reel, and polka, and waltz, until the morning hours, when broiled bones and whisky-punch finished up the saturnalia.

Next day every peg fitted into its proper place. The people on bail gave themselves up. The judge sat. The Crown prosecutor thundered his charges against the men with whom he had hob-nobbed the night before. And the two young fellows tried for tar-ring and feathering got three years' "hard."

As G. V. Brooke, one of the company observed, "They never did it better in Ireland."

Tales of "Jaynial Dan" O'Connor

Daniel O'Connor, popularly known as "Jaynial Dan," was a prominent and colourful political figure in New South Wales during the latter years of the last century. His flow of oratory was unsurpassed. From a fund of anecdotes about him, I have selected two that were recounted by E. H. Collis in his enter-taining book, *Lost Years* (1948).

Daniel O'Connor, a white-whiskered, picturesque and pompous figure in frock coat and silk hat, was Postmaster-General in the last Parkes administration. One day E. W. O'Sullivan, the mem-ber for Queanbeyan, who liked to be called "The Keystone of the Democratic Arch," asked the Postmaster-General if he would ap-point a telegraph messenger to Michelago, then a village in the Queanbeyan electorate.

A week later the Minister read the official answer that, as the number of telegrams received and dispatched at Michelago was only fifteen a week, the appointment of a telegraph messenger was deemed unnecessary.

"On a supplementary question, Mr. Speaker," said O'Sullivan, eager to have some vote-catching propaganda in Hansard, "has the honourable Postmaster-General considered the future needs of Michelago? There may not be many telegrams today, but soon a sturdy yeoman settled on the fertile slopes around Michelago will need a communication with the outside world. More than that, when we get a protectionist tariff, factories will spring up around Michelago, and when the smoke from a thousand chim-neys ascends to the evening sky, the industrious operatives will be telegraphing to other parts of the colony. Has the Postmaster-General, in brief, looked into the future?"

Daniel O'Connor had had enough of this. He arose, his whiskers quivering with determination, and his arm outstretched.

"I would remind the honourable member for Queanbeyan," he said, "that I am Daniel the Postmaster-General, not Daniel the Prophet. I have not looked into the future."

It was almost the only consciously humorous thing that he ever uttered. But once he was unconsciously humorous.

This was also during Parkes' last administration. Madame Sarah Bernhardt, the great French actress, visited Australia. The Ministers desired to honour her, and Daniel O'Connor was selected on account of his picturesque whiskers, his florid language and his resonant oratorical tribute to what he called the fair sex —to his dying day he could always obtain free drinks in a hotel bar by giving his famous toast of "The Ladies"—to do the honours on behalf of his Cabinet colleagues. After communing with his soul for a space, Daniel was struck with the delightful notion of escorting the actress up the tower of the General Post Office. To further honour her, he decided to address her in French.

Now Daniel knew no French, but on the evening before the great day he studied Ollendorf's *First French Course,* a work recommended to him by some of his officials. After wrestling with it for some hours, he mastered a few phrases, which he thought would suffice.

On the next morning the actress arrived at the General Post Office and found a noble figure awaiting her. Daniel's silk hat glittered in the sunlight, and a gentle breeze caressed his whiskers.

"Bonjour, madame," he began as, with the courtesy of his race, he raised his glittering silk hat aloft and bent over her gloved hand. "Parlez-vous français?" he inquired tenderly. "Est-se que vous avez le couteau do votre neveu?" (Do you have your nephew's knife?)

Dan noted with an inward triumph the astonishment which showed on Sarah's face. "You might think that I am French," he went on, with the assurance of complete success, "but I'm not. I'm Irish."

World's Worst Juggler Goes Down Under

By Fred Allen

Early in 1914 the then twenty-year-old Fred Allen was appearing in the Midwest as Freddy James, the World's Worst Juggler, and a single in vaudeville. His act was caught by Ben Fuller, owner of a group of variety theatres in Australia. He liked Fred's act and booked him for a tour of Australia. In his biography *Much Ado About Me*, Fred Allen, whose real name was John Florence Sullivan, describes his trip to Down Under via the *S.S. Sierra*. Incidentally, his salary in Australia was £19, or $92.34, which contrasted with his later earnings as a Broadway star and as the celebrated author and performer in his highly amusing hour-long radio program "Town Hall Tonight," which ran for years.

The *S.S. Sierra* was a ten-thousand-ton vessel. Today, lifeboats bigger than the *Sierra* are found on the *Queen Mary* and other luxury liners. In rough weather the *Sierra* was tossed up and down in a blanket of spray as though she were being hazed as part of her initiation into some briny sorority. In an angry sea the *Sierra* resembled a female housefly caught in a fizzing Alka Seltzer. She was in the middle of everything, but had no control over the situation.

My stateroom was a form-fitting gullhole (on a ship, a pigeonhole is a gullhole). As you squeezed into the room, on the right against the wall were two bunks, upper and lower. Jutting out between the bunks and the door there was a small sink, above which hung a tiny mirror and a rack that held a carafe of fresh water and two glasses. At the opposite end of the stateroom, for purposes of ventilation and lighting, there was a porthole. My ticket called for the lower bunk, but when the passenger who was to share the stateroom with me turned out to be an elderly gentleman, I insisted that he take my lower space. The old man remonstrated feebly, but I argued that I, being younger, was more agile and better equipped to bound up into the upper bunk. He consented.

I demonstrated my superior bounding ability on only one occasion. The first night out of San Francisco I bounded up into my upper quarters; for the next four days I just lay there, an inanimate lump—seasick. I not only couldn't keep any food down; my digestive apparatus got ahead of me: my stomach was rejecting meals I had hoped to eat the following week. My mal de mer didn't seem to bother my roommate. Oblivious to my moaning and retching, he slept soundly through the nights, left early every morning for breakfast, and spent his entire days on deck. When he returned late in the evenings, he washed, quaffed a final drink of water from one glass, and filled the second glass with water into which he submerged his false teeth. The second glass was my glass. After the old man had gone to bed, if my throat was parched and I was dying for a glass of water, I could look down and see my glass laughing up at me. To quench my thirst I had to upend the carafe. Later, the old man told me that he raised sheep in New Zealand and had made more than forty crossings to the States.

The day before we arrived in Honolulu, I was able to crawl out of the bunk and creep up on deck. The second-class passengers were confined to a small area amidships. A few deck chairs were placed around the boat's two funnels. There was no room to play deck games of any sort, although this didn't matter, since there were no games available to play. One small group of passengers, huddled together near the rail, I took to be actors. I didn't know any of them. But since I hadn't eaten anything solid for four days, I must have had that half-starved look that people used to associate with the small-time actor, for one of the huddled actors unhuddled himself, came over to me, and invited me to join the others.

I was instantly brought up to date with the ship's scuttlebutt. There were six acts going to Australia to play the Fuller circuit. There was Madge Maitland, the Megaphone Lady; Madge was an abbreviated woman who sang in a booming voice through a large megaphone. There was Estelle Wordette and Company, presenting their own original playlet, When the Cat's Away. The Company consisted of a middle-aged gentleman who smoked a potent pipe incessantly. There were the Flemings, two muscular young men who did an acrobatic act that consisted of Grecian posing and hand balancing. Also present were the Littlejohns, the Dia-

mond Jugglers, a man and wife who wore costumes studded with
rhinestones, and appeared before a black velvet curtain covered
with rhinestones, and juggled Indian clubs which were bedecked
with rhinestones. And then there was Doranto, a rather serious-
looking elderly man who made up as a Chinese and provoked discordant melodies from strange-looking Oriental instruments.
Doranto billed himself the "Human Xylophone." At the finish of
his act he made good his billing by causing alleged melodies to
emerge from his mouth as the result of spanking his false teeth
with two short sticks while manipulating his orifice. I was the
sixth on the program.

There were five or six other acts on the boat going to Australia, but they were booked to play the Tivoli circuit. The Tivoli
theaters were considered big time and imported stars from England and America. The Tivoli paid much higher salaries, but the
acts only played three cities—Sydney, Melbourne, and Adelaide—
and were guaranteed only twelve weeks' work. The Fuller circuit,
on the other hand, booked vaudville shows into every city of importance in Australia, New Zealand, and Tasmania. Our salaries
were small, but we had sixteen or twenty weeks guaranteed, and
if an act did exceptionally well, it could work steadily on the
Fuller circuit for a year or more.

All of the American acts books for Australia were furnished
second-class transportation. In vaudeville, class distinction was invariably observed. The headliner on the bill ignored the lesser
acts, and the lesser acts in turn snubbed the acrobats or the people with animal acts. The Fuller acts on the *Sierra* were victims of
this class distinction. After the boat had left San Francisco, the
Tivoli acts discovered that they had to associate with the Fuller
acts, who were also traveling second class. The Tivoli group
promptly moved into first-class accommodations, paying the
difference out of their own pockets. To get their money's worth
during the trip, the Tivoli actors came to the rail at the rear of
the first-class deck every day to look down at the Fuller acts in
their restricted quarters. The Fuller acts were not above practicing a bit of snobbery themselves. They walked to the back of
their second-class deck to look down on a few sorry-looking individuals who were traveling steerage. Who knows: the steerage
passengers were probably sitting on their bare deck practicing class

distinction by looking down at the porpoises because they weren't even on the boat.

Another band of scarred citizens going to Australia second class represented the boxing profession. It was headed by Jimmy Dine, a boxing manager from Newcastle, Pennsylvania, who was taking George Chip, a famous heavyweight of the day, and a stable of fighters to appear in Sydney. Chip was to fight Les Darcy, the Australian favorite.

Honolulu, as the *Sierra's* captain had hoped and the travel folder had promised, was there awaiting our arrival on the fifth day. As the boat crept into the harbor, a noisy school of natives swam out to greet us. After a hasty welcome in their native tongue, the natives got down to business in broken English, and demanded that the passengers throw money into the water. If the natives had known there were so many actors on board, they would have postponed their swim schedule for that day. A few first-class passengers tossed coins to watch the natives dive for them. The instant a coin struck the surface, the nearest native followed it down into the water, bobbing up a second later, laughing and showing the coin in his outstretched hand. During their diving exhibition the natives kept the coins they had salvaged in their mouths. As I watched this demonstration of aquatic panhandling for the first time, it seemed to me that a Hawaiian native with a big mouth and a little luck could make more money in a few days than any actor going to Australia to play the entire Fuller circuit.

In 1914, Honolulu's meager attractions were Waikiki Beach and a small colony of artists and writers. The only celebrity whose name was dropped during our six-hour stay there was Jack London. Today, the tourist is welcomed by the Honolulu Ukulele Philharmonic; he is entertained at gustatory rites known as luaus; and as he departs, the tourist's Adam's apple is nestled in a lei furnished by the Honololu Chamber of Commerce and buxom native girls gather at the plane or boat to dance and sing "Aloha." In 1914, nobody in Honolulu knew what a tourist was. Walking down the main street, if you had clothes on, you knew you belonged on the boat that was in the harbor; if you had no clothes on, you were a native. Today, the natives who swim out to meet the boats are the unemployed and the riffraff. In 1914 when the natives swam out, among them you saw some of the best people in town. When our boat, the *Sierra*, left Honolulu, the natives swam out again to see us off and dive for a few final coins. Today, they do not bother to swim along with the departing boats. The natives know that by the time the tourist leaves Honolulu he has no money left to throw.

Pago Pago was a six-day trip from Honolulu. The seasick interlude had left me weak. I was better, but my stomach still felt as though it had slipped its mooring. One morning I fell asleep in a deck chair, and one side of my face was terribly sunburned. After it had blistered and peeled, I looked like a portrait of myself done by a color-blind artist. The peeled side of my face had a covering of new rosy skin; the epidermis on the other side looked dirty. Traveling with us second class was a missionary, an exponent of some vague denomination, and with him was his daughter. The missionary was on his way to the Samoan Islands, where he planned to teach the natives what they were doing wrong. Meantime, he was not averse to having an impromptu tussle with Satan on the way. His daughter was quite pleasant, but the missionary shunned his fellow passengers as if he had caught them throwing stones at a belfry. The first time the missionary saw my face with the two-tone effect, he went into action. I was summoned to the captain's quarters, and when I arrived the ship's doctor was present. The captain told me that the missionary had reported that a leper, or a man with a serious social disease, was rampant in the second class. I explained my semi-raw appearance. The doctor examined my face and corroborated my story. The captain apologized. There was nothing I could do to the missionary. I knew his daughter was sleeping with one of the acrobats, and I thought about suggesting a title for a future sermon: "Look Around, Brother: Sin as well as Charity Often Begins at Home." I didn't, though; I merely turned the other cheek—the one that hadn't been sunburned.

On a long boat trip, the days seem like the waves, each one alike. The *Sierra* turned into the *S.S. Monotony*, doing the same number of knots per hour, hour after hour. At first, the boxers with their training routines, bag punching, rope skipping, and boxing provided some diversion, but this soon lost its novelty. Traveling second class, it was impossible to enjoy any privacy. Our deck space was small. Lying on a deck chair you heard everyone's conversation. This was no relief. At meals there were two

sittings, with the diners squeezed together at one long table, passing the meat, bread, butter, and side dishes along to each other.
Below deck there was a small lounge in which an eternal card
game was in progress. If you went to your stateroom, you had
either to stand up by your bunk or lie down in it. There was no
room to accommodate any other plan you had in mind that involved movement. Any diversion to relieve the irksome redun-
dancy of existence was welcome. On the day that word swept the
Sierra that we would pass another boat at two in the morning,
every passenger stayed up to enjoy the sight. The boat passed us
miles away. The night was dark, we saw no people, we couldn't
see the name of the boat. All we saw were the lights gliding by in
the distance and finally disappearing into the blackness of the
night. Our passengers felt well repaid for the hours they had
spent sitting and silently staring at the horizon. They retired happily, chattering about the experience, guessing the type of boat
whose lights they had seen, the sort of passengers on it, and the
boat's eventual destination. The important thing was that the
monotony had been broken. The night before we arrived in Pago
Pago many of the passengers stayed up all night. They couldn't
wait to see land again.

Pago Pago, an island in the Samoan group, was then an American coaling station. The arrival of the *Sierra* was an island event.
The natives lined the dock, exhibiting their handicraft to the passengers as they left the boat. Tropical fruits, trinkets for souve-
nirs, crude plaited straw hats, toy birchbark canoes, and minia-
tures carved from island woods were lying along the dock to
tempt the tourist. Native men and women hawked their wares in
broken English and in their tribal tongue. As Max Fleming, one
of the acrobats, and I came down the gangplank, a kindly looking
old native, wearing a loincloth and a tattered white shirt that
some tourist must have given him months before, rushed up to us
muttering one word over and over again and pointing to the
hills. The native walked along the dock with us, still repeating
the same word. Finally, Max said, "I think the old guy is trying to
say 'girls.' " At the word "girls" the native smiled and pointed to
the hills. Max and I nodded, and answered, "Girls" together. The
old man nodded back and said, "Flends?" Max decided that this
meant friends, and the native wanted us to augment our party.
We rounded up three of the boxers and two of the other fellows

from the ship. The old man looked us over approvingly, muttered his version of "girls" again, pointed to the hills, and started off down a dirt road.

After we had gone about a half mile, the old man stopped before a path that led up a hill. When we had all caught up to him, the old man started up the path with the seven of us tagging along, single file. We zigzagged up through the thick foliage for fifteen or twenty minutes until we came to a clearing in which we saw a cluster of crude huts. It was obviously a small village, but its inhabitants were not in sight. The old man led us to what appeared to be a meeting hut. A wooden floor covered the ground. A thatched roof shaded the floor from the sun, but the hut had no walls. Anyone in the hut could be seen by any native in the vicinity. The old man motioned us to sit down. After he had arranged us all in a large circle, the old man beamed knowingly, muttered "Girls" again, and added four more words to what had been, up to now his one-word vocabulary. The new words were "flifty cents" and "half clown." His "half clown" rate was for patrons coming back from Australia with English money. We all handed over fifty cents apiece; the old man clinked the silver in his hands, smiled, muttered "Girls," and trotted out of the hut. In no time at all he was back again, followed by five big-breasted and Percheron-buttocked native women. The old man smiled all around, muttered "Girls" again, and then sat on the floor, joining us. The "girls" lumbered into place. The old man started to pound the floor with both and hands and to chant an eerie refrain; the "girls" began some primitive form of mambo. The elephantine gyrations of these village housewives, the slapping of their massive feet on the wooden floor, the perspiration cascading down their fatty parts, and their droning a cappella to amplify the old man's bleating could arouse only one desire in a male: the desire to flee. But there was no escape. The provocative cavorting had to run its course. We were sitting there, crossed-legged, watching these Swamp Rockettes for nearly an hour before the old man stopped bongoing the floor and dismissed the thundering ensemble. The "girls" giggled as they rumbled by us on their way out of the hut. The old man, still smiling, beckoned us to follow him as he started back down the path to the boat. On the way we were caught in a tropical rainstorm and got soaked to our collective skin. I am sure that if the missionary later ran afoul of the old man and his sinful racket, the old man's hut was closed, the native women were saved, and tourists walking down the gangplank at Pago Pago in later years were never accosted by the smiling jungle Minsky muttering "Girls."

Fortunately, this escapade consumed most of our time in Pago Pago.

When the distant Australian coastline came into view, it was a welcome sight. After spending twenty-one days cooped up with the same people in the confining second-class space, I understood how one Siamese twin often had a desire to get away someplace by himself. The boat was all abustle as the passengers collected their baggage and assembled on the main deck, eager to land and explore the new country. I had donned one of my new fifteen-dollar suits, a three-piece gray shepherd-plaid ensemble. According to San Francisco dictates, I was dressed in the height of style: narrow trousers, double-breasted vest, and a coat pinched in at the waist that gave the lower part a skirted effect; my shoes were patent leather with gray cloth tops and white pearl buttons. To crown this I wore a large leghorn hat with the brim turned down in front and in back. Max Fleming and I stood by the rail watching the passengers crowd down the gangplank. Max was also an example of what the well-dressed American vaudeville actor was wearing. As we stood contemplating the exodus, we heard someone laughing. Looking down, we saw three Australian stevedores on the dock looking up, and discovered that they were laughing at us. Our clothes seemed funny to them. Their clothes, with the sloppy-looking suits and the pen-wiper caps they had on, seemed funny to us. Max and I started laughing at them. Their clothes must have been funnier than ours; Max and I were so busy laughing that we walked down the gangplank right past the official who was checking the passengers' credentials. It wasn't intentional, but it was perhaps fortunate, for I had neither birth certificate nor passport. It didn't seem too important at the time, since the steamship-company agent in San Francisco had promised to forward them to me in the mail, so I knew that eventually they would arrive. Meantime, Max and I, still laughing, were met by the representative of the Fuller circuit, who rounded up all the Fuller acts and took us and our baggage into Sydney.

Irish Songs and Ballads

Irish Songs and Ballads

"The Irishman's wars are always merry, even if his songs are always sad," once said G. K. Chesterton. This is a sage observation. You go through thousands of Irish songs and ballads, and you find that many deal with disappointments, suffering, and death. Very often, too, with persecution.

This seems in contrast to the character of the Irish people themselves. Being Celtic, you would think that most of their tunes would be lighthearted and lilting. However, only a few of the Irish balladeers did this. One was Victor Herbert. Although born in Dublin, Herbert spent most of his time in America, where the Irish were better off than they were in the old country.

Of course, when you go through these songs and ballads, you must remember that the Irish were repeatedly persecuted and were subject to many acts of coercion and penal laws. Besides, life was hard because it meant wringing an existence from the land, which in many parts of Ireland is anything but yielding and bountiful. Also there were times of pestilence and famine. On top of all this, there was the constant imigration from Ireland. This meant the breaking up of families with the departure of their youth overseas. The Irish are a nostalgic race and like to look back; even though they might not be suffering, they like to think they are. The great Thomas Moore, who wrote many Irish classics, also supplied many touches of sadness in his pieces.

In this selection, we have tried to assemble those going from away back to current days. It is interesting that many of these are what is known as "Come All Ye's." This comes from the idea that the Irish would amuse themselves by singing, and the expression, "Come all ye" means everyone join in song.

In the old days Irish families would gather around in their cabins and cottages and sing. Even in Dublin, Cork, Galway, and other Irish towns today, the most popular pubs are those in which there is singing. Some of the songs that you hear in the pubs today are those reproduced here. In fact, today, Ireland could be called "Isle of Saints and Singers" rather than the traditional "Isle of Saints and Scholars." The average visitor to that isle sees more of the churches and hears more songs than he sees of libraries and scholars therein.

If all the history books were destroyed, Ireland's story would still live in her songs and ballads.

Singing seems to come as naturally to an Irishman as breathing. And a lad who would find it a struggle to compose a good letter will toss off a ballad with ease.

Like the famous Dr. Gogarty, they all cry, "Now let me have my say, in my own lyric way."

BIDDY O'TOOLE'S WEDDING DAY

Near the town of Kilkenny dwelt Biddy O'Toole,
    A buxom young crathur of twenty,
With a figure not after the delicate school,
    Be me faith but of muscle she'd plenty.
No ditch was too wide to cross in a lep,
    No hedge was too stiff to be scalin',
Till Cupid an obstacle threw in her way,
    In the person of sly Micky Phalen.

Chorus
      Biddy was young, Biddy was fair,
      Like the red risin' sun was the hue of her hair,
      Divil a man in the county her anger would dare,
      Till conquered by sly Micky Phalen.

Mick's courtship it proved too strong to resist,
    She agreed to the day of the wedding.
When herself and her fortunes would all become Mick's,
    Not to spake of the pots and the bedding;
With a bouquet of roses as red as her hair,

Her heart was as light as a feather,
As she took Micky's arm " 'twas an illegant pair"
That wint off to the preacher's together.

When the marriage was over the feasting began,
There was never such drinking and atin',
Till a word from McGinnis excited McCann,
Then they all fell a-fightin' an batin'.
Poor Mick in the battle took sides with a friend,
To whom Biddy was giving a whalin',
But a whack from her fist gave Mickey his end,
And made of herself Widdy Phalen.

BARNEY BRALLAGHAN

'Twas on a frosty night, at two o'clock in the morning,
An Irish lad so tight, all wind and weather scorning,
At Judy Callaghan's door, sitting upon the palings,
His love tale did pour, and this was part of his wailings:

Chorus
Only say you'd have Mister Brallaghan
Don't say nay, charming Judy Callaghan.

Oh, list to what I say, charms you've got like Venus,
Own your love you may, there's only the wall between us;
You lay fast asleep, snug in bed and snoring,
Round the house I creep, your hard heart imploring:

I've got nine pigs and a sow, I've got a stye to sleep them,
A calf and a brindle cow, I've got a cabin to keep them;
Sunday hose and coat, an old gray mare to ride on,
Saddle and bridle to boot, which you may ride astride on:

I've got an old Tom cat, although one eye is staring,
I've got a Sunday hat, a little the worse for wearing;
I've got some gooseberry wine, the trees have got no riper on,
I've got a fiddle so fine, which only wants a piper on:

I've got an acre of ground, I've got it set with praties,
I've got of backey a pound, and got some tea for the ladies;
I've got the ring to wed, some whiskey to make us gaily,
A mattress and feather bed, and a handsome new shillelah:

You've got a charming eye, you've got some spelling and reading,
You've got, and so have I, a taste for genteel breeding.
You're rich and fair and young, as every one is knowing,
You've got a decent tongue whene'er 'tis set a-going:

For a wife till death I am willing to take ye,
But, och! I waste my breath, the devil himself can't wake ye;
'Tis just beginning to rain, so I'll get under cover,
I'll come tomorrow again and be your constant lover.

FATHER MOLLOY

Paddy McCabe was dying one day,
    And Father Molloy he came to confess him;
Paddy prayed hard he would make no delay,
    But forgive him his sins and make haste for to bless him.
"First tell me your sins," says Father Molloy,
    "For I'm thinking you've not been a very good boy."
"Oh," says Paddy, "so late in the evening, I fear
    'Twould throuble you such a long story to hear,
For you've ten long miles o'er the mountains to go,
    While the road I've to travel's much longer you know.
So give us your blessin' and get in the saddle,
    To tell all my sins my poor brain it would addle;
And the docther gave ordhers to keep me so quiet—
    'Twould disturb me to tell all my sins, if I'd thry it;
And your Reverence has towld us, unless we tell all,
    'Tis worse than not makin' confession at all.
So I'll say in a word I'm no very good boy—
    And therefore your blessin', sweet Father Molloy."

"Well, I'll read from a book," says Father Molloy,
    "The manifold sins that humanity's heir to;
And when you hear those that your conscience annoy,

You'll just squeeze my hand, as acknowledging thereto."
Then the father began the dark roll of iniquity,
    And Paddy, thereat, felt his conscience grow rickety,
And he gave such a squeeze that the priest gave a roar—
    "Oh, murdher!" says Paddy. "Don't read any more,
For, if you keep readin', by all that is thrue,
    Your Reverence's fist will be soon black and blue;
Besides, to be throubled my conscience begins,
    That your Reverence should have any hand in my sins,
So you'd bether suppose I committed them all,
    For whether they're great ones, or whether they're small,
Or if they're a dozen, or if they're fourscore,
    'Tis your Reverence knows how to absolve them, asthore;
So I'll say in a word, I'm no very good boy—
    And therefore your blessin', sweet Father Molloy."

"Well," says Father Molloy, "if your sins I forgive,
    So you must forgive all your enemies truly;
And promise me also that, if you should live,
    You'll leave off your old tricks, and begin to live newly."
"I forgive ev'rybody," says Pat, with a groan,
    "Except that big vagabone Micky Malone;
And him I will murdher if ever I can—"
    "Tut, tut!" says the priest. "You're a very bad man;
For without your forgiveness, and also repentance,
    You'll ne'er go to heaven, and that is my sentence."
"Poo!" says Paddy McCabe, "that's a very hard case—
    With your Reverence and heaven I'm content to make pace;
But with heaven and your Reverence I wondher—Och hone—
    You would think of comparin' that blackguard Malone—
But since I'm hard-press'd and that I must forgive,
    I forgive—if I die—but as sure as I live
That ugly blackguard I will surely desthroy!—
    So, now for your blessin', sweet Father Molloy!"

THE LITTLE OLD DUDDEEN

There's a bit of clay on a little stim that's sweet enough to ate;
Whin filled up wid tobacco 'twould put a man to slape.

'Twas introduced in Ireland in the days of Brian Boru;
I'd rather lose my life, my boys, than lose my honey-dew,
Some call it "Cavendish," or any name you'd wish,
And they dale it out in plug, you know, when it is fresh and green;
When from my work I tire, I set down by the fire
An' I watch the smoke roll up and curl from my little ould dud-
deen.

Chorus

My duddeen, you are so sweet to me, I love to see your smoke go
up
Whin I get through my tea; my duddeen, you are in the family.
I'd surely die if I found out you were stole away from me.

If ye have studied history, ye'll read where William Pinn
Bought the State of Pinnsylvania from the wild red Injin men;
He never used a sword or gun when he met them face to face,
But they all sit down continted, and they smoked the pipe of
peace.
If ye'd only take a puff, shure, one would be enough
To put you in a slumber, a stupor, or a dream.
Ye might say it's not ginteel, but so beautiful I feel
Whin I sit down in the corner, boys, wid my little ould duddeen.

A Frenchman smokes the little thing they call the cigarette,
It makes him feel uneasy, as he blows and puffs and frets;
The Chinese smokes the opium till it puts him in a doze;
And the Yankee smokes the bad cigar, wid one end to his nose;
But every Irishman—bould Patsey, Mike or Dan—
That was born in dear old Ireland, where the grasses grow so
green;
If they've no coat to their back, they've that bit of clay so black;
It's a consolation to them, is the little ould duddeen.

THE IRISHMAN'S SERENADE

The full moon is old, my love,
You've got plenty of money, I'm told, my love;

So your knocker I'll ring, and to court you I'll sing,
Though I've got a most shocking bad cold, my love.

Then awake—for my love is so hot, my dear,
That without you I'll soon go to pot, my dear!
For my shirt at your clack would stick close to my back,
But the devil a shirt have I got, my dear!

Like a cat my watch I'm keeping, love,
For no bed have I got to sleep in, my love;
So, honey, look down and smile me a frown,
From your eye so beautiful peeping, love.

Old time, like the guitar, does run, my dear,
So pray thee much modesty shun, my dear;
Have me, I'll have you, and though still we'll be two,
All Kilkenny will take us for one, my dear.

KATTY AVOURNEEN

'Twas a cold Winter's night, and the tempest was snarlin',
   The snow, like a sheet, covered cabin and stye,
When Barney flew over the hills to his darlin'
   And tapped at the window where Katty did lie.
"Arrah! jewel," said he, "are ye sleepin' or wakin'?
   The night's bitter cold, an' my coat it is thin;
Oh! the storm 'tis a-brewin', the frost it is bakin',
   Oh! Katty Avourneen, you must let me in."

"Arrah! Barney," cried she, an' she spoke thro' the window,
   "Ah, would ye be taken me out of my bed?
To come at this time it's a shame an' a sin, too—
   It's whiskey, not love, that's got into your head.
If your heart it was true, of my fame you'd be tender,
   Consider the time, and there's nobody in;
Oh! what has a poor girl but her name to defend her?
   No, Barney Avourneen, I won't let you in."

"Ah! cushla," cried he, "it's my heart is a fountain
   That weeps for the wrong it might lay at your door;
Your name is more white than the snow on the mountain,
   And Barney would die to preserve it as pure.
I'll go to my home, though the Winter winds face me
   I'll whistle them off, for I'm happy within;
An' the words of my Kathleen will comfort and bless me:
   'Oh! Barney Avourneen, I won't let you in.' "

THE BOY FROM COUNTY CLARE

My name is Pat, now look at that, I am an Irishman.
I have a stick to do the trick, so beat me if you can;
Of all the boys that make a noise at wake or pattern fair,
The divil a one so full of fun as the boy from County Clare.

Chorus
For to turn a stick smart and quick, bothers them completely,
Divil a wrist can do the twist, roll it 'round so neatly;
Of all the boys that make a noise at wake or pattern fair,
The divil a one so full of fun as the boy from County Clare.

A neat colleen and sweet potheen, bedad! I love the two,
And to the both I took an oath, and mean to keep it true;
For when away too long I stay, I sigh to think of that,
And take a drain to stay the pain and warm the heart of **Pat.**

Nell O'Grady is a lady, sweet as buttermilk,
Although she wears no quality airs, nor yet the gown of silk;
She has no hat, but what of that? and though her arms are bare,
She is a jade to suit a blade, like Pat from County Clare.

I told my love I'd weep above a teapot full of tears,
Unless she'd say she'd come my way, and comfort Paddy's years.
"I will," said she, and smothered me with kisses on the nose,
"I'm fond of that," said she, "that's flat, but not shillalah blows."

So Paddy's life and Paddy's wife are both as bright as day,
Not anywhere in County Clare are two so blithe as they;

With dance and song they jog along, in fair and stormy weather,
And when they die they mean to try, and so do both together.

I'M A RANTING, ROVING BLADE

Whoo! I'm a ranting, roving blade,
Of never a thing was I ever afraid;
I'm a gentleman born, and scorn a trade,
And I'd be a rich man if my debts were paid.

But my debts are worth something, this truth instill—
That pride makes us fall, all against our will;
For 'twas pride that broke me—I was happy until
I was ruined all out by my tailor's bill.

I'm the finest guide that ever you see,
I know ev'ry place of curiosity,
From Ballinfad unto Tanderagee;
And if you're for sport, come along wid me.

I'll lade you sportin' round about;
We've wild ducks and widgeons, and snipe and throut,
And I know where they are, and what they are about,
And if they're not at home, then I'm sure they're out.

The miles in this country much longer be,
But that is a saving of time, you see;
For two of our miles is equal to three,
Which shorten the road in a great degree.

And the roads in this place is so plenty, we say,
That you have nothing to do but find your own way;
If your hurry's not great, and you have time to delay,
You can go the short cut—that's the longest way.

HARRIGAN AND HART

Though little known today, the famous comedy team of Ned
Harrigan and Tony Hart had a great vogue in the 1870's and

lasted until the death of Tony Hart in 1891.

Their partnership started in 1871 with Ned Harrigan as "Pete" in their original blackface act. The handsome Hart, who had a beautiful tenor voice, often played female roles. When together, the team specialized in Irish songs and later worked up elaborate musical comedies which toured all over America. Ned Harrigan wrote the words of their famous songs, and the music was composed by David Braham, their orchestra leader.

One of their long-standing hits was "The Mulligan Guard" which made great fun of the amateur military marching organizations which had thrived as political and social organizations following the Civil War. The biting satire of "The Mulligan Guard" practically laughed these marching clubs out of existence.

Another show of theirs, "The Mulligan Guard Ball" became one of the most beloved Harrigan and Hart songs, along with "The Babies on Our Block," a forerunner of "The Sidewalks of New York," which Al Smith used as a campaign song when he ran for the Presidency of the United States in 1928.

THE BABIES ON OUR BLOCK

If you want for information, or in need of merriment,
Come over with me socially to Murphy's tenement;
He owns a row of houses in the first ward, near the dock,
Where Ireland's represented by the babies on our block.
There's the Phalens and the Whalens from the sweet Dunochadee,
They are sitting on the railings with their children on their knee,
All gossiping and talking with their neighbors in a flock,
Singing "Little Sally Waters," with the babies on our block.
Oh, little Sally Waters, sitting in the sun,
A-crying and weeping for a young man;
Oh, rise, Sally, rise, wipe your eye out with your frock;
That's sung by the babies a-living on our block.

Of a warm day in the summer, when the breeze flows off the sea
A hundred thousand children lay on the Battery;
They come from Murphy's building, oh, their noise would stop a
    clock!

Oh, there's no perambulatory, with the babies on our block.
There's the Clareys and the Learys from the sweet Blackwater side
They are laying on the Battery and they're gazing at the tide;
All royal blood and noble, all of Dan O'Connell's stock,
Singing "Gravel, Greeney Gravel," with the babies on our block.
For all the pretty fair young maidens that I see;
Oh, "Green Gravel Green," wipe your eye out with your frock;
That's sung by the babies a-living on our block.

It's good morning to you, landlord; come now, how are you today?
When Patrick Murphy, Esquire, comes down the alley way,
With his shiny silken beaver, he's as solid as a rock,
The envy of the neighbors' boys a-living off our block,
Singing "Little Sally Waters," with the babies on our block.
Oh, little Sally Waters, sitting in the sun,
A-crying and weeping for a young man;
Oh, rise, Sally, rise, wipe your eye out with your frock;
That's sung by the babies a-living on our block.

THE NIGHT THAT
PADDY MURPHY DIED

Another very popular song which has survived from the Harrigan and Hart days is "The Night that Paddy Murphy Died." The ballad concerns one Paddy Murphy who came to America from Cork and spent his lifetime beating his wife and supposedly died of acute alcoholism. His relatives gave him a handsome wake.

Curiously, at Northwestern University, founded by teetotalers, in Evanston, Illinois, the alcoholic exploits of Paddy Murphy annually receive appropriate funeral rites sponsored by the local Sigma Alpha Epsilon.

The students line up in a procession three blocks long and parade to the outskirts of Evanston. The marchers are garbed in green and tearfully draining beer bottles as they follow the corpse which is composed of dead beer bottle with a red lamp for a nose. When the procession reaches the grave which has been dug by pledges, the mourners light candles and break into the Paddy Murphy song.

Of course, attempts are made by a rival fraternity, Sigma Chi, to steal the corpse, but the SAE's usually see "Murphy" successfully to his grave as the Irish ballad lives on.

The night that Paddy Murphy died
I never shall forget,
The whole damn town got stinkin' drunk
And some ain't sober yet.

The only thing they did that night
That filled my heart with fear,
They took the ice right off the corpse
And put it in the beer.

Chorus

That's how they showed their respect for Paddy Murphy,
That's how they showed their honor and their pride,
Ho-ho-ho, that's how they showed their respect for Paddy Murphy,
On the night that Paddy died.

When they finished with the beer, they started on the corpse.
They took him from his coffin and put him on the porch,
And then they went next door and stole a neighbor's pig
And brought it back to Paddy's house and tied it on his leg.

DOWN WENT MCGINTY

By JOSEPH FLYNN

Another Irish song popular in 1870 written by Joseph Flynn was "Down Went McGinty." Snatches of this ballad remain today in a college song of the University of Pennsylvania.

Sunday morning just at nine, Dan McGinty dress'd so fine,
Stood looking up at a very high stone wall;
When his friend young Pat McCann, says, I'll bet five dollars, Dan,

I could carry you to the top without a fall;
So on his shoulders he took Dan, to climb the ladder he began,
   And he soon commenc'd to reach up near the top;
When McGinty, cute old rogue, to win the five he did let go,
   Never thinking just how far he'd have to drop.

Chorus

Down went McGinty to the bottom of the wall,
And tho' he won the five, he was more dead than alive,
Sure his ribs, and nose, and back were broke from getting such a
   fall,
Dress'd in his best suit of clothes.

From the hospital Mac went home, when they fixed his broken
   bone,
   To find he was the father of a child;
So to celebrate it right, his friend he went to invite,
   And he soon was drinking whisky fast and wild;
Then he waddled down the street in his Sunday suit no neat,
   Holding up his head as proud as John the Great;
But in the sidewalk was a hole, to receive a ton of coal,
   That McGinty never saw till just too late.

Chorus

Down went McGinty to the bottom of the hole,
Then the driver of the cart gave the load of coal a start,
And it took us half an hour to dig McGinty from the coal,
Dress'd in his best suit of clothes.

Now McGinty raved and swore, about his clothes he felt so sore,
   And an oath he took he'd kill the man or die;
So he tightly grabb'd his stick and hit the driver a lick,
   Then he raised a little shanty on his eye;
But two policemen saw the muss and they soon join'd in the fuss,
   Then they ran McGinty in for being drunk;
And the Judge says with a smile, we will keep you for a while
   In a cell to sleep upon a prison bunk.

Chorus

Down went McGinty to the bottom of the jail,
Where his board would cost him nix and he stay'd exactly six,

They were big long months he stopp'd for no one went his bail,
Dress'd in his best suit of clothes.

Now McGinty, thin and pale, one fine day got out of jail,
 And with joy to see his boy was nearly wild;
To his house he quickly ran to meet his wife Bedaley Ann,
 But she'd skipp'd away and took along the child;
Then he gave up in despair, and he madly pull'd his hair,
 As he stood one day upon the river shore,
Knowing well he couldn't swim, he did foolishly jump in,
 Although water he had never took before.

Chorus
Down went McGinty to the bottom of the say,
And he must be very wet for they haven't found him yet,
But they say his ghost comes round the docks before the break of
 day,
Dress'd in his best suit of clothes.

The Limerick

The Irish City of Limerick is reputedly responsible for the origin
and name of what is perhaps the most popular modern form of
English verse in existence—the Limerick.

At convivial gatherings in Ireland in the 1820's, there was a
popular song in which each of an interminable set of verses dealt
with the adventures of an inhabitant of a different Irish town,
and had to be invented on the spur of the moment, each line by a
different singer, after which the whole company roared out a
chorus commencing with:

> "Won't you come up, come up, come up
> Won't you come up to Limerick town?"

Unfortunately, since the Limerick form of verse is so popular,
it lends itself to great misuse and abuse. In fact, most of the very
best Limericks are so distinctly Rabelaisian that they are not for
publication.

In 1924, Langford Hand Reed, who was compiling *The Com-*

plete Limerick Book, wrote to a number of leading literary figures of that era requesting Limerick contributions from them. Answered Bernard Shaw: "There are several personal Limericks by D. G. Rossetti and some by Swinburne, which became known in their generation, but like a large number of geographical Limericks which preceded them are mostly unfit for publication. They must be left for oral tradition." Arnold Bennett endorsed Shaw's opinion with: "In reply to your letter, all I have to say about Limericks is that the best ones are entirely unprintable."

However, despite the opinion of literary authorities, Limericks have had great popularity with the public. For years, newspapers and magazines have used Limericks as bait to get circulation. In one newspaper contest held in England in 1907–1908, which offered all kinds of prizes but which required an entrance fee of sixpence, entries vaulted from 70,000 monthly to 11,400,000. The big prize offer was one which sought a last line for:

> "There was a Young Lady of Ryde
> Whose locks were considerably dyed.
> The hue of her hair
> Made Everyone stare."

The winning last line was:

> " 'She's piebald, she'll die bald,' they cried."

Interestingly, during all of the great popularity of Limerick contests by newspapers down through the years, one paper which has steadfastly refrained from holding any such contest is the Limerick, Ireland, *Times.* The reason is that people from all over the world are constantly sending unsolicited Limericks to the editor or requesting him to send them some Limericks so they can win prizes. The Limerick *Times* is simply fed up with Limericks.

The late Dr. Oliver St. John Gogarty, who was the "Buck Mulligan" character in James Joyce's *Ulysses,* has the reputation of being the best Irish author of Limericks. I can personally attest that this reputation is not without foundation. I spent many happy hours in the good doctor's company and was privileged to hear some magnificent Limericks on almost every prominent Irish and British personage and subject, too. However, only one of his and one by Joyce which he liked to recite are printable.

In their youth in the early 1900's, Gogarty, then a medical student, and Joyce, a budding author with a beautiful tenor voice, used to roister in Dublin's red light district, known as Nighttown and where the brothels were called Kips. Gogarty used a Limerick to describe his friend Joyce of those days:

"There was a young fellow called Joyce
Who possesseth a sweet tenor voice.
    He goes to the Kips
    With a psalm on his lips
And biddeth the harlots rejoice."

When Lady Gregory, the talented Irish playwright and generous sponsor of the Abbey Theatre, Dublin, once advertised for new talent to write plays for the Abbey, her Ladyship, according to Gogarty, was appalled at the flood of poetry-stricken applicants and fled. In telling this story, Gogarty would always recite Joyce's Limerick on the event.

"There was a kind Lady called Gregory
Said: 'Come to me, poets in beggary'
    But found her impudence
    When thousands of students
Cried: 'All we are in that category!' "

President Woodrow Wilson, whose forebears came from County Tyrone, was not exactly the type to be carousing with Gogarty and Joyce. However, he had some Celtic humor in him as his fondness for this Anthony Ewer Limerick proves:

"As a beauty I am not a star.
There are others more handsome by far,
    But my face, I don't mind it
    Because I'm behind it,
'Tis the folks out in front that I jar."

Diplomat Hugh Gibson, who served several times as Ambassador to Belgium, was of Irish stock; he composed this:

"There was a young man from New York
Whose morals were lighter than cork
    'Young chickens,' said he,

'Have no terrors for me.
The bird I fear is the stork.' "

Two other Limericks with an Irish angle are:

"At a bistro, a chap named O'Reilly
Said: 'I've heard these martinis praised heilly
But they're betterly far
At the neighboring bar
Where they are mixed more smoothly and dreilly.' "

"There was a young lady of Clare
Who was hotly pursued by a bear.
When she found she was tired,
She abruptly expired,
That unfortunate lady of Clare."

This compiler is sincerely sorry that in this publishable department of Limericks, the usually abundant Irish are so sparse. However, the Limerick fan on his next visit to an Irish pub or club can find, as Shaw says, that the Limerick is being done justice to in the oral tradition.

Old Irish Proverbs

Old Irish Proverbs

Most Irishmen are born philosophers. Intrigued with life, the Irish love to come up with reasons why things happen as they do. Also in their philosophy is a strong tinge of fatalism—what occurred was bound to occur regardless of what one may have done in advance to avoid it.

Coupled with this ingrained philosophical attitude, the Irish have a natural picturesque style of saying simple things. Out of these colorful Celtic sayings down through the years, have come not a few pertinent proverbs such as:

The doorstep of a great house is slippery.
Laziness is a heavy burden.
You'd be a good messenger to send for death (said of a slow person).
Better be bald than have no head at all—but the devil a much more than that.
Better the end of a feast than the beginning of a fight.
Let him cool in the skin he warmed in.
A man is shy in another man's corner.
The pig in the sty doesn't know the pig going along the road.
Cows far from home have long horns.
'Tis a good story that fills the belly.
A drink is shorter than a story.
The man that's up is toasted,
The man that's down is trampled on.
A mouth of ivy and a heart of holly.
A soft word never broke a tooth yet.
He comes like the bad weather (i.e., uninvited).
Who lies down with dogs will get up with fleas.
The eye of a friend is a good looking glass.

'Tis the fool has luck.

A blind man can see his mouth.

To die and to lose one's life are much the same.

The three sharpest things at all—a thorn in a mire, a hound's tooth, and a fool's retort.

The jewel most rare is the jewel most fair.

He that loses the game, let him talk away.

A heavy purse makes a light heart.

He is like a bagpipe—he never makes a noise till his belly's full.

Falling is easier than rising.

A woman has an excuse readier than an apron.

A bad wife takes advice from every man but her own husband.

The daughter of an active old woman makes a bad housekeeper.

Never take a wife who has no faults.

She burnt her coal and did not warm herself (i.e., when a woman makes a bad marriage).

A ring on the finger and not a stitch of clothes on the back.

A big belly was never generous.

There is hope from the sea, but no hope from the cemetery.

When the hand ceases to scatter, the mouth ceases to praise.

Big head and little sense.

One cockroach knows another.

A heavy load are your empty guts.

The young thorn is the sharpest.

Sweet is wine, bitter its payment.

Whoever drinks, it is Donall that pays.

The man on the fence is the best hurler (against critics and idle lookers-on).

A closed hand gets but a shut fist.

It is not all big men that reap the harvest.

Easy, oh, woman of three cows (against pretentious people).

Fair words won't feed the friars.

Not worried till married.

Three without rule—a wife, a pig, and a mule.

When your hand is in the dog's mouth, draw it out gently.

Better a drop of whisky than a blow of a stick.

The four drinks—the drink of thirst, the drink without thirst, the drink for fear of thirst, and the drink at the door.

A woman is more obstinate than a mule—a mule than the devil.

All the world would not make a racehorse of a jackass.

Death is the poor man's doctor.

If 'tis a sin to be yellow, thousands will be damned.

There's no good crying when the funeral is gone.

Buttermilk is no milk, and a pudding's no meat.

Though near to a man his coat, his shirt is nearer (i.e., blood is thicker than water).

Better a fistful of a man than a basketful of a woman.

What cannot be had is just what suits.

An unlearned king is a crowned ass.

'Tis the end of the little pot, the bottom to fall out of it.

A woman's desire—the dear thing.

A man without dinner—two for supper.

The man without a resource is hanged.

Poor women think buttermilk good.

Harsh is the poor man's voice—he speaks all out of place.

'Tis a fine horse that never stumbles.

A man loses something to teach himself.

A hen carried far is heavy.

The day of the storm is not the day for thatching.

Winter comes on the lazy.

A crow thinks its own young white.

Truth is bitter, but a lie is savory at times.

'Tis a bad hound that is not worth whistling for.

Better today than tomorrow morning.

Patience is the cure of an old complaint.

Have your own will, like the women have.

An old cat does not burn himself.

A foolish woman knows the faults of a foolish man.

The law of lending is to break the ware.

No heat like that of shame.

A candle does not give light till lit.

Don't praise your son-in-law till the year's out.

The glory the head cannot bear, 'twere better not there.

He that does not tie a knot will lose his first stitch.

The fox never found a better messenger than himself.

Better a little fire that warms than a large fire that burns.

Better a short sitting than a long standing.

Better be idle than working for nothing.

Do not show your teeth when you cannot give a bite.

Better come empty than with bad news.

Trust him as far as you can throw a cow by the tail.

Praise the end of it.

Never was door shut but another was opened.

The heaviest ear of corn bends lowliest.

He who is bad at giving lodging is good at showing the road.

Where there's women there's talk, and where there's geese there's
   cackling.

More beard than brains, as the fox said of the goat.

A trade not learned is an enemy.

An empty house is better than a bad tenant.

He knows as much about it as a dog knows of his father.

He'd say anything but his prayers.

A vessel will only hold the full of it.

A blind man is no judge of colors.

Fierceness is often hidden under beauty.

When the cat is out, the mice dance.

There is often anger in a laugh.

No one claims kindred with the homeless.

An empty vessel makes most sound.

He that gets a name for early rising may sleep all day.

Talk is cheap.

When the hand grows weak, love gets feeble.

If you have a cow, you can always find somebody to milk her.

Long-lived is a man in his own country.

Forgetting one's debts does not pay them.

Nearer is God's aid than the door.

Bad is the walk that is not better than rest.

Diseases without shame are love and thirst.

Might is not lasting.

Wrath speaketh not true.

Wakes and Wags

Irish Wakes

A considerable slice of Irish social life revolves around those fes-
tivities known as "wakes," which are held entirely apart from
Christian funeral services, and surpass in community interest
even the movies or politics. In the wild country of County Donegal, whole villages will participate in a wake. As soon as news of a
relative's death reaches members of the clan, they pack supplies of
foodstuffs, spirits and stout to last several days, assemble at a convenient meeting place and, in a group, proceed to the cottage of
the deceased. There they spend the entire first night in keening.
Keening is one of those ancient Irish customs, dating back into
pre-Christian times, which have outlived both the Christian and
Roman inundation. Crowded around the coffin, the relatives
weep and wail weirdly and in perfect unison, and the effect upon
listeners is soul-searing. The first time you catch it, even as far off
as I did one summer night, you are hard put to reconcile it with any
sound you have heard before. It's so primitive, so eerie, so pagan
that you almost believe the Druids are holding a ceremony high
up in the hills.

The deceased's friends make their calls the next few evenings.
All the people in the home village and nearby towns consider
themselves friends. As they enter the house, they go directly to the
casket, get on their knees and say a few prayers. Immediate members of the family are lined up close to the coffin. Following his
prayers, the caller pays his respects to them, then adjourns to a
back room, where he settles himself for a night of genuine socia-
bility. The women gather in one room, the men in another.

In Ireland, the mister is still the privileged person. Therefore, in
the rooms reserved for men there will be food, whiskey and stout
aplenty, batches of new clay pipes and lots of tobacco. After a few
kind words about the lamented host of the house, the lads fill up

their pipes and go to work on the food, spirits and stout. Tongues unloosen. And the wake is on! Every topic known to mankind is discussed; every personage in Irish public and private life is verbally trotted forth and his reputation literally torn to shreds. Not until the sun comes up does it occur to anyone to stop yarning and go home. Even then, they go reluctantly.

Constant Mourner

No miscellany of Irish gaffs and laughs is complete without a funeral story. To the Irish, funerals, though sad, can oft be sociable too. And many an amusing tale has come out of them. Frank Tinney, the one-time great Broadway comedian, in his earlier days was an undertaker's assistant in Philadelphia. In that time, before World War I, the standing of any Irish family was established by the number of carriages attending a family funeral. It was not uncommon for a Philly Irish funeral cortege to include as many as 125 carriages.

Tinney tells of an Irish oldster named Burke who was a constant mourner at Philadelphia wakes and funerals, even though, frequently, he was not even acquainted with the deceased or the family. He took his leads out of the newspaper obituary columns. Of course, it was not a bad pastime, for the wakes and funerals provided Burke with plenty free food, drinks and smokes. In those times, the Philadelphia Irish wakes, like those in the ould country, went on all night. The long carriage rides out to the Catholic cemeteries in the suburbs called for regular stops at the saloons en route for watering the horses as well as replenishing the carriage's beverage supplies.

Burke turned up at so many Irish funerals that he became an accepted personage, especially since he was a prominent weeper at the graveside, always giving the impression that he had lost his best friend.

One day, Burke, appeared at a society funeral at the Protestant Cathedral in Philadelphia. Here, for once, undertaker assistant Tinney figured, Burke was out of luck. Protestant funerals were strictly private for the immediate family. At this particular one, there were only six carriages.

However, bird dog Burke managed to get into the one of the six which had a liquid supply. Hence, when he arrived at the cemetery, Burke, in his usual fine crying fettle, was soon weeping copiously at the graveside. Whereas at the Irish funerals Burke was accepted, the society folk who had never seen him before were looking at him as though he was a side dish that they had not ordered. Such stares never phased Burke, who was relishing every last morsel of his weeping.

As the body was lowered into the grave, the presiding Episcopal bishop intoned solemnly: "God giveth. God taketh away."

Whereupon, Old Man Burke, with tears streaming down his face, turned to the startled assembled mourners, arms outstretched, and cried out: "Now, what the hell could be fairer than that?"

Unique Will

The Registrar of Wills in Philadelphia constantly receives requests from all over the world for a copy of the will of the late millionaire, John B. Kelly. A former Olympic sculling champion, Kelly began life as a bricklayer and completed it as one of Philadelphia's honored citizens. His daughter is Princess Grace of Monaco. His son, John Jr., also an Olympic sculling champ, won the coveted Diamond Sculls in London, from which his father was banned in 1920 because he was a bricklayer.

Incidentally, when Kelly Sr. Won the Olympic rowing title, beating the titled British winner of the Diamond Sculls, he mailed his Kelly-green rowing cap with his compliments to King George at Buckingham Palace.

Jack Kelly Sr. was not the only celebrity to come from the Kelly clan in the then Irish section of East Falls in Philadelphia. His brother George was the Pulitzer prize-winning playwright, and another brother, Walter, was the Virginia judge of vaudeville fame.

The reason for the steady demand for the will of Jack Kelly Sr. is not from missing heirs seeking a slice of his fortune. Far from it. People just want the copy to read. No, it was not drawn by a

Philadelphia lawyer. Instead, it was compiled by Jack himself and is probably one of the most informal and understanding wills ever written. Also, unlike most millionaires, especially those with large Irish families, Kelly long before his death circulated copies of it to each member of his family.

Wrote John B Kelly in his will:

"For years I have been reading last wills and testaments, and I have never been able to understand any of them clearly at one reading.

"I will therefore attempt to write my own will in the hope that it will be both understandable and legal.

"Kids will be called 'kids' and not issue,' and it will not be cluttered up with 'parties of the first part,' 'perpetuities,' 'to wit,' and lots of other terms that are used only to confuse those for whom the will is written.

"This is my last will and testament and I believe I am of sound mind (some lawyers will question this when they read it; however, I have my opinion of some of them, so that makes it even) ."

After providing for the various members of his family, Mr. Kelly concluded: "I will try to give each of you all that I can during my lifetime so that you will have money in your own right.

"As for me—just shed a respectful tear if you think I merit it, but I am sure you are all intelligent enough not to weep all over the place.

"I have watched a few emotional acts at graves, such as trying to jump into it, fainting, etc., but the thoroughbred grieves in the heart."

The will concluded: "In this document I can only give you things, but if I had the choice to give you worldly goods or character I would certainly give you the latter."

The Governor Was There

By Edwin O'Connor

At 7:30, Adam was waiting; Governor Frank Skeffington, on the other hand, was not. His unpunctuality inviolable, he was fifteen minutes late, and as the long official car pulled up he said genially, "Hop in. As a taxpayer, you're entitled to. Try the comforts of the vehicle you thoughtfully provided for me."

Adam got in. Determined to remove all mystery from the outset, he said, "By the way, when we were talking this afternoon I completely forgot to ask you where we were going."

"So you did," Skeffington said. "I took it as a rare mark of confidence; now I find it was only a lapse of memory. One more illusion lost." He chuckled and said, "Actually, we're going to a wake. Knocko Minihan's wake."

"A *wake?*"

"Surprised? I had an idea you might be: there was just the possibility that you weren't in the habit of spending your free evenings in visiting deceased strangers. But I felt that tonight it might be useful for you to come along. In its way, a wake can be quite an occasion."

"You may be underestimating me," Adam said. "I've been to a few wakes. Not many, but a few."

"I don't doubt it. Probably not exactly like this one, however. Not that poor Knocko's will be unique, but it might be a little different from those you've been to."

Adam was not prepared to dispute this. The car drove on, and he said, "His name wasn't Knocko, surely?"

"No. It was Aram. The mother was part French, and he was named for an uncle in Quebec. The old gentleman had some money, and the Minihans cherished the fond hope that one happy day it would fall into the lap of little Aram. Unfortunately there was a tragic development. The uncle went crazy and gave away all of his money to a convent outside Montreal; two months later he went to a Canadian lunatic asylum where he subsequently died. The Minihans naturally tried to prove that he'd been a madman before he gave the money to the convent. It seemed a reasonable assumption, especially when you consider that the old man suffered from the delusion that he was an air rifle and went around spitting BB's at squirrels. But as anybody can tell you who's ever tried to recover a bequest from an order of nuns in Quebec, the assumption wasn't quite reasonable enough. So no legacy was forthcoming for the little Aram. Meanwhile, of course, he'd been stuck with the name: I don't think he ever forgave his parents for that. It was a terrible start in life for a boy in this city. That's why he gladly became Knocko."

"And how did he make out after this terrible start?"

"Not too well. Save in one respect, that is. He married a grand woman who was a close friend of my wife's—your aunt's," he said. "In every other way he was a failure. He had a hardware store that he ran into the ground almost before the opening-day sale was over. Then he tried several other businesses, all of which petered out in no time at all. I don't know that people trusted him especially, and they certainly didn't like him. And neither," he said, rather surprisingly, "did I. However, *de mortuis . . .*"

"If nobody liked him," Adam said, "I imagine we'll run into a fairly slim attendance tonight."

"Not at all," said Skeffington. "The place'll be crowded to the doors. A wake isn't quite the same as a popularity contest. There are other factors involved. Ah, here we are."

They had arrived in front of a two-story frame tenement house which was in need of paint; the door on the left held a wreath with a large purple ribbon. Skeffington placed a hand just beneath this ornament and then, before pushing the door open, paused to regard the unlovely premises. He shook his head. "Charming," he said. "Come on, let's go in."

A heavy-set woman, dressed in black, and with the face of some large and extremely suspicious bird, came out of the darkness to greet them.

"Hello, Frank," she said.

"Hello, Agnes. Mrs. Burns, my nephew, Adam Caulfield. Mary's boy." There were nods, an exchange of greetings; Skeffington asked, "How's Gert taking it?"

"Pretty good. She cries a little," said the woman. Adam could not help but observe that she was herself noticeably dry of eye. In explanation she added, "She remembers all the nice things he done."

"She has a remarkable memory," Skeffington said dryly.

Mrs. Burns accepted this with a short nod of agreement, then pointed to a door on the right of the narrow hall. "He's in the parlor," she said. "I think no one is in there now; it's still a bit early. Go right in, Frank. He looks lovely."

Adam followed Skeffington into the parlor: he saw a tall,

glum room which might have been designed specifically with this
melancholy event in mind. Heavy dull plush furniture had been
pushed back against the walls: stretching from side to side across
the room were rows of thin metal chairs, of the kind furnished by
catering services. At the moment these were empty; looking at
them through the gloom Adam wondered whether this was indeed due to the hour of their arrival, or rather to the simple fact
that Knocko Minihan had not been widely loved.

At the far end of the parlor, decorated with wreaths and floral
sprays, was a gray coffin; to Adam it seemed huge, a sarcophagus
fit for a giant. He advanced upon it with his uncle; they knelt by
the side of the coffin and Adam saw Knocko in death. He lay
stiffly among billows of white satin, a diminutive man lost in the
recesses of his mighty container. Across the top of his head occasional strands of yellowish-white hair had been combed strate-
gically; a taut, grudging smile, which somehow fell short of suggesting an interior peace, had been worked into position. His
small hands were folded across his chest, clasping a rosary, and
over the coffin a large crucifix, heavily studded with rhinestones,
had been suspended. Someone of ingenious mind—undoubtedly
the undertaker, thought Adam—had fixed a baby spotlight so that
it played full upon the crucifix; high above Knocko's final, alien
smile, the rhinestones glittered and danced.

Adam said a prayer for this man he had not known. Skeffington, after a moment, got to his feet slowly, looking about him, at
the coffin, at the crucifix. "A lavish display," he said. "And you
couldn't get the man near a theater in his life." He put his hand
lightly on Adam's shoulder and said, "Will you do me a favor and
stay here a moment? I have to go in and say a word to the widow."

Adam looked up, surprised; he rose quickly. "You mean, wait
here?"

Skeffington smiled slightly. "I'm afraid I do; it seems to be
about the only place. You could wait in the car, but I've sent the
chauffeur on an errand. In any event, it won't be too bad; I'll be
back directly. Why don't you just sit down in one of those chairs
in back? People will be coming in shortly, and anyway the whole
thing is an experience you ought to have; it's a custom that's dying out. Besides, you can regard it as a meritorious act; you'll be
keeping poor Knocko company."

Adam nodded reluctantly. There seemed nothing to do but agree, although he was scarcely happy over the prospect of the solitary vigil. Feeling vaguely that he had once again been outgeneraled all along the line, he moved towards the back of the room, as far as possible from the dead Knocko, the rhinestones, and the baby spotlight. Here in the dim light of the evening, he sat down to await the return of his uncle.

In the first few minutes of his wait, the quiet, as well as the gloom became increasingly uninviting. All light from the outside seemed to fade; the macabre cruciform dazzle above the coffin dominated the room. From somewhere there came the sound of a banging door; no one entered. Adam had indeed, as he had said earlier to Skeffington, attended a few wakes, but his memory of them was obscure. Now in this silent gloom he had a disquieting recollection of a story of Synge's about a wake in the Aran Islands: the long procession of shawled and sobbing women gathering at the bier, rocking back and forth to the wail of the keen. That such a scene could be duplicated in the parlor of Knocko Minihan tonight was wildly improbable; nevertheless, Adam found himself speculating upon it in some detail. Suddenly, from somewhere to his right, there came a sound. *"Sssst!"* it hissed.

He jumped, startled. He turned and at first saw no one; then in a corner which was darker than the rest of the room because of the shadow of a partially opened door, he saw a small, puckered woman, peering out at him with lively eyes.

"Did I *scare* you?" she said. The possibility seemed to delight her.

"No," Adam lied stoutly. "You startled me. I didn't see you come in."

"Ah, I was in," she said. "I was here in my corner when you come in with Frank. Are you the nephew?"

Adam nodded. It seemed to him that with the discovery of this silent little watcher of the shadows a new dimension of eeriness had entered the room. She had spoken of *"my* corner" with a proud possessiveness, almost as if she had come in with the coffin and would remain in her appointed place, firm, open-eyed and irremovable, until it was taken away.

"I'm Delia Boylan," she said. "I knew your pa and I knew your ma and I knew you when you was a baby." Pepper-and-salt eye-

brows rose as she considered him now. You was homely as spit,"
she said.

"Ah," said Adam. How did one respond more fully to such
frankness? He had no idea. He said, changing the subject hopefully, "I'm surprised there are so few people here to see Mr.
Minihan."

"Ah, they'll be in," she said confidently. "They'll all want to
get a good last look at old Knocko. There's them that's been waiting for it a long time. We're early. I always like to be a bit early."
She raised herself to a half-standing posture and gazed critically at
the coffin. "He looks grand with the cheeks all puffed out, don't
he?" she asked.

She spoke of the corpse with the nonchalant detachment possible only to those who have had vast experience with death. "He
looks very nice," Adam said. He was painfully aware of his own
lack of the special vocabulary of compliment appropriate to just
such an occasion; he was sure that one existed. "Of course," he
added, "I didn't know him when he was alive."

This, too, was maladroit; but Mrs. Boylan did not appear to
mind. Her narrow little shoulders shrugged in contempt and she
said, "A little runt of a man. Thin as a snake and no color to him
at all. He was part French, you know."

"I know."

"That makes all the difference," she said mysteriously. *"Aram.
Ah, well, that's small matter now."* She spoke as one forgiving
him the injury of his ancestry. "God be good to the man," she
said. "He was mean as a panther, but good luck to him."

Adam said nothing. Once more, there seemed to be nothing to
say. The silence was broken by the entrance of a trio of mourners
who came in, looked slowly about the room, nodded to Delia,
then filed up to the coffin.

"The Carmichael girls," Delia explained, "with the brother
Tim. *They* come early, as a general rule." She moved abruptly in
her chair, stretching out to face the door. *"Sssst!"* she hissed.

Adam followed her glance. He saw a stout, balding young man,
spruce and smooth in the discreet clothing of his profession, moving with purposeful yet superlatively respectful steps towards the
coffin.

"Sssst!" Delia said again. "Johnnie!"

The young man paused and looked in their direction; Adam thought he appeared to be annoyed. In response to Delia's frantically beckoning hand he came over to them with an obvious reluctance.

"Johnnie Degnan," Delia said to Adam, adding unnecessarily, "the undertaker. We always like to have our little talk."

"Good evening, Mrs. Boylan," the undertaker said unenthusiastically.

"Ah, Johnnie," Delia said. She introduced Adam. "Frank Sheffington's nephew, Johnnie. The sister's boy."

The undertaker brightened; he made a short, formal bow. "Very pleased to meet you, sir," he said. "I've always been a great admirer of your uncle, although I've never had the pleasure of making his acquaintance. I hope that will be remedied tonight. Ah . . . was there anything in particular, Mrs. Boylan?"

"He looks grand, Johnnie," she said, waving towards the coffin. "Just grand. Did he take a lot of doing?"

An expression of slight strain appeared on the undertaker's round face; clearly, thought Adam, questions from the laity were not encouraged. "Mr. Minihan was in remarkable condition, Mrs. Boylan, for one of his advanced years," he said. He spoke in a low voice and with extraordinary rapidity, as if in the hope that by a sudden sprint through his words he might bring this interview to a close. It was a forlorn hope; Delia had reached out and grabbed the sleeve of his coat.

"And, Johnnie," she said, "you laid him out in the *big* coffin! Ah, you rascal, you!" She rolled her eyes and released a little whoop of laughter; down by the coffin the Carmichael triumvirate turned in unison to stare. The undertaker made a swift, imploring pass with his hands, and Delia lowered her voice to a stage whisper. "My God," she said delightedly, "wouldn't it kill the man if he knew!"

The undertaker gave her a look of pain. "Mr. Minihan has a very fine casket," he said, emphasizing the final word. "As I'm sure he would have wished it."

"Ah," Delia said, "but the cost of it all! The cost. Johnnie!"

"Mr. Minihan," said the undertaker swiftly, "was a very prominent figure in the community. Very prominent."

Delia nodded agreeably. "He was the cheapest old devil that

ever lived," she said. "And you know it. Well, he's gone now, poor man, and you done an elegant job on him, Johnnie." As a grace note she added, "No matter what you charge."

"Ah ha ha ha," said the undertaker tonelessly, giving Adam a nervous smile, presumably meant to imply that they both were familiar with the irrespressible Mrs. Boylan. "Well, I must go now, Mrs. Boylan. Many duties. A pleasure to have met you, sir. I hope to meet your uncle." He bowed again and hurried away on muted feet.

"There's a great rogue," Delia said approvingly. "Only thirty years old and he'd steal the skin off your bones. Just give him the chance and it's the big coffin, ten limousines, and the Holy Name Choir to sing you good-by."

"And is he responsible for the crucifix?" Adam asked, pointing to the dazzling object above the coffin.

"The pride and joy," she assured him. "It all goes on the bill." She shook with a sudden rusty flutter of reminiscent mirth. "I says to him one day, I says, 'Don't you dare to stick that big sparkler over me when I'm gone, Johnnie Degnan! Don't you dare!' And he damn well won't; he knows he won't get a ten-cent piece out of me. Ah, he's a sly one," she said, "but he knows I'm on to him. *Sssst!*"

The sound, while no longer unfamiliar, was unexpected; Adam jumped again. An angular woman of forbidding aspect had come into the room and was now engaged in making hand signals to Delia.

"Aggie Gormley," Delia said. "I wonder has she news about the will? I'd best go see. I'll be back in a minute."

She hustled away with jerky, efficient steps, and Adam was alone once more. He looked at Delia, conversing with her newsy friend; he looked at the Carmichaels, talking quietly to Johnnie Degnan; he looked at the coffin and the jewelry above it. He looked, too, at his watch, and wondered absently when his uncle would return. Rather to his surprise, he did not greatly care, for he discovered to his horror that here in this presepulchral room, reserved for mourning, and in the appalling company of Delia Boylan, he was undoubtedly enjoying himself.

Skeffington, when he had left the parlor, had gone back along the hall until he came to a closed door. He knocked softly, then walked in. He was in the kitchen; on the far side of the small, neat room he saw, dressed in black, the tall, stooped figure of his wife's old friend. She was still, even now, a pretty woman, but faded, very faded; life with Knocko, thought Skeffington, must have been a fading experience. A quick rush of pity came over him as he looked at her; this was succeeded by quite another feeling, unexpected and hardly less painful: *My God*, he thought, *we're the same age almost to the day!* He shook his head quickly and said, "I'm sorry, Gert."

"I know you are, Frank." Obviously she had been weeping; now, however, she had stopped. Skeffington sat down across the kitchen table from her.

"Gert, I'm not going to commiserate with you. That'd be nice, but it wouldn't help much. But I do want to have a little talk with you on practical matters. I know you don't feel much like discussing anything like that now, but I want you to. Will you do that for me?"

There was a faint nod. "I will, Frank," she said.

"That's the girl. Now, first of all, do you have any idea of how you're situated? What did Knocko leave you? Was he able to leave you anything?"

One thin hand rubbed the narrow forehead wearily. "I'm not sure what he did or didn't leave, Frank. I haven't thought much about it at all."

Skeffington gently persisted. "Of course you haven't. But I want you to think about it now. That's why I made you promise you would. Sometimes at a time like this you need to change your thoughts every now and then. And sometimes you have to. You've got to think just a little bit of how you're going to live, Gert." He added, although he felt no confidence in this at all, "Knocko would have wanted you to."

She began to cry again, quietly. "He was a good man, Frank. You had to know him."

He let her cry, and said elusively, "I know he would have provided for you if he could. But we can't always do what we'd like to do. Now, I know he had nothing in the bank; he told me that himself. Was there any insurance?"

"There was some once," she said vaguely, "but I think it's gone. They were charging him too much for the premiums, he said. Ah, I don't know. He told me very little about money,

Frank. He had such bad luck."

"Yes." Bad luck, he thought, which had lasted no less than fifty years: a new world's record. "Any other holdings he might have had? War Bonds, for instance?"

She shook her head. "Since the store closed it seemed hard to put anything by. I know he got discouraged at times. You couldn't blame him. There was so much went wrong for the poor man."

"I know, Gert," he said soothingly, but to himself he said savagely: *and all of it of his own making.* It was tragic: this once-lively, once-lovely woman, whom he had known since childhood, who had been his wife's closest friend, now left old and beaten and penniless thanks entirely to her marriage to a dour, improvident boob! And yet she had loved him. It was utterly improbable, utterly irrational, and, he thought ironically, it happened all the time. Yet in this case it had happened to someone of whom he was fond; now it was up to him to do what the loved one had failed to do.

"Well, Gert," he said, "I guess now's as good a time as any to make good on a promise." He reached into an inner pocket of his coat and brought out an envelope. "Just before Kate died, she left me a little present for you. I would have given it to you before but there was a condition attached to it—she said I was to hold onto it until I was sure you really needed it. I guess you could say that time is now."

He handed her the envelope, and she took it silently. Still looking at him, she opened it; it was only when she felt the contents slipping out that she looked down. In her lap were ten one-hundred-dollar bills. She said instantly, "I won't take it, Frank. Thank you, but I won't."

He had anticipated this: the woman was not a fool. He reached over and took the bills in his hand. "All right," he said, "it's up to you, Gert. I'm not going to force you into anything. But I'll tell you this: The money belongs to you. Kate gave it to me to give to you, and if you don't use it, I can promise you nobody else will . . . I mean that, Gert."

She shook her head. "I saw Kate before she died. She said nothing about leaving me any money, and she knew I didn't want it. That money comes from you, Frank, and God bless you for it.

But I won't take it."

She looked at him steadily, the tired old eyes regarding him for what seemed a very long time; then her hand reached out, touched the money, then drew back. She said, "*Was* it Kate's, Frank? *Is* it mine? Do you swear it?"

"I do, Gert," he said solemnly. And he knew that he had won.

She took the money, holding it awkwardly against her lap. Looking up at Skeffington, she smiled with an odd, almost a young, shyness. "God bless you, Frank," she said.

"Why, I hope He will," he said, "but hardly for this. I'm just the messenger boy here. All blessings go to Kate, and I'm sure she doesn't need them by now." He got up and patted her on the hand. "I'm going back out front now," he said. "You ought to come out yourself a little later."

"I will, Frank." She thanked him again: for the money, for coming in to see her husband. As he was leaving, she said, "Frank?"

"Yes, Gert?"

She looked at the money in her hand and said, "I still don't believe you."

He smiled. "That's your privilege as an old friend. I find that very few of my old friends ever believe me. Maybe that's how they got to be old friends in the first place." She knew, he thought, but she didn't *quite* know, and that was all right: as long as there was the doubt, her pride was saved. He had reached the door when she stopped him again, and this time there was anxiety in her voice.

"I suppose they'll come tonight?" she said. "There haven't been many up to now." She added defiantly, "He was a difficult man in his way, but he had his friends. He had many friends, Frank."

"He had indeed," Skeffington said reassuringly. "They've just been waiting for the final night, that's all. They'll be here tonight, Gert. You'll see. Your only difficulty will be to fit them all in."

As he walked from the room, he thought: Poor woman. If friendship with Knocko were to be the basis for attendance at his wake, it could have been held in a phone booth. . . . However, because of Gert, he had that afternoon taken steps to increase substantially the number of mourners tonight. He had issued an order to all department heads that delegations were to be sent; as a less compulsory, but possibly even more effective measure, he let it be known that he himself would be on hand. While walking along the hallway back to the parlor, he thought of the crowded rooms, in which he would now have to remain at least another half hour; he thought of Gert; he thought, with no particular pity, of the miserable Knocko, whose death, in a sense, gave point to the evening.

To the thousand dollars he had just given away, however, he gave no especial thought, for, as Charlie Hennessey had once pointed out, the opponents of Skeffington who believed him to be an avaricious man, or one even concerned with money as such at all, could hardly have been farther from the truth.

He came into the parlor to discover that the crowd had begun to arrive. The rows of chairs, empty before, were now rapidly being filled; as he entered the room the heads turned towards him at once. He looked for Adam and signaled to him; Adam approached, only slightly behind Delia Boylan.

"Ah, now, Frank," she said eagerly, "how is she taking it back there?"

His reply was brief. "As well as could be expected." He added dryly, "I'm happy to see that you're bearing up under the strain, Delia."

Once more Adam heard the derisive whoop of laughter; it rang through the gloomy room; heads turned; at his position of duty down by the coffin Johnnie Degan frowned reprovingly and did a plump little dance step of despair. "I'll live," Delia said. "Well, me and the nephew has been having a lovely talk about poor Knocko, the old devil."

"I wish I'd been here to join you," Skeffington said. Turning to Adam, he added, "Mrs. Boylan's pious reflections on the faithful departed never fail to uplift the spirit. She has a splendid attendance record at the deathbed of her many friends."

"I go to them all," she said proudly. "I don't miss a one."

"Everybody has to have a hobby," Skeffington said. "Now if you'll excuse us, Delia, I want to take my nephew into the next room and introduce him to some people. Give my best to Tom and the family."

"I will, Frank." The sharp little eyes glinted maliciously and she said, "And will I tell them you wouldn't mind hearing from them come Election Day?"

"I always treasure the Boylan vote," Skeffington said, "and yours in particular, Delia. Every time I get thinking about the wisdom of giving the women the vote I think of you and my fears become quiet."

She crowed with delight. "Ah, that's all mush, Frank. But you know we're with you every single time. The whole family."

"I do, Delia. I appreciate it. And now," he said, with no change of expression, "we'll leave you to your prayers. Good-by, Delia."

Out in the hall he drew Adam aside and said, "I hope you see how things work out for the best. If I hadn't left you alone in there, you wouldn't have met Mrs. Boylan and had your little devotional chat. Your field of experience has been immeasurably widened in the space of but a few minutes."

"I won't deny it," Adam said. "I've certainly never met anyone quite like her before. She's a fantastic woman."

"I suppose she is," Skeffington said carelessly. "I'm so used to her I don't notice any more. It takes a fresh eye to fully appreciate Delia. I may add that she's a woman it's far better to have with you than against you. She has the tongue of a cobra."

"And does she really spend all of her time going to wakes?"

"Apart from a few hours of sleep each night, I believe she does. As she said, she doesn't miss a one. You must remember that she's a singularly devout woman. Also," he said reflectively, "it's somewhat cheaper than going to the movies."

While they stood in the hall, more people came in; clearly, the wake of Knocko Minihan was expanding. As it did, Adam was struck by the altered deportment of his uncle; it was almost as if, from being one of the visiting mourners, he had suddenly become the host. He nodded and spoke briefly to all the new arrivals; without exception, all responded in identical fashion: a muttered acknowledgment of the pitiful fact of Knocko's death, followed by a perceptibly more fervent statement of good wishes for Skeffington in the coming elections. A short, round woman with a serene face approached them with slow, heavy steps; to her

Skeffington spoke at somewhat greater length.

"Glad to see you, Annie," he said. "I gather that everything got here all right?"

"It did, Frank. You wanted no whisky or anything like that?"

"No. What have you got out there?"

"Coffee and tea, sandwiches, and cake. There'll be plenty for everybody, no matter how big it gets."

"Good. Where are you setting it up, in the kitchen?"

"There's a problem there, Frank. God knows there's no place else we can put it, but that's where Gert is, sitting all by herself. I don't like to bother the poor woman."

"Go right ahead and bother her," Skeffington said decisively. "That's what she needs right now, someone bustling around, something to take her mind off things for a few minutes. It's not good for her to be sitting out there all alone. See if you can't get her to come in here, just to go through the motions. If she doesn't want to do that, try to get her doing something out there. If you have any difficulty, let me know."

"All right, Frank, I will." The woman went down the hall with her calm, weighty tread, and Skeffington, who had been noting with some amusement his nephew's polite if imperfect attempt to conceal his curiosity, said, "That's a role I occasionally practice: the combination physician, caterer and master of ceremonies. It's something I might have to fall back on one day when I retire from politics."

"I am impressed," Adam said truthfully. "I hadn't realized that all this was a part of your job."

"Well, this is rather a special case. The widow's an old friend, and in her present condition she's in no shape to arrange for the usual civilities. So I just had a few things sent over." It was a detail he had taken care of that afternoon; the food had come from the ample commissariat of the Wadsworth Hospital. As this was a city institution, the food had been provided for by public funds; it was, in a word, a tax-supported wake. And all for Knocko Minihan; the beneficiary, thought Skeffington, was unworthy of the occasion. He said to Adam, "I'm not so sure that all the arrangements would meet with Knocko's approval, but then, of course, when you come right down to it, he's not really in much of a position to complain, is he? Come along, I want to go in here."

They entered the next door down the hall; Adam found himself in a room which compared favorably with the parlor in its
size and general hideousness, but which contained many more
people and a great deal more noise. It was not until he had been
in this room for a moment that he realized that there was still another difference: here, the mourners were exclusively male. To
his surprise, he recognized some of them as the old familiars of his
uncle's outer office. They had disdained the chairs which had
been set out for them in a severe row which paralleled the wall;
they preferred to stand, talking, smoking, moving, waiting. When
Skeffington came in, the waiting was over. They surged around
him, the noise grew, and Adam was soon separated from his uncle
by a tight, struggling double ring of the self-appointed palace
guard. He caught Skeffington's eye; in return he received a quick
but unmistakable wink, the meaning of which was quite clear.
For the moment at least, he was again on his own; Skeffington
had decided that it was time for his field of experience to be widened still further.

"I think we might move along up to the parlor," the Governor
said to Adam. "I saw a priest come in as I was coming back down
here; I imagine they'll be saying the Rosary any moment now.
We'll join them, and then we'll go."

Led by Skeffington, the men left the kitchen and trooped up to
the parlor; there, at the door they were met by a priest. Or, more
accurately, by a Monsignor; it was the Cardinal's secretary.

"Good evening, Governor," he said pleasantly.

"Well, well," Skeffington said, some slight surprise in his voice.
"Monsignor. This is an unexpected pleasure. Nice to see you
again. Are you here as an emissary of His Eminence?"

"No, no," the Monsignor said. "I'm on my own tonight. Mrs.
Minihan is something of an old friend. When I was a boy in this
part of town I used to drop in to see her fairly often. Most of the
children of the neighborhood did, I think."

"Yes," Skeffington said thoughtfully. "So they did. I'd almost
forgotten. Poor Gert." Then, speaking less to himself and more to
the Monsignor, he said, "Well, it's very good of you to remember
and drop in now. Tell me, how's your boss these days?"

"Very well. I'll tell him I saw you, Governor."

"Do that," Skeffington said. "He'll be overjoyed."

The Monsignor smiled. "You may be misjudging His Eminence, Governor. It's a case of the bark being a good deal worse than the bite."

"I wouldn't know," Skeffington said. "I've never been bitten. There were a few quick snaps in my direction, but I managed to avoid them. However, that's neither here nor there at the moment, I suppose; there's no reason why you should be bothered with these old-time vendettas, Monsignor. By the way, have you met my nephew, Adam Caulfield?"

The Monsignor, who would have given rather a lot to be bothered about the old-time vendettas, greeted Adam with an automatic affability, but his mind was on Skeffington. The old politician captivated his imagination; he saw him a unique, a rich, extraordinary personality who contained within himself a part of local history which soon would be no more and which never again would reappear. It was a vein that called out to be tapped before it disappeared, first, from view, then even from memory; for just a moment the Monsignor thought of suggesting to Skeffington the possibility of a luncheon, a meeting, a talk. Then he thought of the Cardinal, and of the old, tough, knobby face darkening with rage and disappointment when he learned—as he surely would—of the deliberate encounter, planned by his own subordinate. It would be imprudent; worse, it would be unfair. For the time being, at least, any such meeting was impracticable; a little later, perhaps . . . And so the Monsignor, nodding towards the parlor, merely said, "I suppose we'd better go in now."

They went in, they knelt, and the Monsignor led them in the Rosary. They recited in unison the five decades of the beads which commemorate the Sorrowful Mysteries of the Church; they prayed for the immortal soul of Aram Minihan. And as they prayed, their responses low, rhythmic, and at times not quite distinct, riding high over all other voices came one which to Adam was familiar, clear, unhesitating, and infinitely fervent. It was the voice of Delia Boylan.

The Rosary over, it was time to go. Skeffington swiftly and efficiently made the rounds, saying the necessary good-bys; then he signaled to Adam, and uncle and nephew walked towards the front door together. They had almost reached the door when Skeffington, suddenly halting, said, "Hold on a minute. I want a word with that undertaker before we go."

They both turned and saw the head of Johnnie Degnan, poking out of the kitchen at the far end of the hall; obviously he had been watching their departure. Skeffington beckoned, and he came running quietly to them.

"Ah, good evening, Governor," he said, in his swift hushed tones. "A very sad occasion. I wanted to see you before this evening, to make your acquaintance, but the pressure of my duties didn't quite allow. I'm John Degnan, Governor."

"Glad to know you, Mr. Degnan," Skeffington said. "As you say, it's a sad occasion. I'm happy to see you've done your best by it, however. I've been admiring your handiwork with the deceased."

"Thank you, Governor. Thank you very much. That's nice to hear. I did my best," the undertaker said modestly. "I don't mind telling you, Governor, that Mr. Minihan presented a very difficult case. Because of the age and the sunken cheeks and the wrinkles. I'm sure you can appreciate the difficulty of the task, Governor. Everything had to be smoothed out delicately, the youthful contours restored, and so forth."

"Yes. Now, Mr. Degnan, only one feature of your work disturbs me and that is the probable cost. You don't mind if I say that I was rather struck by the fact that the coffin, and what might be called the general deathroom décor, seem a trifle splendid for someone who was in decidedly modest circumstances?"

The undertaker smiled; it was, Adam thought, a nervous smile. "I see what you mean, Governor," he said swiftly. "I appreciate that point of view. And yet I always think the family is more satisfied if the final homage, as I like to think of it, is really nice in its every aspect. Something that the deceased would have been proud of if he could have seen it."

"Why, those are the feelings of an artist," Skeffington said. "They do you credit, Mr. Degnan. I presume, incidentally, that you've discussed all this with Mrs. Minihan?"

"Well, no. Not exactly, that is, Governor. I thought it best not to in her distraught condition. Just a few words here and there. I think you could say, more or less, that it was left to my discretion, as it so often is. I always believe in taking as many worries as possible from the shoulders of the family."

"That's very thoughtful of you. Now then, you're a young man, Mr. Degnan, but I understand you've had quite a bit of professional experience. As you might put it, you've been in charge of a good many final homages. Or as I might put it, you've buried a good many people. What would you say was the lowest price you've ever buried anyone for?"

"The lowest *price,* Governor?" The smile remained; it wavered uncertainly. "I don't quite understand. . . . What I mean to say is, Governor, I don't believe that's anything I've ever quite figured out."

"Try," Skeffington urged him. "Make a rough estimate. Would it be . . . oh, say thirty-five dollars?"

"Thirty-five dollars!" The gasp of astonishment and pain broke through the modulated occupational tones; the undertaker looked wildly at Skeffington and said, "You couldn't *begin* to bury anyone for that price today, Governor!"

"I'll bet you could if you really tried," Skeffington said pleasantly. "I'll bet you could both begin and end. And just to prove my confidence in your resourcefulness, Mr. Degnan, why don't you do that very thing with Mr. Minihan? Let's give it a real try. I think you can do it. I'm sure the final bill won't read over thirty-five dollars. Matter of fact, I'll instruct the widow to that effect immediately."

"But, Governor, you can't be serious!" Degnan cried. The smooth round face had become agonized; the soft hands were united in front of him in a tight, beseeching clasp. He looked as if he were about to hurl himself at his persecutor's feet, and Adam, who had not until a moment ago realized just what it was that his uncle was doing, now felt a sudden pity as well as disgust for this abject little profiteer. "The costs alone, Governor," Degnan moaned. "They're going up every day. I couldn't possibly do it. It's all *arranged—*"

"Fine," Skeffington said. "Then let it go through as arranged. But for thirty-five dollars."

"But, *Governor* . . ."

Skeffington pulled his watch from a vest pocket and examined it with apparent surprise. "It's later than I thought," he said. "Well, then, Mr. Degnan, it's all settled. I'll leave the details to you. A suitable funeral conducted for thirty-five dollars, with no cutting of corners. All the normal courtesies extended, the usual paraphernalia available. I'll have a few men on hand just to see that everthing goes along well. I know you'll do a grand job. In any event, I'll be sure to hear about it: my observers will give me a full report."

The undertaker's face, which for some moments had been the color of putty, now had turned a vivid red. "But, Governor! I hope you know how eager I am to co-operate in anything you suggest. How eager I *always* am. But what you're asking is *impossible. . . .*"

"Why, that's one of the words that doesn't belong to the bright lexicon of youth," Skeffington said reprovingly. "I've always believed that nothing is impossible when one has youth and ambition. I hope you won't be the one to shake this treasured belief. Because if you do," he said, regarding Degnan with a stare which its recipient suddenly found to be as unpleasant as anything he had ever experienced, "you might shake my confidence in you. What's worse, you might even begin to shake public confidence in you. That is a bad thing to have happen to a young undertaker with dreams, Mr. Degnan. You never can tell how far it might reach. It might even reach the members of the licensing board for your profession. You never know. But we mustn't keep you from your labors any longer. I suppose you have many things to do at a time like this. Possibly even more than you'd anticipated. Good night, Mr. Degnan. Glad you introduced yourself."

They went out the door and down the steps; Degnan's anguished voice trailed them to their car. "Thirty-five dollars!" it wailed. "Governor, I *appeal* to you . . ."

When they were under way, Skeffington said: "I hadn't planned on rounding your evening off in just that way. I hope you weren't too shocked by my treatment of the widow's helper."

Adam shook his head. "It seemed to me that the widow's helper rather had it coming. And will he do it for thirty-five dollars, do you think?"

Skeffington chuckled. "I wouldn't be surprised," he said dryly.

The Burial

By St. John Ervine

The funeral procession from the girl's home to the graveyard was due to begin at half-past two, but long before that hour the crowd

of mourners began to collect. They stood about the entrance to
the lane leading to the churchyard and waited. The home of the
dead girl faced the lane, and the procession, therefore, would
reach its journey's end in a few moments from the time when it
began to move. Townsmen and neighbours mingled with men
from the country and the hills, and fishermen from the bay where
the girl was drowned; and each man, as he came up to a group of
his acquaintances, spoke of the terribleness of the disaster, and
then the talk circled round the affairs of the small town.

John Mawhinney came along the old road to Ballyshannon,
and when he was by the lane, he hailed James O'Hara.

"How're ye, James?" he said.

James O'Hara, a lean, foxy-looking man, turned at the sound of
Mawhinney's voice, "Och, I'm just middlin'," he replied, "I've
the quare cowl on me! How is yourself?"

"Ah, I'm not so bad. Man-a-dear, this is a tarr'ble sad thing
about this young girl!"

"Aye, it is that. Man, I mind her when she was that height, the
same wee girl!" He allowed his hand to fall to the level of his
knees as he spoke. "An' a smart wee girl she was, too! Aye! She always had an answer for ye, whatever ye said, she was that sharp!"

He looked up as he spoke, and saw John McClurg approaching.
"Is that you, John?" he said.

McClurg, a large, moon-faced man, with little, smiling eyes,
came puffing up to them.

"It is surely," he replied to O'Hara's greeting.

"I saw ye in the market the fair day," said Mawhinney, "but ye
wurn't lukkin', an' ye didden see me. Did ye do well wi' yer
cattle?"

"Ah, I didden do so bad. I might 'a' done better, an' I might 'a'
done worse!"

"Did ye sell thon wee heifer ye had wi' ye?"

"I did not. I wudden take the price—"

O'Hara tapped him on the arm. "I s'pose ye come to the
funer'l?" he said.

John McClurg glanced across the road to the door of the
house where the dead girl lay. "Well," he said, "I thought I wud
just dander into the town an' show me respect til the dead, God
rest her sowl!" The three men raised their hats at his prayer.

"What time does it begin?" he asked.

"They wur talkin' about half-after-two," replied Mawhinney. "But I'm thinkin' it'll be later'n that. Sure, the mail train's not in thrum Bilfast yet, an' there's fren's comin' thrum there an' thrum Derry, too, an' they'll be wantin' their denner when they git here. It'll be three o'clock afore iver they stir out o' the dure!"

"Aye, it will that," said James O'Hara, and then he turned and spoke to John McClurg. "Wur ye wantin' much for yer wee heifer?" he asked.

McClurg bit a piece of tobacco off a long twist of dark villainous stuff, and when he had chewed it in his mouth a while, he spat yellow juice over the kerb, and then said: "You might think I was wantin' too much, an' I might think meself I was wantin' too little!"

"I saw her meself," exclaimed Mawhinney, "afore she went intil the sea, laughin' an' jokin' like annythin'! Aw, God save us all thrum a death the like o' her death!"

"They wur a quare long time findin' her!"

"They wur."

"Wud ye be wantin' five poun's fur yer wee heifer, John McClurg?" said James O'Hara.

"I wud, indeed, an' a bit more on top of it!"

"They foun' her jus' where she went down," continued Mawhinney, in the voice of a man who is reciting an oft-told tale. "Man, it's quare the way the body returns like that!"

"Aye!"

"Who's thon man wi' the tall hat an' the long coat on him, d'ye know?" asked one that stood by of Mawhinney, as a man in a frock coat knocked at the door.

"I nivir seen him afore," replied Mawhinney. "He's a stranger in this town, I'm thinkin'. D'ye know him, James?"

"I do not," replied O'Hara. "Mebbe he's come be the train. The mail's in now. Thonder's Patrick Magrath with the mailcart comin' roun' the corner!"

"Ye're mebbe right!" Mawhinney resumed the recital of his tale. "Did ye see the piece in the Derry paper about her?" he said. "Thon was the quare bit. An' there was a piece of portry be the young wumman in the post affice!"

"Aye, I saw that. It was quare an' nice. I didden know thon

wumman cud do the like o' that!"

"Ah, sure she's in Government sarvice, issen she? . . ."

"The paper said she was the quare, clivir, wee girl, an' tuk a lotta prizes at the school in Derry her da sent her to. They must 'a' spent a power o' money on her trainin'!"

"They did that. They nivir grudged her nathin'. It's a quare pity of them!"

"Aye, it only shows ye shudden make a god of yer childher! . . ."

Two young men, one of whom carried a costly wreath in his hands, went up to the door and presently were admitted to the house.

"Fur dear sake, luk at thon wreath!" exclaimed John Mawhinney. "Man, thon must 'a' cost somethin'!"

"Aye, it's thrum the young men at the Y.M.C.A. She was goin' to be married to one o' them. Did ye nivir hear about it?"

"Naw. What was his name?"

"I think it wus young McCracken!"

"What! Thon lad?"

"Aye. It'll be a cut-up for him, this! . . . John McClurg, will ye take six poun' ten for yer heifer?"

"Mebbe I wud if it was affered to me! . . ."

"There's manny a Cathlik would be willin' to give a wreath, too, I'm thinkin'!" said John Mawhinney.

"Aye, that's true enough. Sure, there's no room for bigitry where death is! . . . Wur ye thinkin' o' makin' me the affer, James?"

O'Hara walked a little way from the group, and then, squirting tobacco juice before him, returned to it. "Ah, I was just wondherin' if ye wud take it if it was affered t' ye. I wudden affer more'n five poun' for it meself! . . ."

"Ah, well, it wudden be no good you afferin' that amount. I wudden part wi' it fur the money!"

"There's a brave crowd here now," said O'Hara, turning towards the crowd. "It'll be a big procession, I'm thinkin'!"

"It will that. But I've seen bigger. There was the time Dr. Cochrane died. D'ye mind that? That was a procession an' a half!"

"Aye, it was indeed. Near a mile long that was! . . ."

The door of the house opened, and a number of persons entered.

"They'll be startin' soon," said Mawhinney.

"Ah, well, God help her, she'll soon be oura all this. It's the long sleep til the Day o' Judgment!"

"Ye're right there. Ye are indeed! . . ."

The door slowly reopened, and men came forth bearing the yellow coffin on their shoulders. A great quietness descended upon the village street, and each man in it removed his hat and, if he were a Catholic, crossed himself and prayed for the repose of the dead girl's soul. Here and there a woman wrapped her shawl about her face and wept. The bearers carried the coffin across the street to the lane leading to the churchyard, and the people in the street fell in behind and marched slowly towards the grave. A bell tolled softly, and in the house from which the body had just been borne a woman was heard crying and lamenting.

"I'll give ye six poun's fur yer wee heifer," said James O'Hara, as the body went by.

"Ah, God rest her sowl!" murmured McClurg, marking himself with the sign of the cross on the head and breast. "I cudden take less nor six poun' ten!"

"I cudden given more nor six poun'! . . ."

"Well, ye'll not get it fur the price. It's six poun' ten or nathin'!"

"Ye're the hard man to bargain wi'! . . ."

"I'm not hard at all! . . . Mebbe, they're better dead young nor dead oul'!"

"Will ye not budge yer price?"

"I will not!"

"They're in the graveyard now. . . . Come on down til Maloney's public house, an' I'll sale the bargain wi' ye."

Index